Grammar Links 1

A Theme-Based Course for Reference and Practice

SECOND EDITION

Linda Butler
Janet Podnecky

M. Kathleen Mahnke
Series Editor
Saint Michael's College

Houghton Mifflin Company   **Boston**   **New York**

Publisher: Patricia A. Coryell
Director of ESL: Susan Maguire
Senior Development Editor: Kathleen Sands Boehmer
Editorial Assistant: Evangeline Bermas
Senior Project Editor: Margaret Park Bridges
Senior Manufacturing Coordinator: Marie Barnes
Marketing Manager: Annamarie Rice
Marketing Associate: Laura Hemrika

Cover image: Stock Illustration Source © 2003 David Ridley, *Multicultural Figures*

Photo credits: p. 1: © Comstock Images; p. 9: © Scott Cunningham, Stone/Getty Images;
p. 29: © Steve Allen/Getty Images; p. 40: John Lamb, Stone/Getty Images; p. 43: © George
Shelley/Corbis; p. 65: © C. Lee/PhotoLink/Getty Images; p. 79: © Agance France Presse/
Getty Images; p. 92: © Wally McNamee/Corbis; p. 97: © Jim Cummins, Taxi/Getty Images;
pp. 109, 363: © Getty Images; p. 115: © Craig Aurness/Corbis; p. 124: Stephen Trimble
Photography; p. 143: © Sandy Felsenthal/Corbis; p. 144 left: © Ariel Skelley/Corbis;
p. 144 right: © Robert Landau/Corbis; p. 157: © Paul A. Souders/Corbis; p. 160: © Morton
Beebe/Corbis; p. 191: © Corbis; p. 215: © Reuters/Corbis; pp. 225, 395, 406 bottom, 424:
© Bettmann/Corbis; p. 231: © Dave Nagel, Stone/Getty Images; pp. 244, 248: Washington
State Historical Society; p. 263: © Franz-Marc Frei/Corbis; p. 273: © Reuters/Corbis;
p. 281: © Richard Coomber, Taxi/Getty Images; p. 282: © Rosanne Olson, The Image
Bank/Getty Images; p. 315: © Alex Mares-Manton, Stone/Getty Images; p. 323: © Jason
Furnari/Corbis Sygma; p. 390: © Rob Lang, Taxi/Getty Images; p. 405: © Chris Harvey/
Getty Images; p. 406 top: © Rob Atkins, The Image Bank/Getty Images

Printed in the U.S.A.

Library of Congress Control Number: 2003115110

ISBN: 0-618-27412-X

123456789-HES-08 07 06 05 04

Contents

Introduction

WELCOME TO *GRAMMAR LINKS*!

Grammar Links is a comprehensive five-level grammar reference and practice series for students of English as a second or foreign language. The series meets the needs of students from the beginning through advanced levels:

- *Grammar Links Basic*: beginning
- *Grammar Links, Book 1*: high beginning
- *Grammar Links, Book 2*: intermediate
- *Grammar Links, Book 3*: high intermediate
- *Grammar Links, Book 4*: advanced

Available with each *Grammar Links* student text are an audio program and printable Web-based teacher's notes; the teacher's notes are accompanied by the answer key and tapescripts for each book. Tests and other materials are also available on the Houghton Mifflin Website and are described below. In addition, *Grammar Links 1–4* feature workbooks for further practice of all grammar points introduced in the student books.

NEW IN THIS EDITION

- A fresh, new design with eye-catching art, realia, and a focus on ease of use
- Streamlined, easy-to-read grammar charts showing structures at a glance
- Succinct explanations of grammar points for easy understanding
- Simplified content coverage accompanied by vocabulary glosses to let students focus on grammar while learning about topics of interest
- An even greater number and variety of activities than before, now signaled with icons for easy reference:

  Listening activities for receptive practice of grammar structures in oral English

  Communicative activities that lead to fluent use of grammar in everyday speaking

  Writing activities for productive practice of targeted structures in extended written discourse

   Links to the World Wide Web for:
  - Model paragraphs for writing assignments
  - Practice tests, both self-check tests for student use and achievement tests for teacher use
  - Links to interesting sites related to unit themes for further reading and discussion
  - Vocabulary flashcards for review of the content-related vocabulary that is used in text readings and exercises
  - Much more! See for yourself at www.hmco.com/college/esl.

TO THE TEACHER

Series Approach

Recent research in applied linguistics tells us that when a well-designed communicative approach is coupled with a systematic treatment of grammatical form, the combination is a powerful pedagogical tool.

Grammar Links is such a tool. The grammar explanations in *Grammar Links* are clear, accurate, and carefully sequenced. All points that are introduced are practiced in exercises, and coverage is comprehensive and systematic. In addition, each grammar point is carefully recycled in a variety of contexts.

The communicative framework of *Grammar Links* is that of the theme-based approach to language learning. Unlike other approaches, theme-based models promote the development of both communicative and linguistic abilities through in-depth contextualization of language in extended discourse. The importance of this type of contextualization to grammar acquisition is now well documented. In *Grammar Links*, content serves as a backdrop for communication; high-interest topics are presented and developed along with the grammar of each chapter. As a result, *Grammar Links* exercises and activities are content-driven as well as grammar-driven. While learning about adjective clauses in Book 3, for example, students explore various aspects of the discipline of psychology. While they are practicing gerunds and infinitives in Book 2, they read about successful American entrepreneurs. And while practicing the simple present tense in Book 1, students learn about and discuss North American festivals and other celebrations. Throughout the series, students communicate about meaningful content, transferring their grammatical training to the English they need in their daily lives.

Complementing the communicative theme-based approach of the *Grammar Links* series is the inclusion of a range of successful methodological options for exercises and activities. In addition to more traditional, explicit rule presentation and practice, we have incorporated a number of less explicit, more inductive techniques. Foremost among these are our discovery exercises and activities, in which students are asked to notice general and specific grammatical features and think about them on their own, sometimes formulating their own hypotheses about how these features work and why they work the way they do. Discovery exercises are included in each unit opener. They are frequently used in chapter openers as well and are interspersed throughout the *Grammar Practice* sections, particularly at the higher levels.

In short, the *Grammar Links* approach provides students with the best of all possible language learning environments—a comprehensive, systematic treatment of grammar that employs a variety of methods for grammar learning within a communicative theme-based framework.

About the Books

Each book in the *Grammar Links* series is divided into approximately 10 units. Each unit looks at a well-defined area of grammar, and each unit has an overall theme. The chapters within a unit each focus on some part of the targeted unit grammar, and each chapter develops some specific aspect of the unit theme. In this way, chapters in a unit are linked in terms of both grammar coverage and theme, providing a highly contextualized base on which students can build and refine their grammatical skills.

Grammar coverage has been carefully designed to spiral across levels. Structures that are introduced in one book are recycled and built upon in the next. Students not only learn increasingly sophisticated information about the structures but also practice these structures in increasingly challenging contexts. Themes show a similar progression across levels, from less academic in Books 1 and 2 to more academic in Books 3 and 4.

Grammar Links is flexible in many ways and can be easily adapted to the particular needs of users. Although its careful spiraling makes it ideal as a series, the comprehensive grammar coverage at each level means that the individual books can also stand alone. The comprehensiveness and careful organization also make it possible for students to use their text as a reference after they have completed a course. The units in a book can be used in the order given or can be rearranged to fit the teacher's curriculum. Books can be used in their entirety or in part. In addition, the inclusion of ample practice allows teachers to be selective when choosing exercises and activities. All exercises are labeled for grammatical content, so structures can be practiced more or less extensively, depending on class and individual needs.

Unit and Chapter Components

■ **Unit Objectives.** Each unit begins with a list of unit objectives so that teachers and students can preview the major grammar points covered in the unit. Objectives are accompanied by example sentences, which highlight the relevant structures.

■ **Unit Introduction.** To illustrate grammar use in extended discourse, a reading and listening selection introduces both the unit grammar and the unit theme in a unit opener section entitled *Grammar in Action*. This material is followed by a grammar consciousness-raising or "noticing" task, *Think About Grammar*. In *Think About Grammar* tasks, students figure out some aspect of grammar by looking at words and sentences from the *Grammar in Action* selection, often working together to answer questions about them. Students induce grammatical rules themselves before having those rules given to them. *Think About Grammar* thus helps students to become independent grammar learners by promoting critical thinking and discussion about grammar.

■ **Chapter Introduction.** Each chapter opens with a task. This task involves students in working receptively with the structures that are treated in the chapter and gives them the opportunity to begin thinking about the chapter theme.

■ *Grammar Briefings.* The grammar is presented in *Grammar Briefings*. Chapters generally have three or four *Grammar Briefings* so that information is given in manageable chunks. The core of each *Grammar Briefing* is its **form** and **function** charts. In these charts, the form (the *what* of grammar) and the function (the *how, when,* and *why*) are presented in logical segments. These segments are manageable but large enough that students can see connections between related grammar points. Form and function are presented in separate charts when appropriate but together when the two are essentially inseparable. All grammatical descriptions in the form and function charts are comprehensive, concise, and clear. Sample sentences illustrate each point.

■ *Grammar Hotspots.* *Grammar Hotspots* are a special feature of *Grammar Links*. They occur at one or more strategic points in each chapter. *Grammar Hotspots* focus on aspects of grammar that students are likely to find particularly troublesome. Some hotspots contain reminders about material that has already been presented in the form and function charts; others go beyond the charts.

■ *Talking the Talk.* *Talking the Talk* is another special feature of the *Grammar Links* series. Our choice of grammar is often determined by our audience, whether we are writing or speaking, the situations in which we find ourselves, and other sociocultural factors. *Talking the Talk* treats these factors. Students become aware of differences between formal and informal English, between written and spoken English.

■ *Grammar Practice.* Each *Grammar Briefing* is followed by comprehensive and systematic practice of all grammar points introduced. The general progression within each *Grammar Practice* is from more controlled to less controlled, from easier to more difficult, and often from more receptive to more productive and/or more structured to more communicative. A wide variety of innovative exercise types is included in each of the four skill areas: listening, speaking, reading, and writing. The exercise types that are used are appropriate to the particular grammar points being practiced. For example, more drill-like exercises are often used for practice with form. More open-ended exercises often focus on function.

In many cases, drill-like practice of a particular grammar point is followed by open-ended communicative practice of the same point, often as pair or group work. Thus, a number of exercises have two parts.

The majority of exercises within each *Grammar Practice* section are related to the theme of the unit. However, some exercises depart from the theme to ensure that each grammar point is practiced in the most effective way.

■ **Unit Wrap-ups.** Each unit ends with a series of activities that pull the unit grammar together and enable students to test, further practice, and apply what they have learned. These activities include an error correction task, which covers the errors students most commonly make in using the structures presented in the unit, as well as a series of innovative open-ended communicative tasks, which build on and go beyond the individual chapters.

■ **Appendixes.** Extensive appendixes supplement the grammar presented in the *Grammar Briefings*. They provide students with word lists, spelling and pronunciation rules, and other supplemental rules related to the structures that have been taught. The appendixes are a rich resource for students as they work through exercises and activities.

■ **Grammar Glossary.** A grammar glossary provides students and teachers with definitions of the grammar terms used in *Grammar Links* as well as example sentences to aid in understanding the meaning of each term.

Other Components

■ **Audio Program.** All *Grammar Links* listening exercises and all unit introductions are recorded on audio CDs and cassettes. The symbol 🎧 appears next to the title of each recorded segment.

■ **Workbook.** *Grammar Links 1–4* student texts are each accompanied by a workbook. The four workbooks contain a wide variety of exercise types, including paragraph and essay writing, and they provide extensive supplemental self-study practice of each grammar point presented in the student texts. Student self-tests with TOEFL® practice questions are also included in the workbooks.

■ **Teacher's Notes.** The *Grammar Links* teacher's notes for each student text can be downloaded from <http://www.hmco.com/college/esl/>. Each contains an introduction to the series and some general and specific teaching guidelines.

■ **Tapescript and Answer Keys.** The tapescript and the answer key for the student text and the answer key for the workbook are also available at the *Grammar Links* Website.

■ **Links to the World Wide Web.** As was discussed above, the *Grammar Links* Website www.hmco.com/college/esl/ has been expanded for the second edition to include student and teacher tests, teacher notes, model writing assignments, content Web links and activities, and other material. Links are updated frequently to ensure that students and teachers can access the best information available on the Web.

TO THE STUDENT

Grammar Links is a five-level series that gives you all the rules and practice you need to learn and use English grammar. Each unit in this book focuses on an area of grammar. Each unit also develops a theme—for example, business or travel. Units are divided into two or three chapters.

Grammar Links has many special features that will help you to learn the grammar and to use it in speaking, listening, reading, and writing.

FEATURE	BENEFIT
Interesting Themes	Help you link grammar to the real world—the world of everyday English
Introductory Reading and Listening Selections	Introduce you to the theme and the grammar of the unit
Think About Grammar Activities	Help you to become an independent grammar learner
Chapter Opener Tasks	Get you started using the grammar
Grammar Briefings	Give you clear grammar rules in easy-to-read charts, with helpful example sentences
Grammar Hotspots	Focus on especially difficult grammar points for learners of English—points on which you might want to spend extra time
Talking the Talk	Helps you to understand the differences between formal and informal English and between written and spoken English
Grammar Practice	Gives you lots of practice, through listening, speaking, reading, and writing exercises and activities
Unit Wrap-up Tasks	Provide you with interesting communicative activities that cover everything you have learned in the unit
Vocabulary Glosses	Define key words in readings and exercises so that you can concentrate on your grammar practice while still learning about interesting content
Grammar Glossary	Gives you definitions and example sentences for the most common words used to talk about English grammar—a handy reference for now and for later
Websites	Guide you to more information about topics of interest
	Provide you with self-tests with immediate correction and feedback, vocabulary flashcards for extra practice with words that might be new to you, models for writing assignments, and extra practice exercises

All of these features combine to make *Grammar Links* interesting and rewarding—and, I hope, FUN!

M. Kathleen Mahnke, Series Editor
Saint Michael's College
Colchester, VT USA

ACKNOWLEDGMENTS

■ Series Editor Acknowledgments

This edition of *Grammar Links* would not have been possible without the thoughtful and enthusiastic feedback of teachers and students. Many thanks to you all!

I would also like to thank all of the *Grammar Links* authors, from whom I continue to learn so much every day. Many thanks as well to the dedicated staff at Houghton Mifflin: Joann Kozyrev, Evangeline Bermas, and Annamarie Rice.

A very special thanks to Kathy Sands Boehmer and to Susan Maguire for their vision, their sense of humor, their faith in all of us, their flexibility, their undying tenacity, and their willingness to take risks in order to move from the mundane to the truly inspirational.

M. Kathleen Mahnke, Series Editor

■ Author Acknowledgments

I would like to thank the teachers whose comments on the first *Grammar Links 1* helped to shape this new edition, especially Jeanie Francis of the University of Missouri at Columbia. I would particularly like to thank reviewers Marilyn Santos of Valencia Community College (FL) and Nancy Price of the University of Missouri at Columbia and developmental editor Jane Sturtevant for their insightful feedback on drafts of this edition. For their work on materials for the *Grammar Links* Website, I thank Karen Davy, Virginia Martin, Owen Murray of International Pacific University (New Zealand), and Nevitt Reagan of Kansai Gaidai University (Japan).

As always, I thank Series Editor Kathleen Mahnke for her outstanding leadership. Special thanks are due as well to Susan Maguire, Director of ESL Programs, and her dedicated team at Houghton Mifflin. I would also like to thank Janet Podnecky for her work on the first edition and Emily Klyza and Daniel Butler for research assistance. Developmental Editor Randee Falk made an enormous contribution to this edition, balancing a sense of the big picture with superb attention to detail, for which I am very grateful. Finally, I would like to thank Jim, Miles, and Clare for their love and patience.

Linda Butler

Useful Words and Expressions

Words for the Classroom

OBJECTIVES

- the alphabet
- cardinal numbers
- nouns
- subject pronouns
- singular and plural
- adjectives and prepositions
- verbs

The Alphabet

Capital Letters and Small Letters

The capital letters are: A B C D E F G H I J K L M N O P Q R S T U V W X Y Z

The small letters are: a b c d e f g h i j k l m n o p q r s t u v w x y z

Vowel and Consonants

The vowels are: *a, e, i, o, u,* and sometimes *y**.

The consonants are: *b, c, d, f, g, h, j, k, l, m, n, p, q, r, s, t, v, w, x, z,* and sometimes *y*†.

*y has a vowel sound in *happy*, *my*, and *Lydia*.
†*y* has a consonant sound in *yes*, *yo-yo*, and *New York*.

PRACTICE

 1. Listen and repeat the letters of the alphabet.

2. Say the letters in each group.

Group 1: a h j k

Group 2: b c d e g p t v Z

Group 3: f l m n s x

Group 4: i y

Group 5: o

Group 6: q u w

Group 7: r

3. Say the vowels.

4. Say the consonants.

5. Work with a partner. Practice the conversation.

Cardinal Numbers

1	2	3	4	5	6	7	8	9	10
one	two	three	four	five	six	seven	eight	nine	ten

11	12	13	14	15	16	17	18	19	20
eleven	twelve	thirteen	fourteen	fifteen	sixteen	seventeen	eighteen	nineteen	twenty

21	22
twenty-one	twenty-two

		30	40	50	60	70	80	90	100
		thirty	forty	fifty	sixty	seventy	eighty	ninety	one hundred

See Appendix 1 for ordinal numbers.

PRACTICE

1. Listen and repeat the numbers.

2. Listen and write the number.

a. 3 _____   c. _____   e. _____   g. _____

b. _____   d. _____   f. _____   h. _____

3. Work with a partner. Student A: Point to a number in the chart. Student B: Say the number. Take turns.

4. Work with a partner. Practice spelling numbers. Take turns.

Nouns*

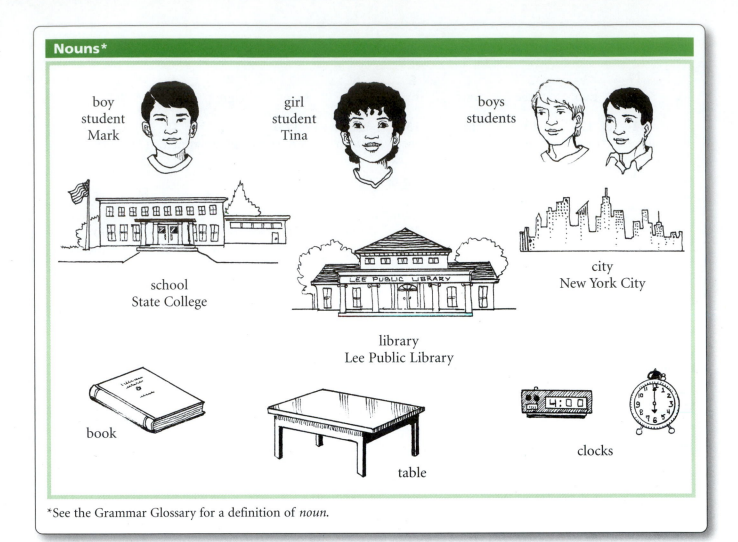

boy
student
Mark

girl
student
Tina

boys
students

school
State College

library
Lee Public Library

city
New York City

book

table

clocks

*See the Grammar Glossary for a definition of *noun*.

PRACTICE

1. Write nouns.

a. _____

b. _____

c. _____

2. Circle the nouns.

a. The (students) are at (school.)

b. The boy is a student.

c. Is Tina from Washington?

d. The clock is on the table.

e. Tina has three books.

f. Mark is at the library.

3. Write three more nouns. _____ _____ _____

Subject Pronouns*

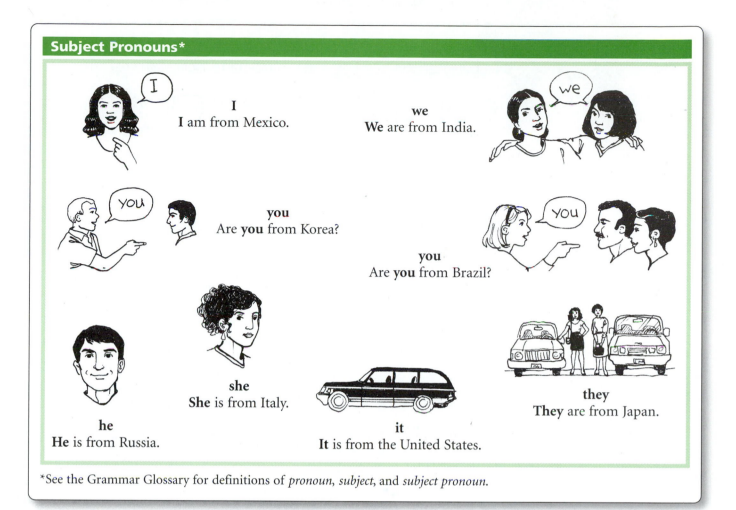

I
I am from Mexico.

we
We are from India.

you
Are you from Korea?

you
Are you from Brazil?

she
She is from Italy.

it
It is from the United States.

he
He is from Russia.

they
They are from Japan.

*See the Grammar Glossary for definitions of *pronoun*, *subject*, and *subject pronoun*.

PRACTICE

1. Listen and repeat the sentences in the chart.

2. **A.** Complete the sentence.

    I am from _____.

    B. Work with a partner. Ask, *Where are you from?* Complete the sentence about your partner. Circle *He* or *She*.

    He / She is from _____.

3. Cross out the subject nouns. Write the subject pronouns *He*, *She*, *It*, and *They*.

    a. ~~The man~~ *He* is from Russia.   e. The two girls are smiling.

    b. The girl is speaking.   f. Yoko and Miki are from Japan.

    c. The man is happy.   g. The car is from the United States.

    d. Paola is from Italy.   h. The books are on the table.

Singular and Plural*

	SINGULAR (ONE)	PLURAL (MORE THAN ONE)
Nouns	He has one **book**.	She has three **books**.
	She has a **pen**.	They have two **pens**.
	There is one **person**.	There are two **people**.
Pronouns	I, you, he, she, it	we, you, they

*See the Grammar Glossary for definitions of *singular* and *plural*.

PRACTICE

1. Listen to the nouns and pronouns. Write *S* for singular words and *P* for plural words.

a. __P__   c. _____   e. _____   g. _____

b. _____   d. _____   f. _____   h. _____

2. Circle the correct word.

	Singular	Plural
a. I have two _____.	book	(books)
b. You have one _____.	pencil	pencils
c. He has seven _____.	pen	pens
d. She has one _____.	backpack	backpacks
e. We have four _____.	notebook	notebooks
f. They have one _____.	teacher	teachers

3. Listen and repeat the sentences in Exercise 2.

Adjectives and Prepositions*

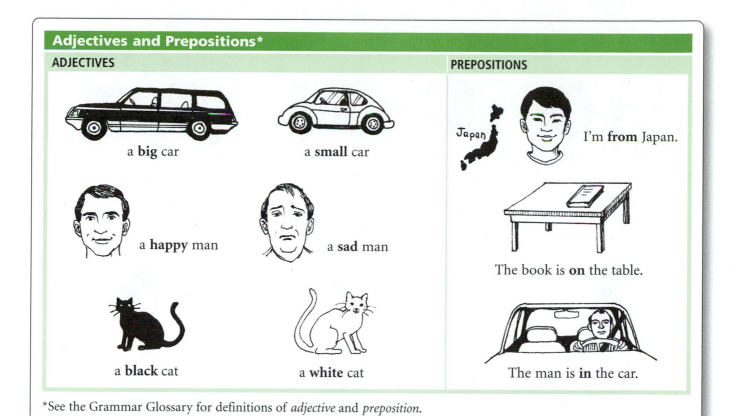

ADJECTIVES

a **big** car

a **small** car

a **happy** man

a **sad** man

a **black** cat

a **white** cat

PREPOSITIONS

Japan

I'm **from** Japan.

The book is **on** the table.

The man is **in** the car.

*See the Grammar Glossary for definitions of *adjective* and *preposition*.

PRACTICE

1. Look at the **boldfaced** words. Circle *adjective* or *preposition*.

a. Tina is **sad**.   (adjective)   preposition

b. Mark is **from** New York City.   adjective   preposition

c. Is the newspaper on the **white** table?   adjective   preposition

d. Write the answer **on** the board   adjective   preposition

e. Is the dog **small**?   adjective   preposition

f. Are you **in** school now?   adjective   preposition

2. Write two more adjectives. _____ _____

Verbs*

listen
The students are listening.

read
She is reading the newspaper.

write
Write your telephone number.

say
Did Mark say, "Yes?"

ask
Ask your partner's name.

repeat
They are repeating the vowels.

*See the Grammar Glossary for a definition of *verb*.

PRACTICE

1. Write the verbs.

a. <u>listen</u>   b. _____   c. _____   d. _____

2. Circle the verbs in the sentences.

a. (Ask) your partner the questions.

b. We listen in class.

c. Mark and Tina read their books.

d. Please write your name.

e. The teacher says the numbers.

f. Please repeat it.

3. Write three more verbs: _____ _____ _____

4. Ask your teacher about the meanings of these verbs:

erase   give   take   look   underline   draw

Present Tense of *Be*

People and Places

UNIT OBJECTIVES

- **subject pronouns**
  (*He* is from New York. *It* is a big city.)

- **statements with the verb** *be*
  (I *am* a student. The teacher *is* not here.)

- **contractions with the verb** *be*
  (*I'm* from Colombia. It *isn't* in the United States.)

- ***yes/no* questions and short answers with the verb** *be*
  (*Are you* from Japan? Yes, *I am. Is* Miami in Texas? No, *it's not.*)

- ***wh-* questions and answers with the verb** *be*
  (*What is* your name? Antonio. *Where are* the maps? In the classroom.)

Grammar in Action

A. *Name That City!* is a TV game show. Read and listen to the conversation on the show.

Announcer: Good evening, ladies and gentlemen, and welcome to *Name That City!* We are in New York City with our host, Alan Adams. He is here with three new contestants. They are from three different cities. Here's Alan!

Alan: Hello, everyone! Welcome to the show! Contestants, please introduce yourselves. What are your names? Where are you from?

May: Hi, everybody. I'm May Parker. I am from Evergreen, Colorado.

Sara:	Hello. My name is Sara Jordan. I'm from Los Angeles, California.
Dan:	Hi, I'm Dan Ferreira, and my hometown is Philadelphia.
Alan:	Philadelphia! So, you're from "The City of Brotherly Love"!
Dan:	Yes, that's right.
Alan:	Well, May, Sara, and Dan, it's nice to have you on the show. Contestants—are you ready?
May/Sara/Dan:	Yes, we are.
Alan:	Okay. Part One is "Cities in the United States." Here are four clues. First, this city is in the South. Second, it's a state capital. Third, it's on a river. Fourth, the name of this city isn't an English word. May?
May:	Is it Santa Fe?
Alan:	No, it's not. Sara?
Sara:	Is it Baton Rouge?
Alan:	Yes, it is! Okay, Sara, where is Baton Rouge?
Sara:	It's in Louisiana.
Alan:	You are right! Congratulations, Sara. Ladies and gentlemen, she is the winner!

B. Practice the conversation in a group of five. Take turns as different people.

Think About Grammar

A. Complete these sentences from the reading.

1. Announcer: We __are__ in New York City with our host, Alan Adams.

2. Announcer: He _____ here with three new contestants.

3. Announcer: They _____ from three different cities.

4. May: I _____ from Evergreen, Colorado.

5. Alan: Yes, it _____!

6. Alan: You _____ right! Congratulations, Sara.

7. Alan: Ladies and gentlemen, she _____ the winner!

Look at the words you wrote. They are **verbs**. They are **present tense forms of the verb *be***. There are three forms. What are they?

Write them here: _____, _____, and _____

B. Circle the word or words before *am*, *is*, or *are*.

1. (Alan Adams) is the host of the show.

2. He is in New York.

3. May and Dan are on the show.

4. Los Angeles is a city.

5. It is in California.

6. Sara is from Los Angeles.

7. She is the winner.

8. We are on page 12.

9. I am a student.

10. You are a student.

Look at the words you circled. These words are the **subjects** of the sentences. A sentence always has a subject and a verb.

Chapter 1

New People, New Places

Statements With *Be*

Introductory Task: Please Introduce Yourselves

> **HELLO**
>
> I'm ___Sara_____.
> I'm from ___the United States_____.

> **HELLO**
>
> I'm _____.
> I'm from _____.

A. Fill out your card:

B. Work with a partner. Practice the conversation.

> I'm Luz. I'm from Puerto Rico.

> I'm Yoshi. I'm from Japan.

> It's nice to meet you.

> Nice to meet you, too.

C. Introduce yourself to your classmates.

Subject Pronouns*

FORM

SINGULAR	PLURAL
I	we
you	you
he	
she	they
it	

FUNCTION

Subject Pronouns in Sentences

1. **Subject pronouns** take the place of subject nouns.

   He
   ~~Antonio~~ is from Colombia.

   They
   ~~The books~~ are here.

2. Use a subject noun OR a subject pronoun. Do not use both.

   Mr. Rees is at school.

   He is at school.
   NOT: Mr. Rees ~~he~~ is at school.

3. Use *it* for:

   • The time.

   It is 9:00 a.m.

   • The day.

   It is Monday.

   • The date.

   It is January 1.

   • The weather.

   It is cold and sunny today.

*See page 5 for more information on subject pronouns.

Subject Pronouns

1 **Subject Pronouns:** Who's Who

Write the subject pronoun *I*, *We*, or *You*.

2 **Subject Pronouns:** Hometowns

Cross out the subject in **bold**. Write the subject pronoun *He*, *She*, *It*, or *They*.

1. Luz is a student. ~~Luz~~ *She* is from Puerto Rico.

2. Yoshi is a student. **Yoshi** is from Tokyo.

3. The teacher is a man. **The teacher** is Mr. Rees.

4. Teresa is a girl from Brazil. **Teresa** is in Chicago now.

5. Kai and Bruce are students. **Kai and Bruce** are Taiwanese.

6. Taipei is their hometown. **Taipei** is in Taiwan.

7. **The time** is 9:00 a.m. in Chicago.

8. San Francisco and Los Angeles are cities. **The cities** are in California.

9. **The weather** is nice and sunny today.

10. **The day** is Monday.

Present Tense of *Be* in Affirmative Statements

FORM

SINGULAR		
SUBJECT	*BE*	
I	am	
You	are	
He		in class.
She	is	
It		
The boy		

PLURAL		
SUBJECT	*BE*	
We		
You		
They	are	friends.
The boys		

FUNCTION

Affirmative Statements with *Be*

1. A **statement** is one kind of sentence. It has a subject and a verb. A statement ends with a period (.).

   a statement   a period
   <u>Luz</u> **is** a student.

2. The subject of a statement can be:

   • A noun.

   Alan is here.

   • A subject pronoun.

   He is in New York.

3. The statement can have subject + *be* +:

   • A noun.

   It is a **map**.

   • An adjective.

   It is **big**.

   • A prepositional phrase.

   It is **in the classroom**.

Present Tense of *Be* in Affirmative Statements

3 **Subject Pronouns and Forms of *Be*:** It's Nice to Meet You

Read the conversation and complete the sentences. Use each subject pronoun + verb from the box. Use a capital letter at the beginning of a sentence: <u>He</u> is from Cartagena.

> I am   you are   he is   she is   it is   we are   they are

Mr. Rees and Antonio are in their school in Chicago. They are in the hall outside their ESL classroom.

Mr. Rees: Hello. <u>I am</u> ₁ Mr. Rees, the ESL teacher.

Antonio: Hello. _____ ₂ Antonio Vargas.

Mr. Rees: It's nice to meet you, Antonio. _____ ₃ in my class, right? Where are you from?

Antonio: Cartagena. _____ ₄ in Colombia.

Mr. Rees: Teresa! Good morning. Antonio, this is Teresa.

_____ ₅ a new student, too. Teresa, this is Antonio.

Teresa: It's nice to meet you.

Antonio: It's nice to meet you, too.

Mr. Rees: Teresa, Antonio, _____ ₆ both from South America. Antonio is from Colombia.

_____ ₇ from Cartagena. Teresa is from Brazil. _____ ₈ from Rio de Janeiro.

You are both from South America.

We are late!

Teresa: Now there are five students from South America.

Three students are from Venezuela.

_____ ₉ in the classroom.

Mr. Rees: In the classroom? I'm surprised. What time is it?

Teresa: It's 9:05.

Mr. Rees: Oh, no! Antonio, Teresa, _____ ₁₀ late!

4 Affirmative Statements with *Be*: People in the Class

A. Work with a partner. Use words from boxes A, B, and C. Make true statements. Take turns.

A	B	C	
Mr. Rees Antonio Antonio and Teresa I You	am is are	a student an ESL teacher	(nouns)
		new friendly	(adjectives)
		in Chicago from South America	(prepositional phrases)

Example: Student A: Antonio and Teresa are in Chicago.

Student B: Antonio is new.

B. Work alone or with a partner. Write about students in your class. Check the spelling of names. Ask, *How do you spell your name?*

1. _____ is a student.

2. _____ and _____ are students.

3. _____ is from _____.

4. _____ and _____ are from

_____.

5 Affirmative Statements with *Be*: Regions and Cities of North America

Work with a partner. Look at the map. Student A: Say a phrase from the box on page 19. Student B: Listen and make a statement about a city or cities. Use *is* and *are*. Take turns.

Example: Student A: in Canada

Student B: Toronto is in Canada.

Student B: in the South

Student A: Raleigh and Atlanta are in the South.

Remember! You can ask for help with pronunciation.

Example: Student: How do you say this word?

Teacher: RAW-lee

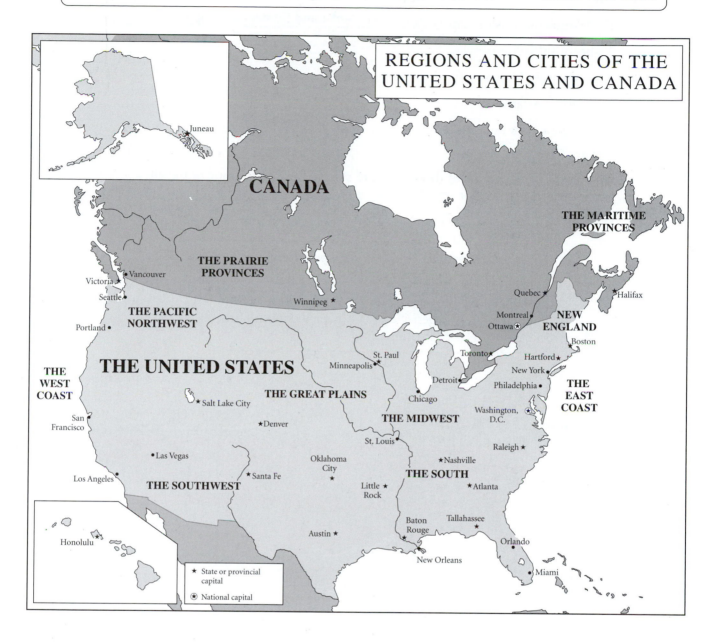

REGIONS AND CITIES OF THE UNITED STATES AND CANADA

6 *Be* + Noun/Adjective/Prepositional Phrase: Cities Near and Far

A. Put the words in order. Write statements.

1. Atlanta and Boston/capitals/are   Atlanta and Boston are capitals.

2. beautiful/is/Vancouver   _____

3. is/warm in Honolulu/it   _____

4. a city/is/Miami   _____

5. big/New York and Los Angeles/are _____

B. On a piece of paper, write three or more statements about your home city. Use words in the box, or use your own words.

Example: I am from Tokyo. It is in Japan. It is big and exciting.

Adjectives		Prepositional Phrases
big	crowded	on a river
small	comfortable	on the coast
quiet	expensive	near the mountains
noisy	beautiful	

On a River

On the Coast

Near the Mountains

C. Read your sentences to a partner. Write one new sentence about your partner's city. Is it correct? Ask your partner.

Affirmative Contractions with *Be*

FORM

A. Singular

FULL FORMS		CONTRACTIONS
SUBJECT	*BE*	SUBJECT + *BE*
I	am	**I'm**
you	are	**you're**
he		**he's**
she	is	**she's**
it		**it's**
the girl		**the girl's**

B. Plural

FULL FORMS		CONTRACTIONS
SUBJECT	*BE*	SUBJECT PRONOUN + *BE*
we		**we're**
you	are	**you're**
they		**they're**
the girls		—

FUNCTION

Using Contractions

1. A **contraction** combines two words into one word. An apostrophe (') takes the place of a letter.

    I am → **I'm**
    she is → **she's**

2. Contractions of *be* are common with:

    • Subject pronouns.

    They're from Mexico.
    It's ten o'clock.

    • Singular nouns.

    Teresa's here.
    The **weather's** cold.

TALKING THE TALK

Use contractions for speaking and for informal writing. In formal writing, use full forms, not contractions.

SAY OR WRITE TO A FRIEND	WRITE IN A PAPER FOR SCHOOL
It's true.	**It is** true.

Affirmative Contractions with *Be*

7 **Changing Full Forms to Contractions:** Identities

Underline the subject and verb. Write the contraction. Remember capital letters.

1. *You're*
   <u>You are</u> a teacher.

2. I am a student.

3. It is a big city.

4. They are big cities.

5. You are a good friend.

6. He is a teacher.

7. You are students.

8. We are friends.

9. Sara is the winner.

10. Washington is the capital.

8 **Contractions in Affirmative Statements:** Time for the Show

Complete the sentences about the people on *Name That City!* (page 10).
Use contractions with subject pronouns.

1. Dan is on the TV show *Name That City!* _He's_____ a young man.

2. Sara is on the show, too. _____ from Los Angeles.

3. May is on the show with Dan and Sara. _____ a contestant, too.

4. Sara: May, you and I are lucky.

   May: Yes, we are. _____ lucky to be here.

5. Tom is Dan's friend. _____ in New York, too.

6. Dan and Tom are at a hotel. _____ in their room now.

7. Their room is nice. _____ big.

8. Dan: Oh no! _____ 8:30. It's time for me to go.
   　　　　　　　　　a

   Tom: I hope you win! _____ lucky to be on TV.
   　　　　　　　　　　　　　b

   Dan: I'm lucky? Yes, but _____ nervous!
   　　　　　　　　　　　　　　　　c

---

lucky = having good luck (good things happening by chance).

Negative Statements with *Be*

FORM

A. Singular

FULL FORMS				CONTRACTIONS (2 FORMS)						

SUBJECT	*BE*	*NOT*		SUBJECT + *BE*	*NOT*			SUBJECT	*BE + NOT*	
I	am			I'm				—	—	
You	are			You're				You	aren't	
He				He's				He		
She	is	not	old.	She's	not	old.		She	isn't	old.
It				It's				It		
John				John's				John		

B. Plural

FULL FORMS				CONTRACTIONS (2 FORMS)						

SUBJECT	*BE*	*NOT*		SUBJECT PRONOUN + *BE*	*NOT*			SUBJECT	*BE + NOT*	
We				We're				We		
You	are	not	old.	You're	not	old.		You	aren't	old.
They				They're				They		
The boys				—				The boys		

GRAMMAR **HOT**SPOT!

1. There are two ways to make contractions with *is* and *are* in negative statements:

   - Contract the subject and *is/are*, and add *not*.

     (The subject can be a pronoun or a singular noun only.)

He's **not** here.
They're **not** here.
The teacher's **not** here.

   - Contract *is/are* and *not*.

He **isn't** here.
They **aren't** here.
The teacher **isn't** here.
The students **aren't** here.

2. Remember! Use an apostrophe (') in place of the missing letter in a contraction.

she i̸s not → she's not
she is no̸t → she isn't
NOT: she ~~is'nt~~

Negative Statements with *Be*

9 **Statements with *Be* and *Not*:** Two Friends

A. Read about Dan.

> Dan's from Philadelphia. His parents are teachers.
> 1   2
>
> He's 21 years old. His eyes are blue. His hair is blond.
> 3   4   5

Dan and His Parents

B. Write negative statements about Tom using the statements about Dan in Part A. Use full forms, not contractions.

Tom

Tom is different from Dan.

1. <u>Tom is not from Philadelphia.</u>   He's a New Yorker.

2. _____ They're dentists.

3. _____ He's 20.

4. _____ They're brown.

5. _____ It's black.

10 Negative Contractions with *Be* in Negative Statements: Two Ways to Say It

These statements are false. Rewrite them as true negative statements. Change noun subjects to pronouns. Use contractions.

	Pronoun + *'m/'s/'re not*	*isn't/aren't*
1. ~~New York City~~ It is quiet.	It's not quiet.	It isn't quiet.
2. Dan: I'm a New Yorker.	I'm not a New Yorker.	—
3. *Name That City!* is a movie.		
4. Dan/Tom: We're brothers.		
5. Alan Adams is a contestant.		
6. Sara is from Philadelphia.		
7. Dan: I'm lucky.		
8. Dan and Tom are in Boston.		
9. Alan: Dan, you're married, right?		

11 Using *Isn't* and *Aren't*: Map Reading

Work with a partner. Student A: Make a statement with *isn't* or *aren't* + the words in parentheses. Student B: Change part of the statement to make it true and affirmative. Take turns. (You can use the map on page 19.)

Example: Student A: Miami isn't in Canada.
           Student B: Miami is in the United States. OR Toronto is in Canada.

1. (Miami/in Canada)
2. (Denver/in New England)
3. (Seattle and Las Vegas/regions)
4. (the South and the Midwest/cities)
5. (Montreal/a region)
6. (Seattle and Vancouver/on the East Coast)
7. (Washington, D.C./on the West Coast)
8. (Orlando and New York/state capitals)
9. (San Francisco/a state capital)
10. (Vancouver/in the United States)

12 Statements with *Be*: Our Class

Adjectives		Prepositional Phrases
single	hungry	in class
married	thirsty	at home
noisy	sleepy	on vacation
quiet	smart	in a big city
homesick	Canadian	from the United States

 A. On a piece of paper, write six true sentences about yourself. Write affirmative and negative statements with *be*. Use the words in the boxes, or use your own words.

Examples: I'm in class. I'm not sleepy.

B. Work with a partner. Write affirmative and negative statements with *be* about your partner. Then read each other's sentences. Are they true?

Example: Student A: Aviel, you're from Nicaragua.
　　　　　　Student B: That is true.

_____:
　　　　　　(partner's name)

1. You're _____

2. You're not _____

3. _____

4. _____

C. Speak to the class about your partner. Use contractions.

Example: My partner is Omar. He's from Egypt. He isn't noisy. He's hungry.

D. Work as a class. Think about you and your classmates. What is true about all of you? Make affirmative and negative statements with *We are* (not).

Examples: We're smart. We aren't lazy.

Check your progress! Go to the Self-Test for Chapter 1 on the *Grammar Links* Website.

2

Getting the Facts

Questions With *Be*

Introductory Task: Mystery Places in the United States

Work with a partner. Read the clues. Look at the pictures. Write the names of the places. (There are maps on page 19 and in Appendix 9.)

Florida	Hawaii	New York	Texas

Clues

1. Is it a state? Yes, it is.
   What's the nickname of this state? "The Sunshine State."
   Is Disney World in this state? Yes, it is.

   Name: _____

2. Is it a big state? No, it isn't.
   Where is it? In the Pacific Ocean.
   Is Honolulu the capital? Yes, it is.

   Name: _____

3. Is it a small state? No, it isn't.
   Where is it? In the Southwest.
   What's the capital? Austin.

   Name: _____

4. Is it on the East Coast? Yes, it is.
   What's the nickname of this state? "The Empire State."
   Is the Statue of Liberty here?   Yes, it is.

   Name: _____

---

a nickname = a short form of a name (like *L.A.* for *Los Angeles*) or a name used by friends (like *Red* for a man with red hair).

Yes/No Questions and Short Answers with Be

FORM

A. Questions and Answers with Singular Subjects

QUESTIONS			ANSWERS			
BE	SUBJECT		*YES*		*NO*	
Am	I			I **am**.		I'm not.
Are	you			you **are**.		you're not./No, you aren't.
	he	in the picture?	Yes,	he **is**.	No,	he's not./No, he isn't.
Is	she			she **is**.		she's not./No, she isn't.
	it			it **is**.		it's not./No, it isn't.
	the cat					

B. Questions and Answers with Plural Subjects

QUESTIONS			ANSWERS			
BE	SUBJECT		*YES*		*NO*	
	we			we **are**.		we're not./No, we aren't.
Are	you	in the picture?	Yes,	you **are**.	No,	you're not./No, you aren't.
	they			they **are**.		they're not./No, they aren't.
	the cats					

C. Forming Questions

1. A question ends in a question mark (*?*).

   Is he from Texas**?**

2. Use a subject pronoun or a subject noun in a question.

   subject pronoun
   Are **they** in class?

   subject noun
   Are **the students** in class?

3. Use *Am/Is/Are* + the subject +:

   • A noun.

   Is it a **state?**

   • An adjective.

   Is it **big?**

   • A prepositional phrase.

   Is it **on the East Coast?**

GRAMMAR **HOT**SPOT!

1. Use full forms in short answers with *Yes*.

   Q: Is she married?
   A: **Yes**, she **is**.
   NOT: Yes, ~~she's~~.

2. Use contractions in short answers with *No*.

   Q: Is he married?
   A: **No**, he **isn't**.
   NOT USUALLY: No, he is not.

The Statue of Liberty

GRAMMAR PRACTICE 1

Yes/No Questions and Short Answers with *Be*

1 **Short Answers with *Be*:**
In the Big Apple

Circle the correct short answer.

1. Is New York City big?   (Yes, it is.) / Yes, it's.

2. Is it the state capital?   No, it is. / No, it isn't.

3. Is the Statue of Liberty in New York City?   Yes, it is. / Yes, they are.

4. Are the buildings tall?   Yes, they are. / Yes, they're.

5. Is the city quiet?   No, it's not. / No, she isn't.

6. Is New York a vacation place?   Yes, it's. / Yes, it is.

7. Is Dan in New York now?   Yes, he is. / Yes, it is.

8. Are Dan and Tom at school?   No, we aren't. / No, they aren't.

9. Are you at school?   Yes, I am. / No, I'm not.

10. Are you and your classmates in New York?   Yes, we are. / No, we're not.

2 *Yes/No* Questions and Short Answers: In New York with Dan and Tom

A. Change these statements about Dan and Tom to *yes/no* questions.

1. Dan is in New York City.   <u>Is Dan in New York City?</u>

2. Dan: I am on Seventh Avenue. Dan: <u>Am I on Seventh Avenue?</u>

3. Dan is a tourist.   _____

4. New York is exciting.   _____

5. Dan and Tom are together.   _____

6. They're friends.   _____

7. They're at a jazz club.   _____

8. It's almost 2:00 a.m.   _____

9. Tom: You are tired.   Tom: _____

10. Dan: We are out of money.   Dan: _____

> *a tourist* = a person who travels or visits a place for fun.

B. Work with a partner. Student A: Ask the questions in Part A. Student B: Give short answers with *Yes*. Take turns.

Example: Student A: Is Dan in New York City?   Student B: Yes, he is.

C. What is your opinion? Check (✓) your answer.

1. Is New York City an exciting place?   ❏ Yes, it is.   ❏ No, it's not.

2. Are you interested in New York?   ❏ Yes, I am.   ❏ No, I'm not.

3. Is New York a good vacation place?   ❏ Yes, it is.   ❏ No, it isn't.

D. Take a vote in your class: Is New York City a good vacation place?
Write the numbers of votes.   *Yes:* _____   *No:* _____

3 *Yes/No* **Questions and Short Answers:** Another Special City

A. Listen and read about Boston.

A Vacation in Boston

Visit Boston, Massachusetts! It's a great place for a vacation.

Boston is an interesting city. The museums are great, and the city is famous for its universities. There are thousands of students in Boston.

Boston is more than 350 years old. Many tourists are interested in the history of Boston. One important part of Boston's history is the American Revolution.

The four seasons are wonderful in Boston. Spring is lovely. Summer is warm. In winter, the snow is beautiful. And fall is fantastic. In fall, the colors of the trees are wonderful—red, orange, and gold. Fall is perfect for a vacation in Boston.

B. Work with a partner. Student A: Ask a *yes/no* question about Boston. Use *Is* or *Are*. Student B: Give the short answer. Take turns.

Example: Student A: Is Boston in New England?
Student B: Yes, it is.

1. . . . Boston in New England? (Yes)

2. . . . Boston an interesting city? (Yes)

3. . . . it near California? (No)

4. . . . the universities famous? (Yes)

5. . . . the museums 1,000 years old? (No)

6. . . . many tourists in Boston? (Yes)

7. . . . summer cold in Boston? (No)

8. . . . you from Boston?

C. Work with a partner. Ask and answer more *yes/no* questions about Boston.

4 **Yes/No Questions and Short Answers:** Lost in Boston

A. Complete the conversation. Write questions with the words in parentheses ( ) +
a form of *be.* Write short answers.

A tourist is lost in Boston. The tourist is talking to a police officer on horseback.

Tourist: <u>Are you a police officer?</u>
1 (you / a police officer?)

Police officer: <u>Yes, I am.</u>
2 (yes)

_____
3 (you / lost?)

Tourist: _____
4 (yes)

_____
5 (I / on Beacon Street?)

Police officer: _____
6 (yes)

Tourist: _____
7 (we / near the Public Garden?)

Police officer: _____
8 (yes)

_____
9 (you / interested in the Swan Boats?)

Tourist: _____
10 (yes)

Police officer: Look—there they are.

Tourist: Now I'm not lost. Thank you!

B. Work with a partner. Act out the conversation.

1. In formal spoken English, people usually give short answers to *yes/no* questions.

   Q: Are they students?
   A: **Yes, they are.** OR **No, they aren't.**

2. In informal spoken English, there are other ways to answer *yes/no* questions.

INFORMAL WAYS TO SAY *YES*	INFORMAL WAYS TO SAY *NO*
Yeah.	Nah.
Yup.	Nope.
Uh-huh.	Uh-uh.
I think so.	I don't think so.
Sure.	No way.

5 **Informal Ways to Answer *Yes* or *No*:** Ask a Travel Agent

Listen for the informal answers in this conversation. Listen again and circle the short answer with the same meaning.

May is asking Sara about Martha's Vineyard. It's an island, part of Massachusetts.

May: Sara, I'm planning a vacation. Tell me, is Martha's Vineyard a nice place?

Sara: (Yes, it is.) / No, it isn't.
  1

May: Is it nice in the summer?

Sara: Yes, it is. / No, it isn't.
  2

May: What about the beaches? Are they good?

Sara: Yes, they are. / No, they aren't.
  3

May: But are all the hotels expensive?

Sara: Yes, they are. / No, they aren't.
  4

And there's camping on the island. Are you interested in camping?

May: Yes, I am. / No, I'm not.
  5

Tell me, what about the food? Are the restaurants good?

Sara: Yes, they are. / No, they aren't.
  6

May: Okay, sounds good! Thanks for your help, Sara.

Sara: No problem. Have a good vacation!

Wh- Questions with Be: Who, What, or Where

FUNCTION

Using Wh- Questions (or Information Questions)

1. Use *who* in questions about people.	Q: **Who** is she? A: That's Luz.
2. Use *what* in questions about things.	Q: **What** is the nickname for New York City? A: The Big Apple.
3. Use *where* in questions about places.	Q: **Where** is Paris? A: In France.

FORM

A. Wh- Questions and Answers with Be

QUESTIONS			ANSWERS
WH- QUESTION WORD	**BE**	**SUBJECT**	
Who	is	he?	The teacher.
			He's the teacher.
	are	they?	New students.
			They're new students.
What	is	that?	A postcard.
			It's a postcard.
	are	their names?	Al and Sara.
			Their names are Al and Sara.
Where	am	I?	On Beacon Street.
			You're on Beacon Street.
	are	Dan and Tom?	In New York.
			They're in New York.

B. Asking Wh- Questions and Giving Answers

1. Use singular verbs with singular subjects. Use plural verbs with plural subjects.	Where **is** your **book**? Where **are** your **books**?
2. Sometimes the answer to a *wh-* question is a complete sentence. Often it is not.	Q: Who is he? A: He's the teacher. (complete) Q: Who is he? A: The teacher. (incomplete)

Wh- Questions with *Be*: *Who*, *What*, or *Where*

6 Identifying *Wh-* Questions with *Be*: The Name Game

A. Read and listen to this conversation on the TV show *Name That City!* (page 10). <u>Underline</u> the six *wh-* questions with *who, what,* and *where*. The first one is underlined for you.

Announcer:	Ladies and gentlemen, welcome back to the show! <u>Who are the contestants today?</u> May, Sara, and Dan.
Alan:	Dan! Is *Dan* really your first name?
Dan:	No, it's not. *Dan* is short for *Daniel.*
Alan:	What is your last name?
Dan:	*Ferreira.* My full name is Daniel Ferreira. No middle name.
Alan:	And you, Sara—what is your full name?
Sara:	My first name is *Elizabeth*, and my last name is *Jordan.*
Alan:	What is *Sara*? Is it a nickname?
Sara:	No, it's my middle name: *Elizabeth Sara Jordan.*
Alan:	And May! Is *May* your real name or a nickname?
May:	*May* is my American nickname. My real first name is *Meili.* It means *beautiful.*
Alan:	Where is it from?
May:	It's a Chinese name.
Alan:	What is your last name?
May:	*Parker.*
Alan:	*Parker* isn't a Chinese name.
May:	No, my Chinese family name is *Bai.* It means *white. Parker* is my married name. So my full name is *Meili Bai Parker.*

B. Match the questions and answers. Write the letters on the lines.

1. _c_ Who is Alan Adams?
2. _____ Who are the contestants?
3. _____ Where are they?
4. _____ What is May's real first name?
5. _____ Where is this name from?

a. In New York.
b. It's from China.
c. He's the host of *Name That City!*
d. May, Sara, and Dan.
e. Meili.

C. Do you have a nickname? Check (✓) your answer.

❑ No, I don't.   ❑ Yes, I do. My nickname is _____.

D. Work with a partner. Ask your partner these questions. Write your partner's answers.

1. What is your first name? _____
2. What is your last name? _____
3. What is your full name? _____

7 **Choosing *Who, What,* or *Where*: *Name That City!***

Write *Who, What,* or *Where*.

1. Q: _What_ is *Name That City!*?   A: It's a TV game show.
2. Q: _____ is the host of the show?   A: Alan Adams.
3. Q: _____ is the show?   A: In New York.
4. Q: _____ are the contestants?   A: Sara, Dan, and May.
5. Q: _____ is from Evergreen?   A: May.
6. Q: _____ is Evergreen?   A: It's a small town (near Denver).
7. Q: _____ is Denver?   A: In Colorado. (It's the capital.)
8. Q: _____ is from Philadelphia?   A: Dan.
9. Q: _____ is the nickname for Philadelphia?   A: It's "The City of Brotherly Love."
10. Q: _____ is Sara from?   A: Los Angeles.

8 Answering *Yes/No* and *Wh-* Questions with *Be*: The Winner

A. Read and listen to some information about Sara.

Sara Jordan is in New York. She's a contestant on the TV show *Name That City!* Sara's from Los Angeles, California. She is 28 years old, and she's married. Her husband's name is Al Jordan. Al is a reporter, and Sara is a travel agent. Her office is in Los Angeles.

a reporter = a person who learns about events and tells people the news (on TV or radio or in the newspaper).

B. Listen to the questions about Sara. You will hear each question twice. Circle your answers.

1. a. A student.   b. Dan.   c. Sara. *(circled)*
2. a. On TV.   b. Jordan.   c. In New York.
3. a. Yes, she is.   b. *Name That City!*   c. No, it isn't.
4. a. In New York.   b. Los Angeles.   c. A contestant.
5. a. Al.   b. She's 28.   c. Yes, she is.
6. a. He's her husband. b. Alan Adams.   c. No, he's not.
7. a. No, she isn't.   b. A student.   c. She's a travel agent.
8. a. It's in Los Angeles. b. Yes, it is.   c. He's a reporter.

TALKING THE TALK

Contractions of *who/what/where* + *is* are common in speaking and in informal writing.

SAY OR WRITE TO A FRIEND	WRITE IN A PAPER FOR SCHOOL
What's the answer?	**What is** the answer?

9 **Asking and Answering *Wh-* Questions with *Be*: Talk to Antonio**

A. Write questions with *Who*, *What*, or *Where* + *are* or *'s*. Use the subject in parentheses.

Pretend you are in Chicago, and you are talking to Antonio (from page 17). You are at his school.

YOU:	**ANTONIO:**
1. <u>Where are we?</u> (we)	We're in Building 2.
2. _____ (your name)	Antonio.
3. _____ (you)	I'm an ESL student.
4. _____ (your teacher's name)	Mr. Rees.
5. _____ (Mr. Rees)	He's in his office.
6. _____ (the students)	They're in the classroom.
7. _____ (your friends)	Teresa, Kai, and Yoshi.
8. _____ (your hometown)	In Colombia.
9. _____ (Colombia)	In South America.

B. Work with a partner. Take turns asking and answering *wh-* questions. You can use some questions from Part **A.** Think of more questions, too. Give your own answers, not Antonio's answers. Take turns.

Example: Student A: Where's your hometown?
Student B: In Korea.

10 **Questions with *What* or *Where* + *Be*: A Quiz**

A. Work with a partner. Use the maps on page 19 and in Appendix 9. Write *wh-* questions about places. Practice saying the answers.

Example: Student A: What's Little Rock?
Student B: It's a city. It's a state capital.

1. What's _____

2. What's the capital of _____

3. Where is _____

4. Where are _____

5. What is the capital of _____

6. _____

B. Work with a new partner. Take turns asking your questions from Part A. Use the maps.

Example: Student A: *What's Little Rock?*
Student B: *It's the capital of Arkansas.*
Student A: *That's right.*

See the *Grammar Links* Website for more information about the 50 states.

11 **Editing:** **A Good Place for a Vacation**

Read the conversation. Correct the errors. There are nine errors in questions and short answers. The first one is corrected for you.

Sara Jordan isn't in New York now. She's at work. She's at her travel agency in Los Angeles. She's talking to a customer.

Sara: Hello, I'm Sara Jordan.

Dr. Kim: Good morning. I'm Dr. Kim. ~~You~~ ^{Are you} a travel agent?

Sara: Yes, I'm.

Dr. Kim: Tell me, who is a good place for a vacation?

Sara: Is you interested in a cruise?

Dr. Kim: No, I are not! Cruise ships are noisy.

Sara: What your idea of a good vacation?

Dr. Kim: A good vacation is a week on the beach with a good book.

Sara: Well, then, Catalina is a good place for you.

Dr. Kim: What Catalina? Is in California?

Sara: Yes, it's. It's an island with beautiful beaches.

Dr. Kim: Catalina—it's a great idea!

Check your progress! Go to the Self-Test for Chapter 2 on the *Grammar Links* Website.

Wrap-up Activities

1 A Beautiful City: READING

Read this paragraph.

San Francisco is a great place to visit. It is a beautiful city in California. There are many things to do in San Francisco. The city has good museums and restaurants. There are nice parks. It is fun to ride the cable cars. It is fun to shop in Chinatown, too.

A San Francisco Cable Car

See the *Grammar Links* Website for more information about San Francisco.

2 A Nice Place to Visit: WRITING

Choose a place to write about. Complete the sentence: _____ *is a nice place to visit.* Write three or more sentences about this place. Be sure each sentence has a subject and a verb.

> ### Kyoto
>
> Kyoto is a nice place to visit. It is in Japan. It is an old city. It is beautiful. The city has many temples.

See the *Grammar Links* Website for another model paragraph.

3 Austin: EDITING

Correct the six errors in the paragraph. The first error is corrected for you. Some errors can be corrected in more than one way.

> **Austin**
>
> Austin ~~it's~~ _is_ an interesting city. Is in Texas.
>
> The weather it is hot in the summer. It is'nt hot
>
> in the spring or fall. Is nice. Austin is famous for
>
> good music. The people they are friendly.

4 A Race: LISTENING/SPEAKING/WRITING

Form a team. Find a space at the blackboard, or use a piece of paper. Use only one piece of chalk or one pen for your team. (You can take turns, or one person can be the writer.) Listen to your teacher for directions.

> **Rules**
> - Spelling is important.
> - It's okay to ask questions.
> - The first team to finish is the winner.

(Teacher: See page A-1.)

5 A Guessing Game: LISTENING/SPEAKING/WRITING

Step 1 Work with one or two partners. Look at the maps on page 19 and in Appendix 9. Choose three places (cities, states, provinces, or regions.) Write the names of the places on three pieces of paper. Write four statements with *be* (affirmative and negative) about each place. These four statements are **clues** to help people guess the place.

Montreal

1. It is in Canada.
2. It is not a province.
3. It is in Quebec.
4. It is not the capital.

Step 2 Put all the papers from the class in an envelope or on the teacher's desk. Your teacher will take a paper and read the clues on it to the class. What is the place? Guess!

Nouns, Articles and Adjectives; Demonstratives, Possessives, and Conjunctions

TOPIC FOCUS
Families and Possessions

UNIT OBJECTIVES

- **count nouns**
  (My two **sisters** are in California.
  My **brother** is a **teacher**.)

- **the articles** *a/an* **and** *the*
  (He is **a** teacher. My aunt is **an** artist.
  Her son is in **the** army.)

- **descriptive adjectives**
  (The car is **new**. It's a **red** car.)

- **demonstrative adjectives and pronouns**
  (**That** man is my father. **This** is my brother.)

- **possessive adjectives and nouns**
  (**His** name is Mark. This is **Mark's** dog.)

- **conjunctions** *and*, *but*, **and** *or*
  (This house is new **and** expensive. Is that your book, **or** is it from the library?)

Grammar in Action

Read and listen.

Lisa Kalmar and her family are at a street party. All the families on their street are at the party. Lisa's new friend, Anne Santo, is there, too.

Lisa:	Hi, Anne. I'm glad you're here.
Anne:	Me, too. Wow! This **party** is *great*! Are these all your **neighbors**?
Lisa:	Uh-huh. All the **families** on Elm Street are really *friendly*.
Anne:	Is your **family** here?
Lisa:	Yes, the **woman** with the camera is my **mother**. Come on. I'll introduce you.
Anne:	Okay.
Lisa:	Mom, this is my **friend** Anne. Anne, this is my mother, Judy Kalmar.
Anne:	It's nice to meet you, Mrs. Kalmar.
Mrs. Kalmar:	Nice to meet you, Anne. Please call me Judy.

Lisa: My **father** is over at the volleyball game, and those *little* **boys** are my **brothers**. Their names are Jim and Jon.

Anne: How old are they?

Lisa: Eight. They're **twins**. Hey, guys! Come here a minute!

Anne: Hi. I'm Anne. That's a *big* **dog**! Is he your dog?

Jim: No, he's our neighbors' dog.

Anne: Do you have a dog?

Jon: No, but we have some other **animals**. They're really *nice*.

Anne: Oh, really? Where are these **pets** of yours?

Lisa: No! No! Please, no!

Jon: They're right here.

Anne: Oh, yuck!

Lisa: Anne, wait! Thanks a lot, guys. Those **snakes** are *ugly*! People don't like them!

Anne! Wait for me!

Think About Grammar

A. Look at the **boldfaced** words in the conversation. These words are **nouns**. Is each boldfaced noun singular (one thing) or is it plural (two or more things)? Write the nouns in the chart.

Singular Nouns	Plural Nouns
party	neighbors

What is the last letter of the plural nouns? Write it here: _____

B. Look at the words in *italics* in the conversation. These words are **adjectives**. Adjectives describe or tell about nouns.

Look at the **boldfaced** adjectives in these sentences. What do they describe in the conversation? Write the nouns from the box.

boys	dog	families	party	snakes

1. It's a **great** party _____ .

2. There are **friendly** _____ on Elm Street.

3. Jim and Jon are **little** _____ .

4. The neighbors have a **big** _____ .

5. Do the boys have **ugly** _____ ?

The plural nouns end in -*s*. Do the adjectives before the plural nouns end in -*s*?

Circle the answer: Yes   No

Every Family Is Different
Count Nouns, Articles, and Adjectives

Introductory Task: Lisa's Family Tree

Mrs. Kalmar (grandmother)

Mark Kalmar

Mr. and Mrs. Carlson (grandparents)

Judy (Carlson) Kalmar

Jim   Lisa Kalmar   Jon

A. This is a picture of Lisa Kalmar's family. Write the names of the people in Lisa's family on the family tree.

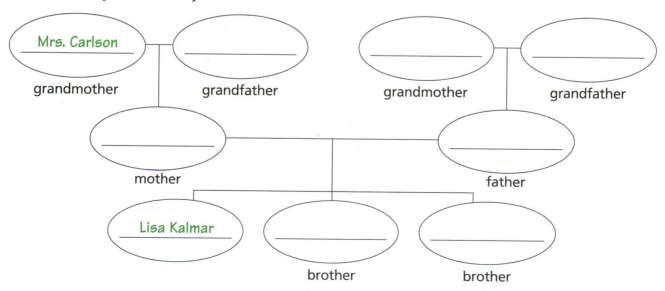

Mrs. Carlson

grandmother   grandfather   grandmother   grandfather

mother   father

Lisa Kalmar

brother   brother

B. Draw a family tree for your family.

C. Work with a partner. Tell your partner about your family.

Example: Natia is my sister.

Male Relatives	Female Relatives
father	mother
brother	sister
husband	wife
son	daughter
grandfather	grandmother

See page 78 for a family tree showing *aunt*, *uncle*, *cousin*, *niece*, and *nephew*.

Nouns

FUNCTION

Using Nouns

1. A **noun** is a word for a person, place, or thing.	My **sister** is in **Dallas**. She has an **apartment**.
2. There are different kinds of nouns.	
• A **proper noun** names a specific person, place, or thing. It begins with a capital letter.	**Aunt Edna** is in **New York City**.
• A **common noun** does not name a specific person, place, or thing. It does not begin with a capital letter.	My **aunt** is in the **city**.
3. A noun is often the subject of a sentence.	**Lisa** has a car.
4. Nouns also come after:	
• *Be*.	Lisa **is** my **sister**.
• A preposition.	She is **at** a **party**.

GRAMMAR PRACTICE 1

Nouns

1 **Proper and Common Nouns:** Anne's Family

A. Circle the 10 proper nouns in the message. The first one is circled for you.

TO: LisaK@welcome.net
FROM: anne_santo@today.net
DATE: 5/15 8:30 p.m.
SUBJ: Hi

Well, Lisa, here I am, back in New York. It's good to be home! I'm especially glad to see my family.

There are four of us: my grandmother, my uncle, my brother, and me. My brother is at school here.

His name is George. He's at Columbia University. My uncle is an art teacher. Uncle Bob is at his

favorite art museum today. It's the Metropolitan Museum of Art. My grandmother is a librarian at the

New York Public Library. It's a great place to study.

There are two other important members of my family, Fluff and Muff. They're my cats! They're here

in my room right now. Come and visit us, OK? We hope to see you soon! Anne

B. Write the 10 proper nouns from Part A in the chart. The first two are done for you.

Common Noun	Proper Noun
girl	Lisa
city	New York City
brother	
school	
uncle	
museum	
library	
cats	
girl	

C. Write some proper nouns for people and places in your life.

Common Noun	Proper Noun
city or town	
school	
brother or sister	
pet	
favorite museum	
friend	

D. Work with a partner. Tell about the people and places in Part C.

Example: I'm from Taipei. It's a city.

Count Nouns

FORM

A. Singular and Plural Count Nouns

	SINGULAR (ONE)		PLURAL (TWO OR MORE)
I have one	**sister**.	Do you have	**sisters**?
There is one	**box**.	There are four	**boxes**.
Austin is a	**city**.	Dallas and Houston are	**cities**.

B. Count Versus Noncount Nouns

1. A **count noun** can be counted. It has a singular and a plural form.

   one **book**, two **books**, three **books**, . . .

2. Some nouns are **noncount nouns**. They have only one form.

   (See Chapter 15 for more about noncount nouns.)

   water

   music

   homework

C. Spelling Rules for Plural Count Nouns

1. For most count nouns, add -*s*.

   room → rooms   snake → snake**s**

   girl → girl**s**   video → video**s**

2. For count nouns ending in *ch*, *sh*, *ss*, or *x*, add -*es*.

   lunch → lunch**es**   brush → brush**es**

   kiss → kiss**es**   box → box**es**

3. For most count nouns ending in a consonant + *o*, add -*es*.

   pota**to** → potato**es**   **zero** → zero**es**

     BUT: one piano, two pianos

           one photo, two photo**s**

           one radio, two radios

4. For count nouns ending in *y*:

   - When there is a vowel (*a*, *e*, *i*, *o*, or *u*) before the *y*, add -*s*.

     day → days   **key** → keys

   - When there is a consonant before the *y*, drop the *y* and add -*ies*.

     story → stor**ies**   penny → penn**ies**

5. For nouns ending in *f* or *fe*, drop the *f(e)* and add -*ves*.

   shelf → shel**ves**   knife → kni**ves**

6. Some count nouns are **irregular**. They do not add -*s* for plurals.

   person → **people**   man → **men**

   child → **children**   woman → **women**

Count Nouns

2 **Singular and Plural Count Nouns:** Anne's Room

A. Read about Anne's room. Look at the **boldfaced** nouns. Write *S* over the singular nouns and *P* over the plural nouns.

Anne is at home in her family's **apartment** in New York. There are
                                          S
                                          apartment
                                          1

six **rooms** in the **apartment**. Anne's **bedroom** is small, but she has
    2   3   4

many **things** in it. There's a **table** next to her **bed**. There are many
     5   6   7

magazines and **CDs** on the **table**. Anne has a lot of **books** on her
8   9   10   11

shelves. She has a **computer** on her **desk** and many **papers**, **pens**, and
12   13   14   15   16

pencils. She also has an English-Spanish **dictionary**. These are **things**
17   18   19

that she uses for **school**.
                   20

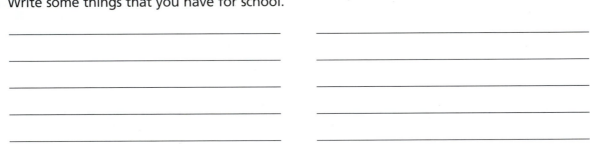

Magazines

A Dictionary

B. Write some things that you have for school.

_____   _____

_____   _____

_____   _____

_____   _____

C. Work with a partner. Read your list to your partner. Listen to your partner's list. Circle the things that are the same on the two lists.

GRAMMAR HOTSPOT!

Use a singular verb with a singular subject. Use a plural verb with a plural subject.	The apartment **is** clean.
	The apartments **are** clean.

The Martins

3 **Subject and Verb Agreement:** Ms. Patti Martin

Look at the **boldfaced** subjects. Are they singular or plural? Write the verb *is* or *are*.

Ms. Patti Martin and her children, Suzy and Jack, _____are_____ neighbors of the

1

Kalmars. **Ms. Martin** _____ a busy person. She has three gardens. She works in her

2

gardens every weekend. The **gardens** _____ not big. One **garden** _____ for

3 4

vegetables. Two **gardens** _____ full of flowers. The **flowers** _____ beautiful

5 6

in the spring and summer.

Ms. Martin _____ a music teacher. She has a piano, a violin, and two guitars.

7

The **piano** _____ old. Ms. Martin plays it every morning. The **violin** _____

8 9

expensive. It sounds beautiful. The **guitars** _____ new. One **guitar** _____

10 11

electric. The other **guitar** _____ from Spain. The Martin family loves music. Their

12

house _____ full of music.

13

A Piano

A Violin

A Guitar

4 **Singular and Plural Forms of Count Nouns:** My Aunt Edna

Lisa Kalmar is talking about her aunt. Read about Aunt Edna. Circle the correct forms of the count nouns.

My Aunt Edna is my favorite ((aunt) / aunts). She's an (artist / artists). Her
                                    1   2
(house / houses) is in San Francisco. She has about 100 (painting / paintings) in the
     3   4
(house / houses). She also has 25 (cat / cats). In the kitchen, she has 25 (dish / dishes)
     5   6   7
for her cats. In the living room, she also has 25 (toy / toys) for the (cat / cats). She has
                                                        8   9
25 (brush / brushes) for the cats and 25 little (bed / beds) for them to sleep in. She has
      10   11
a (comb / combs) for one cat with very long hair. The (cat / cats) are very happy
      12   13
because Aunt Edna is good to them.

TALKING THE TALK

The final -s in plural count nouns has three sounds: /s/, /z/, and /ɪz/.

- Say /s/ after the voiceless sounds /p/, /t/, /k/, /f/, and /th/.

- Say /z/ after vowel sounds and after the voiced consonant sounds /b/, /d/, /g/, /v/, /th/, /m/, /n/, /ng/, /l/, and /r/.

- Say /ɪz/ after the sounds /s/, /z/, /sh/, /ch/, /zh/, /j/, and /ks/. The /ɪz/ sound adds a syllable.

hats (/s/)	bags (/z/)	brushes (/ɪz/)
cups	parents	books
beliefs	months	
boys	families	clubs
kids	dogs	shelves
baths	rooms	pins
things	balls	cars
nieces	houses	dishes
watches	garages	pages
boxes		

---

5 **Plural Count Noun Endings:** Aunt Edna and Her Cats

   A. Listen to the sentences. After each **boldfaced** plural noun, circle the final sound you hear. The first one is done for you.

1. Aunt Edna is one of Lisa's **aunts**. (/ɪz/, /z/, (/s/))

2. She has 25 **cats**. (/ɪz/, /z/, /s/)

3. They are different **sizes**. (/ɪz/, /z/, /s/) Some are big, and some are small.

4. She has eight new **kittens**. (/ɪz/, /z/, /s/)

5. Three are **boys**. (/ɪz/, /z/, /s/)

6. Five are **girls**. (/ɪz/, /z/, /s/)

7. Where are their **dishes**? (/ɪz/, /z/, /s/)

8. They're in the kitchen, next to their **toys**. (/ɪz/, /z/, /s/)

9. Two kittens are asleep in **boxes**. (/ɪz/, /z/, /s/)

10. Three kittens are inside some **bags**. (/ɪz/, /z/, /s/)

11. They are wonderful **pets**. (/ɪz/, /z/, /s/)

B. Work with a partner. Write the plural nouns. Take turns saying the words. Add a syllable when you say the /ɪz/ ending.

/ɪz/	/z/	/s/
brush _____	toy _____	pet _____
watch _____	city _____	cup _____
house _____	piano _____	light _____
size _____	baby _____	plant _____
box _____	kitten _____	bike _____
glass _____	knife _____	month _____

C. Take a class survey. Ask your classmates about pets. Make a chart to show the information.

Example: Student A: *Do you have a pet?*
Student B: *Yes.*
Student A: *Is it a dog?*
Student B: *Yes, it is.*

People in My Class	Do You Have a Pet?		Kinds of Pets People Have				Number of Pets
	Yes	No	Dogs	Cats	Birds	Other	
22	ＨＨＴ ＨＨＴ ＨＨＴ ＨＨＴ //	ＨＨＴ ＨＨＴ	////	ＨＨＴ /	/	1 snake	12

6 | **Singular and Plural Count Nouns:** Classroom Things

Work with a partner. Look at the people and things in the classroom. Write the singular and plural nouns for these people and things. Say the words aloud.

1. _____
2. _____
3. _____
4. _____

5. _____
6. _____
7. _____
8. _____

9. _____
10. _____
11. _____
12. _____

The Articles *A/An* and *The*

FORM and FUNCTION

A. *A/An*

	A + SINGULAR NOUN			*AN* + SINGULAR NOUN
He has	**a cat.**		He has	**an apartment**.
They have	**a garden**.		They have	**an office**.

B. Using *A/An*

1. Use the **article** *a* or *an* with singular count nouns. *A* and *an* have the same meaning. *A/an* often means "one."	I have **a** sister. = I have **one** sister.
• Use *a* before consonant sounds.	**a** bed, **a** dog, **a** hat
• Use *an* before vowel sounds.	**an** apple, **an** island, **an** hour
2. Use *a/an* with a singular noun that is not specific.	I have **a pen** (any pen, not one certain pen).
Do not use *a/an* with plural nouns. Use no article with a plural noun that is not specific.	I like **apples** (all apples, apples in general).
3. Use *a/an* when you introduce a noun for the first time.	Anne has **an apartment**. Her apartment is nice.
4. Use *a/an* to classify or define a person, place, or thing.	**A** dog is **a** pet. **A** kitchen is **a** room.

C. *The*

THE + SINGULAR NOUN			*THE* + PLURAL NOUN	
The apartment	is nice.		**The apartments**	are nice.
The door	is open.		**The doors**	are open.

D. Using *The*

1. Use *the* with singular and plural nouns. Use it when the noun means a specific person, place, or thing.	Mr. Lim is **the teacher** in Room 112.
2. Use *the* when the person, place, or thing is unique. (There is only one.)	Paris is **the capital of France**. **The sun** is hot.

(continued on next page)

D. Using *The* (continued)

3. Use *the* when you use a noun for the second time.

1st use	2nd use

Anne has **an apartment**. **The apartment** is nice.

4. Use *the* when you and your listener both know the person, place, or thing.

Mother: Where is **the dog**?
Son: In **the kitchen**.

(*The dog* is their family dog; *the kitchen* is the kitchen in their house; the speaker and the listener both know them.)

GRAMMAR **HOT**SPOT!

1. Often all the people in a family have the same last name. Use *the* + the plural form of their last name to mean all the family.

The Martins are nice people.

2. Remember! Use *the* only when the noun is specific. Use *a/an* or no article when the noun is not specific.

The cats in this photo are Fluff and Muff.

Pets are animals in people's homes.
NOT: ~~The~~ pets are ~~the~~ animals in ~~the~~ people's homes.

GRAMMAR PRACTICE 3

The Articles *A/An* and *The*

7 Listening for Articles: The Family of the Year

Patti Martin gets a surprising phone call. Listen for the articles *a*, *an*, and *the*. Listen again and write the articles.

Bob: Good afternoon. May I speak to Ms. Patti Martin?

Patti: I'm Ms. Martin.

Bob: Hello, I'm Bob Clark, from *Family Time* magazine. Congratulations! Your family is

_____the_____ Family of the Year!
      1

Patti: What? That's not possible!

Bob: Oh, yes, it is! We have _____ family in Ohio in second place, and _____
2   3

family in New Mexico in third place, but your family is _____ winning family.
                                                         4

_____ Martins of California are _____ Family of the Year! Congratulations!
5   6

Patti: I don't know what to say! Is there _____ prize?
                                          7

Bob: Oh, yes, there is! _____ new car!
                        8

Patti: Oh! I can't believe it!

Bob: But wait. There's more . . . _____ trip to _____ Hawaiian Islands!
                                 9   10

Patti: Oh! _____ trip to Hawaii? What _____ amazing thing! I . . . I . . .
           11   12

Bob: And there's still more! _____ check for fifty thousand dollars!
                             13

Patti: You're kidding! Oh, thank you, Mr. Clark.

Bob: Thank you, Ms. Martin! Now, _____ official letter is in the mail to you. It has all
                                 14

the information about your prizes. And your family photo is on _____ cover of
                                                               15

the new *Family Time* magazine.

Patti: We're on the cover? Wow! Oh, thank you again, Mr. Clark!

Bob: It's my pleasure, Ms. Martin.

8 Using *A* or *An* or No Article: What Do I Want?

A. The Martin family has a check for fifty thousand dollars. What do they want to buy?
Add *a* or *an* to their lists.

Patti Martin: Mother Age: 38	Suzy Martin: Daughter Age: 16	Jack Martin: Son Age: 10
1. _an_ airplane	6. _____ car	11. _____ boat
2. _____ pool	7. _____ CD player	12. _____ computer
3. _____ clock	8. _____ electric guitar	13. _____ island
4. _____ video camera	9. _____ printer	14. _____ elephant
5. _____ air conditioner	10. _____ radio	15. _____ motorcycle

B. Write *a, an,* or — (for no article).

Patti Martin has ___a___ list. The list has ___—___ things
1 2

for everyone in the family. Patti plans to buy _____ air conditioner,
3

_____ CD player and _____ CDs, _____ electric guitar,
4 5 6

and _____ new computer with _____ printer and _____
7 8 9

computer games for Jack. She doesn't plan to buy _____ pool,
10

_____ boat, _____ island, _____ animals of
11 12 13

any kind, or _____ motorcycle.
14

An Air Conditioner

A Boat

A Motorcycle

C. Imagine you have a check for fifty thousand dollars! What do you want?
Write a list of five things on a piece of paper. Use *a* or *an* (+ a singular
noun) or no article (+ a plural noun).

D. Work with a partner. Tell your partner about your five things. What is on your
partner's list? Do you want the same things?

9 **Using *A/An, The,* or No Article:** Prizes

Read about the Martins, their new car, and other prizes. Write *a, an, the,* or —
(for no article).

1. The Martins have ___a___ new car. _____ car is great!
a b

2. _____ Martins' car has _____ computer inside. _____
a b c

computer has _____ maps.
d

3. _____ Martins' car has _____ radio and _____
a b c

CD player. There are _____ speakers in the front and back.
d

4. Suzy Martin: Mom, where's _____ new video camera?
a

Patti Martin: It's in _____ car.
b

5. It's fun to win _____ prizes. Do you think _____ trip to Disney World
a b

is _____ good prize?
c

Descriptive Adjectives

FORM and FUNCTION

A. Descriptive Adjective + Noun

	ADJECTIVE	NOUN	
He has a	nice	camera.	·
The	new	CD	is on the table.
	Big	cars	are expensive.

B. *Be* + Descriptive Adjective

	BE	ADJECTIVE
I	am	ready.
That bike	is	new.
The boys	aren't	hungry.

C. Using Descriptive Adjectives

1. Adjectives describe nouns. They give information about nouns.

    He has a car. It's a **small** car.

2. Descriptive adjectives have only one form. They do not change for singular or plural, male or female.

    Lisa is **friendly**.

    Jim and Jon are **friendly**.

    They are **nice** boys.
      NOT: They are ~~nices~~ boys.

GRAMMAR PRACTICE 4

Descriptive Adjectives

10 **Identifying and Using Descriptive Adjectives:** My Car

A. Read about the cars. Circle the descriptive adjectives. Then match the picture to the description.

_____ 1. My car is a classic. It is an (old) car. It is long and wide. The wheels are shiny and bright. It's an expensive car.

_____ 2. My car is fast and noisy. It's not a big car, but the engine is powerful. My car is low and wide. It's a great car to drive.

_____ 3. My car is not slow, but it's not fast. It's a small car. It's not beautiful, but it's cute. It's a good car for me.

> *a classic* = a very good car from a long time ago.

a. Lisa   b. Felix   c. Hank

B. Look at the owners of the cars. Choose adjectives from the box to describe each person. You can write an adjective once, twice, three times, or not at all.

Adjectives			
bald	heavy	rich	strong
friendly	old	short	tall
good-looking	married	single	thin
happy	pretty	smart	young

a. Lisa   b. Felix   c. Hank

_____   _____   _____

_____   _____   _____

_____   _____   _____

_____   _____   _____

C. Work in a group of three or four. Talk about the people. Use your adjectives for them. Take turns. Are all your lists of adjectives the same?

Example: Student A: Lisa is young. She is happy.

See the *Grammar Links* Website for more information about different kinds of cars.

11 Word Order: Tell Me About the Car Owners

Use the words to write sentences about the people and cars in Exercise 10.
Remember to use capital letters and periods in your sentences.

1. tall/Hank/is   _Hank is tall._ _____

2. a/tall/he/is/man   _____

3. Lisa/lazy/is/not   _____

4. good/is/a/she/student   _____

5. the/different/cars/are   _____

6. is/not/Felix/young   _____

7. the/is/expensive/car   _____

8. car/cheap/a/is/not/it   _____

12 Using Descriptive Adjectives: Describing a Family Member or Friend

A. Think of a friend or family member. Circle the adjectives in the box that
describe the person. You can add more adjectives to the list.

> beautiful/handsome—ugly   hard-working—lazy
> friendly—shy   loud—quiet
> funny—serious   short—tall
> happy—sad   young—middle-aged—old
>
> other: _____   _____   _____

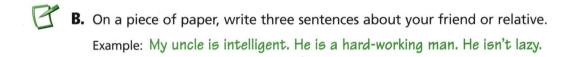

B. On a piece of paper, write three sentences about your friend or relative.

Example: _My uncle is intelligent. He is a hard-working man. He isn't lazy._

C. Work with a partner. Read your sentences to your partner. Listen to your
partner's sentences. In the box in Part A, underline your partner's words. Does
your partner have any other adjectives? Write those new adjectives here:

_____

Check your progress! Go to the Self-Test for
Chapter 3 on the *Grammar Links* Website.

Chapter 4

Families and Their Activities
Demonstratives, Possessives, and Conjunctions

Introductory Task: Where's My Camera?

 A. Listen to the conversation.

The Kalmars are on vacation in Washington, D.C. They're at a hotel. They are almost ready to go to the White House.

  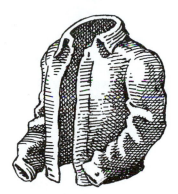

| A Backpack | Sunglasses | A Jacket |

B. Read the statements about possessions. Who owns the **boldfaced** possessions? Listen again to the conversation in Part A, and circle *a* or *b*.

1. You have **your camera**.   (a.) Mrs. Kalmar   b. Jim

2. We have our **backpacks**.   a. Lisa   b. Jim and Jon

3. **Her book** has the map and directions.   a. Mr. Kalmar   b. Lisa

4. I have **my sunglasses**.   a. Lisa   b. Mr. and Mrs. Kalmar

5. Where are **their hats**?   a. Mrs. Kalmar   b. Jim and Jon

6. **His jacket** is here.   a. Lisa   b. Mr. Kalmar

possessions = things that a person owns.

Demonstrative Pronouns and Adjectives

FORM and FUNCTION

A. Overview

Demonstrative pronouns and adjectives "point to" people and things. *This* and *these* are for people or things **near** the speaker. *That* and *those* are for things **not near** the speaker.

This watch is nice. **These** glasses are old.

That is my car.

Those are my friends.

B. Demonstrative Adjectives

SINGULAR			PLURAL		
ADJECTIVE	NOUN		ADJECTIVE	NOUN	
This	watch	is nice.	**These**	glasses	are old.
That			**Those**		

Demonstrative adjectives come before nouns.

I like **that bike**.

Those people are my neighbors.

C. Demonstrative Pronouns

SINGULAR			PLURAL		
PRONOUN	VERB		PRONOUN	VERB	
This	is	my watch.	**These**	are	my glasses.
That		your chair.	**Those**		nice cars.

Demonstrative pronouns take the place of nouns.

That
~~That car~~ is my car.

Q: Who are the new people?

Those
A: ~~The new people~~ are my friends.

Demonstrative Pronouns and Adjectives

1 **Identifying Demonstrative Pronouns and Adjectives:** A Tour of the White House

A. The Kalmars are at the White House. Read and listen. Circle the demonstratives you hear: *this, that, these,* or *those.*

The White House in Washington, D.C.

Tour guide: Welcome to the White House. We're in the Blue Room right now. ((This) / That) room is for meetings. You will see many things from other countries in the
1

White House. (These / Those) chairs are from France. And (this / that) table in
2   3
the center is also French. Please come this way. Now we're in the East Room.

(This / That) is a large room for dances and parties. Do you see (these / those)
4   5
paintings on the wall?

Jim: Hey, is (this / that) George Washington?
6

Tour guide: Yes, you're right. (This / That) is a famous painting of our first president, and
7
(this / that) picture shows his wife, Martha. Now please follow me to the China
8
Room. Is everyone here? Good. (This / That) is a small room with china plates
9
and cups from the past.

Lisa: I like the blue and gold ones. (These / Those) are beautiful.
10

Tour guide: Uh-huh. (These / Those) are from the Lenox Company in Pennsylvania. Step this
11
way, please. (This / That) large room is the State Dining Room. It's for special
12
dinners and parties. And (this / that) painting over there is of President . . .
13

Jim and Jon: Abraham Lincoln!

Tour guide: Yes, indeed. We are now at the end of the tour. (This / That) is the gift shop on
14
your left. Thank you for visiting the White House.

The Kalmars: Thank you!

B. Write *P* over the demonstrative pronouns in Part A. Write *A* over the demonstrative adjectives.

Examples: (This / That) room is for meetings.

                ^A

                  (This / That) is a large room.

                ^P

 See the *Grammar Links* Website for more information about the White House.

2 Demonstrative Pronouns and Adjectives: The Kalmars' Things

A. Write the adjective *this* or *these*.

1. Jon: ___This_____ camera is Mom's.

2. Lisa: _____ watch is Dad's.

3. Lisa: I like _____ sunglasses.

4. Jim: _____ hats are Jon's and mine.

5. Lisa: _____ postcards are for my friends.

6. Lisa: I'm reading _____ book.

B. Write the pronoun *this* or *these* + *is* or *are*.

1. ___These are_____ Lisa's sunglasses

2. _____ Lisa's book.

3. _____ the boys' hats.

4. _____ Mr. Kalmar's watch.

5. _____ Mrs. Kalmar's camera.

6. _____ Lisa's postcards.

C. Write the adjective *that* or *those*.

1. <u>That</u> van is the Kalmars' van.

2. _____ things belong to the Kalmar family.

3. _____ backpacks are Jim and Jon's.

4. _____ suitcase is Lisa's.

5. _____ bags are her parents' bags.

6. _____ umbrella is Lisa's.

TALKING THE TALK

1. The contracted form of *that + is* is *that's*. *That's* is common in conversation and in informal writing.

SAY	WRITE
That's a good book.	**That is** a good book.

2. Demonstratives are common in questions with *What*. Use these questions when you don't know what things are.

Q: **What's this**?
A: It's my CD player.

Q: **What are these**?
A: They're my CDs.

3 **Demonstrative Pronouns in *What* Questions:** What's That?

A. Work with a partner. Student A: Look at pictures in this book. Point to things and ask *What's this?* and *What are these?* Student B: Answer with *That is/Those are*. Take turns.

Example: Student A: What's this?
Student B: That's the White House.

B. Continue working with your partner. Point to things that are **not** near you in the classroom. Ask *What's that?* and *What are those?* Take turns.

Example: Student B: What are those?
Student A: English books.

Possessive Adjectives

FORM and FUNCTION

A. Singular and Plural Possessive Adjectives

SINGULAR	PLURAL	
my	our	
your	your	
his		
her	their	
its		

B. Using Possessive Adjectives

1. Possessive adjectives show that a person owns or possesses something.

   Jack has a book. It is **his** book.

2. Possessive adjectives always come before nouns.

   They have a car. **Their car** is big.

   Whose chair is this? Is this **your chair**?

3. Possessive adjectives agree in number (singular or plural) and gender (male or female) with the owner.

   owners
   Jim and Jon are brothers. **Their** room is large.
   owner
   Lisa has two brothers. **Her** brothers are little.

4. The form of a possessive adjective is the same before a singular noun or a plural noun.

   Our neighbor is friendly.
   Our neighbors are friendly.

GRAMMAR **HOT**SPOT!

1. *It's* and *its* sound the same, but they have different meanings:

   • *It's* = *it is*.

   Jim has a snake. **It's** small.

   • *Its* = a possessive adjective.

   The snake has a name. **Its** name is Boo.

2. Remember! A possessive adjective matches the owner (male or female, singular or plural).

   My **uncle** is Canadian. **His** wife is Chinese
   NOT: ~~Her~~ wife is Chinese.

   Mr. and Mrs. Doe have a son. **Their** son is 21.
   NOT: ~~His~~ son is 21.

Possessive Adjectives

4 **Identifying Possessive Adjectives:** Suzy's Letter from Hawaii

Suzy Martin is in Hawaii with her mother and her brother. Read Suzy's letter to her friend Lisa Kalmar. Circle the nine possessive adjectives. The first one is circled for you.

Dear Lisa,

Well, we're in Hawaii, on the island of Oahu! I can't believe it! (Our) hotel is big and very comfortable. Its restaurant is one of the best on the island. The food is great.

My mother and I love the stores. Our bags are full of new clothes. Her suitcase is so heavy! Jack is happy, too. We go to the beach every day. It's his favorite place. He loves to swim.

The Hawaiian people are very friendly. I think their islands are beautiful. We're having a wonderful time. I hope your trip to Washington is fun, too.

Your friend,

Suzy

5 Choosing Possessive Adjectives: Hawaiian Souvenirs

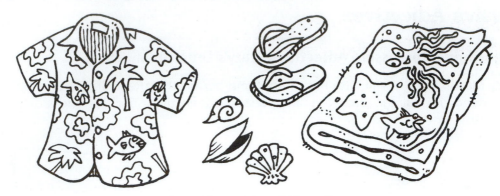

Some Souvenirs of Hawaii

A. Read about the Martins' souvenirs from their trip. Complete the statements with the missing possessive adjectives.

1. Patti: Suzy and I have Hawaiian dresses. <u>Our</u> dresses are comfortable.

2. Jack and Suzy have sunglasses. _____ sunglasses are new.

3. Suzy: My mother has postcards. _____ postcards are of the beach.

4. Jack: I have a Hawaiian shirt. _____ shirt is blue and white.

5. Jack has some shells from the beach. _____ shells are unusual.

6. Suzy: I have new sandals. _____ sandals are pretty.

7. Jack has a T-shirt. _____ T-shirt is big.

8. Patti: We have photos. _____ photos are of places in Hawaii.

9. Patti and Suzy have beach towels. _____ towels are red and white.

10. Jack: I don't have a towel. Mom, can I use _____ towel?

> *a souvenir* = something you bring home from a place you visited.

B. Work with a partner. Do you or people in your family have souvenirs from a trip? Who has a souvenir? What is it? Tell your partner. Use possessive adjectives.

Example: I have a T-shirt from Chicago. My T-shirt is red.
My sister has a hat from New York. Her hat says Yankees.

6 Using Possessive Adjectives: People and Their Things

Work with a partner. Student A: Describe one or two people in the class. Don't say their names. Use possessive adjectives. Student B: Guess who the people are. Take turns.

Example: Student A: Our shirts are green. His backpack is blue. My backpack is black.
Student B: Raúl and you.
Student B: Her jacket is white. Her sunglasses are red.
Student A: Tatiana.

Possessive Nouns; *Whose*

FORM

A. Possessive Nouns

1. Possessive nouns show that a person owns or possesses something.	Jack has a book. It is **Jack's** book.
2. To form a possessive noun:	
• Add *'s* to a singular noun. (' = apostrophe)	My **friend's** car is nice. (singular noun) What is **Luis's** last name? (singular noun)
• Add *'s* to a plural noun that does not end in *s*.	Where is the **men's** room? (irregular plural noun)
• Add only *'* to a plural noun that ends in *s*.	The **boys'** shirts are blue. My **friends'** names are Tim and Kyle.
3. Use a possessive noun + a noun, or use a possessive noun alone.	That is **Mary's shirt**. That shirt is **Mary's**.

B. Questions with *Whose*

1. Use *whose* to ask who owns something.	**Whose** book is that? Is it your book?
2. Use *whose* + a singular or a plural noun.	**Whose cat** is it? **Whose cats** are they?
3. Use *whose* alone when the meaning is clear to the listener.	*Q:* **Whose** are these? Are they your sunglasses? *A:* No, those are Suzy's.

1. These are two different uses for *'s*:

    • As a contraction of *is*.   **Rob's** from Canada.

    • As a possessive form.   **Rob's** wife is French.

2. Do not confuse *whose* and *who's*. They sound the same, but their meanings are different.

    • *Whose* = possessive question word.   *Q:* **Whose** keys are those?
                                                      A: They're my keys.

    • *Who's = who is*.   *Q:* **Who's** your teacher?
                                                      A: Mrs. Cohen.

GRAMMAR PRACTICE 3

Possessive Nouns; *Whose*

7 **Possessive Nouns and *Whose*:** The Kalmars at Home

A. Write the possessive form of the noun in parentheses ( ). Then listen to the conversation.

Mrs. Kalmar is talking to her little boys, Jim and Jon, in their bedroom. She isn't happy.

Mrs. Kalmar: This room is a mess! Listen, boys, your <u>sister's</u> CD player is lost.

                       1 (sister)

                               Is it in here?

Jon: No, it's in _____ bedroom. Hey, whose camera is that?

                   2 (Lisa)

Jim: It's _____ camera.

           3 (Dad)

Jon: Mom, Jim has other _____ stuff under his bed. He has my new

                           4 (people)

                         DVD, my . . .

Mrs. Kalmar: Jim, please put the camera on your _____ desk. No, don't take my
5 (father)

picture! Then get your _____ DVD. What's this? Jon! Is that a dog
6 (brother)

under your bed?

Jim: It's the new _____ dog.
7 (neighbors)

Mrs. Kalmar: That's the _____ dog? Well, take it out! Now!
8 (Smiths)

Jon: Okay, okay. Come, Waldo!

Lisa: Mom? Mom, where are you?

Mrs. Kalmar: I'm up here, in the _____ room.
9 (boys)

Lisa: _____ piano teacher is on the
10 (Jon)

phone. And the _____ cage is empty!
11 (snakes)

Mrs. Kalmar: Jon! Jim! Where are the snakes?

> *a mess* = something that is not neat or in good order. *stuff* = (informal) possessions or things.

B. Work with a partner. Ask questions with *whose* about the people and possessions in Part A. Use possessive nouns in the answers. Take turns.

beds	cage	dog	piano teacher
brothers	camera	DVD	~~room~~
CD player	desk	football	toy

Example: Student A: **Whose room is it?**
Student B: **It's the boys' room.**

8 Possessives Versus Contractions: What's in the Boxes?

Write *C* over contractions. Write *P* over possessive words (possessive adjectives, possessive nouns, and *whose*).

Lisa, Jim, and Jon are at their grandmother's house. There are many boxes there. Lisa is telling her brothers about some of the things in the boxes.

Jon: Is this **Grandma's** picture? She looks so young!
               P
               1

Lisa: Yeah, **it's** from college.
        C
        2

Jon: **Who's** the other woman?
     3

Lisa: That's **Grandma's** friend. Her **name's** Betty.
            4   5

Jon:	Are they still friends? Where is she now?
Lisa:	Yes, **they're** still friends, but I think **Betty's** in Alaska.
	₆ ₇
Jim:	Look at this old magazine. **Its** pages are all yellow.
	₈
Jon:	And this old watch. Is it a **man's** watch? **Whose** is it?
	₉ ₁₀
Lisa:	I don't know, but **it's** really beautiful!
	₁₁
Mrs. Carlson:	Lisa! Boys!
Jim:	**Grandma's** here. Let's ask her about the watch.
	₁₂

9 **Using Possessive Nouns and *Whose*: Whose Is It?**

Form a group of four or five, and sit around a desk. Student A closes his or her eyes. Each other person in the group puts something on the desk. Student A looks at the objects and guesses whose they are. Take turns. Use possessive nouns.

Example: Student A: *This pen is Yuri's. These are Michelle's keys. Are these Carmen's glasses?*

GRAMMAR BRIEFING 4

The Conjunctions *And*, *But*, and *Or*

FORM and FUNCTION

Using Conjunctions

1. **Conjunctions** can connect:

   - Words.

   - Groups of words.

   - Complete sentences.

They are <u>brother</u> **and** <u>sister</u>.
It's <u>on the desk</u> **or** <u>in the drawer</u>.
<u>Jim is at school</u>, **but** <u>Jon is at home</u>.

2. Conjunctions have different meanings:

   - *And* adds information.

   - *But* shows that something is different or surprising.

   - *Or* shows a choice or an alternative.

The dog is black **and** white.
He's the Smiths' dog, **and** his name is Waldo.
My car is old, **but** his car is new.
Pete's car is old **but** fast!
Is Anne at home, **or** is she at school?
Lisa is 19 **or** 20 years old.

(continued on next page)

Using Conjunctions (continued)

3. Use a comma before a conjunction when it connects two complete sentences.

> Is that Jim, **or** is it Jon?
>
> Anne is a nice person, **and** she is a good friend.

4. Don't use a comma when a conjunction connects two words or groups of words.

> Is that Jim **or** Jon?
>
> Anne is a nice person **and** a good friend.

The Conjunctions *And*, *But*, and *Or*

10 **Conjunctions:** American Families

A. Listen to some information about American families. Fill in the conjunctions you hear: *and, but,* or *or.*

What is a family? Families aren't all the same. In the United States, the average family has 3.3 people. Some families have two parents, __*but*__ some families have one parent.
₁

Some families have grandparents _____ other relatives in the home, _____
₂ ₃
some families live far from their relatives.

Homes in the United States are different, too. Some American families live in the country,

_____ most families live in cities _____ towns. Some families have houses,
₄ ₅

_____ some families have apartments.
₆

Most families have a car. Some families have two _____ three cars. Many families
₇

have computers, _____ almost all families have one _____ more televisions. Pets
₈ ₉

are common in American homes, _____ many families have dogs _____ cats.
₁₀ ₁₁

Families are not the same, _____ homes are not the same, _____ families
₁₂ ₁₃

_____ homes are important to people everywhere.
₁₄

> *the country* = land outside of cities and towns, with trees and open fields but not many houses.

B. Work alone or with a partner. Look back at the conjunctions in Part **A**. Do they connect words or sentences? Write *W* over conjunctions that connect words. Write *S* over conjunctions that connect sentences.

Example: Some families have two parents, ___*but*___ some families have one parent.

$\overset{S}{\underset{1}{}}$

11 **Using *Or* in Questions:** Asking for Information

Choose two opposite adjectives for each person or thing, for example, *good/bad* or *beautiful/ugly*. Write questions with *or*. You can use the same adjectives in different questions.

bad	cheap	good	old	ugly
beautiful	expensive	loud	quiet	young
big	female	male	small	

1. A new restaurant: ___Is the restaurant a cheap or expensive?___

2. A friend's new apartment: _____

3. A friend's cat: _____

4. A neighbor's new car: _____

5. A new CD: _____

6. A friend's new roommate: _____

7. A new teacher: _____

12 **Connecting Words and Sentences with *But* and *And*:** What's the Same? What's Different?

A. Form a group of three. What is the same about your two partners? On a piece of paper, write two statements with *and*.

Example: Maria and Ivan are students.

B. What is different about your two partners? On the same paper, write two statements with *but*.

Example: Maria is from Mexico, but Ivan is from Hungary.

C. Share your sentences with your partners. Is all the information correct?

Check your progress! Go to the Self-Test for Chapter 4 on the *Grammar Links* Website.

Wrap-up Activities

1 My Aunt: READING

Read this paragraph.

   This is a picture of my aunt, Sara Jordan. She is 28 years old. She is tall and pretty. Her hair is black, and her eyes are brown. She is nice and friendly. Sara is married, and her husband's name is Al. He is a reporter, and she is a travel agent. They live in a small house in Los Angeles, California.

2 This Is a Picture of . . . WRITING

Draw a picture of a friend or relative. Write a paragraph about the person in the picture. Begin: *This is a picture of my . . .* Then write at least four more sentences about the person. Use descriptive adjectives, possessive adjectives, and nouns.

See the *Grammar Links* Website for a model paragraph for this assignment.

3 My Brother: EDITING

Correct the nine errors in the paragraph. The first error is corrected for you.

My Brother

   ~~These~~ *This* is a picture of my brother Esteban. He is the

doctor. He is married, and her wife name is Liliana. She is

a artist. Esteban is a brother nice. He is a funny, and smart.

We are goods friends.

4 Who Am I? LISTENING/SPEAKING/WRITING

Step 1 On a piece of paper, write five sentences about yourself and something you own. Use descriptive adjectives and possessives. Write *Who am I?* at the end. Fold up your paper very small.

Example: I am a student. I am not old. I am shy and quiet. My car is white and small. It's new. Who am I?

Step 2 Form a group with four or more other students. Put all the papers with your sentences on a desk together. Mix them up. Take a paper and read the description aloud. Guess who the person is. Take turns.

5 **Things in the Room:** LISTENING/SPEAKING

Sit in a circle with your group. Take turns making statements about objects in the room. Use *this*, *that*, *these*, and *those*. Each person talks about four different things. Do not repeat any nouns. You can help one another think of new nouns. How many different things did your group name?

Example: Student A: These are my books.
That's Hiro's jacket.
Those are the teacher's papers.
This is my chair.

Example: Student B: This is my sweater.
Those are Kristin's keys.
That's your CD.
These are our desks.

6 **Who's Missing from the Family Tree?** LISTENING/SPEAKING

Work with a partner. Student A: Use this page. Student B: Go to page A-1 in the Exercise Pages at the end of the book.

Student A: This is Kim Hewitt's family tree. What are the missing names on the family tree? Ask your partner. Write the names. Then answer your partner's questions.

Example: Student A: Who is Julia's husband? He's Kim's grandfather.
Student B: That's Carl, C-a-r-l.
Student B: Who is Kim's father?
Student A: Kim's father is George.

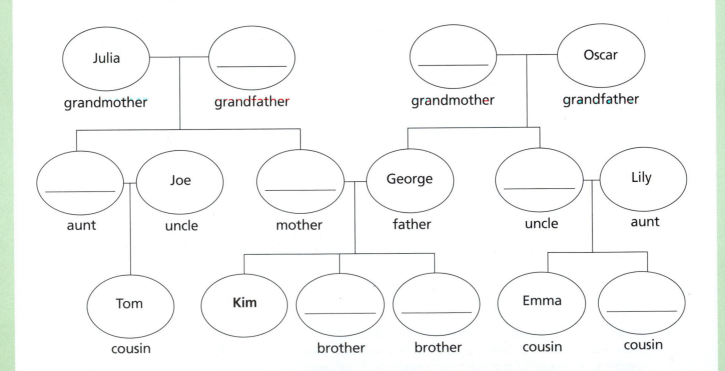

Present Progressive Tense

Working Toward a Goal

UNIT OBJECTIVES

- **affirmative and negative statements in the present progressive tense**
  (I *am learning* English. We *aren't watching* TV.)

- ***yes/no* questions and short answers in the present progressive tense**
  (*Are you wearing* a watch? *No, I'm not. Is he living* with friends? *Yes, he is.*)

- ***wh-* questions and answers in the present progressive tense**
  (*Who is running?* Alice is. *Where are* you *going?* To the pool.)

Grammar in Action

🎧 Reading and Listening: Getting Ready for the Olympics

Alice Kennedy is getting ready for the Olympics. Read and listen.

1   Alice: Hi. I'm Alice Kennedy. I'm a college student, but I'm not at school now. I'm not taking courses this year. What am I doing? I'm getting ready for the Olympic Games!

2   Narrator: Alice is a swimmer. These days, she is thinking about the Olympics and nothing else.

3   At the moment, it's 5:30 a.m. Is Alice sleeping? No, she isn't. She's getting dressed. It's time to go to the pool.

She's swimming in the pool.

4   Alice is happy that she's on the U.S. Olympic team. But the life of an Olympic athlete isn't easy. These days, Alice is swimming, she's running, and she's working with weights. At night, she's very tired! Alice is on a swimmer's diet, too, so she's eating all the right foods. She's living at home, and her parents are supporting her.

She's running at the track.

5   Alice: My friends are all at school, and I miss them. My brother, Mike, is in college, too. His life and my life are very different right now, but one thing is the same: We are working hard to reach our goals. Mike is thinking about life after college. He's getting ready for his career. My goal is an Olympic medal. In my dreams, I'm wearing a medal—a GOLD medal!

She's working with weights.

> *get ready* = prepare. *get dressed* = put on clothes. *support* = give money to live. *his career* = the work he will do in life.

Think About Grammar

A. Complete these sentences from the reading. They tell what is happening.

1. (Paragraph 1)   Alice: What <u>am</u> I <u>*doing*</u>_____?

2. (Paragraph 1)   Alice: I<u>'m</u> _____ ready for the Olympic Games!

3. (Paragraph 2)   Narrator: These days, she <u>is</u> _____ about the

   Olympics and nothing else.

4. (Paragraph 4)   Narrator: She<u>'s</u> _____ at home, and her parents <u>are</u>

   _____ her.

5. (Paragraph 5)   Alice: We <u>are</u> _____ hard to reach our goals.

6. (Paragraph 5)   Alice: Mike <u>is</u> _____ about life after college.

B. Look at the words you wrote in Part A. These are the **main verbs**. The main verbs in these sentences end with the same three letters. Write the three letters.

   – _____ _____ _____

C. Look at the <u>underlined</u> words in Part A. These are **auxiliary verbs**. Write the full forms of these three auxiliary verbs:

   _____, _____, and _____

   The verbs in these sentences are in the **present progressive tense**.

Chapter 5

The Olympic Games

The Present Progressive Tense—Affirmative and Negative Statements

Introductory Task: Getting Ready for the Games

A. Listen and read some information about getting ready for the Olympic Games.

It's almost time for the summer Olympics. The organizers are very busy. They are getting ready for the Games. About 200 countries are sending athletes—thousands of athletes! People are buying their tickets for the Olympics now. They are looking forward to the Games.

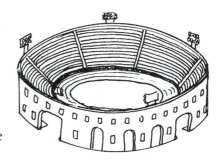

The Stadium

These days, the organizers are working hard. Some people are planning for the buses and trains at the Games. Other people are getting the stadium ready. The stadium is an important place on Opening Day.

The Olympic Village is almost ready. It has rooms for all the athletes. Workers are finishing the athletes' rooms now. Other people are thinking about food. They are planning good meals for the athletes.

The president of the Olympic Committee is busy these days. At the moment, he is talking to reporter Al Jordan. Al is asking many questions. Right now, the president is saying, "I'm looking forward to the Games. We're working hard, and things are going well. Our goal is the greatest Olympic Games in history!"

> *an organizer* = a person who plans something. *an athlete* = a person who is good at sports. *look forward to* = feel happy and excited about something in the future.

B. Underline the 16 present progressive verbs in Part A.

Example: They <u>are getting</u> ready for the Games.

C. Work with a partner. The following sentences about the reading are false. Take turns making true statements in place of each sentence.

Example: People are watching the Olympic Games on TV right now.
Student A: *People are getting ready for the Olympic Games.*
Student B: *They're looking forward to the Games. They're buying tickets.*

1. About 200 athletes are coming to the Games.
2. The athletes are getting the stadium ready.
3. Workers are building rooms for the athletes in the stadium.
4. The organizers aren't thinking about meals for the athletes.
5. Al Jordan isn't working these days.
6. The president of the Olympic Committee isn't talking to reporters.

GRAMMAR BRIEFING 1

Present Progressive Tense—Affirmative Statements

FUNCTION

Using the Present Progressive*

1. Use the present progressive tense for actions happening now.

PAST   NOW   FUTURE

he is sleeping
they are swimming

Use it with time expressions like *now*, *right now*, and *at the moment*.

He is in bed. He **is sleeping**.
They are in the pool. They **are swimming**.

She's talking on the phone **at the moment**.
Hurry! The movie is starting **now**.

2. Use the present progressive for actions happening over a longer time in the present.

PAST   NOW   FUTURE

I am living
Ann is working

Use it with time expressions like *this week*, *this year*, and *these days*.

I **am living** with two friends.
Ann **is working** for Microsoft.

He's taking four courses **this semester**.
You're working a lot **these days**.

*Another name for the present progressive is the present continuous.

(continued on next page)

A. Singular

FULL FORMS			CONTRACTIONS	
SUBJECT	BE	BASE VERB* + ING	SUBJECT + BE	BASE VERB + -ING
I	am		I'm	
You	are		You're	
He		working.	He's	working.
She	is		She's	
It			It's	
Ann			Ann's	

B. Plural

FULL FORMS			CONTRACTIONS	
SUBJECT	BE	BASE VERB + -ING	SUBJECT + BE	BASE VERB + -ING
We			We're	
You	are	working.	You're	working.
They			They're	
The men			—	

* Base verb = the base form of the verb (the verb without an ending like -ing or -s).

Present Progressive Tense—Affirmative Statements

1 **Function of the Present Progressive Tense:** Thinking About Time

Work alone or with a partner. Read these present progressive statements about Olympic swimmer Alice Kennedy. Is the action happening right at this moment, or is the action happening over a longer time? Check (✓) your answers.

At This Moment	Over a Longer Time	
✓	☐	1. Alice is in the pool. She is swimming.
☐	✓	2. Alice is working hard these days.
☐	☐	3. She is living at home with her parents.
☐	☐	4. Alice is in her coach's office. They are talking.
☐	☐	5. She's asking a question.
☐	☐	6. All the swimmers are spending long hours in the pool these days.
☐	☐	7. They are traing for the Olympics. It's a lot of work!
☐	☐	8. They are getting stronger and faster.
☐	☐	9. Alice is putting on her jacket.
☐	☐	10. Her coach is watching some swimmers on TV.

> *a coach* = a person who trains an athlete or a team for a sport.

2 Affirmative Statements with *He*, *She*, *It*, and *They*: Who's Doing What?

A. Match the pictures and the statements. Write the statements on the lines.

a. It is sleeping.

b. He is studying.

c. They are singing.

✓ d. She is smiling.

e. She is writing a letter.

f. It is sitting.

g. He is cheering.

h. They are clapping.

i. She is winning the race.

1. She is smiling.

2. _____

3. _____

4. _____

5. _____

6. _____

7. _____

8. _____

9. _____

B. Work with a partner. Student A: Say the number of a picture in Part A. Student B: Say what is happening in the picture, using a contraction. Take turns.

Example: Student A: **Picture number 2.**

Student B: **He's studying.**

3 Affirmative Statements with *I* and *We*: What Are You Doing?

A. Check (✓) the actions you are doing now.

❑ 1. I'm reading.

❑ 2. I'm sitting in class.

❑ 3. I'm using a pen.

❑ 4. I'm holding a book in my hands.

❑ 5. I'm writing.

❑ 6. I'm listening to music.

❑ 7. I'm looking at the clock.

❑ 8. I'm wearing earrings.

❑ 9. I'm thinking about lunch.

❑ 10. I'm learning English.

B. Tell your partner what you are doing right now. Use the contraction *I'm*.

Example: Student A: I'm sitting in class, and I'm learning English.

C. What is the same about you and your partner? Write three true statements with *We're . . . -ing*.

1. _____

2. _____

3. _____

4 Affirmative Statements with *You*: Act It Out

A. Look at your teacher. Your teacher is showing the class an action. Say what your teacher is doing.

Example:

B. Work with a partner. Student A: Show your partner an action. Use an action from the box below or a different action. Student B: Guess what Student A is doing. Take turns.

Example: Student A: (swimming)
Student B: You're swimming.
Student A: That's right.

> run   walk   eat   drink   clap   sleep   die   read   write   listen   dance   cry

Ask your teacher about any new verbs.

What does "cry" mean?

Spelling Rules for -*ing* Verb Forms

FORM

Spelling Rules

1. Most verbs: Add -*ing* to the base form of the verb.	go → go**ing** carry → carry**ing**	wear → wear**ing** sleep → sleep**ing**
2. Verbs that end in a consonant + *e*: Drop the *e*, and add -*ing*.	writ~~e~~ → wri**ting**	tak~~e~~ → ta**king**
3. Verbs that end in *ie*: Change the *ie* to *y*, and add -*ing*.	**lie** → **l**y**ing**	**die** → **d**y**ing**
4. Most verbs that end in "C V C" (consonant + vowel + consonant): Double the final consonant and add -*ing*.	**cut** → cu**tting**	be**gin** → begi**nning**

GRAMMAR HOTSPOT!

Exceptions to spelling rule 4:

- Do not double the final consonant when the last syllable is not stressed.

  listen → listen**ing**   enter → enter**ing**

- Do not double *w*, *x*, or *y*.

  showing   fixing   paying

5 Writing *-ing* Forms: Spelling Practice

Write the base form of the verb and its *-ing* form in the correct column in the chart.

clean	do	give	live	put	sit	win
cry	drive	hit	make	rain	sleep	write
dance	fly	lie	mix	ride	stop	
die	get	listen	play	run	study	

1. Most Verbs	2. Verbs That End in Consonant + *-e*	3. Verbs That End in *-ie*	4. Verbs That Double the Final Consonant
clean—cleaning	dance—dancing	die—dying	get—getting

6 Present Progressive in Affirmative Statements: Carrying the Olympic Torch

A. Reporter Al Jordan is talking about two events before the Olympics. Write the correct present progressive form of the verb in parentheses. Then listen.

One month before the Olympic Games:

I __am standing__ in the stadium here in Olympia, Greece.
(1) stand

Today, it is one month before the start of the Olympic Games.

Something special _____ here. We _____ the
(2) happen   (3) watch

lighting of a flame, the Olympic flame. A woman _____ a
(4) use

mirror to catch the light of the sun. The sun _____ on the
(5) shine

mirror, and it _____ a fire. This fire will light a torch. Now
(6) start

the torch _____, and the first runner _____ it.
(7) burn   (8) take

The torch _____ its long journey.
(9) begin

One week before the Olympic Games:

Good morning. This is Al Jordan. I _____ to you
(10) speak

from the Olympic stadium. You _____ at the stadium
(11) look

behind me. The Olympic torch isn't here now, but it _____.
(12) come

At this moment, a runner _____ the torch into the city.
(13) carry

Runners _____ turns, and they _____ the
(14) take   (15) bring

torch here. People in the streets _____ for the runners.
(16) cheer

Everyone is excited about the Olympics.

Al Jordan

A Runner with the Torch

B. Work with a partner. Describe the pictures in Part A. Who are the people? Where are they? What are they doing?

See the *Grammar Links* Website for more information about the Olympic Games.

Present Progressive Tense—Negative Statements

FORM

A. Singular

FULL FORMS

SUBJECT	BE	NOT	BASE VERB + -ING
I	**am**		
You	**are**		
He		**not**	work**ing**.
She	**is**		
It			
The man			

CONTRACTIONS

SUBJECT + BE + NOT	BASE VERB + -ING
I'm not	
You're not/**You aren't**	
He's not/**He isn't**	
She's not/**She isn't**	work**ing**.
It's not/**It isn't**	
The man's not/**The man isn't**	

B. Plural

FULL FORMS

SUBJECT	BE	NOT	BASE VERB + -ING
We			
You	**are**	**not**	work**ing**.
They			
The men			

CONTRACTIONS

SUBJECT + BE + NOT	BASE VERB + -ING
We're not/**We aren't**	
You're not/**You aren't**	
They're not/**They aren't**	work**ing**.
The men aren't	

GRAMMAR **HOT**SPOT!

1. Remember! There are two ways to make contractions with *is* and *are* in negative statements.

   - Contract *is/are* and *not*.

     He isn't going. **Jack isn't** going.
     They aren't going. **The boys aren't** going.

   - Contract the subject and *is/are*, and add *not*.

     (The subject can be a pronoun or a singular noun only.)

     He's not going. **Jack's not** going.

     They're not going.
       NOT: The ~~boys're~~ not going.

2. Remember! There is only one contracted form of *I am not*.

     I'm not going.

Present Progressive Tense—Negative Statements

7 **Full Forms and Contractions in Negative Statements:** The Olympic Village at Night

A. Write the correct negative form of the verb in parentheses. Use full forms, not contractions.

1. (not/compete) It's late at night in the Olympic Village. The athletes _are not competing_ right now.

2. (not/shine) It's 3:00 a.m. The sun _____ now.

3. (not/go) The athletes are resting. They _____ to parties.

4. (not/think) Alice is asleep. She _____ about the Games.

5. (not/practice) The teams _____ right now.

6. (not/watch) We _____ the Games at the moment.

7. (not/sleep) I _____.

8. (not/compete) You _____ in these Games.

> *compete* = try to win.

B. Rewrite the statements from Part A. Use both forms of contractions when possible.

[subject + 'm/'s/'re] + not	subject + isn't/aren't
1. (not possible—plural noun subject)	1. The athletes aren't competing right now.
2. The sun's not shining now.	2.
3.	3.
4.	4.
5.	5.
6.	6.
7.	7.
8.	8.

8 | Affirmative and Negative Statements: After the Race

 A. Work with a partner. Look at the photo. What is happening? Talk about what the people are doing and aren't doing. Make affirmative and negative statements in the present progressive. Use the verbs in the box or other verbs.

Example: Student A: **The athletes aren't running now.**
Student B: **This woman is smiling.**

| cry | hold | look at | run | smile | stand | watch | wave | wear |

 B. Write at least eight sentences about the photo in Part A or about another picture in this book. Give the page number of the picture. Tell what is happening. Write affirmative and negative statements in the present progressive.

See the *Grammar Links* Website for a model paragraph for this assignment.

 Check your progress! Go to the Self-Test for Chapter 5 on the *Grammar Links* Website.

Chapter 6

Academic Goals

The Present Progressive Tense— *Yes/No* Questions and *Wh-* Questions

Introductory Task: Academic and Career Goals

A. Listen and read about Mike Kennedy and his roommates.

Mike Kennedy is a college student. He's at a university in California. His major is engineering. He's planning a career as an engineer. That's his goal. He has another goal right now, too. This goal is getting a job. Mike is looking for a job on campus.

Mike isn't living at the university. He's living off campus. He's sharing an apartment with two international students, Ahmed and Jae Yong. Ahmed's goal is the same as Mike's: a career in engineering. Jae Yong isn't sure about his career goals. Right now, he is studying English as a second language, and he's taking business courses. Business and engineering are popular majors for international students in the United States. Fifty percent (50%) of them are majoring in business, engineering, math, or the sciences.

Right now, Mike, Ahmed, and Jae Yong are sitting in the living room of their apartment. They're watching the Olympic Games on TV. They're all cheering for the athletes from their countries.

> *a major* = the main subject of a student's college studies. *engineering* = the work of planning and building machines, roads, bridges, etc. *on campus* = at the college or university.

Majors of International Students in the United States

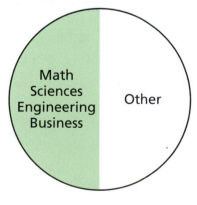

See the *Grammar Links* Website for more information about college students in the United States.

B. Work with a partner. Circle the correct answers. Take turns asking and answering the questions.

1. Is Mike studying in California? (Yes, he is.) / He's a student.
2. What is he majoring in? No, he isn't. / Engineering.
3. Is he planning his career? Yes, he is. / A career as an engineer.
4. Where is Mike living? No, he's not. / In an apartment off campus.
5. Who is Mike living with? Yes, they are. / Two international students.
6. Who's studying business? No, it isn't. / Jae Yong.
7. What are they doing right now? Yes, they are. / Watching TV.
8. Are they watching the Olympics? Yes, they are. / In the living room.

C. Circle your answers to the questions in the chart below. Then ask a partner the questions and circle your partner's answers.

	You	Your Partner
1. Are you living in an apartment?	Yes, I am. / No, I'm not.	Yes, I am. / No, I'm not.
2. Are you living alone?	Yes, I am. / No, I'm not.	Yes, I am. / No, I'm not.
3. Are you working?	Yes, I am. / No, I'm not.	Yes, I am. / No, I'm not.
4. Are you looking for a job?	Yes, I am. / No, I'm not.	Yes, I am. / No, I'm not.
5. Are you taking other courses?	Yes, I am. / No, I'm not.	Yes, I am. / No, I'm not.
6. Are you making career plans?	Yes, I am. / No, I'm not.	Yes, I am. / No, I'm not.

D. Tell the class one or two things about your partner.

GRAMMAR BRIEFING 1

Present Progressive Tense—*Yes/No* Questions and Short Answers

FORM

A. Singular

QUESTIONS			ANSWERS			
BE	**SUBJECT**	**BASE VERB + -ING**	**YES**		**NO**	
Am	I			I **am**.		I**'m not**.
Are	you			you **are**.		you**'re not**/you **aren't**.
	he		Yes,	he **is**.	No,	he**'s not**/he **isn't**.
	she	**winning?**		she **is**.		she**'s not**/she **isn't**.
Is	it			it **is**.		it**'s not**/it **isn't**.
	the team					

(continued on next page)

B. Plural

QUESTIONS			ANSWERS			
BE	SUBJECT	BASE VERB + *-ING*	*YES*		*NO*	
Are	we	**winning**?	Yes,	we **are**.	No,	we**'re not**/we **aren't**.
	you			you **are**.		you**'re not**/you **aren't**.
	they			they **are**.		they**'re not**/they **aren't**.
	the boys					

GRAMMAR **HOT**SPOT!

Remember! Use contractions in negative short answers to *yes/no* questions. Do not use contractions in short answers with *yes*.

Q: Are you leaving?
A: No, I'm not.
  NOT USUALLY: No, I am not.

Q: Is she coming?
A: Yes, she is.
  NOT: Yes, ~~she's~~.

TALKING THE TALK

You can answer a *yes/no* question with:

• A short answer.

Q: Are you coming?
A: Yes, I am./No, I'm not.

• *Yes/No* + more information.

Q: Are you coming?
A: Yes, I'm almost ready./No, I'm staying here.

Present Progressive Tense—*Yes/No* Questions and Short Answers

1 **Identifying *Yes/No* Questions; Short Answers:** A New Job

A. Read the conversation. <u>Underline</u> the four *yes/no* questions in the present progressive tense. The first one is underlined for you.

Mike Kennedy is looking for a part-time job. Most of his friends are working these days. About 75 percent of American college students have jobs. Right now, Mike is at the university tutoring center. Many students get free help with their classes here. Mike is talking to the director of the center.

U.S. College Students with Jobs

About 75%

Director: Are you interested in a job as a tutor?

Mike: Yes, I am. <u>Are you looking for tutors now?</u>

Director: Yes, we're hiring four or five new people.

What are you studying?

Mike: English, physics, math, and engineering.

Director: What courses are you taking?

Mike: English 201, Physics 210, Calculus, and Engineering 151.

Director: Are you majoring in electrical engineering? That's a popular major these days.

Mike: Well, I'm not sure. I'm still thinking about my major.

Director: What about your grades? Are you doing well?

Mike: Yeah, I'm getting all A's and B's.

Director: That's great. Well, Mike, what about tutoring math?

Mike: Math's fine, or physics. Are you hiring tutors for those subjects?

Director: Yes, we are. In fact, you can start your new job right now!

> *tutor* = (noun) a person who helps a student with schoolwork; (verb) teach one student. *hire* = give a job to (someone). *electrical engineering* = the work of designing machines, including computers.

B. Circle the correct short answers. Then work with a partner asking and answering the questions. Take turns.

1. Is the director interviewing Mike? (Yes, she is.) / No, she isn't.

2. Is Mike looking for a job? Yes, he's. / Yes, he is.

3. Mike: Are you looking for new tutors? Director: Yes, we're. / Yes, we are.

4. Is the director hiring new people? Yes, she is. / Yes, she's.

5. Director: Are you majoring in electrical engineering?   Mike: Yes, I'm. / No, I'm not.

6. Are Mike and the director talking about courses?   Yes, they're. / Yes, they are.

7. Is Mike getting good grades?   Yes, he is. / Yes, he's.

8. Mike: Am I starting the job right now?   Director: No, you're not! / Yes, you are!

2 *Yes/No* Questions and Short Answers: Roommates

Read the conversation. Complete the *yes/no* questions and short answers.

The three college students are at their apartment. Mike is in the living room. The TV is on. Ahmed and Jae Yong are in their rooms.

Mike: Jae Yong! The Olympics are on. __Are you coming?__
                                                1 (you / come)

Jae Yong: Yes, __I am.__
                   2

(Jae Yong is coming into the living room.)

Jae Yong: _____
                      3 (Ahmed / come?)

Mike: No, _____. He's studying.
                      4

Jae Yong: Ahmed is studying a lot these days. _____ a paper?
                                                        5 (he / write)

Mike: Yes, _____. We're getting ready for an exam, too.
                      6

Jae Yong: _____ the same course?
              7 (you and Ahmed / take)

Mike: Yes, _____. We're taking math together.
                      8

Jae Yong: But Mike . . . YOU aren't studying a lot these days.

Mike: No, _____, and it's a problem—I'm going to classes, I'm working, I'm
                      9

           watching the Games on TV and I'm not studying very much!

(Ahmed is calling from his room.)

Ahmed: Hey, Mike! *SOME* people are trying to study!

Mike: _____ too much noise?
                      10 (we / make)

Ahmed: Yes, _____! _____ now?
                   11   12 (your sister / compete)

Mike: No, _____. We're watching track. The men's 100-meter dash is starting.
                      13

Ahmed: _____ ready?
                      14 (the runners / get)

Jae Yong: Yes, _____. Come and watch!
                      15

3 Using *Yes/No* Questions and Short Answers: Ahmed and Jae Yong

A. Listen and read about Ahmed and Jae Yong.

Ahmed and Jae Yong are Mike's roommates. They're living in an apartment off campus. Ahmed is from Kuwait. Many students from Kuwait are studying in the United States this year. Ahmed is majoring in engineering, and he's working hard. His government is supporting him. Right now, Ahmed is at the library. He's studying for an exam.

Jae Yong is an international student, too. He's from Korea. Jae Yong is majoring in business. He's not sure about his career goals. He's thinking about business or law. His family is supporting him. Right now, Jae Yong is in the kitchen. He's making dinner. He's thinking about his mother's cooking. She's a wonderful cook, and he's thinking about her delicious dinners. Jae Yong isn't a good cook, but he's learning.

B. Write four *yes/no* questions about Ahmed and Jae Yong. Use the present progressive tense.

Example: Is Ahmed studying business? Is Jae Yong learning to cook?

1. _____

2. _____

3. _____

4. _____

C. Work with a partner. Take turns asking your questions about Ahmed and Jae Yong. Give short answers to your partner's questions.

4 Using *Yes/No* Questions and Short Answers: Find Someone Who

A. Work with a partner. Read the statements below. Practice changing them to *yes/no* questions with *Are you -ing . . . ?*

B. Walk around the room. Ask your classmates the questions. Write names on the lines to make true statements.

Example: Student A: Carmen, are you studying math?
Student B (Carmen): Yes, I am. OR Yes, I'm taking calculus.

Student A writes, " Carmen _____ is studying math."

1. _____ is studying math.

2. _____ is wearing a necklace today.

3. _____ is taking a difficult course.

4. _____ is taking an easy course.

5. _____ is having fun in class.

6. _____ is working toward a goal.

7. _____ is making plans for the weekend.

8. _____ is getting enough sleep these days.

Present Progressive Tense—*Wh-* Questions and Answers I

FORM

Wh- Questions with *Who* or *What* as Subject

QUESTIONS				ANSWERS
SUBJECT (*WHO/WHAT*)	*IS*	BASE VERB + *-ING*		
Who	**is**	**studying**?		Mike and Ahmed.
				Mike and Ahmed are.
				Mike and Ahmed are studying.
What	**is**	**making**	that noise?	The dishwasher.
				The dishwasher is.
				The dishwasher is making that noise.

GRAMMAR HOTSPOT!

The answer to a question with *who* or *what* as subject can be:

- A word or group of words.

  Q: Who is talking on the phone?
  A: Mike./My friend Mike.

- A subject + auxilary verb.

  Q: Who is talking on the phone?
  A: Mike is.

- A complete sentence.

  Q: Who is talking on the phone?
  A: Mike is talking to his sister.

Present Progressive Tense—*Wh-* Questions and Answers I

5 **Questions with *Who* or *What* as Subject:** Dinner Time

Complete the questions with *Who* or *What* + the present progressive of the verb in parentheses.

It's 6:00 p.m. Mike, Ahmed, and Jae Yong are in their apartment.

1. <u>Who is making</u> _____ dinner tonight?   Mike is.
   (make)

2. _____ on the stove?   Spaghetti and tomato sauce.
   (cook)

3. The TV is on. _____ it?   Mike and Jae Yong.
   (watch)

4. _____ on TV?   The Olympic Games are on.
   (happen)

5. _____ that strange noise?   The refrigerator. It's not working right.
   (make)

6. _____ in his room?   Ahmed is.
   (study)

7. The phone's ringing. _____ it?   Mike's getting it.
   (answer)

8. _____ ?   Ahmed's father.
   (call)

9. What's that smell? _____ ?   The tomato sauce!
   (burn)

6 **Questions with *Who* or *What* as Subject:** What's Happening?

A. Write questions with *Who* or *What* as subject. Use present progressive verbs.

1. You hear someone knocking at the door. <u>Who is knocking at the door?</u>

2. You hear something happening outside. <u>What is happening outside?</u>

3. You smell something cooking on the stove. _____

4. You smell something burning. _____

5. You hear someone crying. _____

6. The news is on. Something is happening in the city. _____

7. You hear something making a noise upstairs. _____

8. You hear a game on TV. Someone is winning. _____

9. You hear someone calling you. _____

10. You hear some people fighting. _____

B. Work with a partner. Take turns asking the questions in Part A. Invent your own answers.

Example: Student A: Who is knocking at the door?
Student B: The police!

Present Progressive Tense—*Wh*- Questions and Answers II

FORM

Wh- Questions with *Who(m)*, *What*, and *Where*

QUESTIONS				ANSWERS
WH- QUESTION WORD	*BE*	SUBJECT	BASE VERB + *-ING*	
Who **Whom***	**is**	he	**watching**?	The runners. He's watching the runners.
What	**are**	you	**doing**?	Writing a letter. I'm writing a letter.
	is	she	**drinking**?	Coffee. She's drinking coffee.
Where	**are**	they	**working**?	In the library. They're working in the library.
	is	he	**living**?	Off campus. He's living off campus.

* *Whom* is very formal. It is not common in spoken English.

TALKING THE TALK

	SAY	WRITE
Wh- question words + the contracted forms *'m*, *'s*, and *'re* are common in conversation. The contracted form *'s* is also common in informal writing. Always use the full forms *am*, *is*, and *are* in formal writing.	"What's he making?"	What is he making? What's he making? (informal)
	"Where're they going?"	Where are they going?
	"What'm I doing?"	What am I doing?

Present Progressive Tense—*Wh*- Questions and Answers II

7 *Wh*- **Questions and Answers:** On Campus

A. Work with a partner. Read each conversation aloud. Ask *wh*- questions using the words in parentheses. Use your own ideas to complete each conversation. Then repeat, changing roles.

Example: Student A: Hi, Ahmed. What are you doing?
Student B: I'm studying for a test. What are you doing?
Student B: I'm looking for a book.

1. In the college library:

   Mike: Hi, Ahmed. _____
   a (what / you / do)

   Ahmed: I'm studying for a test. _____
   b (what / you / do)

   Mike: _____
   c

2. At the college tutoring center:

   Director: Hello, Siok. _____
   a (who / you / wait for)

   Siok: My tutor.

   Director: _____
   b (who / you / work with)

   Siok: Mary Jane.

   Director: _____
   c (what / you / work on)

   Siok: _____
   d

3. In the college administration building:

   Ahmed: Look, there's Mike. _____
   a (where / he / go)

   Jae Yong: I don't know. Maybe the Business Office, or the Career Center.

   Ahmed: _____
   b (what / you / do here)

   Jae Yong: _____
   c

4. In the college cafeteria:

   Ahmed: Look at all those students. _____
   a (where / they / go)

   Mike: _____
   b (who / you / talk about)

Ahmed: Look out the window.

Mike: Oh! They're going to the stadium. The football team has a game today.

Jae Yong: _____
                                c (who / they / play)

Mike: _____
                                           d

B. Complete the conversations in Part A in writing.

8 Contractions and Full Forms: Old Friends

A. Listen to the conversation. You will hear informal speech with contractions.
Write the **full** forms of the words you hear.

Mike Kennedy is riding his bike across the campus of his college. An old
friend of Mike's from high school is sitting on the grass. Mike is surprised.

Mike: Jack? Jack Harris!

Jack: Mike Kennedy! Hey, how _are you_____ doing?
                                          1

Mike: Not bad. _____ you doing here?
                             2

Jack: _____ studying journalism.
               3

Mike: Yeah? _____ you living?
                          4

Jack: Here on campus, in Baker Hall. What about you? _____
                                                                           5

        you doing here?

Mike: _____ working on a major in engineering.
               6

Jack: _____ you living?
               7

Mike: Off campus, with a couple of friends. _____ sharing an apartment.
                                                           8

Jack: Oh, yeah? _____ you living with?
                              9

Mike: Two international students.

Jack: _____ they from?
               10

Mike: Kuwait and Korea. _____ studying engineering and business.
                                      11

Jack: What about Alice? _____ she living? _____ she
                                    12   13

        doing these days?

Mike: _____ competing at the Olympics.
               14

Jack: Wow! That's great! _____ swimming, right?
15

Mike: Yeah.

Jack: Is she still seeing that guy from high school?

Mike: Pablo? No, _____ married now, to Debbie Williams.
16

Jack: _____ kidding! Unbelievable. What about Alice?
17

        _____ she seeing now?
18

Mike: Sorry, Jack—she has a boyfriend.

Jack: Yeah? Too bad.

 B. Imagine you are far from home, and you meet a friend from your country. Write your conversation. What is your friend doing in this place? Ask about his or her family. What are they doing these days? Tell this friend about what you are doing. Use the conversation in Part A as a model. Use verbs in the present progressive tense.

 See the *Grammar Links* Website for another model conversation.

C. Share your conversations. Act them out.

9 **Editing: Alice's Race**

Read the conversation. Correct the nine errors in present progressive questions and short answers. The first error is corrected for you.

   Alice's parents, George and Julia Kennedy, are at the Olympic swimming pool. It is time for Alice's race.

George: There's Alice! She's getting ready. Julia,
         are you
         ~~you are~~ feeling okay?

Julia: No, I am'nt. I'm so nervous! My heart

         is racing.

George: Hold my hand. What time is it in California?

         Is Mike watch the race on TV right now?

Julia: I'm sure he is. Oh, George! I'm not watching anymore. It's too hard. What she's doing?

George: Julia, open your eyes! The swimmers are ready to start the race.

Julia: Is smiling Alice?

George: Yes, she's. Listen, the announcer is saying her name, and she's waving. Now she's getting ready. Open your eyes—the race is starting!

Julia: Where she swimming?

George: She's in Lane 4. That's good. Open your eyes, Julia! You're missing the race!

Julia: Who's swim next to Alice?

George: The girl from Australia. Now they're making the turn. Alice is ahead!

Julia: Who winning, George? Who? WHO?!

George: Julia, you're breaking my hand! It's . . . it's . . . it's Alice! She's the winner!

Check your progress! Go to the Self-Test for Chapter 6 on the *Grammar Links* Website.

Wrap-up Activities

1 At the Olympics: READING

Read this paragraph.

    I am sitting in the Olympic Stadium. It is a beautiful day, and I am happy to be here. I am watching the men's track and field events. Some runners are getting ready for their race. I am looking at the runner from my country. He is at the start. He is not moving. He is not smiling. His eyes are closed. What is he thinking about at this moment?

2 Where I Am Now: WRITING

Where are you? What are you doing? What is happening around you? Write a paragraph of five or more sentences. Use affirmative and negative statements in the present progressive tense.

See the *Grammar Links* Website for a model paragraph for this assignment.

3 In My Room: EDITING

Correct the eight errors in present progressive verbs. The first error is corrected for you.

In My Room

        sitting
I am ~~sit~~ in my room. I am at my desk, and I writing. My radio

it is playing. My roommate is here, too. He not listening to the

music. What he is doing? He is lie in bed with a book, but he is

no reading. He is sleep, and he is snoring.

---

4 Draw It: WRITING/SPEAKING/LISTENING

Step 1 Take three small pieces of paper and write a sentence on each one. Write about people or animals and what they are doing. Use present progressive verbs.

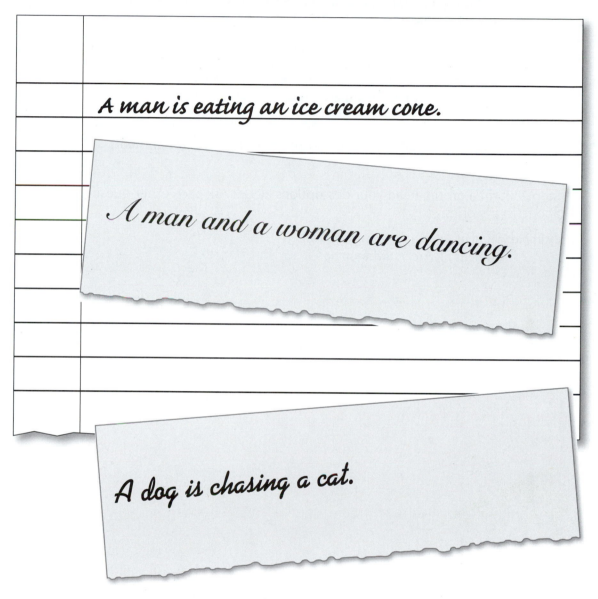

A man is eating an ice cream cone.

A man and a woman are dancing.

A dog is chasing a cat.

Step 2 Form a group with three or four other students. Put all your sentences into a hat or a bag. Then take turns as the Artist. The Artist takes out one sentence and draws a picture of it on paper or on the blackboard. The Artist **does not speak**. The others in the group say what is happening in the picture.

Example: Student A: Eating ice cream!
 Student B: Is it a woman? No, it's a man. A man is eating ice cream, right?

5 An Olympic Story: SPEAKING/LISTENING/WRITING

Step 1 Write the beginning of a story. It's happening at the summer Olympics. Your story is about an athlete, a reporter, or a person watching the Games. (Maybe it's about you!) Tell the place and the time, and tell what is happening. Use present progressive verbs. Write 40 words or more.

Example: It's the second day of the Olympic Games. I'm in the stadium. I'm waiting for my race. I'm wearing my team uniform. It's red, yellow, and black, like the flag of my country. The runners aren't talking. We aren't smiling. We're nervous. Many people are watching.

  See the *Grammar Links* Website for another model for this assignment.

Step 2 Form a group. Read your descriptions aloud. Ask each other questions about your stories.

Example: Student A: Is your family watching?
          Student B: Are you dreaming?

Simple Present Tense

TOPIC FOCUS
Celebrations

UNIT OBJECTIVES

- **affirmative and negative statements in the simple present tense**
  (She *cooks* dinner. They *don't write* letters.)

- **adverbs of frequency and time expressions**
  (He is *usually* late. I *always* go to a party on New Year's Eve. We clean the house *in the spring*. They eat *at 6:00*.)

- **yes/no questions and short answers in the simple present tense**
  (*Does* he *work* every day? *Yes, he does. Do* you *know* Eva? *No, I don't*.)

- **wh- questions and answers in the simple present tense**
  (*When do* you *celebrate* the new year? On January 1. *Why does* she *cook* special food? Because of the holiday.)

- **choosing between the simple present tense and the present progressive tense**
  (We always *eat* special food on Christmas. We *are eating* lunch right now.)

- **non-action verbs**
  (That old bicycle *belongs* to Jack. He *wants* a new bicycle.)

Grammar in Action

🎧 Reading and Listening: New Year's Traditions

Read and listen.

Reporter Al Jordan is describing a New Year's celebration. Al and other people are talking about traditional celebrations in their cultures.

1 **Al Jordan:** It's New Year's Eve in Times Square, New York City. It's almost midnight, and people are counting down the seconds. Five, four, three, two, one! Happy New Year!

2   Some people in the United States celebrate New Year's Eve at home. Many people go to parties. At parties, they eat, drink, dance, and sing. But different groups of people in the United States celebrate the start of a new year at different times and in different ways. Let's listen to some people tell about other kinds of new year celebrations.

3 **Ming Li:** My family and I are Chinese American. We celebrate the Chinese New Year in February or March. It's a special time. We buy new clothes, and we often wear red. The color red brings good luck. I go to the parade in Chinatown with my friends. I also visit my relatives. My grandparents give me red envelopes with money in them. I like Chinese New Year a lot.

4 **Isabel Vargas:** My family follows Mexican traditions on December 31. My mother cooks a big dinner. Just before midnight, everyone takes 12 grapes for good luck in the new year. We eat the grapes in the last 12 seconds of the old year, and we make wishes for the new year. Everybody hugs and kisses!

5 **Myra Rosen:** My family is Jewish. We celebrate the Jewish New Year in September. It's called Rosh Hashanah. My mother makes a special kind of bread for the holiday. It tastes good. My father reads stories aloud. They tell about the history of our religion. My family goes to temple, and we make resolutions for the new year.

6   Daniel Hawk: I am a Native American. I live in New York State. My people are the Iroquois, and we have our new year celebration in the middle of January. Dancers come to our homes. They wear masks, and one person plays a drum. The dancers bring good luck for the year.

7   Al Jordan: Different cultures, different celebrations—but they all say "Happy New Year!"

> *traditions* = ways of doing things that stay the same year after year.
> *a celebration* = a special activity or party because of a happy event.
> *midnight* = 12:00 at night. *resolutions* = plans people make to change things in their lives.

Think About Grammar

A. Complete these sentences from the reading.

1. (Paragraph 2) Some people in the United States __celebrate_____ New Year's Eve at home.
2. (Paragraph 3) We _____ new clothes, and we often _____ red.
3. (Paragraph 3) I _____ Chinese New Year a lot.
4. (Paragraph 5) My mother _____ a special kind of bread for the holiday.
5. (Paragraph 5) It _____ good.
6. (Paragraph 5) My father _____ stories aloud.
7. (Paragraph 6) Dancers _____ to our homes.
8. (Paragraph 6) They _____ masks, and one person _____ a drum.

B. Look at the verbs you wrote. They tell about routines, habits, and facts. These verbs are in the **simple present tense**. Some of the verbs end in *-s*. Write those verbs here.

_____   _____   _____   _____

C. Circle the subject pronouns that go with this *-s* ending.

I   you   he   she   it   we   they

Native American Celebrations

Simple Present Tense—Affirmative and Negative Statements

Introductory Tasks: A Harvest Celebration

A. Listen and circle the verb you hear.

Peter Cox is talking to his friend Jong-Su from Korea. He's telling Jong-Su about a photo from his vacation in New Mexico, USA.

Look, here's a picture of me in New Mexico. This is Maria Concho,

a Native American woman. She (make / makes) these pots.
1

Maria (speak / speaks) three languages: English, Spanish,
2

and Keresan, a Native American language. She (live / lives)
3

in Acoma with her family. The Native Americans in Acoma

(have / has) a special harvest celebration every year in
4

August. It (go on / goes on) for three days. Maria and
5

the other women (cook / cooks) traditional food.
6

Many people (sing / sings) and (dance / dances), and
7   8

some people (wear / wears) traditional clothes.
9

   The United States and Canada (have / has) harvest celebrations, too. We (call / calls)
10   11

this holiday Thanksgiving. Canada (have / has) its Thanksgiving in October.
12

In the United States, we (have / has) it on the fourth Thursday in November. We
13

(cook / cooks) traditional food, but we don't sing or dance or wear any special clothes.
14

> *the harvest* = the time when farmers bring in the things they grew in their fields.

B. Complete the sentences about Maria Concho.

1. Maria Concho lives in _____.

2. She speaks _____.

3. Her family celebrates the harvest in _____.

 **C.** Complete the sentences about yourself. Then tell a partner about yourself. Write about your partner.

Example: I live in Seoul.

I live _____.   _____ lives in _____.
                                              (name)

I speak _____.   He/She speaks _____.

I celebrate _____.   He/She celebrates _____.

GRAMMAR BRIEFING 1

Simple Present Tense—Affirmative Statements

FUNCTION

Using the Simple Present

1. Use the **simple present tense** for the habits and routines (things that people do again and again).

PAST   NOW   FUTURE

▲▲▲▲▲▲▲▲▲

I study
he goes

> I **study** every evening.
>
> He **goes** to movies with his friends.

2. Use the simple present tense for facts (things that are true).

PAST   NOW   FUTURE

they live
it has

> Some Native Americans **live** in New York.
>
> Canada **has** 10 provinces.

(continued on next page)

FORM

A. Affirmative Statements

SUBJECT	BASE VERB*		SUBJECT	BASE VERB + -S	
I			He		
We			She	**works**	every day.
You	**work**	every day.	It		
They			Maria		
Al and Sara					

*Base verb = the base form of the verb (the verb without an ending like -*ing* or -*s*.)

B. Verb Forms

1. In the simple present, use the base form of the verb after *I*, *we*, *you* (singular or plural), *they*, and plural nouns.

   Maria, **you need** a new computer.

   Al and Sara, **you need** new computers.

2. In the simple present tense, third person singular verbs end in -*s*. These are the verbs after:

   - Singular nouns (for example, *a boy*, *Mrs. Brown*, *her book*).

     Jack loves his car.

     The car looks new.

   - Third person singular subject pronouns (*he*, *she*, and *it*).

     He drives a Toyota.

     It runs well.

GRAMMAR PRACTICE 1

Simple Present Tense—Affirmative Statements I

1 **Simple Present Tense Functions:** Learning About Native Americans

Work alone or with a partner. Do these statements describe people's habits and routines, or do they give facts? Check (✓) your answers.

Habit/ Routine	Fact	
✓	☐	1. I often read books about Native Americans.
☐	✓	2. Our public library has many books about Native Americans.
☐	☐	3. We go to the library on weekends.
☐	☐	4. I borrow books and music from the library.
☐	☐	5. The library also has films about Native Americans.
☐	☐	6. Native Americans live in every state in the United States.
☐	☐	7. Some Native American tribes have reservations (areas of land for the people of the tribe).
☐	☐	8. My friend Marta buys Native American pots and rugs for her apartment.

2 Simple Present Tense Forms: Maria Concho and Her Family

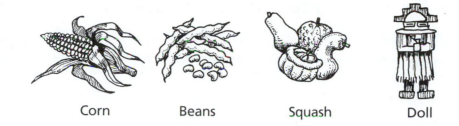

Corn   Beans   Squash   Doll

A. Circle the correct simple present verb.

I'm Maria Concho. I (**live** / lives) in Acoma, New Mexico. The name *Acoma*
                           1
(mean / means) "People of the White Rock." New Mexico is a hot, dry place, but
    2
we (grow / grows) corn, beans, and squash. When the growing season (end / ends),
        3   4
we (celebrate / celebrates) the harvest. Many tourists (come / comes) to our
        5   6
celebration. It (last / lasts) for three days. My son, Ray, (play / plays) his drum at
                7   8
the celebration. Minda, my daughter, (make / makes) dolls, and she (sell / sells) her
                                           9   10
dolls to the tourists. The tourists (take / takes) pictures, and they (listen / listens)
                                        11   12
to our music. We (enjoy / enjoys) this time of year. You are welcome to join us.
                    13

Spelling Rules for Simple Present Tense Verbs

FORM

Spelling Rules for Verbs with Third Person Singular Subjects

1. After third person singular subjects, add *-s* or *-es* to the base form of the verb.	**He likes** baseball. **Paula watches** a lot of TV. **That store opens** at 9:00 a.m.
• For most verbs, add *-s*.	eat → eats play → plays wake up → wakes up
• For verbs ending in *ch*, *s*, *sh*, *x*, or *z*, add *-es*.	kiss → kisses brush → brushes fix → fixes
• For verbs ending in a consonant *+y*, change *y* to *i* and add *-es*.	study → studies carry → carries
2. Remember: After *I*, *you*, or a plural subject, use just the base form of the verb.	**I like** baseball. **We watch** a lot of TV. **Those stores open** at 9:00 a.m.

GRAMMAR **HOT**SPOT!

In the simple present tense, the verbs *have*, *go*, and *do* are **irregular** after third person singular subjects. They do not follow the rules in Grammar Briefing 2.	I **have**/She **has** a full-time job. I **go**/He **goes** to work by car. I **do**/She **does** homework at the library.

Spelling Rules for Simple Present Tense Verbs

3 **Third Person Singular Verbs:** Spelling

Write each base verb (for example, *ask*) and its third person singular simple present form (for example, *asks*). Put them in the correct columns in the chart.

ask	fly	hurry	miss	run
brush	get up	kiss	mix	study
carry	go	listen	say	wake up
do	have	match	push	write

1. Most Verbs	2. Verbs Ending in *ch*, *s*, *sh*, *x*, or *z*	3. Verbs Ending in a Consonant + *y*	4. Irregular Verbs
ask—asks	brush—brushes	carry—carries	do—does

4   **Spelling Third Person Singular Verbs:** Another American Harvest Celebration

Complete the sentences in this e-mail from Peter Cox in the United States to his friend in Korea. Write the correct forms of the verbs in parentheses.

FROM: peter_cox@mymailbox.com
TO: jong-su777@worldwide.com
DATE: 9/2
SUBJ: Thanksgiving

    So you want to know about Thanksgiving? It's a special holiday in the United States. In my family, we do the same things every year. My mother _____ (1. plan) the traditional dinner. She _____ (2. do) the shopping and _____ (3. buy) the turkey. On Thanksgiving morning, our city _____ (4. have) a parade. I always go with my friends. My father _____ (5. march) in the parade. He _____ (6. carry) a flag. My mother _____ (7. stay) home and _____ (8. fix) dinner. My grandmother _____ (9. help). She _____ (10. worry) about the turkey, but every year it's delicious.

    By noon, all our relatives are at our house. Our dinner _____ (11. start) with some quiet words of thanks. It _____ (12. end) with wonderful desserts—pumpkin pie, apple pie, ice cream, and more!

    After dinner, my sister _____ (13. wash) the dishes, and I help. My father _____ (14. lie) on the couch and _____ (15. watch) football on TV. But sometimes he _____ (16. fall) asleep and _____ (17. miss) the game.

A Thanksgiving Turkey

Pies

A Football

TALKING THE TALK

1. There are three ways to pronounce the *-s* ending of third person singular verbs:

   - Say /s/ after voiceless sounds such as /p/, /t/, /k/, and /f/.

jumps	cuts	walks	laughs (gh = /f/)

   - Say /z/ after all vowel sounds and the voiced consonant sounds /b/, /d/, /g/, /v/, /th/, /m/, /n/, /ng/, /l/, and /r/.

goes	plays	rubs	finds	jogs	leaves
bathes	comes	runs	sings	feels	wears

   - Say /ɪz/ after the sounds /s/, /z/, /sh/, /ch/, /zh/, /j/, and /ks/. The /ɪz/ adds a syllable to the word.

misses		buzzes	washes
itches		massages (ge = /zh/)	
judges (dge = /j/)	mixes (x = /ks/)		

2. The third person singular forms of *do* and *say* have a change in the vowel sound.

do → does (/duz/)
say → says (/sez/)

---

5 **Pronunciation of Verb Endings:** Thanksgiving Traditions for One American Family

 A. Listen to the sentences. After each **boldfaced** verb, circle the final sound you hear. The first one is done for you.

1. My family **celebrates** Thanksgiving. (/s/, /z/, /ɪz/)

2. Thanksgiving **comes** in November. (/s/, /z/, /ɪz/)

3. My uncle always **visits** our family. (/s/, /z/, /ɪz/)

4. Sometimes he **brings** me a gift. (/s/, /z/, /ɪz/)

5. My grandmother **cooks** a turkey every year. (/s/, /z/, /ɪz/)

6. My sister **helps**. (/s/, /z/, /ɪz/)

7. Our family **goes** to church. (/s/, /z/, /ɪz/)

8. Our family **eats** a big dinner. (/s/, /z/, /ɪz/)

9. My uncle **takes** some pictures. (/s/, /z/, /ɪz/)

10. My father **watches** football on TV. (/s/, /z/, /ɪz/)

11. Sometimes he **falls** asleep on the couch. (/s/, /z/, /ɪz/)

12. Then he **misses** the game. (/s/, /z/, /ɪz/)

B. Work with a partner. Take turns saying the verbs in Part A. Remember that you add a syllable when you say the /ɪz/ ending.

6 Affirmative Statements: Celebrations with Our Families and Friends

 A. On a piece of paper, write the name of a celebration in your country. Write at least six sentences about this celebration. You can choose subjects and verbs from the box or use other words. Use the simple present tense.

Subjects	Verbs
I	watch (dances, parades)
the children	play (games, a sport)
my family	cook (special foods, a big dinner)
my mother	give (gifts, food)
we	listen to (music, stories)
my friends	take (pictures)
my _____	tell (stories)
	wear (special clothes)

Example: *In my country, we celebrate Carnevale in February. My family has a big dinner. After dinner, I go out with my friends. Some people wear costumes and . . .*

See the *Grammar Links* Website for more model sentences.

 B. Form a group. Tell your group about your celebration.

Simple Present Tense—Negative Statements

FORM

A. Negative Statements

FULL FORMS					CONTRACTIONS			
SUBJECT	DO/ DOES	NOT	BASE VERB		SUBJECT	DON'T/ DOESN'T	BASE VERB	
I					I			
We					We			
You	**do**				You	**don't**		
They					They			
The boys		**not**	**drink**	milk.	The boys		**drink**	milk.
He					He			
She	**does**				She	**doesn't**		
It					It			
Tom					Tom			

B. *Do/Does* in Simple Present Statements

1. *Do* and *does* are **auxiliary verbs** (or **helping verbs**) in negative simple present tense statements.

   • Use *do/does not* with a main verb.

   > Peter **does** not **make** pies.
   >   NOT: Peter ~~does not~~ pies.

   • *Do* and *does* can also be main verbs.

   > They **do** their homework every night.

   > He doesn't **do** the dishes after dinner. She **does** the dishes.

2. Use only the base form of a verb after *does not/doesn't*. Do not add -(*e*)s.

   > He doesn't write letters.
   >   NOT: He doesn't ~~writes~~ letters.

   > She does not have breakfast.
   >   NOT: She does not ~~has~~ breakfast.

GRAMMAR **HOT**SPOT!

1. Remember! Use *do* or *does* + *not* in negative statements.

   > I do not speak French.
   >   NOT: I ~~no speak~~ French.

2. Do not use *isn't* or *aren't* to make a simple present tense verb negative.

   > Jack doesn't live here.
   >   NOT: Jack ~~isn't~~ live here.

Simple Present Tense—Negative Statements

7 **Writing Negative Forms:** A Red Lake Powwow

Read about another Native American celebration. Write the correct negative forms of the verbs in parentheses. Write full forms.

My name is Tom Red Fox. My tribe is the Red Lake Tribe. We live in northern Minnesota. Our

tribe has several powwows during the year. The people of my tribe **do not want**_____ to miss

1 (not / want)

these powwows. In July, we have a very large powwow. It _____ the

2 (not / celebrate)

harvest. It celebrates an agreement made in 1889 between the U.S. government and the Red Lake

Tribe. This powwow is our Independence Day celebration. We _____

3 (not / forget)

the history of our people.

During the week of the powwow, my wife and I _____ to work,

4 (not / go)

and our daughter _____ to school. We all go to the powwow. My

5 (not / go)

family and I _____ our usual clothes during the powwow. We wear

6 (not / wear))

our traditional costumes. They are very beautiful.

All the members of the tribe march in a long parade. The leader

of the parade carries a staff. We _____

7 (not / use)

many different musical instruments, but we have many drums.

I _____ a drum, but I sing.

8 (not / play)

Visitors _____ in the parade,

9 (not / walk)

but they can watch, listen, and take pictures. You

_____ to miss the powwow.

10 (not / want)

It's a great time.

A Staff with Feathers

---

a tribe = a group of Native Americans with the same language, customs, and beliefs. *a powwow* = a traditional meeting of Native Americans. *independence* = being free from the control of another country.

---

8 **Affirmative and Negative Statements:** The Fourth of July, Independence Day

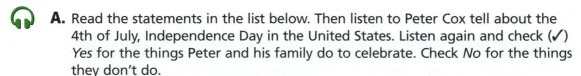 **A.** Read the statements in the list below. Then listen to Peter Cox tell about the 4th of July, Independence Day in the United States. Listen again and check (✓) *Yes* for the things Peter and his family do to celebrate. Check *No* for the things they don't do.

Yes	No
	✓

1. His family celebrates for four days.
2. They have a big picnic.
3. Peter cooks in the kitchen.
4. Peter's parents work.
5. The kids play games.
6. The adults relax.
7. Peter does homework.
8. The family goes to a park.
9. They watch dancers.
10. They listen to a concert.
11. They see a movie.
12. They stay in the park all night.

> *have a picnic* = eat outdoors, for example in a park or on a beach.
> *relax* = rest. *a concert* = a music show with people singing or playing instruments.

B. Look at the *No* statements in Part A. On a piece of paper, rewrite the statements to make them true. Use negative contractions.

Example: 1. His family doesn't celebrate for four days.

C. Talk about these questions in a group: Is Independence Day a celebration in your country, or does your country have a celebration for an important leader? Tell your group about it. Tell what you do and don't do on this day. Use contractions in negative statements.

Example: In France, our Independence Day is July 14. We spend the day with our families, and we have a big dinner. We don't cook outside.

Time Expressions with the Simple Present Tense

FORM and FUNCTION

Statements with Time Expressions

1. Time expressions tell when something happens. They can be:

    • Specific.

    • General.

The bus comes **at 7:25 a.m.**
During the summer, I go to the beach **on weekends**.

2. Time expressions usually go at the beginning or at the end of a sentence.

Every Saturday morning, he washes his car.
He washes his car **every Saturday morning**.

Time Expressions with the Simple Present Tense

9 **Identifying Time Expressions:** A White Mountain Apache Celebration

A. Read about another Native American celebration. <u>Underline</u> the 10 time expressions. The first one is underlined for you.

When a White Mountain Apache girl turns 14, she becomes an adult. Many girls have a special ceremony called the Sunrise Dance. It happens <u>in the summer</u>. The girl learns a dance for the ceremony.

On the first day of the celebration, the girl dances around a fire at night. This is just a short dance. The long dance starts on the second day. In the early morning, the girl begins to run and dance. She doesn't have much rest during the day. The dance is a test: Is the girl strong enough to be an adult in the tribe? At night, the girl dances again. On the third day, she receives a staff. It is hers to keep. In the evening, many people pray, and everyone eats a special dinner. On the fourth day, more people visit, and the ceremony comes to an end.

Girls sometimes cry because the ceremony is long and difficult. These traditions help a girl to become a strong woman.

> *a ceremony* = a traditional set of actions used when celebrating an important event.

B. Write a time expression to answer each question.

1. When does a White Mountain Apache girl become an adult? <u>*at age 14*</u>

2. When does the Sunrise Dance happen? _____

3. On the first day, when does the girl dance around a fire? _____

4. On the second day, when does her dance begin? _____

5. When does the girl receive a staff? _____

6. When does the ceremony end? _____

 See the Grammar Links Website for more information about Native Americans.

GRAMMAR BRIEFING 5

Adverbs of Frequency

FUNCTION

Using Adverbs of Frequency

1. Adverbs can describe verbs. **Adverbs of frequency** tell how often something happens:

always (100% of the time)	I **always** go out on Saturday nights.
usually	I **usually** go out with friends.
often	We **often** go to movies.
sometimes	We **sometimes** go dancing.
seldom	We **seldom** eat in expensive restaurants.
never (0% of the time)	I **never** stay home.

2. Use adverbs of frequency with simple present tense verbs. They are not usually used with present progressive verbs.

> She **often gets up** early.
> **NOT:** She's ~~often getting up~~ early.

3. **Seldom** and **never** have negative meanings. Do not use them in statements with *not*.

> He **never goes** to the mall.
> **NOT:** He ~~doesn't never go~~ to the mall.

(continued on next page)

Adverbs of Frequency in Statements

1. In statements with *be*, adverbs of frequency usually go:

   - After *am/is/are* in affirmative statements.
   - After *not* in negative statements.

   She **is often** busy on weekends.

   They are **not often** late for class.

2. In statements with other verbs, adverbs of frequency usually go before the main verb.

   He **never misses** a football game.

   They **sometimes go** to concerts.

   I don't **usually get up** early.

3. *Sometimes* often comes at the beginning of a statement.

   Sometimes I drink coffee, but I usually drink tea.

GRAMMAR PRACTICE 5

Adverbs of Frequency

10 **Position of Adverbs of Frequency:** Visiting a Powwow

Work with a partner. Student A: Read a sentence aloud. Student B: Say the sentence with the adverb of frequency. Mark the correct place (or places) for the adverb. Take turns.

Example: Student A: Peter Cox reads about Native American traditions.
Student B: Peter Cox often reads about Native American traditions.

1. (often)   Peter Cox reads about Native American traditions.

2. (always)   Peter is ready to learn more about them.

3. (sometimes)   He goes to see Native American powwows and ceremonies.

4. (often)   Visitors are welcome at the powwows.

5. (always)   Religious ceremonies are not open to visitors.

6. (sometimes)   The ceremonies are for Native Americans only.

7. (never)   People talk during the ceremonies.

8. (usually)   Visitors don't understand the songs.

9. (seldom)   Visitors understand the ceremonies.

10. (often)   Peter doesn't forget his camera.

11. (always)   He asks, "Is it okay to take pictures?"

12. (usually)   He takes a lot of pictures.

 11 **Using Adverbs of Frequency and Time Expressions:** Your Routine Activities

A. Work with a partner. Take turns giving facts about your everyday lives. Use the verbs in the box (or other verbs) in affirmative and negative statements. Include adverbs of frequency and time expressions.

Example: Student A: I usually eat dinner at 8:00 or 9:00.
         Student B: I never eat dinner after 7:00. I'm usually hungry at 5:30.

eat dinner	cook	read	be late
watch TV	play (a sport)	get up early	write to my friends
speak English	be happy	be tired	get e-mail

B. Tell the class two facts you learned about your partner.

C. On a piece of paper, write at least eight statements about your everyday life. Use the verbs in the box (or other verbs) in affirmative and negative statements. Include adverbs of frequency and time expressions.

Example: I don't play sports during the week, but on weekends, I sometimes go swimming.

 Check your progress! Go to the Self-Test for Chapter 7 on the *Grammar Links* Website.

Chapter 8

Regional Celebrations

Simple Present Tense—*Yes/No* Questions and *Wh-* Questions

Introductory Tasks: State Fairs

🎧 **A.** Listen and circle the verb form you hear.

Many states in the United States have a state fair every year. A state fair is a big, outdoor event with rides, games, farm animals, food, and music. People also grow things and make things for the fairs, and sometimes they win prizes. Reporter Al Jordan is talking with two prize winners.

Al Jordan: This is Al Jordan reporting to you from Albuquerque

and the New Mexico State Fair. We're at the chili

exhibit, and I'm talking to Santiago Paz. Mr. Paz,

why (**do** / does) you grow chili peppers?
1

Santiago Paz: They are an important part of Southwestern cooking,

and they taste great.

Al Jordan: (Do / Does) all chili peppers **taste** the same?
2

Santiago Paz: No, they (don't / doesn't). Some are hot and spicy, and some are mild.
3

Al Jordan: Now, what (do / does) I see in this bowl—is it salsa?
4

Santiago Paz: Yes, that's salsa. I make it with chili peppers, onions,

and tomatoes.

Al Jordan: (Do / Does) it **taste** hot and spicy, or is it mild?
5

Santiago Paz: Here, (do / does) you **want** to try it? Have some!
6

Al Jordan: Thanks. . . . Wow! That's hot! (Do / Does) you **have**
7

some water?

Chili Peppers

Salsa

> *spicy* = made with seeds or powder from plants that give food a special taste. *hot* = with a burning, spicy taste.

Peaches

A Pie

Al Jordan:	We're here at the Georgia State Fair with Sally Smith. She wins prizes every year for her wonderful pies. Mrs. Smith, what kind of pies (do / does) you make?
	8
Sally Smith:	Strawberry, apple, and peach pies. They're my favorites.
Al Jordan:	These pies smell great! (Do / Does) this pie **have** apples in it?
	9
Sally Smith:	No, that's a peach pie.
Al Jordan:	Where (do / does) the peaches come from?
	10
Sally Smith:	From our farm. Georgia is famous for its peaches.
Al Jordan:	And what (do /does) you put in your pie, besides the peaches?
	11
Sally Smith:	Sorry, but that's a secret!
Al Jordan:	Well, congratulations and thanks for talking with us. This is Al Jordan, from the Georgia State Fair.

B. Look at the two conversations in Part A to answer these questions.

1. Look at the five **boldfaced** verbs. These are the main verbs. Circle the subject of each verb.

   Example: (Do/Does) all chili peppers **taste** the same?
   2

2. The five **boldfaced** main verbs are in simple present *yes/no* questions.

   Do the verbs end in *-s*? ☐ Yes ☐ No

3. What auxiliary verbs do you see in these questions?

   ☐ am/is/are ☐ do/does

4. How do you form *yes/no* questions in the simple present tense? Write the words in the correct order.

subject	base form of verb	*do/does*

   Use: _____ + _____ + base form of verb

Simple Present Tense—*Yes/No* Questions and Short Answers

FORM

Questions and Answers

QUESTIONS					ANSWERS					
DO/DOES	SUBJECT	BASE VERB			*YES*			*NO*		
Do	I					I			I	
	we					we			we	
	you				Yes,	you	**do.**	No,	you	**don't.**
	they					they			they	
	the boys	**need**	help?			he			he	
Does	he					she	**does.**		she	**doesn't.**
	she					it			it	
	it									
	the team									

GRAMMAR **HOT**SPOT!

1. In *yes/no* questions in the simple present, use *do/does* with the base form of the main verb.

    > **Does** he **fix** cars?
    > **NOT:** Does he ~~fixes~~ cars?

2. In negative short answers, use contractions.

    > *Q:* Does he fix cars?
    > *A:* No, he **doesn't.**
    > **NOT USUALLY:** No, he does not.

3. Remember! *Yes/no* questions with the verb *be* do not use *do/does*.

QUESTIONS WITH *BE*	QUESTIONS WITH OTHER VERBS
Are you ready?	**Do** you **want** to go?
Is he a good runner?	**Does** he **run** fast?

Simple Present Tense—*Yes/No* Questions and Short Answers

1 **Identifying Simple Present *Yes/No* Questions and Answers:** Maple Syrup

Listen and read the conversation. Then <u>underline</u> the eight *yes/no* questions in the simple present tense (**not** questions with the verb *be*). The first one is underlined for you.

Reporter Al Jordan is at the St. Albans Maple Festival in Vermont. Vermont is famous for its maple syrup. Al is talking to Mark LaFleur, winner of the maple syrup contest.

Al: Excuse me, are you the winner of the maple syrup contest?

Mark: Yes, I am.

Al: Congratulations. <u>Do you enter this contest every year?</u>

Mark: Yes, this is my sixteenth year here.

Al: So tell me about making maple syrup. I know you get sap from maple trees. Does it hurt the trees?

Mark: Not much. The trees are very big, and the holes for the sap are small.

Al: When do you go out and get the sap? Do you collect it every day?

Mark: Yes, we do. Every day in the late winter and early spring.

Al: Does your family help?

Mark: Yes, my wife and kids help a lot.

Al: Do you make syrup all year?

Mark: Not all year, no. Just for a few weeks.

Al: I know you have to cook the sap. Does it take a long time?

Mark: Yes, about six hours.

Al: Now, I see that this syrup is light, and that's dark. Do they taste the same?

Mark: Well, they're both good and sweet, but they taste a little different. Here, try both kinds!

Al: Thanks! Are you the pancake cook, too?

Mark: No, my wife's making the pancakes today. What do you think? Do you like them?

Al: Mmmm. Yes, these are good.

Collecting Sap
from a Maple Tree

Cooking Sap to Make Syrup

B. Match the questions and answers. Write the letter of the answer on the line.

There is a pancake breakfast at the St. Albans Maple Festival every year.

_b_ 1. Do you come to the pancake breakfast every year?   a. Yes, you do.

_____ 2. Does Mark make syrup for the breakfast?   b. No, I don't.

_____ 3. Does the syrup taste sweet?   c. No, we don't.

_____ 4. Does Mark's wife cook?   d. Yes, it does.

_____ 5. Do many people eat pancakes?   e. Yes, she does.

_____ 6. Do you and your family eat pancakes every day?   f. Yes, they do.

_____ 7. Do I need a ticket for the breakfast?   g. Yes, he does.

2   Simple Present *Yes/No* Questions and Short Answers: Regional Products

A. Complete the *yes/no* questions in the simple present. Use the verb in parentheses.

1. (grow)   _Do_ farmers in the Southwest _grow_ apples?

2. (catch)   _____ people in New England _____ fish?

3. (plant)   _____ farmers in New England _____ cotton?

4. (produce)   _____ the state of Alaska _____ grapes?

5. (produce)   _____ the state of Hawaii _____ oil?

6. (plant)   _____ farmers in the Midwest _____ corn?

7. (grow)   _____ peaches _____ in the South?

8. (have)   _____ the South _____ oil?

9. (grow)   _____ farmers _____ wheat on the Great Plains?

10. (produce)   _____ the East Coast _____ cotton?

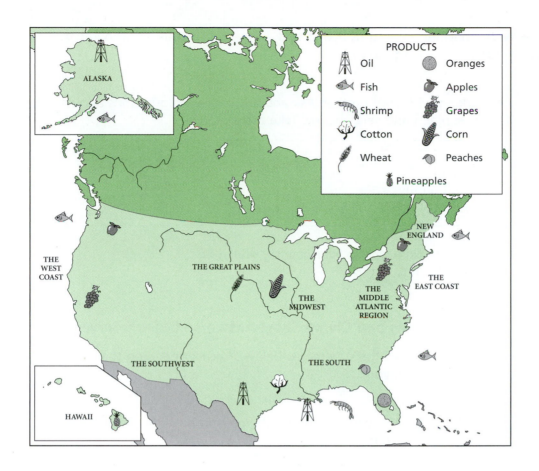

B. Work with a partner. Take turns asking the questions in Part A. Look at the map and give short answers. Then ask and answer two more *yes/no* questions.

Example: Student A: **Do farmers in the Southwest grow apples?**
Student B: **No, they don't.**

3 *Does* Versus *Is* in *Yes/No* Questions and Short Answers: Food Facts

A. Complete the questions with *Does* or *Is*.

1. __Is_____ fish a popular food in Japan?

2. _____ coffee grow in Colombia?

3. _____ Canada produce bananas?

4. _____ Florida a good place to grow oranges?

5. _____ sugar a product of Brazil?

6. _____ France produce grapes?

7. _____ tea a popular drink in China?

8. _____ maple syrup have a sweet taste?

9. _____ maple syrup spicy, like salsa?

10. _____ salsa come from Korea?

B. Work with a partner. Take turns asking and answering the questions in Part A. Check your answers with the class.

C. Continue working with your partner. Ask and answer *yes/no* questions about food. Use the subjects and verbs below. Take turns.

you	eat
your best friend	drink
people in your family	like
people in your country	grow

Example: Student A: Do people in your country drink tea?
　　　　　Student B: Yes, they do.

4　Asking *Yes/No* Questions and Giving Short Answers: Taking a Survey

A. Work with a partner. Read the statements below. Practice changing them to *yes/no* questions with *Do you . . . ?*

B. Walk around the room. Ask your classmates the questions. Write names on the lines to make true statements.

Example: Student A: Do you eat pancakes?
　　　　　Student B (Ahmed): No, I don't.

　　　　　Student A writes: ___Ahmed___ doesn't eat pancakes.

1. _____ doesn't eat pancakes.

2. _____ likes pancakes.

3. _____ likes salsa.

4. _____ doesn't eat salsa.

5. _____ likes to cook.

6. _____ doesn't often cook.

7. _____ often tries new foods.

8. _____ often goes out to eat.

Simple Present Tense—*Wh*- Questions and Answers I

FUNCTION

Overview of *Wh*- Questions

1. Use *wh*- questions to ask for specific information. Use:

   - *Who* or *whom** in questions about people.

     *Whom is very formal. It is not common in conversation.

     | Q: **Who** likes pancakes? |
     | A: Al does. |
     | Q: **Who**(**m**) do you know in the class? |
     | A: I know Nadia and Karel. |

   - *What* in questions about things.

     | Q: **What** happens in August? |
     | A: We have our state fair. |
     | Q: **What** do they grow in Georgia? |
     | A: Peaches. |

   - *Where* in questions about places.

     | Q: **Where** do oranges grow? |
     | A: In Florida. |

   - *When* in questions about time.

     | Q: **When** do they pick the grapes? |
     | A: In the fall. |

   - *Why* in questions about the cause or reason for something.

     | Q: **Why** do you come to the fair? |
     | A: Because it's fun. |

   - *How often* in questions about the number of times something happens.

     | Q: **How often** do you come to the fair? |
     | A: Every year. |

2. A *wh*- question can:

   - Ask about the subject of a verb (who or what does something).

     subject
     Who likes pancakes?

     subject
     What grows in Georgia?

   - Ask for other information (when you know the subject).

            subject
     Who does **Tom** meet for lunch?

            subject
     Where do **people** grow peaches?

(continued on next page)

Answers to *Wh-* Questions

The answer to a *wh-* question can be:

- A complete sentence.

  > Q: Where does he live?
  > A: **He lives in Texas.**
  >
  > Q: Who makes good coffee?
  > A: **Stan makes good coffee.**

- Just the new information.

  > Q: Where does he live?
  > A: **In Texas.**
  >
  > Q: Who makes good coffee?
  > A: **Stan./Stan does.**

GRAMMAR PRACTICE 2

Simple Present Tense—*Wh-* Questions and Answers I

5 ***Wh-* Questions and Answers:** What's a Rodeo?

A. Match the questions and answers. Write the letter of each answer.

A tourist in Cheyenne, Wyoming, is asking questions.

<u>c</u> 1. What's a rodeo?	a. Because it's a Western tradition.
_____ 2. What happens at a rodeo?	b. Cowboys do.
_____ 3. Who rides the bulls?	c. It's a show of cowboy skills.
_____ 4. How often do they have rodeos?	d. In the afternoon.
_____ 5. Why do they have rodeos?	e. They have them every year.
_____ 6. When do they hold the contests?	f. At the ticket window.
_____ 7. Where do people buy tickets?	g. Because I'm a bull rider.
_____ 8. Why do YOU know so much about rodeos?	h. Different contests—bull riding, for example.

> *a skill* = the ability to do something you learned.

B. Work with a partner. Take turns asking and answering the questions in Part A.

 See the *Grammar Links* Website for more information about rodeos.

6 Using *Wh-* Question Words: Stan Nielson, Bull Rider

A. Complete the questions with *who, what, when, where, why,* and *how often.*

Reporter Al Jordan is interviewing a cowboy, Stan Nielson.

Al Jordan asks:

Stan answers:

1. _What_ do you have on your ranch?   Cows and bulls and horses.

2. _____ rides the bulls?   I do, and other cowboys do, too.

3. _____ do you ride bulls?   Because it's exciting.

4. _____ do you get the bulls?   From ranches in Wyoming and Montana.

5. _____ catches the bulls?   The other cowboys and I catch them.

6. _____ do you practice bull riding?   When I have some free time.

7. _____ do you practice?   On the ranch.

8. _____ do you fall?   Very often—every time I ride a bull.

9. _____ happens when you fall?   It hurts!

10. _____ teaches bull riding?   I do. Do you want to try it?

> *a ranch* = a place in the Western United States where people raise horses, cows, sheep, etc.

B. Work with a partner. Ask and answer the questions from Part A.

7 Answering *Wh-* Questions and *Yes/No* Questions: Rodeo Time

Listen to each question about the rodeo. Circle the letter of the answer.

1. a. Every year.   b. No, they don't.

2. a. In Cheyenne.   b. At 10:00.

3. a. At the ticket window.   b. Yes, they do.

4. a. No, it doesn't.   b. Riders race their horses around barrels.

5. a. Yes, it does.   b. They ride horses.

6. a. Yes, they often fall.   b. In the afternoon.

7. a. Cowboys do.   b. Yes, they do.

8. a. In the evening.   b. To keep sun and rain from their eyes.

A Cowgirl Racing Around a Barrel

Simple Present Tense—*Wh-* Questions and Answers II

FORM

A. Questions with *Who* or *What* as Subject

QUESTIONS			ANSWERS
WH- QUESTION WORD	**BASE VERB + -(E)S**		
Who	**rides**	horses?	Cowboys.
			Cowboys do.
			Cowboys ride horses.
What	**happens**	every summer?	A rodeo.
			They have a rodeo.

B. Questions with Other Subjects

QUESTIONS					ANSWERS
WH- QUESTION WORD	**DO/DOES**	**SUBJECT**	**BASE VERB**		
Who **Whom***	**do**	you	**call**	on Sundays?	My parents.
What	**does**	Stan	**do**?		He works on a ranch.
Where	**do**	they	**live**?		In California.
When	**does**	the rodeo	**happen**?		In the summer.
Why	**do**	you	**practice**	the guitar?	Because I want to improve my skills.
How often	**does**	it	**rain**	in the desert?	Almost never.

Whom is very formal. It is not common in conversation.

Simple Present Tense—*Wh-* Questions and Answers II

8 **Wh- Questions with *Who* or *What* as Subject:** Don't Miss Frontier Days!

A. Complete the questions with *Who* or *What* as the subject. Use the verb in parentheses.

1. ___What takes place___ every summer in Wyoming?   Cheyenne Frontier Days.
   (take place)

2. _____ at Frontier Days?   They have a big rodeo.
   (happen)

3. _____ to the rodeo?   Thousands of people!
   (come)

4. _____ at 1:05 every afternoon?   The rodeo events.
   (start)

5. _____ the events?   Cowboys and cowgirls do.
   (enter)

6. _____ prizes?   The winners of all the events.
   (get)

7. _____ in the evening?   There are concerts.
   (happen)

8. _____ at the concerts?   Big name bands do.
   (play)

B. Write a question with *Who* or *What* about the missing information.

1. Some people like rodeos.
   Who likes rodeos?

2. Something happens in Wyoming in July.
   _____

3. Some people ride bulls.
   _____

4. Something starts at 9:00 each night.
   _____

5. Some people perform at the concerts.
   _____

6. Some people have fun at Frontier Days.
   _____

9 *Wh-* Questions with Other Subjects: Wayne Cody, Bronco Rider

A. Read each sentence. Write a *wh-* question about the **boldfaced** words. Use the simple present tense and *what, where, why,* or *how often.*

Visit Wayne Cody's home page:

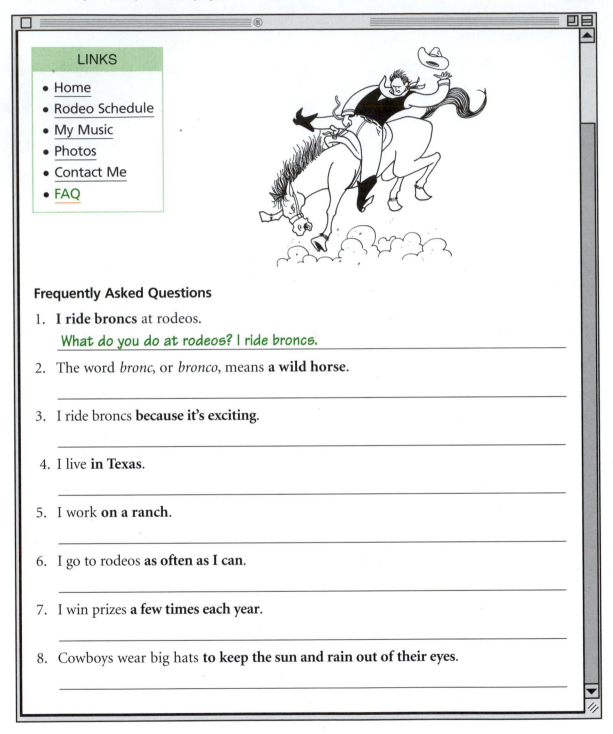

LINKS

- Home
- Rodeo Schedule
- My Music
- Photos
- Contact Me
- FAQ

Frequently Asked Questions

1. **I ride broncs** at rodeos.

   What do you do at rodeos? I ride broncs.

2. The word *bronc,* or *bronco,* means **a wild horse.**

   _____

3. I ride broncs **because it's exciting.**

   _____

4. I live **in Texas.**

   _____

5. I work **on a ranch.**

   _____

6. I go to rodeos **as often as I can.**

   _____

7. I win prizes **a few times each year.**

   _____

8. Cowboys wear big hats **to keep the sun and rain out of their eyes.**

   _____

B. Work with a partner. Ask and answer questions about Wayne Cody. Use the information in Part A.

Example: Student A: *What does Wayne do at rodeos?*
          Student B: *He rides broncos.*

Who and *what* are used in both kinds of *wh-* questions:

- Use *who/what* + a third person singular verb to ask about the subject (S).

S
Q: **Who needs** books?
A: **We** do.

S
Q: **What has** four legs and flies?
A: **A horse.**

- Use *who/what* + *do(es)* + subject + base verb to ask about the object of the verb (O).

O
Q: **Who do you watch?**
A: I watch **the riders.**

O
Q: **What does Al like?**
A: He likes **rodeos.**

10 **Questions with *Who* or *What* as Subject and as Object:** At a Rodeo

Write a question with *Who* or *What* about the missing information.

1. (Some people) go to rodeos.

   Who goes to rodeos?

2. I see (some people) at rodeos.

   Who do you see at rodeos?

3. (Some people) compete in rodeo events.

   _____

4. I watch (somebody) in the events.

   _____

5. (Some people) give prizes.

   _____

6. Cowboys win (something) in rodeo events.

   _____

7. The winners call (some people) with the news.

   _____

8. (Something) happens at 9:00 each night.

   _____

9. Bands play (something).

   _____

10. I like (something) most at the rodeo.

   _____

11 **Using _Wh-_ Questions and Answers:** Interview a Classmate

 Work with a partner. Ask _wh-_ questions in the simple present tense about the common daily activities listed in the box. Use _who, what, where, when, why,_ and _how often_. Take turns.

Example: Student A: When do you eat dinner?
Student B: Usually at 6:00.
Student B: Where do you study?
Student A: In my room. It's quiet, and I have my computer there.

eat (breakfast, lunch, dinner)	read (newspapers, magazines)	visit relatives
go (to the store, to work, to the library)	relax	watch TV
have class	see friends	
play (sports)	study	

Check your progress! Go to the Self-Test for Chapter 8 on the _Grammar Links_ Website.

9

Ethnic Celebrations

Simple Present Tense and Present Progressive Tense; Non-Action Verbs

Introductory Task: Three Holidays

A. Listen and read about three holidays. Then look at the **boldfaced** verbs. Circle the verbs that tell a fact or tell what is usually true. <u>Underline</u> the verbs that describe what is happening now.

Here is some information about three ethnic celebrations in the United States.

At the Saint Patrick's Day Parade

1   Hi, I'm Kevin Murray. My family is Irish American, and we (**live**) in Chicago. Many Irish Americans **live** in the Chicago area. We **celebrate** Saint Patrick's Day on March 17. Every year, the fun **starts** early and **continues** all day and night. For example, we always **have** a parade that day. In this picture, some people <u>**are watching**</u> the parade. Lots of them **are wearing** green—it's the traditional color of Ireland. That's my brother Brandon in the middle. He**'s wearing** a green jacket and a hat with a shamrock on it. He**'s having** a good time.

2   My name is Jazmin Walters. I'm **African American**. In this picture,
I**'m standing** with my mother and my little sister. She**'s lighting** a candle
for Kwanza, and I**'m helping** her. The word "Kwanza" **comes** from Swahili,
an African language. It **means** "first." We **have** a celebration every night from
December 26 to January 1. We **remember** the past and **plan** for the future.

Celebrating Kwanza

Dancers at a Cinco de Mayo Parade

3   Hi, I'm Alicia Rios. My family and I **live** in San José, California. We **speak**
Spanish and English. Like many Mexican Americans, we **celebrate** Cinco de Mayo,
the fifth of May. On this day, we **remember** an important battle. It was between
the Mexicans and the French in 1862. We always **have** a parade and a fair and
fireworks. In this picture, I**'m standing** with my friends. That's me on the right.
We**'re getting** ready to dance in the parade.

> *ethnic* = about people from the same country or culture. *a battle* = a
> fight in a war.

B. Look at the circled and underlined verbs in Part A.

1. Which verbs tell a fact or what usually happens? Write three examples here:

    live   _____   _____

    These verbs are: ☐ simple present tense   ☐ present progressive tense

2. Which verbs tell what is happening at this moment? Write three examples here:

    are watching   _____   _____

    These verbs are: ☐ simple present tense   ☐ present progressive tense

Simple Present Tense Versus Present Progressive Tense

FUNCTION

A. The Simple Present

1. Use the simple present tense for:

   - Habits or routines.

He **drinks** milk every day.
Do you always **give** gifts on holidays?

   - Things that are always true.

The sun **sets** in the west.
Tuesday **comes** after Monday.

2. Adverbs of frequency often go with verbs in the simple present tense.

   (See Chapter 7, Grammar Briefing 5, page 125, for more information on adverbs of frequency.)

I **always** go to bed at 10:00.
Does he **often** have parties?
It **seldom** snows in the winter there.

3. Certain time expressions go with verbs in the simple present tense. These are expressions like *every year*, *on Mondays*, *at night*, and *in the summer*.

We eat vegetables and fruit **every day**.
He doesn't go to school **on weekends**.

B. The Present Progressive

1. Use the present progressive for actions that are happening right now.

   Time expressions that go with this use of the present progressive include *now*, *right now*, and *at this moment*.

Listen! They**'re playing** a great song.
It **is snowing** <u>at the moment</u>.

2. Use the present progressive for actions that are happening over a longer period in the present.

   Time expressions that go with this use of the present progressive include *this week*, *this year*, and *these days*.

Are they **studying** at Ohio State University?
She**'s living** with friends <u>this semester</u>.

Simple Present Tense Versus Present Progressive Tense

1 **Simple Present Versus Present Progressive:** Saint Patrick's Day in Chicago

A. Circle the correct verb.

Kevin Murray is in Chicago. Today he (makes /(is making))
1
a video of the Saint Patrick's Day activities. At this moment, he

(tapes / is taping) with his video camera. He (talks / is talking)
2   3
at the same time. Let's listen:

Kevin: Today is one of my favorite holidays, Saint Patrick's Day.

We (watch / are watching) the parade right now. Every year, many
4

people and groups (march / are marching) in the parade. The bands
5

usually (play / are playing) traditional Irish songs. Right now this
6

band (plays / is playing) "When Irish Eyes Are Smiling." We often
7

(sing / are singing) the songs as the bands play. Over there is the Chicago
8

River. Do you see the color of the river? Don't worry, you're not going

crazy—the river really is green! Every year, the city (changes / is changing)
9

the color of the river to celebrate Saint Patrick's Day.

Now Kevin and a friend, Tanya, are watching his video of Saint Patrick's Day
in Chicago. Tanya is Russian. She's asking questions about the video and about
the holiday.

Kevin: Look, here's the Chicago River.

Tanya: It's green!

Kevin: Yeah. Every year they (color / are coloring) the river for Saint Patrick's Day.
10

Tanya: I don't understand. Why (do they make / are they making) it green?
11

Kevin: I guess it's because green is the traditional color of Ireland.

Tanya: (Do many visitors come / Are many visitors coming) to Chicago on Saint
12

Patrick's Day?

Kevin: Sure! There's always a big crowd. Oh, this part of the tape shows the parade.

Tanya: Who (rides / is riding) in that car?
13

Kevin: That's the mayor. He's in the parade every year.

Tanya: Why (does he always ride / is he always riding) in the parade? Is he Irish?
                                              14

Kevin: No, but he always (likes / is liking) to be in different community
                                        15

celebrations. Okay, now I have some tape from my favorite Irish restaurant.

Tanya: How often (do you go/ are you going) there?
                              16

Kevin: Once or twice a month.

Tanya: Who (sings / is singing) at that table?
                    17

Kevin: That's my brother, Brandon, and some of our friends.

Tanya: I think they (have / are having) a good time!
                                   18

Kevin: Sure. Saint Patrick's Day is a lot of fun.

---

a mayor = a person elected to lead the government of a city.

B. Listen to Part A and check your answers.

---

2 **Simple Present Versus Present Progressive:** **Kwanza, an African American Holiday**

Complete each sentence with the correct tense of the verb in parentheses. Use affirmative and negative verbs. Use the simple present and the present progressive.

Tonight is the fifth night of Kwanza. Read about Jazmin and her family, what they usually do in the evening, and what they are doing tonight.

1. In the evening, Jazmin usually __*does*__ her homework. She
                                      a (do)

   __*doesn't go out*__. But tonight, because it's Kwanza, Jazmin and her family aren't
        b (not / go out)

   at home. They __*are visiting*__ relatives.
                    c (visit)

2. Jazmin: Every night, I _____ on the phone with my friends. Tonight is special,
                           a (talk)

   so I _____ on the phone. I _____ to stories.
          b (not / talk)   c (listen)

3. Jazmin: In my family, we usually _____ dinner at 6:00, and we
                                      a (eat)

   _____ a large meal. Tonight, for Kwanza, we _____
      b (not / have)   c (have)

   a big dinner with our relatives and friends.

4. Jazmin: My father usually _____ TV in the evening, but he _____
                               a (watch)   b (not / watch)

   TV tonight. Because it's Kwanza, he _____ something different. Tonight he
                                         c (do)

   _____ gifts to our friends and family.
      d (give)

3 Using the Simple Present and Present Progressive: Tell Me About Yourself

A. Work with a partner. Take turns asking questions in the simple present tense and present progressive tense. Use the words in parentheses.

Example: Student A: Where do you live?
Student B: I live in Springfield.

Simple Present Tense

1. (where/you/live)
2. (what/you/do on weekends)
3. (where/you/do your homework)

Present Progressive Tense

4. (why/you/take this course)
5. (why/you/study English)
6. (what/you/do to practice your English outside class)

B. Write at least four sentences about your partner. Use the information from Part A.

Example: My partner's name is Tamara. She lives in . . .

 See the *Grammar Links* Website for a complete model paragraph for this assignment.

4 Using the Simple Present and Present Progressive: Giving Gifts

Form a group, and sit in a circle. Choose Picture 1 or Picture 2: Who are the people in the picture, and what is happening? Go around the circle, taking turns to tell a story about the people. Use simple present verbs to tell facts about them. Use present progressive verbs to describe what is happening at this moment. One student writes the group's story. Then share your story with the class.

Example: Student A: The two women are friends. They always go shopping together.
Student B: Their names are Mary and Brittany. They live in Los Angeles.
Student C: Right now they are looking for a present.
Student A: They are . . .

Picture 1

Picture 2

Non-Action Verbs

FORM and FUNCTION

Non-Action Verbs*

1. **Non-action verbs** do not tell about actions. Some non-action verbs are for:

   - Definition or description: *be, seem, sound, look.*

     I **am** tired, but you **seem** full of energy.

     That **sounds** like a good idea.

     This word **doesn't look** right. How do you spell it?

   - Senses: *see, hear, smell, taste.*

     I **don't see** any birds, but I **hear** some.

     The pie **smells** good and **tastes** great.

   - Possession: *have, own, belong.*

     He **has** a guitar. He also **owns** a piano. Both instruments **belong** to him.

   - Thoughts: *know, remember, forget, understand.*

     They **know** my phone number.

     I **remember** his face, but I **forget** his name.

     We **don't understand** the math.

   - Attitudes: *need, want, prefer.*

     I don't **need** new clothes, but I **want** some!

     Baseball is okay, but I **prefer** basketball.

   - Emotions: *hate, like, love.*

     I **like** parties.

     He **loves** rock music and **hates** jazz.

2. Non-action verbs are not usually used in the present progressive. Use the simple present tense.

   I **like** this music.
     NOT: I ~~am liking~~ this music.

   We **need** some more music.
     NOT: We ~~are needing~~ some more music.

*Non-action verbs are also called verbs with stative meaning.

Have can be a non-action verb or an action verb:

- *Have* is a non-action verb when it shows possession. Use only the simple present.

- Sometimes *have* tells about actions. For example, *have* can mean *eat, drink,* or *experience.* Use the present progressive for actions happening now and the simple present for facts and habits.

> I **have** a CD player.
> **NOT:** I ~~am having~~ a CD player.

> She**'s having** dinner right now.
> She always **has** dinner at the same time.

> We**'re having** a party. Come on over!
> We **have** parties almost every weekend.

> I**'m having** trouble with this homework.
> I often **have** trouble with math.

GRAMMAR PRACTICE 2

Non-Action Verbs

5 **Identifying Non-Action Verbs: The Fifth of May**

Work alone or with a partner. Circle the 12 non-action verbs. The first one is done for you.

Alicia Rios is telling about the Cinco de Mayo celebration in San José, California:

I (like) the 5th of May celebration in my town. My little sister and I always go to the fair with our friends. Everybody goes there. Many people wear red, green, and white on the 5th of May. These are the colors of the Mexican flag. My friends and I usually walk around and play some of the games. I like to play, but I hate to lose. The food at the fair smells good. Some of it tastes very hot and spicy. I love spicy food, but my friends prefer ice cream and candy. In the evening, we listen to a concert in the park. After dark, we watch the fireworks. They look beautiful in the sky. My sister hates them because they are very loud. We always get home late at night. The 5th of May is a great day.

6 **Action Versus Non-Action Verbs in Statements and Questions: A Game at the Fair**

Write the correct present tense form of the action and non-action verbs.

Alicia Rios is at the fair on the 5th of May. Her little sister Diana is with her.

Diana: Alicia, what <u>are</u> you <u>doing</u> ?
           1a   b (do)

Alicia: I _____ a dart game.
              2 (play)

Diana: Oh. How do you play?

A Dartboard

Alicia: Well, to begin with, I _____ four darts. Watch.
3 (have)

Now I _____ my last dart. I _____
4 (throw)   5 (try)

to hit the center of the dartboard. Bull's-eye!

Diana: I _____ to try.
6 (want)

Alicia: Okay. _____ you _____ the target?
7a   b (see)

Diana: Yes, yes, I _____. One. Oops.
8 (understand)

Alicia: Try again.

Diana: Two. Oh, no!

Alicia: That _____ okay. Here's another dart. Wait, you _____
9 (be)   10 (hold)

it wrong. Hold it like this.

Diana: Three. Oh, this game _____ easy.
11 (be / not)

Alicia: Try again.

Diana: Okay. Four. I _____ this game! I _____. Why do
12 (hate)   13 (understand / not)

I miss the target every time?

Alicia: You _____ to practice a little. Here's a prize for you.
14 (need)

Diana: But that prize _____ to you.
15 (belong)

Alicia: I _____, but I _____ you to have it.
16 (know)   17 (want)

Diana: Thanks!

7 *Have* **for Possession Versus** *Have* **for Actions:** A Family in San José

A. Read the following sentences. Is *have* an action verb or a non-action verb?
Check (✓) your answers.

Action	Non-action	
☐	☑	1. Alicia has brown eyes.
☑	☐	2. Alicia's family often has parties on holidays.
☐	☐	3. They are having dinner now.
☐	☐	4. They have a small house in San José.
☐	☐	5. Alicia has one sister, Diana.
☐	☐	6. Alicia and Diana don't have brothers.
☐	☐	7. Alicia has fun with her sister at the fair.
☐	☐	8. They always have a good time on the 5th May.

B. Write true statements, affirmative and negative. Use a form of *have* and the words in parentheses. Use the present progressive when you can.

1. My brother Yuri has blue eyes. OR I don't have blue eyes.
    (blue eyes)

2. _____
    (sister)

3. _____
    (fun)

4. _____
    (a good time)

5. _____
    (a car)

6. _____
    (parties)

8 Using *Like* and *Prefer*: Food Choices

A. Work with a partner. Look at the foods in the box. Add three more kinds of food. Tell your partner the things you like and don't like.

Example: Student A: I like ice cream, but I don't like spicy food.
          Student B: I like ice cream and spicy food, too. I don't like hamburgers.

apples	peaches	hamburgers	ketchup	_____
hot chili peppers	pancakes	ice cream	chocolate	_____
maple syrup	pineapple	spicy food	salsa	_____

B. Ask your partner questions about things he or she prefers.

Example: Student A: Do you prefer peaches or apples?
          Student B: Peaches. I prefer peaches.

9 Non-Action Verbs for Thoughts: Inside Your Head

A. Complete the sentences with words from the box.

English spelling	English grammar	my first language	_____'s address
my library card	my book for . . .	my homework	the teacher's name
the schedule for . . .	the phone number for . . .	birthdays	this room number

1. I sometimes forget _birthdays._____

2. I understand _____

3. I know _____

4. I don't know _____

5. I seldom forget _____

6. I always remember _____

B. Work with a partner. Ask questions about things in the list in Part A.

Example: Student A: *Do you sometimes forget your homework?*
Student B: *Yes, I do.* OR *No, I don't forget my homework.*

10 **Using Verbs for the Senses:** Sights and Sounds of a Celebration

A. Close your eyes and imagine that you are at a special holiday or celebration. Then write things you see, hear, and smell.

Example: I smell . . . *our Christmas tree, oranges, a fire in the fireplace*

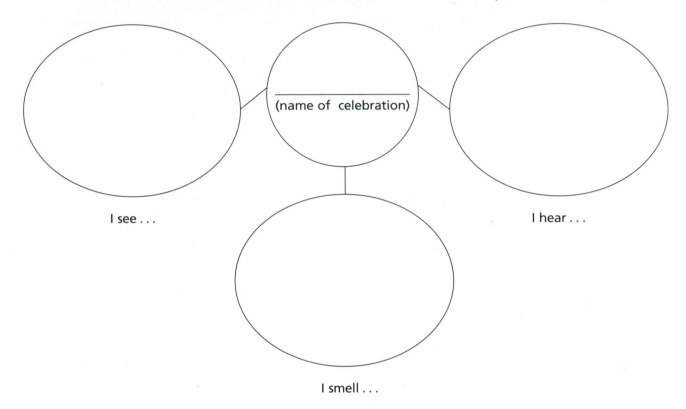

(name of celebration)

I see . . .

I hear . . .

I smell . . .

B. Work in a group. Take turns asking one person in the group to close his or her eyes again and imagine the celebration. Ask questions about the celebration.

Example: *Where are you? What do you hear? What do you see? What smells good?*

Check your progress! Go to the Self-Test for Chapter 9 on the *Grammar Links* Website.

Wrap-up Activities

1 Chinese New Year: READING

Read this paragraph.

Daniel lives in Taiwan. His favorite holiday is Chinese New Year. The new year doesn't start on the same day each year, but it usually starts in February. Daniel doesn't go to school for one week. He loves that! His family visits their relatives during this time. They always have a big dinner. The children get money in red envelopes from the adults. Daniel and his cousins often play cards. Sometimes they go to a parade and watch the dancing. He likes the fireworks at night.

2 When Do You Celebrate? WRITING

Talk to a friend or relative. Ask, *What is your favorite holiday or celebration? What do you usually do at this time?* Write down his or her answers, and use them to write a paragraph. Write six or more sentences. Use adverbs of frequency and verbs in the simple present tense.

See the *Grammar Links* Website for a model paragraph for this assignment.

3 Mardi Gras: EDITING

Correct the eight errors with simple present and present progressive verbs and adverbs of frequency. The first error is corrected for you.

> ### Mardi Gras
>
>   lives
> My friend Emily ~~live~~ in New Orleans. It is a city in Louisiana in the United States.
>
> The city have a Mardi Gras celebration every year. This holiday is usually coming in
>
> February. Always Mardi Gras is on a Tuesday. *Mardi Gras* mean "Fat Tuesday," but
>
> the fun don't last just one day. People are celebrate this holiday for weeks, with many
>
> parties and parades. Every year Emily is going to the parades. She loves Mardi Gras.

4 **A New Holiday:** WRITING/SPEAKING/LISTENING

Form a group, and think of a new holiday or celebration. Give your holiday a name. Talk about when and why you celebrate this new holiday. Then, on a piece of paper, write five sentences about things you do to celebrate the holiday, and write five sentences about things you don't do on this day. Tell the class about the new holiday.

5 **Guess What It Is:** WRITING/SPEAKING

Think of three foods, products, or other items described in Unit Four, and write their names on three small pieces of paper. Fold them up, and give them to the teacher. Student A takes a paper from the teacher. The other students ask *yes/no* questions to guess what is on it. Student A gives only short answers with *yes* or *no*.

Example: *Do you eat it? Is it spicy? Does it grow on trees? Does it grow in the South? Is it a peach?*

6 **Find Out About Holidays:** SPEAKING/LISTENING

Ask an English speaker about one of the holidays in the box. Ask when it is and where people celebrate it. Find out what people do to celebrate. Then share your information with the class.

Some Holidays in the United States		
Valentine's Day	Memorial Day	Halloween
Mardi Gras	Father's Day	Thanksgiving
Mother's Day	Labor Day	Christmas

 See the *Grammar Links* Website for more information about holidays.

Prepositions; *There + Be*

UNIT OBJECTIVES

- **prepositions for describing location**
  (They live *in* a small house. The house is *near* a river.)

- **prepositions for showing direction**
  (We're going *up* the stairs. The stairs lead *to* the second floor.)

- **prepositions for describing time**
  (They met *at* 10:00. They talked *for* an hour.)

- **prepositional phrases**
  (They live *in an apartment*. It is *on the third floor*.)

- **statements with *there + be***
  (*There are* good jobs in that city. *There isn't* a big airport.)

- ***yes/no* questions and short answers with *there + be***
  (*Is there* a dishwasher in the apartment? Yes, *there is. Are there* noisy neighbors? No, *there aren't*.)

Grammar in Action

🎧 Reading and Listening: Houses Around the World

Read and listen to some information about houses.

1   What is a house? <u>There are</u> different answers to this question in different places around the world.

2   Ask a child **in** the United States, "What is a house?" Most American children live in single-family houses, so they usually think "a house" means a building for one family. Inside the house, <u>there are</u> several rooms. <u>There are</u> often two floors, with bedrooms **on** the second floor. Go outside the house, **into** the yard, and there is a place to play.

HOUSE

3   Ask African children in a Shilluk village in the Sudan, "What is a house?" They think of a different kind of house. It's a mud hut. <u>There is</u> a roof of grass on the hut. **Inside** the hut, <u>there is</u> only one room.

A Shilluk Hut

4   Ask a Nenets child in Siberia, "What is a house?" Here the answer is different, too. A traditional Nenets house is called a *chum*. It is made with reindeer skins. This kind of house is easy to move. By tradition, the Nenets people move north **in** the spring. They move **from** the forest **to** the tundra (a cold place where the land is flat and open, with no trees). **After** a few months, they move back to the forest **for** the winter.

5   Why are houses around the world so different? <u>There are</u> many reasons. Here are three.

A Nenets Chum and a Reindeer

- The weather: Is it usually hot or cold in the region? Is there much snow or rain?
- Building materials and technology: Is there wood to build with? What tools do people have?
- The culture: Who lives together in a house? What do they need for their way of life?

6   So houses can be very different. <u>Is there</u> one thing about houses that is always the same? Maybe there is—maybe it's this: A house protects us. It's a place of safety. What do you think: What is a house?

> *a village* = a very small town. *several* = more than three but not many.
> *mud* = a mixture of water and dirt or clay. *a forest* = a place with many
> trees. *technology* = things people make and use and the ways they know
> to use them.

Think About Grammar

A. The **boldfaced** words in the reading are prepositions. The word or words after a preposition are the object of the preposition. Together, they form a **prepositional phrase**.

a preposition   +   its object   =   a prepositional phrase

Look at these sentences from the reading. The <u>underlined</u> words are prepositional phrases. What kind of information do they give? Write *a*, *b*, or *c*.

1. _____ They move <u>from the forest to the tundra</u>.

   a. These prepositional phrases tell when something happens.

2. _____ <u>After a few months</u>, they move back <u>to the forest for the winter</u>.

   b. These prepositional phrases tell where someone or something is.

3. _____ Most American children live <u>in single-family houses</u>. <u>Inside the house</u>, there are several rooms.

   c. These prepositional phrases tell where someone or something is going.

B. Complete these sentences from the reading.

1. (Paragraph 1) <u>There are</u> different _answers_ to this question.

2. (Paragraph 2) Inside the house, <u>there are</u> several _____.

3. (Paragraph 2) <u>There are</u> often two _____, with bedrooms on the second floor.

4. (Paragraph 3) <u>There is</u> a _____ of grass on the hut.

5. (Paragraph 3) Inside the hut, <u>there is</u> only one _____.

6. (Paragraph 5) <u>There are</u> many _____. Here are three.

7. (Paragraph 6) <u>Is there</u> one _____ about houses that is always the same?

C. Look at each of the words you wrote in Part B. Is it a singular noun or a plural noun? Look at the verb *be* in each sentence. Is it singular (*is*) or plural (*are*)?

Complete these rules:

Use *there* + _____ + a singular noun.

Use *there* + _____ + a plural noun.

Chapter 10

Some Unusual Houses

Prepositions

Introductory Task: Life on a Houseboat

A. Listen and read about Debbie Tanaka's home.

Hello! My name is Debbie Tanaka, and I want to tell you about my house *in Seattle, Washington*. It's a houseboat *on Lake Union*. My houseboat is small and made of wood. *Inside it*, there are three rooms. It sits *on the water* right *next to a dock*. It doesn't have a motor, so it doesn't go anywhere. I use a little motorboat to go *across the lake*.

On weekends, I like to fish *in the morning*. I have a good place to sit and fish. I watch the ducks swimming *around the houseboats*. But *on most mornings*, I drive *into the city* and go *to my office*. My office is *at a bank*. I work *until 5:30*, and then I drive *out of the city* and back *to my home*. *In the evening, after sunset*, I often sit and look at the lights of the city. It's my favorite time of day.

> *a dock* = a place where people get on and off boats. *a motor* = the part of a machine that makes the power to move it. *sunset* = the time of day when the sun goes down.

B. Work alone or with a partner. Look at the prepositional phrases *in italics* in Part A. What kind of information do they give? Write them in the chart.

Where Someone or Something Is	Where Someone or Something Is Going	When Something Happens
1. in Seattle, Washington	1. across the lake	1. on weekends
2.	2.	2.
3.	3.	3.
4.	4.	4.
5.	5.	5.
6.	6.	6.

Prepositions and Prepositional Phrases

FORM and FUNCTION

A. Overview

1. A **preposition** can be one word or more than one word.

for	in	near	to	in front of
from	inside	on	in back of	next to

2. A preposition always has an object. The object is a noun or pronoun.
   A preposition + its object = a **prepositional phrase**:

	PREPOSITIONAL PHRASE	
	PREPOSITION	OBJECT
The boat is	**on**	a large **lake**.
Who sits	**next to**	**you**?

B. Uses of Prepositional Phrases

Prepositional phrases often describe:

- Location (place).
- Direction.
- Time.

The lake is **near Seattle**.
We walked **across the street**.
I work **until 5:30**.

C. Placement of Prepositional Phrases

Prepositional phrases can come:

- After *be*.
- After other verbs.
- After nouns.
- At the beginning or end of a sentence.

The boat **is** on the water.
They **are going** into the house.
The **flowers** on your table are beautiful.
In the fall, they move south.
They move south in the fall.

D. Verb + Preposition Combinations

Certain verbs and prepositions often go together. Some common verb + preposition combinations are *agree with*, *belong to*, *listen to*, *think about*, *wait for*, and *worry about*.

That house **belongs to** my friends.
We **wait for** the bus at that corner.
I **listen to** music all the time.

Prepositions and Prepositional Phrases

1 **Prepositions and Their Objects:** Houses on Wheels

Find the 13 prepositional phrases with *after*, *at*, *in*, *inside*, *near*, *on*, and *to*. Circle the prepositions. <u>Underline</u> the objects of the prepositions. The first one is done for you.

A Motor Home

A motor home is like a house (on) <u>wheels</u>. Step inside a motor home. What do you see? There's probably a kitchen, a bathroom, beds, chairs, closets, and a TV. It has all the things you need when you are not at home.

Motor homes are popular in the United States. In the summer, many American families use them as vacation homes. Some people drive them to the ocean and stay in campgrounds near the beach. Other people go to national parks.

Many older Americans like motor homes, too. After retirement, they have time for travel. They can stay in hotels, but hotels are expensive, and meals in restaurants aren't like home cooking. Sometimes a motor home is the answer. Maybe a motor home is in *your* future!

---

a campground = an area for tents and often motor homes. *retirement* = the time when an older person doesn't work at a paid job anymore.

---

2 **Positions of Prepositional Phrases:** Motor Homes

A. Look at the sentences with prepositional phrases in Exercise 1.

1. Copy the two sentences that start with a prepositional phrase.

   _____

   _____

   _____

   _____

2. Write the two sentences again but put each prepositional phrase at the end of the sentence.

   _____

   _____

   _____

   _____

B. In each statement below, underline the prepositional phrase with *in*, *inside*, *near*, *on*, or *to*. Where is it in the sentence? Mark your answer with a check (✓).

The prepositional phrase comes:

	After *Be*	After Another Verb	After a Noun
1. A motor home is like a house <u>on wheels</u>.			✓
2. Step inside a motor home.			
3. The beds are in the back.			
4. Some people go to national parks.			
5. Some people like campgrounds near the beach.			
6. They can stay in hotels, but hotels are expensive.			
7. Meals in restaurants aren't like home cooking.			
8. Maybe a motor home is in *your* future!			

3 **Common Verb + Preposition Combinations:** Al Jordan at the Campground

A. Add the prepositions *about*, *for*, *on*, *to*, and *with*. Circle their objects.

Reporter Al Jordan is at a campground. He has his tape recorder, and he's taping conversations with people about their motor homes.

Al: Excuse me, does this motor home belong __*to*__ (you)?
                                                    1

Max: Yes, it belongs _____ me and my wife. I'm Max Mueller.
                          2

Al: I'm pleased to meet you, Mr. Mueller. My name's Al Jordan. I'm a reporter, and I'm

       talking to people today about life in a motor home. Can I ask you a few questions?

Max: Sure, but let's wait _____ my wife. She loves to talk. Here she is now. Shirl,
                              3

       this is Al Jordan. He's a reporter.

Shirley: Hello! It's nice to meet you!

Al: It's nice to meet you, too, Mrs. Mueller. Do you have time for a few questions?

Shirley: Do I have time? Oh, don't worry _____ that! We're retired—we have all the
                                           4

       time in the world!

Al: Great! Well, then, I'd like you to think _____ life in your motor home—what's
                                                 5

       it like?

Shirley: Well, we just love it, don't we, Max? We think it's a great way to live.

Al: Mr. Mueller, do you agree _____ your wife?
                                  6

Max: You bet. Just listen _____ Shirley, young man, and . . .
                            7

Shirley: Come and sit down, Mr. Jordan!

B. Work with a partner. Student A: Say the beginning of a sentence from the list. Student B: Finish the sentence with a prepositional phrase. Take turns.

Example: Student A: **The tape recorder belongs . . .**
Student B: **. . . to Al Jordan.**

1. The motor home belongs . . .
2. The tape recorder belongs . . .
3. Max and Al wait . . .
4. Al listens . . .
5. Max often listens . . .

6. Shirley doesn't worry . . .
7. Does Max agree . . .
8. Does Shirley listen . . .
9. Shirley doesn't wait . . .
10. What does Shirley think . . .

4 **Common Verb + Preposition Combinations:** An Interview

Work in a group. Take turns asking and answering the questions. Use a verb + preposition in your answers.

Example: Student A: **Who do you usually agree with?**
Student B: **I usually agree with my friend Yoko. We usually see things the same way.**

1. Who do you usually agree with? Is there someone you *never* agree with?

2. Is there someone you often wait for? When and why do you wait for this person?

3. What kinds of things do you worry about? Who worries about *you*?

4. What kind of music do you usually listen to?

5. Look at _____. What is (he/she) thinking about?
   (classmate)

Prepositions for Describing Location

FORM and FUNCTION

A. Overview

Some prepositions help describe location (place). They tell where someone or something is. These prepositions include *above, behind, between, in, in back of, in front of, inside, near, next to, on, outside,* and *under.*

The table is **in front of** the window.

The window is **in back of** (or **behind**) the table.

The window is **near** the door.

The tree is **outside** the house.

The table is **inside** the house.

The book is **on** the table.

The glass is **next to** the book.

The spoon is **in** the glass.

The shoe is **under** the table.

The table is **between** the door and the fireplace.

The painting hangs **above** the fireplace.

B. Uses of *In, On,* and *At*

1. Use *in* + a city, a state or province, a country, or a continent.

    They live **in Toronto**. Toronto is **in Ontario**. Ontario is **in Canada**. Canada is **in North America**.

2. Use *on* + a street or floor.

    His building is **on Park Road**.

    He works **on the second floor**.

3. Use *at* + a building or specific address.

    She's **at the bank**.

    The bank is **at 222 Main Street**.

Prepositions for Describing Location

5 **Meanings of Prepositions:** A Two-Family House

Work alone or with a partner. Look at the floor plans of a two-family house. Read the clues and write the names of the rooms in the right places.

Mrs. Romano owns this house. She lives alone on the first floor. Barbara and Paul Lambert and their son, David, live on the second floor.

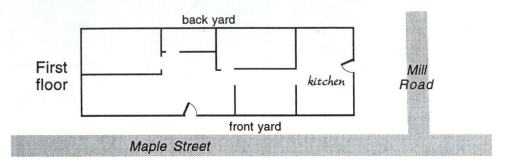

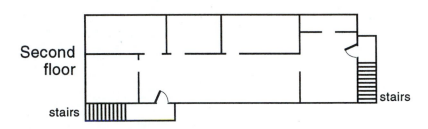

CLUES

First Floor

1. Mrs. Romano's **kitchen** is on the Mill Road side of the house.

2. She has two **bedrooms** at the back of the house.

3. There is a **bathroom** between the bedrooms.

4. Her **dining room** is next to the kitchen at the front of the house.

5. The big room next to the dining room is her **living room**. The front door is in the living room.

Second Floor

6. The Lamberts' **kitchen** is above Mrs. Romano's kitchen.

7. They have a small **bathroom** next to the kitchen.

8. The big room at the front of the house is their **family room**.

9. Barbara Lambert's **office** is near the front door.

10. There is a **bathroom** between **David's bedroom** and his parents' bedroom.

11. **Paul and Barbara's room** is not near the kitchen.

6 Writing Prepositions: In the Kitchen

A. Look at the picture of Mrs. Romano's kitchen. Complete the statements with these prepositions:

> above, between, in, in back of, in front of, inside, near, on, under

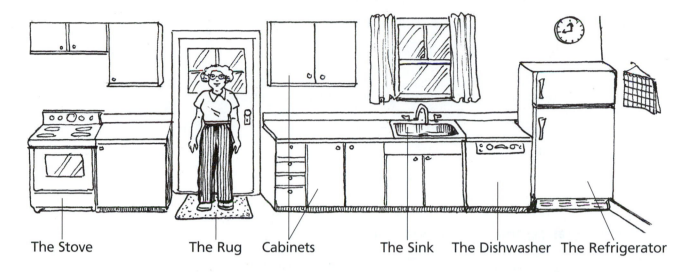

The Stove   The Rug   Cabinets   The Sink   The Dishwasher The Refrigerator

1. Mrs. Romano's refrigerator is __in_____ a corner of the kitchen.

2. Her dishwasher is _____ the refrigerator and the sink.

3. There is a clock _____ the wall _____ the refrigerator.
                       a   b

4. The sink is _____ a window.

5. Mrs. Romano is standing _____ the kitchen door. The door is
                                  a
    _____ her.
         b

6. _____ the cabinets, there are dishes and food.

7. There is a calendar on the wall _____ the refrigerator.

B. Work with a partner. Ask about the things in Mrs. Romano's kitchen. Take turns asking questions with *Where is/are . . . ?* Use prepositional phrases as answers.

Example: Student A: *Where are the cabinets?*
               Student B: *Near the door.*

7 *In, On,* and *At:* The Places We Live

A. Use *in, on,* or *at* to complete these sentences about Mrs. Romano.

1. Mrs. Romano lives _in_ Erie. Erie is her hometown.

2. Erie is _____ Pennsylvania.

3. Mrs. Romano lives _____ Maple Street.

4. Her house is _____ 127 Maple Street.

5. She lives _____ the first floor.

B. Complete these sentences about the place where you live.

1. I live in _____

2. I live on _____

3. I live at _____

8 Using Prepositions: In Your Classroom

A. On a piece of paper, write eight statements about the locations of people and things in the room. Use six different prepositions.

Example: Alexi is sitting in back of Parinda.
The desks are in the classroom.

B. Work with a partner. Student A: Ask questions with *Where is/are* about the people and things you wrote about in Part A. Student B: Use two or more prepositional phrases in each answer. Take turns. (Your partner's answers can be different from your statements.)

Example: Student A: Where is Alexi?
Student B: Alexi is sitting near the door, in back of Parinda and in front of Janez.

Prepositions for Showing Direction

FORM and FUNCTION

A. Overview

climb **up**
the ladder

climb **down**
the ladder

go **from** the
window **to**
the door

go **out**
the door

get **out of** bed

get **in(to)** bed

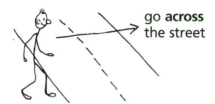

go **across**
the street

walk **through** the forest

go **around** the chair

jump **on(to)**
the chair

jump **off (of)**
the chair

Some prepositions help show movement or direction. They tell where someone or something is going. These prepositions include *across, around, down, from, in, into, off, off of, on, onto, out, out of, through, to,* and *up.*

He always runs **up** the stairs.

She is walking **out** the door.

The cat jumps **onto** the bed.

B. Prepositions with Vehicles

1. Use a verb + *into* (or *in*) and *out of* with cars and trucks.

   The driver gets **into the car** on the left.

   She's stepping **out of the taxi** now.

2. Use a verb + *onto* (or *on*) and *off* (or *off of*) with bicycles and with big vehicles such as buses, trains, and planes.

   He's climbing **onto his bicycle**.

   We get **off the train** at the last station.

Prepositions for Showing Direction

9 **Prepositions for Describing Direction:** A Visit to a Tree House

A. Listen to this description of an unusual house. Write the prepositions you hear.

Reporter Al Jordan is speaking into his tape recorder.

This is Al Jordan, reporting __*from*__ Florida. Today I'm taking you
                                  1

_____ an unusual house. We're going _____ a tree! Most people
          2   3

think of tree houses as places for children's games. But tree houses are homes and offices, too.

In fact, there's a World Treehouse Association, for people who build and live in tree houses.

Come with me now and visit a tree house. It belongs to Jim Cooper, a young man who designs

and builds tree houses.

I'm walking _____ a forest near the Sleepy River. Now I'm at Jim's tree, and
                       4

I'm climbing _____ the ladder. Jim's tree house is about 20 feet above the
                      5

ground. The climb _____ the ladder isn't hard, but I'm not so sure about going
                            6

_____ it! Now I'm stepping _____ the deck. Jim isn't home, but
         7   8

here is a note on the door. It says, "Hi, Al, come _____ the house and look
                                                              9

around!" Okay, I'm going _____ the main room.
                                   10

There are chairs, a table, bookshelves, a stove, a sink—it looks very comfortable! Let's go

_____ the room and climb _____ another ladder. This ladder goes
          11   12

_____ the second floor bedroom. Now I'm looking _____ the
          13   14

windows. What a beautiful view! The air smells wonderful here, and it's very quiet. Do you

hear those birds? Now I understand why Jim lives in a tree house.

> *design* = draw or plan something, such as clothes, a building, etc.
> *a deck* = a wooden floor attached to the outside of a house. *a view*
> = an area that you see from a place.

B. Take a vote in class: Is a tree house a good place for a home or office? Write the numbers of votes.

For a home: YES: _____   NO: _____

For an office: YES: _____   NO: _____

How many people in the class would like to live or work in a tree house? _____

See the *Grammar Links* Website for more information about tree houses.

10 Listening to Prepositions: The Runaway Puppy

A. Mrs. Romano has a little dog. He's a puppy, only three months old. At the moment, she's outside her front door, and the puppy is running away from her. Listen to Description 1, and draw the line on the floor plan to show where the puppy goes.

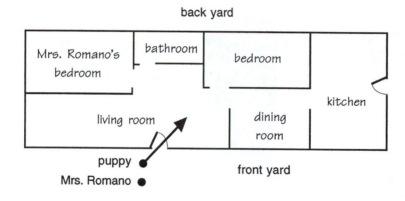

B. Work with a partner. Compare your line on the floor plan with your partner's line. Are they the same? If they are not the same, listen again or check the floor plan on page A-1.

C. The puppy is running away again! Listen to Description 2, and draw the line on the floor plan.

D. Work with a partner. Student A: Trace one of the lines with a finger, and tell where the puppy is going. Student B: Listen to your partner, and then trace the other line and tell where the puppy is going.

Example: Student A: The puppy is going into the house. He's running around the living room.

11 Prepositions with Vehicles: What's the Story?

Work in a group. Take turns asking and answering questions about what is happening in the pictures. Use your imagination! Include *get* + *in*, *into*, *out of*, *onto*, *off*, or *off of* + *the car/plane/bus* in your answers.

Example: Student A: **What is the man in Picture A doing?**
Student B: **He's getting into the car.**
Student C: **Where is he going?**
Student B: **He's going to a party for someone rich and famous.**

Picture A

Picture B

Picture C

Picture D

Prepositions for Describing Time

FORM and FUNCTION

A. Overview

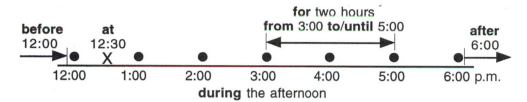

1. Some prepositions help describe time. They tell when something happens. These prepositions include *after, at, before, during, for, from, to,* and *until.*

   My classes end every day **before** 12:00.

   I meet my friend Chris for lunch every day **at** 12:30.

   I usually see all my friends at some point **during** the afternoon.

   I'm always in the library **from** 3:00 **to** 5:00.

   I study there **for** two hours.

   I stay there **until** 5:00, and then I usually leave.

   I'm never in the library **after** 6:00.

2. Prepositional phrases that describe time can come at the beginning or the end of sentences.

   After lunch, I go to the library.

   I go to the library **after lunch**.

B. Uses of *In, On,* and *At*

1. Use *at* + a specific time.

   The class starts **at 8:00 a.m.**

2. Use *on* + a day or date.

   They eat out **on Fridays.**

   His birthday is **on June 5.**

   I don't work **on holidays/weekends.**

3. Use *in* + a month, season, or year.

   They go back to Canada **in June.**

   In the fall, the birds fly south.

   She was born **in 1990.**

4. Use *in* + a part of the day.

   He works **in the morning/in the afternoon/in the evening.**

   BUT use *at* + *night.*

   He works **at night.**

Prepositions for Describing Time

12 Choosing Prepositions for Describing Time: A Mobile Lifestyle

Circle the correct preposition.

Bob and Martha Kelley live in a mobile home (**for** / to) most of the year. There
                                              1
are almost eight million mobile homes in the United States, many of them in the

Sunbelt. Some people—like the Kelleys—move to the Sunbelt (until / after)
                                                              2
retirement.

The Kelleys' mobile home is in Arizona. Bob

and Martha stay there (before / from) September
                              3
(at / to) June each year. Then (until / in) June,
  4   5
they travel north to Canada by car. (After / From)
                                         6
two weeks on the road, they arrive at their daughter's

Mobile means easy to move, but a
mobile home usually doesn't move
much. The homeowner parks it on
a piece of land, and it stays there.

house near Vancouver. It's a big house and a nice change from their mobile home.

(Before / During) the summer, they take care of their grandchildren. They stay
   7
(until / on) the start of the new school year. Then (until / at) 8:00 a.m. (on / in) the
  8   9   10
first day of school, they say good-bye and start south. They always stop and visit old

friends in Oregon, their home (during / before) their retirement. Then they go back
                                      11
to their everyday lives at their mobile home.

> *the Sunbelt* = the southern part of the United States, where winters are
> not very cold.

13 Choosing Prepositions for Describing Time: A College Student's Schedule

Complete the sentences with the prepositions in the boxes.

> for   ✓from   on   to

Lily Chen is a college student in Montreal. She lives at college __*from*__ September
                                                              1
_____ May. She shares a room with a roommate, but _____ Fridays, her roommate
        2   3
always goes home _____ the weekend.
                      4

at	from	to	until

Lily loves weekends. She usually sleeps _____ 10:00 or 11:00 a.m. She skips breakfast
                                        5
but goes to the snack bar for lunch _____ 12:00 or 12:30. The snack bar is open
                                    6
_____ 6:00 a.m. _____ 2:00 p.m.
   7   8

after	before	for	in	on

Then, _____ lunch, Lily sometimes studies in her room, but only _____ a
        9   10
couple hours. _____ weekends, she always goes out with her friends _____ the
               11   12
evening, and she always stays out late. She never gets in _____ 2:00 a.m.
                                                          13

14 Using Prepositions to Tell When: Your Everyday Life

 A. Work with a partner. Student A: Complete a statement about your life. Use a prepositional phrase with *after*, *at*, *before*, *for*, *from*, *to*, or *until*. Student B: Is your partner's prepositional phrase correct? Take turns.

Example: Student A: I usually get up before 7:00, but on weekends, I get up at 9:00 or 10:00.
                    Student B: I usually get up a 6:00. I'm a morning person.

1. I usually get up . . .
2. I eat . . .
3. I go out . . .
4. I study . . .
5. I exercise . . .
6. I see my friends . . .
7. I have lunch . . .
8. I have dinner . . .
9. I like to be at home . . .
10. I go to bed . . .

B. Write 10 sentences about things you do every day or on a typical weekend day. Tell when you do them. Use prepositional phrases with *after*, *at*, *before*, *for*, *from*, *to*, and *until*.

Example: In the morning, I get up at 7:30.
         I take a shower before breakfast.

Check your progress! Go to the Self-Test for Chapter 10 on the *Grammar Links* Website.

City Life

There + Be

Introductory Task: An Apartment Building in the City

A. Look at the picture of an apartment building in the city, and read the statements about it. Check (✓) the boxes next to the true statements. Correct the false statements.

☐ 1. There are ~~nine~~ *six* floors in the apartment building.

☐ 2. There's a restaurant next to the building.

☐ 3. There are trees in front of the building.

❑ 4. There are no people on the sidewalk in front of the building.

❑ 5. There's a bus stop near the building.

❑ 6. There are two doors on this side of the building.

❑ 7. There isn't a mailbox near the building.

❑ 8. There aren't any flowers in the windows of the building.

B. Work with a partner. Check your answers to Part A.

C. Is an apartment building in the city a good place to live? Check (✓) the box next to your answer. Then ask a partner. Check (✓) the box next to your partner's answer.

Your answer: ❑ Yes, it is.   ❑ No, it isn't.   ❑ Sometimes it is, and sometimes it isn't.

Your partner's answer: ❑ Yes, it is.   ❑ No, it isn't.   ❑ Sometimes it is, and sometimes it isn't.

Talk about the reasons for your opinions.

GRAMMAR BRIEFING 1

There + Be

FUNCTION

Using *There + Be*

1. Use *there + be* to talk about someone or something for the first time.	*Tim:* **There's** a great restaurant near here. *Kate:* Really? What restaurant?
2. Sentences with *there + be* show that someone or something exists. Sometimes they also:	**There is** one problem with the plan. **There are** different opinions about city life.
• Show the location (place) of someone or something.	**There is** a map on the table. **There are** six people at the bus stop.
• Tell the time of something.	**There's** always a movie at 8:00 p.m. **There are** buses every 10 minutes.

Function of *There* + *Be*

1 Function of *There* + *Be*: Life in the City

Work alone or with a partner. Why does the speaker use *there* + *be*? Write the number of your answer in the box.

1 = *There* + *be* is used just to show that something exists
2 = *There* + *be* is also used to give a location.
3 = *There* + *be* is also used to tell a time.

1. Sam: I don't like cities.

   [1] Tim: Really? But **there are** lots of great cities.

2. Sam: What's so good about city life?

   [ ] Tim: Well, **there are** great restaurants.

3. Sam: Do you have a favorite restaurant?

   [ ] Tim: Yes, **there's** a good one on the corner near my apartment.

4. Sam: But cities have no trees or flowers or green spaces.

   [ ] Tim: That's not true—**there's** a great park in my neighborhood.

5. Sam: What do you do in the park?

   [ ] Tim: I go running, and **there are** concerts on weekends.

6. Sam: Do you have a car?

   [ ] Tim: No, **there's** good public transit, so I don't need one.

7. Sam: Do you ever take taxis?

   [ ] Tim: I usually take the bus. **There are** buses until 2:00 a.m.

8. Sam: What do you do in the evening?

   [ ] Tim: Sometimes I go to the movies. **There's** a theater on my street.

> *public transit* = city-owned ways for people to travel (such as buses or subways).

There + *Be*—Affirmative and Negative Statements

FORM

A. Affirmative Statements

Singular

FULL FORM				CONTRACTION		
THERE	BE	SINGULAR NOUN		THERE + BE	SINGULAR NOUN	
There	is	a **problem**	with my TV.	There's	a **problem**	with my TV.
		one **bookstore**	on Main Street.		one **bookstore**	on Main Street.

Plural

FULL FORM			
THERE	BE	PLURAL NOUN	
There	are	some **problems**	with my TV.
		two **bookstores**	on Main Street.

B. Negative Statements

Singular

FULL FORM					CONTRACTIONS			
THERE	BE	NOT	SINGULAR NOUN		THERE + BE	NOT	SINGULAR NOUN	
					There's	not	a **cloud**	in the sky.
					THERE	BE + NOT	SINGULAR NOUN	
There	is	not	a **cloud**	in the sky.	There	isn't	a **cloud**	in the sky.

Plural

FULL FORM					CONTRACTION		
THERE	BE	NOT	PLURAL NOUN		THERE	BE + NOT	PLURAL NOUN
There	are	not	many **people**	here.	There	aren't	many **people** here.

C. Use of Quantifiers

Quantifiers are often used with the nouns following *there* + *be*. Quantifiers include *some*, *any*, *many*, *no*, and *a lot of*.

(See Chapter 16 for more information on quantifiers.)

There are **some letters** for you on the table.

We have tea, but there is **no coffee**.

There aren't **a lot of students** in my class.

In conversation and informal writing, use the contracted form *there's*.

SAY OR WRITE TO A FRIEND	WRITE IN A PAPER FOR SCHOOL
There's a problem.	There is a problem.

GRAMMAR PRACTICE 1

There + *Be*—Affirmative and Negative Statements

2 **Affirmative Statements:** Reasons to Live in the City

A. Read the telephone conversation. Write *there's* or *there are*.

Kate and Tim are on the phone. She is at home in Smallville, and he is in his new apartment in the city.

Kate: So, how is life in the city?

Tim: Great! My job is pretty interesting, and _____ $\underset{1}{}$ lots of things to like about city living.

Kate: Really? Like what?

Tim: Well, _____ $\underset{2}{}$ a great bus system, so I don't need a car.

Kate: That's good, because _____ $\underset{3}{}$ no parking places!

Tim: And _____ $\underset{4}{}$ things to do all the time. _____ $\underset{5}{}$ clubs and concerts and movies. _____ $\underset{6}{}$ a movie theater near my building. _____ $\underset{7}{}$ good stores in my neighborhood. And _____ $\underset{8}{}$ a nice park, too. In fact, _____ $\underset{9}{}$ a view of it from my window.

Kate: You sound pretty happy. I guess the city has everything.

Tim: No, _____ one problem.
          10

Kate: What's that?

Tim: I don't have you here.

B. On a piece of paper, write affirmative statements with *There + be*.

1. Write five statements with *There are*. Write about the good things in cities.

   Example: There are many stores in cities.

2. Write two statements with *There is*. Write about two good things in the city or town where you are now.

   Example: There is a nice park next to the river.

See the *Grammar Links* Website for more model sentences for this assignment.

3 Affirmative and Negative Statements: City Scene

Look at the picture on page 176. Complete the statements about the picture. Write *There is, There isn't, There are,* or *There aren't*.

1. _There aren't_____ any horses on the street.

2. _____ a restaurant in the picture.

3. _____ windows in the apartment building.

4. _____ any people in the windows.

5. _____ people outside the building, on the sidewalk.

6. _____ any stores in the picture.

7. _____ a bus stop near the apartment building.

8. _____ a police officer in the street.

9. _____ a mailbox on the sidewalk.

10. _____ cars on the street.

4 Affirmative and Negative Statements: How Is Your Memory?

A. Work with a partner. Think about the picture on page 176, but do not look at it. What do you remember about it? Take turns making statements about the picture. Use *There's* or *There are, There isn't* or *There aren't*.

Example: Student A: There's an apartment building in the picture.

B. Continue working with your partner. Look at this picture of the apartment building from page 176. What is missing? Take turns making statements about this picture. Make six or more statements using *There isn't* or *There aren't*. (Look back at page 176 if you need to.)

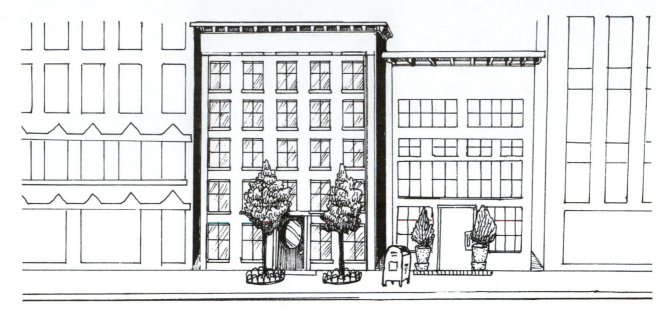

GRAMMAR **HOT**SPOT!

1. Do not confuse *it is* with *there is*. Do not confuse *they are* with *there are*.

   • Use *there is/are* to introduce a noun.

   There is a good movie at the King Cinema.

   There are many restaurants in the city.

   • Use *it* or *they* to take the place of a noun instead of repeating the noun.

                                 It
   The **movie** is at 8:00. ~~The movie~~ is two hours long.

                               They
   Cities have many attractions. ~~Cities~~ are nice places to visit.

2. *There*, *they're*, and *their* sound the same, but they have different meanings.

   • Use *there + is/are* to talk about something or someone for the first time.

   There are two new families in our building.

   • Use *they're* in place of *they are*.

   They're from Mexico.

   • Use *their* to show possession.

   Their last names are Cruz and Garcia.

5 *There Is* Versus *It Is,* and *There Are* Versus *They Are*: At the Café

A. Circle the correct words.

(There is / It is) a café in the
1
picture. It has a French name.

(There is / It is) the Bonjour Café.
2

(There is / It is) in San Francisco.
3

(There is / It is) a man at one of
4

the tables. His name is Paul. On

the table, (there are / they are) two
5

coffee cups. (There are / They are)
6

for Paul and his friend Chris.

(There are / They are) some books on the table, too. (There are / They are) Paul's books.
7   8

Under the table, (there are / they are) some shopping bags. (There are / They are) Chris's bags.
9   10

Paul and Chris live near the Bonjour Café. (There is / It is) their favorite café. Right now,
11

(there aren't / they aren't) any other people at the café. That's unusual. The Bonjour Café is a
12

popular place. (There is / It is) busy most of the time. (There are / They are) many coffee
13   14

lovers in San Francisco.

B. Listen to Part A. You will hear contracted forms. Check your answers. Then with a partner, practice saying the sentences with the contracted forms.

6 *There Are* Versus *They Are*: The World's Megacities

Write *there are* or *they are*.

Read about the biggest cities in the world.

1. __There are__ more than six billion people in the world. Many of these people
   a

   are now moving into big cities, often because _____ looking for jobs.
   b

2. What are megacities? _____ cities with very big populations.
   a

   _____ millions of people in the world's megacities.
   b

3. _____ megacities on four continents. Which continents are they?
   a

   _____ Asia, Africa, North America, and South America.
   b

4. Beijing and Shanghai are two megacities. _____ in China.
   a

   _____ about 12 million people in Beijing and about 15 million
   b

   in Shanghai.

5. Tokyo and Yokohama are growing fast. _____ cities in Japan. In the
   a

   Tokyo/Yokohama area, _____ about 27 million people.
   b

6. _____ two megacities in South America. _____
   a   b

   São Paolo and Buenos Aires.

---

population = the number of people living in a place.

---

7 *There, They're,* or *Their*: City Lovers

Circle the correct words.

At an Outdoor Market in Rome

Read about Silvano and Nicla and their neighborhood in Rome, Italy.

1. Silvano and Nicla love Rome. (They're / There) happy living in the city.

2. They live in an apartment building. (Their / There) are 10 apartments in all.

3. (They're / Their) apartment is on the second floor.

4. The name of (there / their) street is via Panicale.

5. (There / They're) are many stores and restaurants on the street.

6. (There / They're) always full of people.

7. Every Thursday, (there / their) is an outdoor market on the street.

8. (There / Their) is always music in the street and crowds of people.

9. Silvano and Nicla enjoy the music and the crowds. (There / They're) city lovers.

10. (They're / Their) neighborhood is a busy, noisy place.

8 *There*, *They're*, or *Their*: Life in the City

Complete the sentences. Write *there*, *they're*, or *their*.

Cities have <u>their</u> problems. <u>   </u> usually very noisy
  1   2

places. <u>   </u> are many people with cars, and <u>   </u> cars make
          3   4

a lot of noise. Also, <u>   </u> are often problems with dirty air and water.
                        5

In the city, most people live in apartments. <u>   </u> apartments are usually
                                               6

small, and <u>   </u> often expensive. People in cities often worry about crime, too.
             7

Sometimes <u>   </u> afraid to leave <u>   </u> homes after dark.
            8   9

But cities also have a lot to offer people. Many people live in cities because of

<u>   </u> jobs. <u>   </u> are other good reasons, too: schools, stores,
  10   11

exciting places to go at night, and so on. About 75 percent of the people in the United States now

live in cities. Every day, <u>   </u> are more and more people in cities around the world.
                            12

There + *Be*—*Yes/No* Questions and Short Answers

FORM

Questions and Answers

QUESTIONS				ANSWERS				
BE	THERE	NOUN		YES			NO	
Is	**there**	an **airport**	in your city?	Yes,	**there**	**is.**	No,	there's not.
								there isn't.
Are		good **places**	to eat?			**are.**		**there aren't.**

There + Be—*Yes/No* Questions and Short Answers

9 *Yes/No* **Questions:** *Money* **Magazine's Top Cities**

Complete the questions with *Is there* or *Are there*.

There is an American magazine called *Money*. Every year, the editors of *Money* make a list of

the best cities in the United States to live in. The editors look at more than 300 cities. They ask

questions like these about each city: <u>Is there</u> _____ a good supply of clean water?
                                          1

_____ good schools? _____ good hospitals?
    2   3

_____ museums and theaters? _____ an area of the city with
    4   5

good restaurants? _____ nice public parks? _____ sports teams
                      6   7

to watch? The editors at *Money* ask about problems in these cities, too, for example:

_____ a problem with crime? _____ a high cost of living?
    8   9

_____ long, cold winters? Then, they look at all the answers to these questions,
    10

and they write their report.

> *an editor* = a person who works on stories for a magazine, newspaper, etc.
> *the cost of living* = the amount of money that people need to spend on
> food, housing, clothes, etc.

10 *Yes/No* **Questions and Giving Short Answers: The Best in the West**

A. *Money* magazine says that Minneapolis and Seattle are great cities to live in.
Find them on the map on page 19.

B. Look at the chart for information about these cities.

	Minneapolis		Seattle	
Advantages	**Yes**	**No**	**Yes**	**No**
Good jobs	✓		✓	
Many theaters and museums	✓		✓	
Good sports teams to watch	✓		✓	
Many sunny days	✓			✓
Disadvantages				
A high cost of living		✓	✓	
A bad problem with crime		✓		✓
Long, cold winters	✓			✓

C. Work with a partner. Take turns asking and answering *yes/no* questions with *Is/Are there* about Minneapolis and Seattle. Use the information in the chart to ask questions and give short answers.

Example: Student A: **Are there good museums in Seattle?**
Student B: **Yes, there are.**

 D. Take turns asking *yes/no* questions about your partner's city or hometown. Use *Is/Are* there. Give short answers.

Example: Student A: **Are there many people in your hometown?**

See the *Grammar Links* Website for more information about some great cities.

11 *Is There*, *Are There*, and *Are They*; Short Answers: Looking for an Apartment

A. Complete the questions with *Is there*, *Are there*, or *Are they*. Complete the short answers.

Tim and Kate are looking for an apartment. They're talking to a landlord. He has an apartment for rent.

Tim: <u>Are there</u> many apartments in your building?
         ₁

Landlord: No, there are only four. There are two on the first floor and two on the second.

Kate: _____ an apartment for rent on the second floor?
                2

Landlord: Yes, _____. It's a very nice apartment, too.
              3

Tim: _____ three rooms in the apartment?
                        4

Landlord: Yes, _____. There's a kitchen, a bedroom, and a living room.
                        5

Of course, there's a bathroom, too.

Kate: What about the neighbors? _____ quiet?
                                                    6

Landlord: Yes, _____. I live on the first floor, and it's a very quiet building.
                        7

Tim: What about heat and electricity—_____ included in the rent,
                                                            8

            or _____ separate?
                        9

Landlord: They're separate. You pay your own bills for heat and electricity.

Kate: _____ a time today that you can show us the apartment?
                        10

Landlord: How about right now?

> *a landlord* = a person who owns a building and rents it to others.
> *included in the rent* = part of the money paid to use an apartment
> or house.

B. Form a group of three. Read the conversation aloud. Take turns reading the
different parts.

 **C.** Work in a group. Imagine that you are looking for an apartment in the city.
You are talking to a landlord or to someone who lives in the building. Think of
important questions to ask. Use *Is there* and *Are there* in your questions.

 **D.** Work with a partner. Act out a conversation, using your questions from Part C.
Student A is looking for an apartment, and Student B is a landlord or someone
who lives in the building.

**Check your progress! Go to the Self-Test for
Chapter 11 on the *Grammar Links* Website.**

Wrap-up Activities

1 A Place in the Country: READING

Read this paragraph.

I love my grandparents' house. It is in on a farm in the country. It is about two hours from my home in the city. I have my own room at their house. It is on the third floor. There are animals on the farm: goats, chickens, rabbits, cats, and dogs. They all live in the big, red barn. There are flowers and vegetables and fruit trees on the farm, too. Near the farm there is a small lake. We always go swimming in the summer. There is a big tree next to the lake. I like to climb up the tree and jump into the water.

2 A Place You Like: WRITING

Choose statement 1 or 2: (1) *I like life in the city.* (2) *I like life in the country.* Make it your first sentence in a paragraph. Tell why you like city life or country life. What are some good things in the city or in the country? Use sentences with *There + be.*

See the *Grammar Links* Website for a model paragraph for this assignment.

3 Country Life: EDITING

Correct the 10 errors in the paragraph. There are six preposition errors and four errors in sentences with *there*. The first error is corrected for you.

Life in the Country

                                    to
I like life in the country. I go ∧ the country in weekends with my family.

We visit my aunt and her family. They live a small town next a lake. There is

a nice lake. There is not many cars or people, but they're many farms with

horses. My cousins are lucky. There house is near to a beautiful forest. The air

smells clean and fresh. In night, we look up and see the stars.

---

4 A Guessing Game: SPEAKING/LISTENING

Step 1 Think of people and things in the classroom. Think of some sentences with prepositional phrases about these people and things. These sentences are clues.

Step 2 Work with a partner and take turns. Student A: Say your clues about a person or thing. Student B: Guess who or what Student A is describing.

Example: Student A: *This thing is on the teacher's desk. It's next to his books.*
Student A: *Is it a coffee cup?*
Student A: *Yes, it is.*

5 Places You Like: SPEAKING/LISTENING

Work in a group. Think of places you like. Take turns telling about the places and the reasons why you like these places. Use statements with *there + be*. Listen and ask questions.

Example: Student A: *I like the park next to the river. There's a great bike path through the park.*
Student B: *Do you have a bike?*

6 A Dream House: WRITING/READING/SPEAKING

Step 1 Imagine that you have the perfect house. Maybe your house is in a different part of this country, or maybe it is in a different part of the world. Write a short description of your house. Describe you favorite time of year there, and tell why you like it then. Use prepositional phrases. Use statements with *there + be*.

Step 2 Put your paper up on the wall or blackboard with all your classmates' papers. Read their papers and talk with them about their houses. Choose two houses to visit.

Examples: *I have a house in Hawaii. It is on the beach. There are 15 rooms in my house . . .*

My dream house is small and pretty. It is on a mountain in Mexico. There are flowers and trees all around the house, and there is . . .

Simple Past Tense

TOPIC FOCUS
Inventors and Inventions, Great and Small

UNIT OBJECTIVES

- **the past tense of** *be*
  (Thomas Edison *was* an inventor. Wilbur and Orville Wright *were* inventors, too.)

- **the simple past tense of regular verbs**
  (She *called* me last night. We *talked* for an hour.)

- **the simple past tense of irregular verbs**
  (We *went* to the store and *bought* some food.)

- **negative statements with simple past tense verbs**
  (The story *was not* true. I *did not believe* it.)

- **questions in the simple past tense**
  (*Did* you *see* the movie? How *was* it? *Did* you *like* it? Who *went* with you?)

- **past time expressions**
  (We went to the museum *yesterday*. It opened *ten years ago*.)

Grammar in Action

🎧 Reading and Listening: Inventors Through History

Read and listen to some information about inventors and inventions.

1   Do you know the word *inventor*? An inventor is a person who makes a new product or finds a new way to do something. Inventors have many ideas, and they try to turn these ideas into things we can use.

2   Sometimes an inventor changes the world. For example, in 1450, Johannes Gutenberg **invented** the printing press. Before that time, people **copied** books by hand. This **was** very slow work, so books **were** rare. Most people never **learned** to read. After 1450, books and reading **became** more common. In this way, Gutenberg **changed** the world.

3   Most inventors are not as important. Consider Thomas Adams, for example. Adams **was** an inventor in the 1800s. He **tried** to make a new kind of rubber, but he **made** something else by mistake. What did he invent? Chewing gum!

4   Many important things in our lives are from thousands of years ago. We know nothing about their inventors. For example, who **invented** the wheel? Who **built** the first boat? We don't know.

5   There are some things we do know about inventions from long ago. We know that people in China **invented** the abacus and that people in Egypt **were** the first to make glass. But who **were** the inventors of these wonderful things? Nobody knows their names.

6   Sometimes we forget the names of inventors. Ada Byron **wrote** the first computer program, and Yoshiro Nakamata **invented** the floppy disk. Did you know their names?

7   We don't always remember their names, but thanks to inventors, our lives are different in many ways, large and small.

> *rare* = unusual, hard to find. *consider* = think about. *rubber* = a material made from the sap of certain trees and used for tires, balls, boots, etc.

The Wheel, About 5,500 Years Ago

The Abacus, About 1,700 Years Ago

Gutenberg's Printing Press, 1450

The Floppy Disk, 1950

Think About Grammar

A. Find the following sentences in the reading. Fill in the past tense forms of *be*.

1. (Paragraph 2) This _____ very slow work, so books _____ rare.

2. (Paragraph 3) Adams _____ an inventor in the 1800s.

3. (Paragraph 5) But who _____ the inventors of these wonderful things?

What are the two past tense forms of *be*? _____ and _____

B. The chart lists the base forms of some verbs used in the reading. Find the **boldfaced** simple past tense forms of these verbs and copy them in the chart.

Regular Verbs		Irregular Verbs	
Base Form of the Verb	Simple Past Tense	Base Form of the Verb	Simple Past Tense
1. change	changed	6. be	was/were
2. copy	_____	7. become	_____
3. invent	_____	8. build	_____
4. learn	_____	9. make	_____
5. try	_____	10. write	_____

Regular verbs always end with the same two letters in the simple past tense. What are the two letters? - _____

C. Talk with a partner. Think of some inventions.

1. Some inventions changed the world. Give two or more examples:

   _____

2. Some inventions made life more fun. Give two or more examples:

   _____

Discuss your answers with the class.

12

Some American Inventors

The Past Tense of *Be*

Introductory Task: The National Inventors Hall of Fame

Read and listen to the conversation. Circle the verbs you hear.

Reporter Al Jordan, his wife, Sara, and their seven-year-old niece, Carol, are visiting Akron, Ohio. They are at the National Inventors Hall of Fame. It's a museum in honor of American inventors.

Sara: Carol, look at the men in this photo.

Carol: Oh, I know those guys! Their picture ((was)/ were) in my book at school.
        1

Sara: Who (was / were) they? Do you remember?
       2

Carol: (Was / Were) they . . . the Wright brothers?
        3

Sara: Yes, they (was / were). Wilbur and Orville Wright. And why (was / were)
       4   5
        their picture in your book? Do you remember?

Carol: They invented the . . . telephone—no, wait! The airplane!

Sara: That's right.

Al: Carol, it says "1867–1912" under Wilbur's picture. What does that mean?

       Do you know?

Carol: Oh, of course I know, Uncle Al! It means he (was / were) born in 1867, and he
                                                  6
        died in 1912. What about that picture over there—who (was / were) that guy?
                                                               7

Al: Thomas Alva Edison. He (was / were) born here in Ohio, in Milan. We
                              8
        (was / were) in Milan yesterday.
        9

Carol: So, what did Thomas Edison invent?

Al: Well, the light bulb and the microphone—

but those (was / were) just two of his ideas.
10

Edison (was / were) responsible for more
11

than 1,000 inventions. The man (was / were)
12

a genius.

Edison's Light Bulb

A Modern Microphone

> *in honor of* = showing special respect for. *a genius* = a very smart person.

GRAMMAR BRIEFING 1

Past Tense of *Be*—Affirmative Statements; Past Time Expressions

FUNCTION

Past Tense of *Be*

1. Use the past tense of *be* to talk about states in the past:

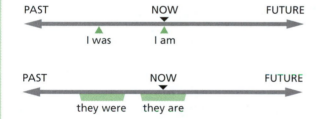

PRESENT TENSE	PAST TENSE
I **am** here today.	I **was** here yesterday, too.
They **are** investors now.	They **were** teachers 10 years ago.

2. Sentences with the past tense of *be* often have past time expressions. The time expressions tell when something happened.

> We were in Washington **last month**.
>
> He was in business **from 1980 to 1999**.

(continued on next page)

A. Affirmative Statements

Statements with Subject Nouns or Pronouns

SUBJECT	WAS		SUBJECT	WERE	
I			We		
He			You*		
She	was	here.	They	were	here.
It					
Jack			My friends		

*Use *were* with the singular or plural *you*.

Statements with There + Be

THERE	WAS	SINGULAR NOUN		THERE	WERE	PLURAL NOUN	
There	was	one man	in the photo.	There	were	two men	in the photo.

B. Past Time Expressions

Past time expressions usually come at the beginning or end of a sentence. They include:

- *Yesterday* and *yesterday* + *morning*, *afternoon*, or *evening*.

  I was absent **yesterday**.

  Yesterday evening, there was an accident at the corner of High Street and Main.

- An amount of time + *ago*.

  He was here **five minutes ago**.

  A week ago, it was very cold.

- *Last* + a specific period of time.

  The weather was nice **last Monday**.

  Last year, they were in Florida.

- Prepositional phrases of time.

  (See Chapter 10, Grammar Briefing 4, page 173, for more information on prepositional phrases of time.)

  She was born **in 1985**.

GRAMMAR HOTSPOT!

1. Use *two days ago* or *the day before yesterday*.
   BUT: Do not use "one day ago." Use *yesterday*.

   There was no class **yesterday** or **the day before yesterday/two days ago**.

2. Do not use *yesterday* + *night*. Use *last night*.

   We were home **last night**.
     NOT: We were home ~~yesterday~~ night.

Past Tense of *Be*—Affirmative Statements; Past Time Expressions

1 *Was* Versus *Were*: Three American Inventors

A. Read about two American inventors. Circle *was* or *were*.

Thomas Edison (1847–1931) ((was) / were) a famous American inventor.
                       1

The electric light bulb (was / were) one of his inventions. The microphone
               2

(was / were) his idea, too. These (was / were) just two of his many inventions.
 3   4

There (was / were) hundreds of them! Edison (was / were) the first inventor in
     5   6

the National Inventors Hall of Fame.

James Naismith (1861–1939) (was / were) a teacher, and he
               7

(was / were) the inventor of basketball. In the first basketball games,
 8

the balls (was / were) soccer balls. The first baskets (was / were)
     9   10

peach baskets. There (was / were) a problem with using peach
     11

baskets. They (was / were) not like basketball nets today. There
     12

(was / were) no hole in the bottom, so the ball stayed up in the basket.
 13

Naismith's New Game

B. Write *was* or *were*.

Madame C. J. Walker
(1867–1919)

I _____ an inventor of hair and beauty products. My products
       1

_____ for African-American women. At first, my kitchen _____
     2   3

my laboratory. It _____ a hard place to have a laboratory.
       4

My daughter and I _____ in business together. She _____
       5   6

my business partner. After a lot of hard work, we _____ very successful.
       7

I _____ a rich and famous woman!
     8

a laboratory = a room where a scientist works and does special tests.

2 Past Time Expressions: A Bad Week

Read a letter from a worker in the laboratory of inventor Thomas Edison.
Write *last*, *ago*, or *yesterday*.

April 1, 1887

Dear Mother and Father,

_____Last_____ week at work, Mr. Edison was very unhappy. Too many
     1

people were absent from the lab. _____ Monday, three workers
                                  2

were out sick. Then _____ Tuesday, two more were absent.
                   3

Three days _____, I started to feel sick, too. The day before
              4

_____, I went to work, but that was a mistake. So
     5

_____, I stayed in bed. I slept 15 hours _____ night!
     6   7

I woke up just an hour _____. Now I feel much better. I had some
                     8

tea about 10 minutes _____.
               9

    I hope you are well. I will write again soon.

Your loving son,

Andrew

P.S. _____ evening, a friend from work came by. He says
      10

Mr. Edison is sick now, too.

3 Using Affirmative Statements with *Be* and Past Time Expressions: Where Were You?

A. Work in a group. Look at the time expressions in the list. Take turns telling
where you were at these times and who was with you. Do not make true
statements. Invent stories.

Examples: Three hours ago, I was with the president. We were in a TV studio.
Yesterday evening, I was at a restaurant in Hollywood with . . .

1. three hours ago
2. yesterday evening
3. last Sunday
4. last month
5. six months ago
6. a year ago
7. in 1999
8. _____

B. Did someone in your group invent a good story? Tell it to the class.

Example: Student A: Artem has a good story. He says last week, he was in a meeting with Bill Gates. Bill Gates wants Artem's ideas for computer games.

GRAMMAR BRIEFING 2

Past Tense of *Be*—Negative Statements

FORM

A. Statements with Subject Nouns or Pronouns

FULL FORMS

SUBJECT	BE	NOT	
I			
He			
She	was		
It			
The cat		not	in the room.
We			
You			
They	were		
The cats			

CONTRACTED FORMS

SUBJECT	BE + NOT	
I		
He		
She	wasn't	
It		
The cat		in the room.
We		
You		
They	weren't	
The cats		

B. Statements with *There + Be*

FULL FORMS

THERE	BE	NOT	NOUN	
There	was	not	a computer	in the office.
	were		any computers	

CONTRACTED FORMS

THERE	BE + NOT	NOUN	
There	wasn't	a computer	in the office.
	weren't	any computers	

GRAMMAR PRACTICE 2

Past Tense of *Be*—Negative Statements

4 **Negative Statements with *Was/Were*; Full Forms and Contractions:** Verb Forms

Complete each statement with the past tense of *be + not*, using the full form. Then rewrite the statement with the contracted form.

1. I __was not__ home last night. __I wasn't home last night.__

2. You _____ late. _____

3. The teacher _____ in her office. _____

4. She _____ at school. _____

5. We _____ ready. _____

6. You _____ friends last year. _____

7. I _____ asleep. _____

8. He _____ in class. _____

9. There _____ many seats. _____

Negative Statements with *Was/Were*; Contractions: More Facts About Inventors and Inventions

Write negative statements. Use the words in parentheses ( ) and the correct form of *be + not*. Use contractions.

1. a. (Thomas Edison's inventions/always big money-makers)

   Thomas Edison's inventions weren't always big money-makers. _____

   But some of them were.

   b. (Edison/a great businessman)

   _____

   He made many mistakes.

   c. (he/a good student)

   _____

   He had trouble in school.

   d. (he/lazy)

   _____

   He worked very hard.

2. a. (the first airplanes/very safe)

   _____

   They were dangerous.

   b. (the Wright Brothers/afraid to fly)

   _____

   They were brave.

   c. (they/engineers)

   _____

   They were the owners of a bicycle shop.

6 Affirmative and Negative Statements with *Was/Were*: True and False

 A. Write three statements about you, your family, and friends with *was/were* or *wasn't/weren't* + a past time expression. Write only one true statement. Write two lies (false statements).

Example: 1. I wasn't in school one year ago. (False)
2. My parents were in Hawaii last month. (False)
3. My roommate was a waiter in an Italian restaurant last year. (True)

B. Work in a group. Tell the group your three statements. The other students try to guess which statement is true. Take turns.

Example: Student A: 1. Last Saturday was my birthday.   2. I was in bed at 9:00 last night.   3. There weren't any girls at my high school.
Student B: Number 2 is false! You were in the computer lab. I guess number 1 is true.
Student C: I guess number 3.
Student A: You're right—my high school was all boys.

GRAMMAR BRIEFING 3

Past Tense of *Be*—Yes/No Questions and Short Answers

FORM

A. Questions with Subject Nouns and Pronouns

QUESTIONS			ANSWERS				
WAS/WERE	SUBJECT		YES			NO	
Was	I			I			I	
	he			he			he	
	she			she	**was.**		she	**wasn't.**
	it		Yes,	it		No,	it	
	the train	late?						
Were	we			we			we	
	you			you	**were.**		you	**weren't.**
	they			they			they	
	the boys							

B. Questions with *There + Be*

QUESTIONS			ANSWERS			
WAS/WERE	*THERE*	NOUN	YES		NO	
Was	**there**	a problem?	Yes,	there was.	No,	there wasn't.
Were		any problems?		there were.		there weren't.

To answer a *yes/no* question, use:

- A short answer.

- *Yes/No* + more information.

> Q: Were they successful inventors?
> A: Yes, they were./No, they weren't.

> Q: Were they successful?
> A: Yes, they were very successful./No, their inventions never worked.

(See Chapter 2, Talking the Talk, page 33, for other ways to say *yes* or *no*.)

GRAMMAR PRACTICE 3

Past Tense of *Be*—*Yes/No* Questions and Short Answers

7 *Yes/No* **Questions and Short Answers:** I Don't Remember a Thing

A. Use the words given to write *yes/no* questions with *be*. Write the short answers.

The Wright Brothers, Inventors of the Airplane, One Day in 1904

1. I/in an accident?   yes

    Was I in an accident? Yes, you were.

2. it/bad?   yes

    _____

3. you/with me?   yes

    _____

4. it/a plane crash?   no

_____

5. we/in the car?   no

_____

6. I/on my bicycle?   yes

_____

7. those men/doctors?   yes

_____

8. you/worried about me?   yes

_____

B. Work with a partner. Use a piece of paper to cover the picture of the Wright Brothers. Take turns asking and answering questions about the picture with *Was/Were there* + the words in parentheses. Then think of two more questions to ask.

Example: Student A: **Were there three men in the picture?**
Student B: **No, there weren't.**

1. (three men/in the picture)
2. (a bed/in the picture)
3. (a cat/on the bed)
4. (pictures/on the wall)

5. (lights/in the room)
6. (chairs/in the picture)
7. (a mirror/on the wall)
8. (a window/in the room)

8 **Using *Yes/No* Questions and Short Answers:** French and American Inventors

A. Work with a partner. Student A: Look at the chart on this page. Student B: Turn to page A-2. The people in the chart were all French or American inventors. Each person was also a scientist, a teacher, or a businessperson. Find the missing information about them by asking your partner *yes/no* questions with *be*. Give short answers or *yes/no* + more information. Take turns.

Example: Student A: **Was Louis Pasteur a man?**
Student B: **Yes, he was. Was Louis Braille a scientist?**
Student A: **No, he was a teacher.**

Inventor's Name	Man/Woman	Profession	Nationality
Edouard Benedictus	a man		French
Louis Braille		a teacher	
Elizabeth Lee Hazen	a woman		American
James Naismith	a man		
Louis Pasteur	a man	a scientist	French
Ruth Wakefield		a businessperson	
Madame C. J. Walker	a woman		American

B. Student A: Choose an inventor from the chart on page 203. In a past life, you were that inventor. Student B: Ask *yes/no* questions with *be*. Try to guess who your partner was. Take turns.

Example: Student B: *Were you a man?*
Student A: *No, I was a woman.*

 See the *Grammar Links* Website for more information about inventors.

Past Tense of *Be*—*Wh*- Questions and Answers

FORM

Wh- Questions and Answers

QUESTIONS			ANSWERS
WH- QUESTION WORD	*WAS/WERE*		
Who		Henry Ford?	An inventor and maker of cars.
What	**was**	the Model T?	The first popular car.
Whose* idea		was it?	It was Henry Ford's idea.
When		your classes yesterday?	At 9:00 and 11:00 a.m.
Where	**were**	you?	At home.
Why		you absent?	I was sick.

*Use *whose* (+ noun) to ask who the owner of something is.

TALKING THE TALK

The answer to a *wh*- question can be:

- A complete sentence.

  Q: Where were you last night?
  A: I was home, watching TV.

- A word or group of words.

  Q: Where were you last night?
  A: At home./Home.

Past Tense with *Be*—*Wh*- Questions and Answers

9 ***Wh*- Questions:** Levi Strauss and the California Gold Rush

Write *who, what, when, where, whose,* or *why.* Circle *was* or *were.*

Read about Levi Strauss and his invention.

1. ___Who___ (was / were) Levi Strauss?
A German-American businessman.

2. _____ (was / were) Strauss in business?
In California.

3. _____ (was / were) he in California?
In the 1850s.

4. _____ (was / were) many people in California then?
Because of the Gold Rush.

5. _____ (was / were) Levi Strauss's great invention?
The first blue jeans.

6. _____ (was / were) his customers?
California gold miners.

7. _____ (was / were) his blue jeans so popular?
Because they were useful and long-lasting.

8. _____ name (was / were) on the first blue jeans?
Levi's.

> *the California Gold Rush* = the time in the 1850s when many people
> hurried to California to look for gold. *a miner* = a person who works
> in a mine, digging for gold, silver, coal, etc.

10 ***Wh*- Questions and Answers:** Pants for Women, Too

A. Work alone or with a partner. Write questions about bloomers to match
the answers. Do not use the **boldfaced** words. Use a *wh*- question word,
was/were, and the other words from the answer.

1. ___What were bloomers?_____

Bloomers were **a combination of pants and a short skirt.**

2. _____

They were in the news **in the 1850s.**

3. _____

They were **Elizabeth Miller's** idea.*

A Woman Wearing
Bloomers

* Mrs. Miller was the inventor of bloomers, but the word *bloomers* comes from
the name of Amelia Bloomer. She was a newspaper editor. She said women needed
easy-to-wear clothes.

4. _____

The first women in bloomers were **American women interested in equal rights**.

5. _____

The usual clothes for women were **long dresses and skirts**.

6. _____

Bloomers were a good idea **because long dresses were a lot of trouble**.

7. _____

Most Americans were against the idea of bloomers.

8. _____

Bloomers were popular in the 1890s **because they were good to wear on a bicycle**.

> *equal rights* = the same rights for women as for men, such as the chance to vote.

B. Work with a partner. Take turns asking the questions you wrote in Part A. Say only the **boldfaced** words as answers.

Example: Student A: What were bloomers?
         Student B: A combination of pants and a short skirt.

11 Questions and Answers with *Was/Were*: Remembering Someone

Work in a group. Think of a person from your past. The person could be a childhood friend, a family member, a teacher, or anyone who affected your life. Tell the name of the person and something about him or her. The others in the group ask *wh-* and *yes/no* questions with *was* and *were*. Answer their questions.

Example: Student A: I remember my friend Yulia.
         Student B: Was she a friend from a long time ago?
         Student A: Yes, from when I was a child.
         Student C: Why was she important to you?

 Check your progress! Go to the Self-Test for Chapter 12 on the *Grammar Links* Website.

Chapter 13

Unusual Inventors

The Simple Past Tense—
Affirmative and Negative Statements

Introductory Task: Accidental Inventions

🎧 **A.** Listen and read about how inventions happen in different ways.

Sometimes an inventor has an idea and follows a plan, step by step. For example, take the case of Thomas Edison and the light bulb. Edison **wanted** to make a light bulb, and he **needed** the right material for it. So he and the workers in his lab **did** a series of tests. They **tested** more than 1,600 kinds of materials. Finally, he **found** the right one. Careful work **brought** him good results.

But not all inventions happen this way. Some inventions happen by accident. For example, some popular American foods **started** as mistakes. Chocolate chip cookies, Coca-Cola™, and potato chips all **surprised** their inventors.

Accidents sometimes happen in scientists' laboratories, too; for example:

- In 1903, a French chemist **broke** some glass. Something surprising **happened** to the glass, and it **gave** him an idea. Because of that accident, we now have safety glass in cars.

- In 1928, there was an accident in the lab of a Scottish scientist. It was a lucky accident. It gave us penicillin, an important new medicine.

We usually think of accidents as bad things. But smart people sometimes find good things in them.

---

a lab = (short for) *laboratory*, a room where a scientist works.
by accident = by chance, in a way that was not planned.

B. Work alone or with a partner. Find the simple past tense forms of the verbs below in the reading. Write both forms of each verb in the chart. Verbs ending in *-ed* in the simple past tense are regular.

break   bring   do   find   give   happen   need   start   surprise   test   want

Regular Verbs (*-ed*)		Irregular Verbs	
Base Form of the Verb	Simple Past Tense	Base Form of the Verb	Simple Past Tense
want	wanted	do	did

GRAMMAR BRIEFING 1

Simple Past Tense—Affirmative Statements; Regular Simple Past Verbs

FUNCTION

Simple Past Tense

1. Use the simple past tense to describe actions or states in the past:

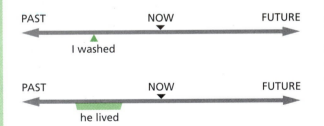

SIMPLE PRESENT TENSE	SIMPLE PAST TENSE
I **wash** my hair every day.	I **washed** my hair yesterday.
He **lives** in Italy now.	He **lived** in Italy from 1990 to 1998.

2. Sentences with simple past tense verbs often have past time expressions.

   (See Chapter 12, Grammar Briefing 1, page 196, for more on past time expressions.)

   We cleaned the house **yesterday**.

   They invented it **200 years ago**.

   He worked there **in 1998**.

(continued on next page)

A. Affirmative Statements

SUBJECT	SIMPLE PAST VERB	
I		
You		
He		
She		
It	**worked**	yesterday.
We		
You		
They		
Anna		
The men		

B. Simple Past of Regular Verbs

Most verbs are regular. For the simple past, add -*ed* or -*d* to the base form of the verb. Follow the spelling rules.

walk → walk**ed**

play → play**ed**

live → live**d**

C. Spelling Rules

1. For verbs ending in *e*: Add -*d*.

   smil**e** → smil**ed**   danc**e** → danc**ed**

   believ**e** → believ**ed**

2. For all other verbs: Add -*ed*.

   turn → turn**ed**   want → want**ed**

   stay → stay**ed**   listen → listen**ed**

   Sometimes another change is also needed:

   - For verbs ending in a consonant + *y*: Change *y* to *i* and add -*ed*.

     cry → cr**ied**   stu**dy** → stud**ied**

   - For verbs ending in a consonant + vowel + consonant: Double the final consonant and add -*ed*.

     stop → sto**pped**   plan → plan**ned**

     cont**rol** → contro**lled**

   BUT:

   Do not double *w* or *x*.

   snow → snow**ed**   fix → fix**ed**

   Do not double the final consonant when the last syllable is not stressed.

   *Last syllable **not** stressed*:   énter → enter**ed**

   Last syllable stressed: preférr → prefe**rred**

Simple Past Tense—Affirmative Statements; Regular Simple Past Verbs

1 **Regular Simple Past Verbs:** The History of Coca-Cola

Read about the invention of Coca-Cola. Write the simple past form of the verb in parentheses.

1. In 1886, Dr. John Pemberton ___invented___ Coca-Cola.
   (invent)

2. He really _____ to invent a new medicine for headaches.
   (want)

3. He _____ some ingredients together in a big pot over a fire in his backyard.
   (mix)

4. He _____ some of the medicine into a glass.
   (pour)

5. He _____ plain water and ice to the medicine.
   (add)

6. It was ready to drink, so Dr. Pemberton and his assistant _____ it.
   (try)

7. It _____ good!
   (taste)

8. It was so good that Dr. Pemberton _____ his mind.
   (change)

9. Now he _____ to sell it as a drink, not a medicine.
   (plan)

10. He _____ to have another glass of it.
    (decide)

11. By accident, his assistant _____ carbonated water with the medicine.
    (use)

12. But Dr. Pemberton _____ the drink with bubbles even better.
    (like)

13. Both men _____ it that way.
    (prefer)

14. Dr. Pemberton _____ very little money in his first year of selling Coca-Cola.
    (earn)

> *ingredients* = things that go into a mixture to make something, as in cooking. *an assistant* = a helper.

2 **Regular Simple Past Verbs:** The Invention of Potato Chips

A. Complete the sentences with the simple past tense of the verbs in parentheses.

George Crum was a cook in a restaurant in Saratoga Springs, New York. One day in 1853,

a customer at the restaurant ___refused___ to eat a plate of potatoes. "They're too
1 (refuse)

thick," he _____ to the waiter. The man _____ more
2 (complain)   3 (order)

potatoes, but he wasn't happy with those either. "They're not cooked enough," he said. Again,

he _____ for more.
    4 (ask)

George Crum was proud of his cooking, so he was angry at this customer. He

_____ to cut some potatoes very, very thin. Then he _____
    5 (decide)   6 (fry)

the potatoes in hot oil for a long, long time, and he _____ them with salt.
                                                          7 (cover)

He _____ the customer to hate these potatoes, but the man
    8 (expect)

_____ them! The news about Crum's new style of potatoes
    9 (love)

_____ fast. Soon potato chips were popular all over the United States.
    10 (travel)

Today, more than 3 billion pounds of potatoes a year become potato chips.

 B. Work with a group. Tell about a time when you tried a new food. What was it? Where did you try it? Who prepared it? Did you like it?

Example: Student A: A long time ago, I tried octopus. I was at a neighbor's house. She wanted me to try it, but I didn't like it.

See the *Grammar Links* Website for more information about food-related inventions.

TALKING THE TALK

There are three ways to pronounce the -*ed* on simple past tense regular verbs:

- Say /t/ when the base form of the verb ends in the voiceless consonant sound /k/, /p/, /s/, /ch/, /sh/, /f/, or /ks/.

- Say /d/ when the base form of the verb ends in a vowel sound or the voiced consonant sound /b/, /g/, /j/, /m/, /n/, /ng/, /l/, /r/, /th/, /v/, /z/, or /zh/.

- Say /ɪd/ when the base verb ends in /t/ or /d/. The sound /ɪd/ adds one syllable.

/-kt/ picked		/-pt/ sto**pp**ed
/-st/ dre**ss**ed		/-cht/ wa**tch**ed
/-ft/ lau**gh**ed		/-kst/ mi**x**ed
/-eed/ carri**ed**		/-oed/ show**ed**
/-bd/ ro**bb**ed		/-jd/ ju**dg**ed
/-md/ clim**b**ed		/-nd/ plan**n**ed
/-rd/ prefe**rr**ed		/-thd/ brea**th**ed
/-zd/ refu**s**ed		/-zhd/ massa**g**ed
/-tɪd/ wan**t**ed		/-dɪd/ nee**d**ed
/-tɪd/ inven**t**ed		/-dɪd/ loa**d**ed

3 **Spelling and Saying Verb Endings:** A Delicious Mistake

A. Circle the simple past tense verbs. Number them from 1 to 12.

One day in 1933, a lucky accident (happened) in the kitchen of the Toll House

Inn in Whitman, Massachusetts. That day, Ruth Wakefield wanted to make some

chocolate cookies, but she needed to make them fast. Usually, she melted some

chocolate first. But that day, to save time, she used small pieces of a chocolate

candy bar. She expected the pieces to melt in the oven and make the cookies all

chocolate. But the cookies surprised her—the chocolate pieces stayed separate.

People liked these "mistakes" very much. They asked for more, so Mrs. Wakefield

baked more. Many more! She named them Toll House Cookies. Today, we also

call them chocolate chip cookies. In the United States today, people eat *billions* of

these cookies each year.

> *an inn* = a small hotel. *melt* = use heat to make (something) soft and
> liquid; or become soft and liquid because of heat.

B. Copy the 12 verbs from Part A. Then check answers with a partner.

1. _happened_ /t/ /d/ /ɪd/   7. _____ /t/ /d/ /ɪd/
2. _____ /t/ /d/ /ɪd/   8. _____ /t/ /d/ /ɪd/
3. _____ /t/ /d/ /ɪd/   9. _____ /t/ /d/ /ɪd/
4. _____ /t/ /d/ /ɪd/   10. _____ /t/ /d/ /ɪd/
5. _____ /t/ /d/ /ɪd/   11. _____ /t/ /d/ /ɪd/
6. _____ /t/ /d/ /ɪd/   12. _____ /t/ /d/ /ɪd/

C. Listen to 12 statements about the reading. Circle the final sound of each simple
past verb in Part B.

Example: 1. _happened_ /t/ (/d/) /ɪd/

D. Work with a partner. Practice the pronunciation of the 12 simple past tense verbs.

4 **Using Regular Simple Past Verbs:** This Past Week

 A. Work with a partner. Student A: Use verbs from the list to make six true statements about things you did in the past week. Student B: Listen and circle the verbs you hear. Then take your turn to make statements while Student A listens and circles.

Example: Last night, I studied in my room.

ask	cook	help	play	talk	wash
clean	fix	listen	study	use	watch

B. Write eight true statements with the simple past tense of verbs in Part A. Try to use a past time expression in each sentence.

Example: I talked to my sister on the phone yesterday.

GRAMMAR BRIEFING 2

Irregular Simple Past Verbs

FORM

Overview

Irregular verbs do not add -(e)d in the simple past. Here are some common irregular verbs:

BASE FORM	SIMPLE PAST TENSE FORM	BASE FORM	SIMPLE PAST TENSE FORM	BASE FORM	SIMPLE PAST TENSE FORM
be	was/were	eat	ate	make	made
begin	began	fall	fell	read	read
break	broke	find	found	say	said
buy	bought	get	got	see	saw
come	came	go	went	speak	spoke
do	did	have	had	think	thought
drink	drank	leave	left	write	wrote

(See Appendix 7 for a list of irregular verbs.)

Only the verb *be* has two simple past tense forms. The other irregular verbs have one form for all subjects.

(See Chapter 12 for more information about the past tense of *be*.)

| I **was** at school yesterday. |
| They **were** at school yesterday. |
| I **went** to school yesterday. |
| They **went** to school yesterday. |

GRAMMAR PRACTICE 2

Irregular Simple Past Verbs

5 **Irregular Simple Past Verbs:** A Lab Accident

Write the simple past tense of the irregular verb in parentheses.

In 1903, there _____was_____ an accident in the laboratory of Edouard
      1 (be)

Benedictus, a French chemist. A glass flask _____ on the floor, and it
                                              2 (fall)

_____. Benedictus looked down, and he _____ something
   3 (break)   4 (see)

surprising. The pieces of broken glass _____ still together in the shape
                                          5 (be)

of the flask.

A Flask

Benedictus _____ about the flask. A while ago, this flask
              6 (think)

_____ a liquid in it. The liquid _____ cellulose
   7 (have)   8 (be)

nitrate, a kind of plastic. Benedictus studied the flask. He _____ a thin
                                                               9 (find)

plastic film covering the inside of the flask. The cellulose nitrate _____
                                                                       10 (leave)

this film. It _____ the pieces of broken glass stay together. "Très
               11 (make)

intéressant . . ." he _____. ("Very interesting . . .")
                       12 (say)

Benedictus _____ to think about ways to use cellulose nitrate.
              13 (begin)

A few days later, he _____ in the newspaper about a problem:
                       14 (read)

In car accidents, car windshields often _____, and the broken glass
                                            15 (break)

cut people. When Benedictus _____ this
16 (see)
story in the paper, he _____ the idea for
17 (get)
safety glass. Now car windshields are safer, thanks to
an accident in a French laboratory.

> *a liquid* = something like water (not a solid, not a gas). *plastic* = a
> strong, light material often used for toys, credit cards, etc.

6 **Irregular Simple Past Verbs:** Quiz Your Partner

Work with a partner. Student A: Choose a verb from the list and say it aloud.
Student B: Say the simple past tense form of the verb. Take turns.

begin	come	eat	get	leave	say	think
break	do	fall	go	make	see	write
buy	drink	find	have	read	speak	

7 **Affirmative Statements with Irregular Simple Past Verbs:** A Memory Game

A. Work in a group. Form a circle. Student A: Tell something you did last
weekend, using an irregular verb in the simple past tense. Student B: Repeat
that statement, and add your own sentence with a different verb. (**Note:** See
Appendix 7 for more irregular verbs.) Go around the circle as many times as
you can. How many activities can you remember? The group with the longest
list is the winner.

Example: Student A: Last weekend, I went to my friend's party.
          Student B: Last weekend, Mina went to her friend's party. I bought
                      new shoes.
          Student C: Last weekend, Mina went to her friend's party. Abdul
                      bought new shoes. I saw a movie.

B. Write a paragraph about last weekend. Tell what you did. Use both regular and
irregular simple past tense verbs in your paragraph.

See the *Grammar Links* Website for a model paragraph for this assignment.

8 Affirmative Statements with Irregular Simple Past Verbs: Interview

Work with a partner. Student A: Ask a question with *Do you ever* + a verb from the list below. (You can use the words in parentheses in your question or any other words.) Student B: Answer *No, I don't*, or answer *Yes*, and tell one time in the past when you did it. Take turns.

Example: Student A: Do you ever write letters?
Student B: Yes, I wrote a letter last weekend.

1. buy (books, CDs)
2. do (your homework, the dishes)
3. drink (coffee, Coca-Cola)
4. eat (apples, candy bars)
5. get (phone calls, e-mail messages)
6. go (to the beach, to sports events)
7. have (headaches, parties)
8. make (your bed, mistakes)
9. read (English magazines, the newspaper)
10. see (movies, old friends)
11. speak (to strangers, on the phone)
12. write (letters, poems)

GRAMMAR BRIEFING 3

Simple Past Tense—Negative Statements

FORM

A. Negative Statements

FULL FORM

SUBJECT	DID	NOT	BASE VERB	
I				
You				
He			**work.**	
She				
It	**did**	**not**		
We				
You			**do**	the job.
They				
Ann				
The men				

CONTRACTED FORM

SUBJECT	DIDN'T	BASE VERB	
I			
You			
He		**work.**	
She			
It	**didn't**		
We			
You		**do**	the job.
They			
Ann			
The men			

(continued on next page)

B. Regular and Irregular Verbs

1. With both regular and irregular verbs (except *be*), use *did* + *not* to form negative statements in the simple past tense.

REGULAR VERB	IRREGULAR VERB
It started at 9:00. It **didn't start** late.	It began at 9:00. It **didn't begin** late.

2. The irregular verb *be* is different from all other irregular verbs. Do not use *did*.

(See Chapter 12, Grammar Briefing 2, page 199, for negative past tense statements with *be*.)

I **wasn't** ready.
   NOT: I ~~didn't was~~ ready.

They **weren't** at home.
   NOT: They ~~didn't be~~ at home.

3. *Did* is the past tense form of the auxiliary verb *do*. *Did* can also be the main verb in a statement.

DID AS AUXILIARY VERB	DID AS MAIN VERB
I **did** not <u>see</u> him.	He **did** a nice job.
She **didn't** <u>do</u> the dishes.	I **did** my homework.

GRAMMAR PRACTICE 3

Simple Past Tense—Negative Statements

9 **Affirmative and Negative Statements:** Edison's Childhood

Write the simple past tense of the verb in parentheses. (See Appendix 7 for the past tense forms of *build*, *catch*, *sell*, *spend*, *teach*, and *tell*.)

The great inventor Thomas Edison __*didn't have*__ a typical childhood. For
                                                        1 (have, not)

example, he _____ very little time in school. He _____
                      2 (spend)   3 (do, not)

well there, and he _____ long—only three months. People today think Edison
                            4 (stay, not)

_____ a genius, but his teacher _____ this at all. In fact,
         5 (be)   6 (think, not)

she _____ his parents that he _____ smart. So Mrs. Edison
      7 (tell)   8 (be, not)

_____ her son at home. At age nine, he _____ his first
      9 (teach)   10 (read)

scientific books. Soon he _____ a science laboratory in the basement of his house.
                          11 (build)

At age twelve, he _____ his business career. Every morning, he _____
                      12 (begin)   13 (catch)

the train to the city and _____ newspapers, candy, and sandwiches to the people on
                      14 (sell)

the train. But he _____ all his time selling things. He _____ a
                  15 (spend, not)   16 (build)

lab on the train and _____ science experiments there, too!
               17 (do)

10 Affirmative and Negative Statements: Your Childhood

Work with a partner. Tell if you did or didn't do the things in the list when you were a child. Give more information about each statement.

Example: Student A: **1. I wasn't born in the United States. I was born in Korea.**
2. I started school at age five. I went to a girls' school near my home.

1. be born in the United States
2. start school at age five
3. have a school uniform
4. walk to school
5. love school
6. speak English in school
7. eat lunch in school

8. always get good grades
9. study every day
10. play sports after school
11. have friends in the neighborhood
12. spend a lot of time alone
13. live in the city
14. go on family vacations

11 Editing: Mary Shelley's Frankenstein

Correct the 12 errors in verbs and past time expressions. The first one is corrected for you.

One famous invention ~~did'nt~~ **didn't** exist in the real world. People first

learnd about this invention in a book. Later they see it in the movies.

This invention were the monster known as Frankenstein.

Mary Shelley was an English writer. In 1818, she writed the book

Frankenstein. In the book, the monster had not a name. "Frankenstein"

was the name of a young student. The student invent the monster as

an experiment. He get parts of bodies, sewed them together, and was use electricity

to give life to the monster. (Ago many years, people did no understand electricity, so

maybe they believed this idea.) The monster didn't had a happy life. In the end, he

killed the young inventor.

Mary Shelley's Monster

Check your progress! Go to the Self-Test for Chapter 13 on the *Grammar Links* Website.

Chapter 14

From Saving Lives to Just Having Fun

The Simple Past Tense—*Yes/No* Questions and *Wh-* Questions

Introductory Task: Garrett Morgan, Inventor and Hero

A. Listen to a sixth-grade teacher and his students. Circle the verb you hear in each simple past tense question.

The Morgan Safety Hood and Smoke Protector

Mr. Garcia: For homework, you read about Garrett Morgan.

What did you (learn / learned) about him? Mike?
1

Mike: He was an African-American inventor, and he

invented a kind of gas mask.

Serena: And he was a hero.

Mr. Garcia: Why did people (say / said) he was a hero?
2

Did he (do / does) something brave? Serena?
3

Serena: Well, there was a gas explosion in a tunnel under Lake Erie. It killed a lot of

workers in the tunnel, but some workers were still alive. So the police and some

firefighters went into the tunnel to help them.

Mr. Garcia: And did they (save / saved) the people? Katie?
4

Katie: No, they didn't come out.

Mr. Garcia: So then what? What did they (try / tried) next? Go ahead, Katie.
5

Katie: Nobody else wanted to go into the tunnel. Then somebody called Garrett Morgan,

and he came and he put on his safety hood, and he went into the tunnel. The

hood protected him from the gas—that was the whole idea of it.

Mr. Garcia: Did he (save / saved) any of the workers? Serena?
6

Serena: Yes, he did, and he saved some of the police and firefighters, too.

Mr. Garcia: When did this (happen / happened)? Mike?
7

Mike: In 1916.

> *a hero* = a brave person who does something difficult. *a tunnel* = a long passage that goes underground or through a mountain. *protect* = keep someone safe.

B. Work alone or with a partner. Look at the seven simple past tense questions in Part A. Answer the following questions.

1. What kinds of main verbs are there? Circle your answer.

   a. regular verbs   b. irregular verbs   c. both regular and irregular verbs

2. What is the auxiliary verb in these questions? _____

3. What form are the main verbs in the questions?

   a. the simple past tense form   b. the base form   c. the base form + -(e)s

GRAMMAR BRIEFING 1

Simple Past Tense—*Yes/No* Questions and Short Answers

FORM

A. *Yes/No* Questions and Short Answers

QUESTIONS			ANSWERS					
DID	SUBJECT	BASE VERB	YES			NO		
	I			I			I	
	you			you			you	
	he			he			he	
	she			she			she	
Did	it	**win?**	Yes,	it	**did.**	No,	it	**didn't.**
	the team							
	we			we			we	
	you			you			you	
	they			they			they	
	the men							

(continued on next page)

B. Regular and Irregular Verbs

1. With both regular and irregular verbs (except *be*), use *did* to form *yes/no* questions in the simple past.

REGULAR VERBS	IRREGULAR VERBS
Did it **start** on time?	**Did** it **begin** on time?
Did you **own** a car?	**Did** you **have** a car?

2. Don't use *did* with the irregular verb *be*.

Were you at home last weekend?
   NOT: ~~Did you were~~ at home?

Was the weather nice?
   NOT: ~~Did the weather was~~ nice?

(See Chapter 12, Grammar Briefing 3, page 201, for past tense *yes/no* questions with *be*.)

GRAMMAR PRACTICE 1

Simple Past Tense—*Yes/No* Questions and Short Answers

1 **_Yes/No_ Questions with _Did_, _Was_, and _Were_; Short Answers:** Two Heroes

A. Complete the questions with *Did*, *Was*, or *Were*.

Part One: Inventor Gertrude Belle Elion

1. ___Was___ Gertrude Belle Elion a successful inventor? (Yes.)

2. ___Did___ she invent a drug to fight one kind of cancer? (Yes.)

3. _____ this drug save people's lives? (Yes.)

4. _____ Elion earn a place in the National Inventors Hall of Fame? (Yes.)

5. _____ she and her team the winners of a Nobel Prize? (Yes.)

Part Two: Inventor Stephanie Kwolek

6. _____ Dr. Stephanie Kwolek a chemist? (Yes.)

7. _____ she always want to be a chemist? (No. At first she wanted to be a doctor.)

8. _____ Dr. Kwolek invent a special fiber? (Yes. It's called Kevlar, and it's stronger than steel.)

9. _____ people use this fiber to make bulletproof vests? (Yes.)

10. _____ her invention save police officers' lives? (Yes.)

11. _____ Dr. Kwolek's invention a lucky accident? (No. It was the result of hard work.)

A Bulletproof Vest

> *a Nobel Prize* = an important international prize given each year.
> *fiber* = thread, usually used to make cloth.

B. Work with a partner. Take turns asking the questions in Part A. Give short answers.

Example: Student A: Was Gertrude Belle Elion a successful inventor?
Student B: Yes, she was.

TALKING THE TALK

	WRITE	YOU WILL OFTEN HEAR
People sometimes pronounce *did you* as "didja" or "ja."	Did you go out?	"Didja" go out?
		"Ja" go out?

---

2 **Pronunciation of *Yes/No* Questions with *Did*:** Assignments Due

Listen to a conversation between two college students. Write the auxiliary verb + subject pronoun you hear.

Marina: <u>Did you</u> try to call me last night?
            1

Carlo: Yeah. _____ go out?
                      2

Marina: Uh-huh, to the library. I needed to look up Garrett Morgan—you know, the inventor.

Carlo: I never heard of him. _____ invent something important?
                                          3

Marina: A kind of gas mask. Soldiers used it in World War I.

Carlo: _____ have an assignment on this guy?
              4

Marina: Yeah, it was due today. What about you? _____ finish that paper
                                                                          5

for econ?

Carlo: Not yet. I asked the professor for an extension.

Marina: Oh, Carlo, really! What _____ say?
                                            6

Carlo: "No!"

Marina: See? What _____ tell you?
                            7

---

look up = try to find information about. *an assignment* = a job given to someone to do, such as a college paper. *econ* = (short for) *economics*, the study of how money and things are made and used. *an extension* = extra time allowed to finish something.

---

3 **Asking *Yes/No* Questions and Giving Short Answers:** Find Someone Who

A. Read the past activities in the boxes below. Write another past activity in the middle box.

B. Work with a partner. Take turns forming *yes/no* questions about the activities using *Did you* or *Were you*.

Example: Student A: Did you watch TV last night?
Student B: Were you out yesterday evening?

C. Walk around the room. Ask your classmates the *yes/no* questions. Write a name on each line to make true statements. The winner is the first person to write three different names in three boxes in a row.

_____ watched TV last night.	_____ was out yesterday evening.	_____ read a newspaper today.
_____ made a phone call yesterday.	_____	_____ got some good news recently.
_____ was in bed at 10:00 last night.	_____ had a big breakfast today.	_____ went shopping last weekend.

GRAMMAR BRIEFING 2

Simple Past Tense—*Wh-* Questions and Answers

FORM

A. Questions with *Wh-* Question Word as Subject

QUESTIONS			ANSWERS
WH- QUESTION WORD/SUBJECT	SIMPLE PAST VERB		
Who	**washed**	the floor?	I did.
Whose phone	**rang**?		My phone.
Which* team	**won**	the game?	Our team did.
What	**happened**	at the party?	Everybody had a good time.

*Use *which* + noun to ask about one person or thing out of two or more.

(continued on next page)

B. Questions with Other Subjects

QUESTIONS					ANSWERS
WH- QUESTION WORD	DID	SUBJECT	BASE VERB		
Who	did	you	call	on Sunday?	My parents.
Whom*					
What	did	she	do?		She went shopping.
When	did	he	call	you?	An hour ago.
Why	did	you	buy	the guitar?	Because I want to learn to play.

*Whom is very formal. It is not common in conversation.

C. Regular and Irregular Verbs

	REGULAR VERB	IRREGULAR VERB
1. Wh- questions in the simple past tense are the same for regular and irregular verbs.	When **did** it **start**? Who **started** it?	When **did** it **begin**? Who **began** it?
2. Do not use did in wh- questions with the irregular verb be.	When **was** it? NOT: When ~~did it was~~?	
3. Do not use did when the wh- question word is the subject.	**Who** called? NOT: Who ~~did call~~?	

Simple Past Tense—Wh- Questions and Answers

4 **Wh- Questions and Answers:** Frisbee History

Complete the wh- questions. Use the words in parentheses.

1. Q: __Who played_____ with the first Frisbees?
      (who / play)

   A: College students did.

2. Q: _____ to school?
      (where / they / go)

   A: At Yale University in New Haven, Connecticut.

3. Q: _____ at first?
      (what / they / use)

   A: Metal pie plates from the Frisbie Bakery.

4. Q: _____ the Frisbie Bakery?
      (where / be)

   A: In Bridgeport, Connecticut.

5. Q: _____ the plates?
   (why / they / throw)

   A: Because it was fun.

6. Q: _____ the first plastic Frisbees?
   (who / make)

   A: Walter F. Morrison.

7. Q: _____ plastic?
   (why / he / use)

   A: Because it is light and strong.

8. Q: _____ Morrison's idea?
   (who / buy)

   A: The Wham-O Company.

9. Q: _____ making Wham-O Frisbees?
   (when / they / start)

   A: In 1955.

10. Q: _____?
   (what other famous toy / Wham-O / make)

   A: The Hula Hoop.

Hula Hoops, 1958

5 *Wh-* Questions and Answers: Bicycle History

A. Work alone or with a partner. Read about early bicycles. Write a *wh-* question about each sentence.

(1) The draisine was a kind of bicycle. (2) Men rode draisines in the early 1800s. (3) The draisine was a German inventor's idea. (4) His name was Karl von Drais von Sauerbronn. (5) He introduced his invention to the public in Paris and Frankfurt.

1. What _was the draisine?_____

2. When _____

3. Whose idea _____

4. What _____

5. Where _____

The Draisine

(6) Kirkpatrick Macmillan built the first real bicycle. (7) Macmillan was an inventor in Scotland. (8) He built his bicycle in 1839. (9) John Dunlop improved the bicycle. (10) In the 1880s, Dunlop added tires filled with air.

6. Who _____

7. Who _____

8. When _____

9. Who _____

10. What _____

B. Work with a partner. Take turns asking and answering your questions about the readings.

C. Work with a partner. On a piece of paper, write more *wh-* questions with simple past tense verbs. Your questions can be about the invention of the bicycle or about a different toy, game, or piece of sports equipment. Share your questions with the class. Can anyone answer them?

Examples: **Who made the first yo-yo? Where did people first play ping-pong (table tennis)?**

See the *Grammar Links* Website for more infomation about the history of toys and games.

TALKING THE TALK

In conversation, contractions of *wh-* question words + *did* are common.

WRITE	YOU WILL OFTEN HEAR
Who did he call?	"**Who'd**" he call?
What did she say?	"**What'd**" she say?
Where did they go?	"**Where'd**" they go?

6 Pronunciation of *Wh-* Questions in the Simple Past Tense: A Great Idea

Listen to a conversation between two sixth-graders. Write the missing words: *wh-* question words, *did*, and subject pronouns.

Serena: <u>Did you</u> _____ write your paper?
            ₁

Mike: Yeah. _____ do yours?
                        ₂

Serena: Uh-huh. I wrote about Garrett Morgan. _____ do Henry Ford?
                                                                    ₃

Mike: No, I picked another guy, a Japanese inventor.

Serena: _____ change?
                    ₄

Mike: Ford was boring.

Serena: So _____ write about?
                    ₅

Mike: Akio Morita.

Serena: Who's he? _____ invent?
                            ₆

Mike: The Sony Walkman.™

Serena: Cool! _____ do that?
                        ₇

Mike: In 1979. He wanted to listen to music and play golf at the same time.

Serena: _____ hear about him?
                    ₈

Mike: From my dad.

7 Questions and Answers: Learn About Each Other

A. On a small piece of paper, write a statement about an important event or time in your past.

Examples: I was in a car accident last summer.
My baseball team won a national championship.

B. Work in a group. Put all the slips of paper in an envelope or a hat. Take turns drawing out a slip and reading it aloud. Guess who wrote it, and then find out more about that person's experience. Take turns asking *yes/no* and *wh-* questions in the simple past tense.

Examples: Where did this happen?
Was your baseball game on TV?

Check your progress! Go to the Self-Test for Chapter 14 on the *Grammar Links* Website.

Wrap-up Activities

1 Growing Up: READING

Read this paragraph.

I had a good childhood. I grew up in a big family. There were six of us: my parents, my two brothers, my sister, and me. My grandmother lived with us for a few years, too. I started school at age five, and I went to a school near my house. I had a lot of friends at school, but I didn't like my teachers very much. They were very strict with us. I was always very happy on the last day of the school year. Summer was the best time for me. I played with my friends in my neighborhood, and my family sometimes went to the beach. I have good memories of those days.

2 Your Childhood: WRITING

What do you remember from your childhood? Write a paragraph about growing up (your family, your school, your friends), or write about a happy time you remember (one special day, a family trip, fun with a pet). Use simple past tense verbs to describe things that happened in the past.

See the *Grammar Links* Website for a model paragraph for this assignment.

3 Sasha and Me: EDITING

Correct the 10 errors in the paragraph. They are errors in simple past tense verbs. The first error is corrected for you. Some errors can be corrected in more than one way.

Sasha

wanted
When I was a child, I always ~~want~~ a dog, but I hadn't any pets. My parents did

no like animals in the house. Our neighbor was have a dog, and I play with her

a lot. Her name were Sasha. Sometimes I go for a walk with her. We usually visit

the candy store, and I buy candy for her and for me. Now I know the candy no

was good for her, but she liked it very much.

---

4 Mystery Inventions: SPEAKING/LISTENING

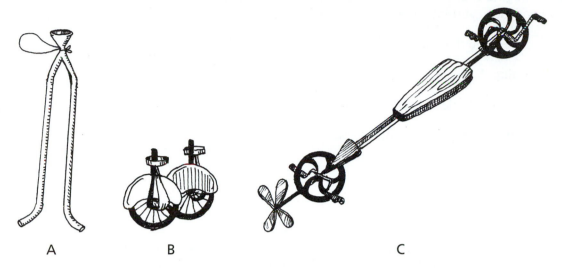

A   B   C

Work in a group. Look at pictures A, B, and C above. These are inventions from the past. What were these things? What did they do? Who used them? When and where did they use them? Discuss these inventions with your group. Use the simple past tense. Make guesses about the inventions, and tell the class your ideas. Then find the answers on page A-2.

5 Guess the Inventor: SPEAKING/LISTENING

Work in a group. Student A: Think of an inventor from this unit. Other students: Get information about the inventor by asking *yes/no* questions. Student A: Give only short answers.

Example: Student B: Was this inventor a man?
               Student A: Yes, he was.
               Student C: Did he invent something in this room?
               Student A: No, he didn't.

Other students: When you are sure of the inventor's name, make a guess. For example, *Was this inventor Garrett Morgan?* A correct guess means the group wins. A wrong guess means Student A wins.

6 **An Interview:** SPEAKING/LISTENING/WRITING

Step 1 Imagine that it is the year 2050. You are an old and famous inventor. Many years ago, you invented one of these things:

- A car engine that uses only water

- Clothing that cleans itself

- A way for people to learn while they sleep

- A drug that makes sleep unnecessary

- A cure for _____

- Other: _____

Step 2 Work with a partner. Student A: You are the inventor. Student B: You are a journalist. You want to know about the inventor's life and work. Ask *wh-* and *yes/no* questions, for example, *What did you invent? Why did you want to invent this? Did you get rich?* Student A: Answer the questions.

Step 3 Switch roles.

Step 4 Write a paragraph as the inventor. Tell about your life and your invention.

Example: Forty years ago, I had a great idea. It was an idea for a new kind of engine for cars. My engine didn't need gas. It ran on water . . .

More About Nouns and Pronouns; Quantifiers

TOPIC FOCUS
Money, Money, Money!

UNIT OBJECTIVES

■ **count and noncount nouns**
(I have twenty *dollars*. They don't need *money*.)

■ **articles with count and noncount nouns**
(He has *a map* of *an island*. He is looking for Blackbeard's *treasure*. Is *the treasure* on *the island*?)

■ **quantifiers and measure words**
(There were *many* things on his shopping list. He bought a *pound* of sugar.)

■ ***wh-* questions with *how much* and *how many***
(*How much* gold did they find? *How many* coins were in the box?)

■ **subject pronouns and object pronouns**
(*We* heard some stories. Anna heard *them*, too.)

■ **possessive adjectives, possessive pronouns, and possessive nouns**
(Mr. Smith keeps *his* money in a safe. We keep *ours* in the bank. *Mr. Smith's* safe is in his office.)

■ **indefinite pronouns with *some-*, *any-*, and *no-***
(*Somebody* tried to rob the bank. Did they take *anything*? *No one* saw them.)

■ ***one* and *ones* as indefinite pronouns**
(He works in a bank, the *one* on Appleton Street. There are two big banks in town and several small *ones*.)

Grammar in Action

🎧 Reading and Listening: Money in the United States

Read and listen to reporter Al Jordan's talk on money in the United States.

A Dollar Bill

A Penny

A Quarter

A Nickel

A Dime

1   This is Al Jordan, reporting to you from Denver, Colorado. Today, our topic is **money**. We all use money, right? You probably have some **cash** with you right now. But how much do you know about it? Where does it come from? What is it made of?

2   Take your money out, and take a look at it. First, look at the coins. On some coins, there is a small letter near the date. The letter "D" means that the coin is from the building behind me, the Denver Mint. The letter "P" means that the coin is from Philadelphia. Some pennies have no letter. They're also from Philadelphia. Denver and Philadelphia are the only two places where the U.S. government makes coins.

3   Here at the Denver Mint, many people take tours through the building. Inside, there are many machines. Some machines make the coins, using metals such as **silver** and **copper**. One machine checks the weight of the coins. Another one counts them. All these machines work very fast. How many coins do they make? About 750 coins every minute. That's a lot of coins!

4   Now take a look at a bill. The paper is special. It feels different from the paper in a book or notebook. The government uses **cotton** and other materials for the paper in dollar bills. But the bills don't come from Denver. The government prints paper money in Washington, D.C., and Fort Worth, Texas. How many bills do they print in one year? About 9 billion. And how much cotton is in all those bills? About 14 million pounds. That's a lot of cotton and a lot of money!

Cotton

9 billion = 9,000,000,000. 14 million = 14,000,000.

Think About Grammar

A. Look at the six nouns that are <u>underlined</u>. Write them on the left side of the chart. Look at the five nouns that are **boldfaced**. Write them on the right side of the chart.

Count Nouns	Noncount Nouns

Look at the nouns in the chart. Then circle your answers below.

1. (Count nouns / Noncount nouns) have two forms, singular and plural.

2. (Count nouns / Noncount nouns) have only one form.

Complete the questions with the missing words from the reading.

1. (Paragraph 3)   How _____ coins do they make? About 750 coins every minute.

2. (Paragraph 4)   And how _____ cotton is in all those bills? About 14 million pounds.

Look at the questions you completed. Then circle the correct words below.

Use *how many* + (a plural count noun / a noncount noun).

Use *how much* + (a plural count noun / a noncount noun).

15

Money and Treasure
Count and Noncount Nouns

Introductory Task: The Riches of the "New World"

A. Read and listen to some information about Christopher Columbus. Listen again and complete the statements with the words in the box.

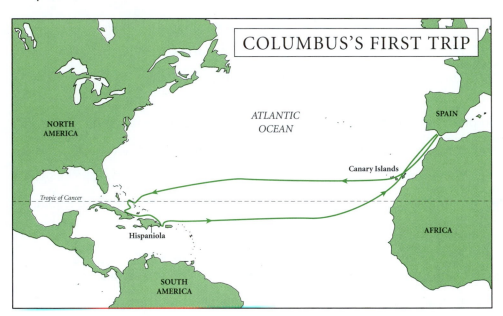

| cotton | food | gifts | ✓ money | spices | water |
| fish | fruit | land | oil | supplies | wood |

Christopher Columbus was an explorer who lived from 1451 to 1506. He received

<u>money</u> from the king and queen of Spain to find a new way to Asia. They wanted
₁

valuable things from Asia: _____ and gold.
₂

On August 3, 1492, Columbus began his first trip. He and his men took many

_____ with them on their ships. They had dried _____ and
₃ ₄

vegetables, _____ for cooking, and _____ for making fires.
₅ ₆

They had drinking _____, soap, pots, and tools. They also took _____
                        7   8
and things to trade for spices and gold.

Columbus and his men stopped first at the Canary Islands. There, they loaded more fresh

water and _____ onto their ships. During their voyage, they also ate
                  9

_____ from the ocean. The good food helped Columbus and his men stay healthy.
      10

After many weeks of sailing west, Columbus finally reached _____. He visited
                                                                      11

several islands and met the people there. He believed he was near India, so he called the people

"Indians." They introduced him and his men to new customs and types of food. Columbus traded

for gold and _____, and then he sailed for Spain with news of a new world.
                    12

> *an explorer* = a person who travels to find something new. *spices* = seeds
> or powder from plants used to give food a special taste. *supplies* = things
> available for use when they are needed. *trade* = give one thing to get
> another.

B. Match the parts of the sentences.

_c_____ 1. The money   a. was for making fires.

_____ 2. The fish   b. were valuable in Spain.

_____ 3. The wood   c. was from the king and queen of Spain.

_____ 4. Water   d. were friendly.

_____ 5. Spices   e. was important for drinking on the ships.

_____ 6. The people in the New World   f. were fresh from the ocean.

Count and Noncount Nouns

FORM and FUNCTION

A. Count Nouns

1. Count nouns name people, places, and things that we count. They can be singular or plural.

   Singular: one **student**, one **dollar**

   Plural: two **students**, ten **dollars**

2. All regular plural nouns end in *-s.*
   (See Chapter 3, Grammar Briefing 2, page 51, for spelling rules for plural count nouns.)

pens	watches	famil**ies**
books	boxes	stor**ies**

3. Some count nouns are irregular:

   • Some have special plural forms.

SINGULAR	PLURAL
person	people
child	children
man	men
woman	women
tooth	teeth
foot	feet
one deer	two deer
one fish	three fish
one sheep	ten sheep
—	clothes
—	jeans
—	pants
—	sunglasses

   • Some have the same singular and plural form.

   • Some have only a plural form.

(continued on next page)

B. Noncount Nouns

1. Noncount nouns name things that we do not count. Noncount nouns have only one form. Some common noncount nouns are:*

FOOD				OTHER			
bread	food	salt		advice	dust	jewelry	rain
butter	fruit	soda		air	equipment	luck	silver
cereal	juice	soup		cash	furniture	money	snow
cheese	meat	sugar		clothing	gold	music	weather
coffee	milk	tea		cotton	homework	oil	wood
corn	rice	water		dirt	information	peace	work

*See Appendix 6 for more specific categories of common noncount nouns.

2. Many noncount nouns name groups of things. The things in the groups are countable.

GROUPS	COUNTABLE THINGS
fruit	apples, bananas, oranges
furniture	tables, chairs, beds
money	nickels, quarters, dollars

C. Subject–Verb Agreement with Count and Noncount Nouns

1. Singular count noun subjects take singular verbs.

His <u>car</u> **is** red.

That <u>man</u> **works** here.

Plural count noun subjects take plural verbs.

<u>Cars</u> **are** expensive.

Those <u>men</u> **work** here.

2. Noncount noun subjects take singular verbs.

The <u>homework</u> **seems** easy.

Does <u>that cheese</u> **come** from France?

Was there <u>much cash</u> in the wallet?

Count and Noncount Nouns

1 **Identifying Count and Noncount Nouns:** Looking for Gold

Look at the **boldfaced** nouns. Write *SC* over singular count nouns, *PC* over plural count nouns, and *N* over noncount nouns.

          PC

Many **countries** sent **explorers** to the Americas. They wanted **gold**.
       1   2   3

Christopher Columbus was an **explorer** for Spain. He made four **trips** to the
                             4   5

Americas. Columbus didn't find a lot of gold there, but he learned important

information about the New World.
  6

Columbus wrote **letters** about each **trip**. In his letters, he described many
              7   8

islands. The **weather** was always warm on these islands. Columbus also wrote
  9   10

about the **men** and **women** of the islands and their **clothing**. Many of the
         11   12   13

people in the New World had **jewelry**. They wore **bracelets** and **necklaces** of gold.
  14   15   16   17

Columbus was also interested in the **animals** and **plants** in the New World.
                                      18   19

He and his men tasted many new kinds of **food** there. For example, they ate
                                       20

corn for the first time. Corn was a **plant** that didn't grow in Europe. Columbus
  21   22

took **vegetables** and gold back to Spain. Soon other explorers sailed west to
      23

look for more treasures in the New World.

2 Subject–Verb Agreement with Count and Noncount Nouns: On an Island with Columbus

A. Christopher Columbus is writing in his journal. Circle the correct form of the verb in each sentence.

1. I'm sitting on a beach. The beach (is / are) long and wide.

2. I see many flowers. The flowers (looks / look) beautiful.

3. The leaves on the trees (is moving / are moving) in the wind.

4. The water (is / are) deep and blue.

5. This island (is / are) beautiful.

6. The weather here (is / are) always warm.

7. Some people here have earrings of gold. The gold (is / are) heavy.

8. The food here (is / are) new and strange. I like it.

9. My men (is / are) happy to be here.

10. Some women (is playing / are playing) music on drums.

11. Children (is singing / are singing).

12. The music (sounds / sound) nice.

B. Work with a partner. Imagine you are with Columbus and his men. You are making plans for the trip back to Spain. What do you want to take on the ship? Look at the list, and tell what is and isn't important to have. Choose no more than 10 things.

List of Supplies			
bananas	corn	music	sugar
books	eggs	oranges	tea
bread	fresh water	potatoes	vegetables
chocolate	gold	rice	warm clothing
coffee	meat	salt	

	is/isn't	important.
_____	are/aren't	

Example: Student A: **Bananas aren't important.**

Articles Before Count and Noncount Nouns*

FORM and FUNCTION

A. Articles Before Count Nouns

Before count nouns, use *the*, *a/an*, or no article:

- Use the definite article, *the*, before singular and plural nouns. Use *the* only when the noun is specific.

  Is **the teacher** here today? (one specific teacher)

  The books for that class are heavy. (specific books)

- Use the indefinite article, *a* or *an*, before singular nouns. Use *a/an* only when the noun is not specific.

  A nickel is five cents. (any nickel, not one specific nickel)

  Take **an umbrella** with you. (any umbrella, not one specific umbrella)

- Use no article before plural nouns when they are not specific.

  Apples are good for you. (plural, not specific)
  Compare: **The apples** from that tree taste good. (plural, specific)

B. Articles Before Noncount Nouns

Before noncount nouns, use the article *the* or no article:

- Use *the* before noncount nouns that are specific.

  You're a good cook. **The food** is great!

  She is counting **the money** in her wallet.

- Use no article before noncount nouns that are not specific.

  Everyone needs **food**.

  People keep **money** in banks.

*See Chapter 3, Grammar Briefing 3, page 56, for an introduction to articles.

GRAMMAR **HOT**SPOT!

Nouns that are specific and nouns that are not specific take different articles:

	COUNT NOUNS		NONCOUNT NOUNS
	SINGULAR	PLURAL	
NOUNS THAT ARE SPECIFIC	the	the	the
NOUNS THAT ARE NOT SPECIFIC	a/an	—	—

Articles Before Count and Noncount Nouns

3 *The* **Versus No Article:** **Is It Specific?**

Work alone or with a partner. The **boldfaced** nouns in these sentences are
either plural count nouns or noncount nouns. Decide if each noun is specific
or not. Then write *the* or write a dash (—) for no article.

1. Do you like ___—___ **music**? I do, but I don't like ___the___ **music** on the radio right now.
   a   b

2. Let's open a window. We need _____ **air**. _____ **air** in this room isn't fresh.
   a   b

3. This store takes _____ **cash** but not credit cards. You can use _____
   a   b

   credit cards at all the other stores in this mall.

4. _____ cold **weather** usually doesn't bother me. Do you like _____ **snow**?
   a   b

5. _____ **jeans** are comfortable to wear. My friends and I buy our jeans at _____
   a   b

   same **stores**.

6. Is _____ **coffee** in that pot still hot? I love _____ hot **coffee**.
   a   b

7. Some coins are made of _____ **silver**. _____ **silver** is a kind of metal.
   a   b

8. _____ **pennies** are made of copper. _____ **coins** in my pocket are all pennies.
   a   b

9. My history course is interesting, but _____ **homework** for the class is hard.

10. _____ **pictures** in that book are nice. Do you like _____ **photo** on the cover?
    a   b

4 Articles: An Exchange of Gifts

A. Circle the correct article for the noun. Circle the dash (—) for no article.

One day, long ago, ((an) / the) explorer from Spain
                    1

walked into (a / —) city in South America. He carried
              2

(a / —) Spanish flag and wore armor over his clothes.
  3

The king of (a / the) city went to see this strange man
              4

with white skin. (An / The) explorer looked at (a / the)
                  5   6

king. He saw (an / the) earrings and (a / the) necklaces
              7   8

of the king. (A / The) jewelry was made of (the / —)
              9   10

gold, and the explorer wanted it.

The king welcomed the explorer and gave him (a / —) food. There was (a / —)
                                              11   12

corn, and there were (the / —) tomatoes and peppers. The explorer tasted (a / the)
                      13   14

new food, and he liked it. Then he gave (the / —) gifts to the king. In return, the king
                                          15

gave (a / —) gold to the explorer. The explorer went away the next day to tell other
      16

explorers about (the / —) gold.
                  17

> *armor* = clothing made of metal to protect fighting men.

5 Articles: El Dorado

Write *a*, *an*, *the*, or a dash for no article.

Long ago, __—__ explorers in the New World heard stories about _____ cities of
           1   2

_____ gold. They heard _____ amazing story about one city, a city called El Dorado.
   3   4

_____ city was near _____ lake. _____ people of El Dorado believed that a
   5   6   7

monster lived in the lake. _____ monster was very large and had _____ big teeth.
                            8   9

The people were afraid of the monster, and they wanted to keep it happy. So they had special

ceremonies twice a year, and they put _____ gold and _____ jewels into the lake for
                                        10   11

the monster. First, all the men in the city made _____ boat. Then, on the day of the ceremony,
                                                  12

they put gold dust on their king. After that, _____ king went to the lake and sat in the boat.
                                               13

All _____ women of El Dorado carried _____ pieces of gold to the boat.
                14   15

_____ children of the city waited by the lake and watched. Finally, the men and the king
      16

took the boat to the middle of the lake and dropped the gold and jewels into _____ water.
                                                                                    17

> *a jewel* = a valuable stone such as a diamond.

 See the *Grammar Links* Website for more information about explorers in the New World.

6 **Using Articles:** **A New Place with Different Things**

A. Think about a time you arrived in a new place. What new things did you see? What new things did you eat? Write them on the chart. Use count and noncount nouns.

Things I Saw	Things I Ate

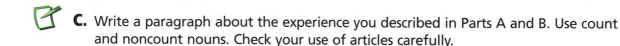 **B.** Sit with a small group, and tell your classmates about these new things.

Example: Student A: In Florida, I saw orange trees. The flowers on the trees were
            beautiful. In Florida, I ate Cuban food for the first time.

C. Write a paragraph about the experience you described in Parts A and B. Use count and noncount nouns. Check your use of articles carefully.

See the *Grammar Links* Website for a model paragraph for this assignment.

 Check your progress! Go to the Self-Test for Chapter 15 on the *Grammar Links* Website.

Gold!

Quantifiers and Measure Words

Introductory Task: Gold in the Klondike

🎧 **A.** Read and listen to this letter. Circle the words you hear.

Luke and Harry are two gold miners. They are trying to get to the town of Dawson in the Klondike (a region in northwestern Canada). Luke is writing to his wife, Molly, about the trip.

Lake Lindeman

December 14, 1898

Dear Molly,

We finally arrived at the lake. (Many / Some) people are coming
to the Klondike this year. (A lot of / Several) people are from the
United States, and (a few / some) people even come from Australia
and Europe. We all are looking for gold.

The trip up the mountains was not easy. It took (a little / a few)
time. (Some / A lot of) miners take their supplies up the White Pass
with horses. Those miners have (a lot of / a little) money. They buy
(a few / many) horses and enough food for a year. This year, there's
been (a little / a lot of) bad weather. (A few / A little) men and animals
died on the pass last month.

The other way up the mountain is the "Golden Stairs." (Many / A few) miners walk up this trail with heavy bags of food and boxes of tools. That's what we did. Harry and I went up and down the stairs 40 times with our supplies. The Golden Stairs are hard to climb and dangerous, and (a lot of / a few) miners quit. After that, we walked the 33 miles to Lake Lindeman. We are waiting here until spring, when we'll make the trip to Dawson by boat. I heard that (a lot of / a few) miners here had (a few / a little) luck last year. They found (a lot of / some) gold, and now they're rich.

I miss you.

Your husband,

Luke

a *miner* = a person who digs for minerals or metals, such as gold.
a *pass* = an opening or break through some mountains.

B. Work alone or with a partner. Look at the five quantifiers in the chart below. Quantifiers tell about the general amount or quantity. Find and <u>underline</u> these five quantifiers in Luke's letter. What nouns follow the quantifiers? Write each noun in the correct column.

Quantifiers	Count Nouns	Noncount Nouns
a lot of	*people*	*money*
many		
some		
a few		
a little		

C. Look at the chart in Part B. Complete the statements. Write the quantifiers.

1. Use __*a lot of*__ and _____ with either count or noncount nouns.

2. Use _____ and _____ with plural count nouns only.

3. Use _____ with noncount nouns only.

GRAMMAR BRIEFING 1

Quantifiers

FORM and FUNCTION

A. Overview

Quantifiers tell about quantity—the general amount or number of something. They do not tell specific amounts or numbers. Use quantifiers before nouns.

a large quantity (*many coins, a lot of money*)

a small quantity (*a few coins, a little money*)

(continued on next page)

B. Meanings of Quantifiers

1. Use *many, much, a lot of,* or *lots of* to mean a large number or amount.

> There were **many** people, more than 100.
>
> There was **a lot of** noise from all the cars.
>
> There wasn't **much** time—only minutes.

2. Use *several, a few,* or *a little* to mean a small number or amount.

> **Several** students were absent.
>
> I made **a few** mistakes.
>
> We had only **a little** homework.

3. Use *some* to mean a number or amount that isn't known or isn't definite.

> They ate **some** cookies.
>
> We have **some** time but not much.

4. Use *no* to mean zero or none.

   Do not use *no* and *not* together.

> There are **no** classes on weekends.
>
> We have **no** homework.
>   **NOT:** We ~~don't~~ have no homework.

5. Use *enough* to mean the amount or number that is needed or correct.

> There aren't **enough** cups for all of us.
>
> Did you have **enough** money?

C. Quantifiers with Plural Count Nouns and with Noncount Nouns

A large quantity

None

	WITH PLURAL COUNT NOUNS	WITH NONCOUNT NOUNS	WITH BOTH
	many	**much**	**a lot of/lots of**
			enough
	several		**some**
	a few	**a little**	
			no

1. Some quantifiers can be used with only one kind of noun:

   - Use *many, several,* and *a few* with plural count nouns only.

   > **Several boys** came to the party.
   >
   > **A few girls** sat at the back of the room.

   - Use *much* and *a little* with noncount nouns only.

   > Is there **much work** to do?
   >
   > He drank **a little coffee**.

2. Some quantifiers can be used with both plural count nouns and noncount nouns. These include *a lot of, lots of, some, no,* and *enough.*

   > He has **a lot of friends**.
   >   They have **a lot of fun** together.
   >
   > She wore **no earrings**. She wore **no jewelry** at all.

	WRITE	YOU WILL OFTEN HEAR
1. In conversation, the quantifier *a lot of* often sounds like "allota." The quantifier *lots of* sounds like "lotsa."	He had **a lot of** friends.	He had "alotta" friends.
	We have **lots of** time.	We have "lotsa" time.
	WRITE IN A PAPER FOR SCHOOL	**WRITE OR SAY TO A FRIEND**
2. *Lots of* has the same meaning as *a lot of*, but it is more informal.	There was **a lot of** information.	There was **lots of/a lot of** information.

GRAMMAR PRACTICE 1

Quantifiers

There were 30,000 people in Dawson in the summer of 1898.

1 **Quantifiers:** Klondike Entertainment

A. Read this tourist information about the town of Dawson in northwestern Canada. Circle the correct quantifiers.

Welcome to Dawson! Dawson was famous in the late 1800s. There were

(many / much) gold mines there. Today Dawson is a small town with (a few / a little)
  1   2

old cabins, (many / much) new buildings, and (several / a little) gold mines. The city
              3   4

is still busy and exciting. There are (enough / much) things to do in Dawson to keep
                                        5

visitors happy. Here are (a few / a little) ideas of places to go.
                          6

Do you want (a few / a little) entertainment? *Diamond-Tooth Gertie's* has
7
(a lot of / much) games. When you go there, you need (several / some) money and
8   9
(a lot of / many) luck. Do you want gold? *Claim 33* sells a pan with (several / some)
10   11
dirt in it for $5. But there's gold in the pan, too! You just need to do (a few / a little)
12
work to find it.

Are you hungry? Try *Nancy's*. You can get delicious soup and sandwiches there. The
coffee is good, too. Do you need (a few / a little) supplies for camping or (several / some)
13   14
food for a picnic by the river? *Dawson General Store* has everything you need.

Maybe you are worried about the weather. Dawson has (many / a lot of) snow in
15
the winter—about four feet of snow every month—but there's (several / no) snow in
16
the summer, and there isn't even (many / much) rain. There's always (many / a lot of)
17   18
fresh air. Come and visit us in Dawson!

> *entertainment* = (noncount) things people can watch or do for fun.
> *a cabin* = a small house made of wood, usually in the mountains or forest.

 B. Work with a partner. Tell about the place where you are from or a place you once
visited. Use the quantifiers below with nouns from the list or your own nouns.

Example: I visited Tampa, Florida. There are lots of tourists. There is no cold weather.
There are some nice beaches.

Quantifiers

some	a lot of	lots of	no	enough

Nouns

entertainment	mountains	restaurants	tourists
gold mines	places to hear music	snow	_____
houses	rain	stores	_____

 C. Write a paragraph about the place you described in Part B. Include statements
with quantifiers.

See the *Grammar Links* Website for a model paragraph for this assignment.

2 Quantifiers: Lucky Luke and Sad Harry

A. Work alone or with a partner. Complete the statement about Lucky Luke with the correct quantifier. Use the other quantifier to write a statement about Sad Harry.

Luke and Harry arrived in Dawson in 1899. Their experiences in the Klondike were very different. Luke had good luck. Now people call him "Lucky Luke." Harry had bad luck. People call him "Sad Harry."

Quantifiers	Lucky Luke	Sad Harry
a lot of, no	1. I had __no__ trouble on the trail. Not a single problem!	I had a lot of trouble. I had problems all the time.
a lot of, a little	2. There was only _____ rain in the area where I was.	_____
many, a few	3. I caught _____ fish in the river. I was never hungry.	_____
no, enough	4. I had _____ supplies for the whole summer.	_____
a lot of, no	5. I was very lucky. I found _____ gold.	_____
many, a few	6. I saw only _____ wolves, and they soon went away.	_____
no, many	7. There were _____ other miners near me. I had the place all to myself.	_____
no, enough	8. I have _____ money now, but I don't want to leave. I love it here.	_____

B. Work in a group. Share your statements about Sad Harry. Add more information about Sad Harry's experiences.

Example: Student A: *Sad Harry had a lot of trouble. He had some problems with bears.*

3   Using *A Lot Of*, *Lots Of*, *A Little*, and *A Few*: Lots of Luck

Work in a group. Read the things in the following box. Think about your friends and family. Tell about the amounts they have. Use *a little*, *a few*, *a lot of*, or *lots of*. Add more information.

good luck	bad luck	free time
money	friends	photos
CDs	homework	fun

Example: Student A: *My mother has lots of good luck. She always wins in card games with her friends. But she doesn't win lots of money.*

Student B: *My friend had a lot of bad luck last year. He broke his arm—twice!*

GRAMMAR BRIEFING 2

Measure Words

FORM and FUNCTION

A. Types of Measure Words

Use measure words to tell about specific quantities of things. There are different types of measure words:

• Words for containers.	a **bag** of apples, a **bottle** of milk, a **box** of cookies, a **can** of beans, a **jar** of jam
• Words for weights.	an **ounce** of gold, a **pound** of nails, a **ton** of dirt
• Words for volume (how much space something fills).	a **cup** of sugar, a **gallon** of gas, a **quart** of blueberries, a **teaspoon** of salt
• Words to measure how long or deep something is.	a **foot** of string, a **yard** of cloth, an **inch** of snow

(continued on next page)

B. Words Used with Measure Words

1. Use measure words with both plural count nouns and noncount nouns.	*With count nouns*: a box of **matches**, two bags of **apples** *With noncount nouns*: a box of **cereal**, two bags of **rice**
2. Use an article, a number, or a quantifier before a measure word. Use *of* after it.	He bought: **a** can **of** juice. **two** cans **of** juice. **a few** cans **of** juice.

Measure Words

4 **Listening for Measure Words:** Shopping in Dawson

Read the supplies on Luke's list. Then listen to the conversation and complete the list. Use singular and plural forms of the words from the box. Some words are used more than once.

It's August 10, 1899. Lucky Luke is at the general store in Dawson. He's getting supplies from Irma, the store owner.

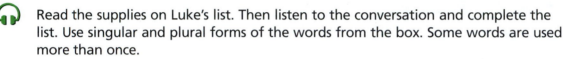

bag	can	pound
bottle	foot	quart
box	ounce	yard

Luke's List

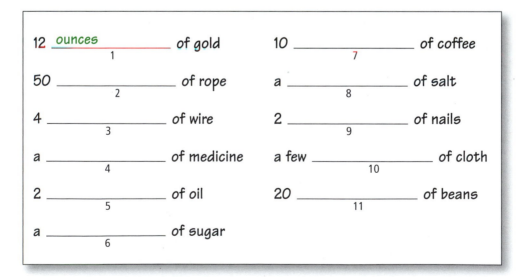

12 _ounces_ of gold — 1
50 _____ of rope — 2
4 _____ of wire — 3
a _____ of medicine — 4
2 _____ of oil — 5
a _____ of sugar — 6

10 _____ of coffee — 7
a _____ of salt — 8
2 _____ of nails — 9
a few _____ of cloth — 10
20 _____ of beans — 11

5 **Measure Words:** The Usual Amounts

A. Look at the pictures below. They show the way stores in the United States often sell certain foods.

B. Work with a partner. Student A: Say a type of food listed in the picture. Student B: Say the food with its measure word. Take turns.

Example: Student A: *Cheese.*
           Student B: *A pound of cheese.*

C. With your partner, make a shopping list of 10 or more items for a class party. Think of food, drink, and other supplies. Include measure words with numbers, articles, and quantifiers. Then tell the class some of the things you need.

Example: *two bags of potato chips, a few bottles of soda, a lot of paper cups, . . .*

GRAMMAR BRIEFING 3

Quantifiers and Measure Words in Affirmative and Negative Statements

FORM

A. Measure Words and Most Quantifiers

Measure words and most quantifiers can be used in both affirmative and negative statements:

AFFIRMATIVE	NEGATIVE
I **bought** a **bag** of apples.	I **didn't buy** a **bag** of apples.
He **has many** friends.	He **doesn't have many** friends.

(continued on next page)

B. The Quantifiers *No, Some, Any,* and *Much*

1. Use *no* + noun only in statements with affirmative verbs. In statements with *not,* use *any* + noun instead.

We **have no** books.

We **don't have any** books.
    NOT: We ~~don't have no~~ books.

There **is no** paper.

There **isn't any** paper.
    NOT: There ~~isn't no~~ paper.

2. Use *some* in affirmative statements. *Any* usually replaces *some* in negative statements.

We **ate some** sandwiches.

They **didn't eat any** sandwiches.

I **had some** coffee.

I **didn't have any** tea.

3. Use *much* only in negative statements. Use *a lot of* or *lots of* in affirmative or negative statements.

We **don't have much** free time, but they **have a lot** of free time.
    NOT: They have ~~much~~ free time.

Quantifiers and Measure Words in Affirmative and Negative Statements

6 *No, Some,* and *Any* in Affirmative and Negative Statements:
Trying to Make Gold

A. Read about a man who tried to make gold. Complete the statements with *no* or *any.*

Johann Böttger was a scientist in Germany about 300 years ago.

He lived in small rooms in a large castle. Johann didn't go to school

to study science. There were <u>   no   </u> schools for scientists
                                    1

where he lived. Instead, he learned from old books. Johann had a

lab, but he didn't have _____ modern equipment. There
                               2

wasn't _____ electricity for lights, so he probably used candles. Johann probably had
            3

_____ assistants and usually worked alone. He probably didn't have _____ ways
       4   5

to meet other scientists, either.

A Castle in Germany

B. Complete the statements with *some* or *any*.

Johann had __*some*__ interesting ideas about chemistry. He believed it was possible to
1

make gold. To test his ideas about gold, he tried several experiments. In one experiment,

Johann put _____ chemicals together in a jar, but the chemicals didn't change into
2

gold. Next, he poured _____ chemicals on _____ silver, but he didn't get
3   4

_____ gold that way, either. Finally, he cooked _____ chemicals in a jar, but he
5   6

still didn't have _____ luck making gold. But when he looked in the jar, Johann found
7

something else very valuable. It was porcelain! At that time, people from Europe needed to

travel to Asia to buy porcelain. Johann didn't find _____
8

new ways to make gold, but he became famous for his porcelain.

Chinese Porcelain

> *chemistry* = the study of substances and how they change or
> combine with other substances. *a chemical* = a substance used in
> or made by a scientific process.

7   *No* and *Any* in Affirmative and Negative Statements: The Life of a Scientist

A. Work with a partner. Student A: Read a statement with *no* about life for
Johann Böttger and other people in the 1700s. Student B: Change it to a
negative statement with *any*. Take turns.

Example: Student A: **Johann had no computers.**
          Student B: **He didn't have any computers.**

1. Johann had no computers.
2. He had no electric lights.
3. He had no helpers in his lab.
4. There were no microscopes.
5. There were no radios at that time.
6. Most people had no books.
7. They had no telephones.
8. Most people had no time for vacations.

A Microscope

B. Continue with your partner. Student A: Read a statement with *any*. Student B: Change it to a statement with *no*. Take turns.

1. There weren't any children in Johann's lab.

2. He didn't have any safety glasses or gloves to wear.

3. Johann didn't have any time for a vacation.

4. He didn't have any modern equipment.

5. He didn't have any assistants.

6. There weren't any computers.

7. People didn't have any electricity.

8. Johann didn't have any luck making gold.

8 **Using *Some* and *Any* in Affirmative and Negative Statements: Böttger's Lab**

Work with a partner. Look at the picture of Johann Böttger's science laboratory. Make statements about the supplies he had or didn't have. Use *some* and *any* in your statements. Take turns.

Example: He didn't have any electric lights.

9 *Much* and *A Lot Of* in Affirmative and Negative Statements: The 1700s and Today

A. Complete the statements about life in the 1700s and life today. Use *much* when possible. When *much* is not possible, use *a lot of*.

1. In the 1700s, there wasn't <u>much</u> science equipment. Today,
   a

   there is <u>a lot of</u> science equipment.
   b

2. Today, we have _____ information about the moon. In the
   a

   1700s, there wasn't _____ information about it.
   b

3. Today, we have _____ entertainment: movies, TV, music, and
   a

   so on. People in the 1700s didn't have _____ entertainment.
   b

4. Doctors didn't earn _____ money back then. Most doctors
   a

   earn _____ money today.
   b

5. People didn't buy _____ food back then. They grew
   a

   _____ their food.
   b

B. Work alone or with a partner. Write four more statements about life in the 1700s and four more statements about life today. Use *much* and *a lot of* + noncount nouns (such as *education*, *time*, *information*, and so on).

10 **Measure Words and Quantifiers in Statements:** What's in Your Refrigerator?

Work with a partner. Imagine that you just went food shopping and spent a lot of money. Now you have a refrigerator full of the things you like to eat and drink. Student A: Name a kind of food or drink. Student B: Tell if you do or don't have it in your refrigerator. Take turns. Use *some*, *any*, *no*, *much*, and *a lot of* and measure words in your statements.

Examples: Student A: Soda.
Student B: I have a lot of cans of soda. Milk.
Student A: I don't have much milk. Ice cream . . .

Quantifiers and Measure Words in Questions; *Wh-* Questions with *How Much* and *How Many*

FORM and FUNCTION

A. Measure Words and Quantifiers in Questions

1. Measure words and most quantifiers can be used in questions.	Do you have a **cup** of sugar? Were there **any** problems?

2. The quantifier *any* is more common than *some* in *yes/no* questions.

MORE COMMON	LESS COMMON
Is there **any** paper?	Is there **some** paper?
Did you buy **any** gifts?	Did you buy **some** gifts?

3. The quantifier *no* is not usual in *yes/no* or *wh-* questions. Use *any* instead, or don't use a quantifier.	Didn't you have **any money**?
	
	Didn't you have **money**?
	  NOT USUALLY: Did you have no money?
	
	Why didn't you have **any money**?
	
	Why didn't you have **money**?
	  NOT USUALLY: Why did you have no money?

B. Asking and Answering Questions with *How Much* and *How Many*

1. *How much* and *how many* are *wh-* question words. Use them to ask about quantities or amounts.

- Use *how much* to ask about noncount nouns.

  How much time do we have?
  How much information did you find?

- Use *how many* to ask about count nouns.

  How many students are in the class?
  How many children do they have?

2. Quantifiers and measure words are common in answers to questions with *how much* or *how many*.

Q: How much money do you need?
A: Only **a little**.
Q: How many oranges did you buy?
A: Five **pounds**.

Quantifiers and Measure Words in Questions; *Wh-* Questions with *How Much* and *How Many*

11 *Any* **in Questions:** Treasure Island

Robert Louis Stevenson wrote *Treasure Island*, a book about pirates and buried treasure. Read the answers about the book. Then write the *yes/no* questions with *any* that the **boldfaced** sentences answer.

1. _Are there any pirates in the story?_

   Yes, there are some pirates in the story. Jim Hawkins, a young English boy, has the pirates' treasure map.

2. _____

   Yes, Jim tells some other people about the map. These men get a ship and find sailors to take them to the island on the map.

3. _____

   No, no women go on this trip.

4. _____

   Yes, there is some trouble on the ship. The sailors are really pirates.

5. _____

   Yes, there are some fights on the ship.

6. _____

   No, no "good guys" die in the story. But the pirates take control of the ship.

7. _____

   Yes, there is one person already on the island. His name is Ben Gunn.

8. _____

   Yes, there is some treasure on the island. But it isn't buried in the sand.

9. _____

   Yes, Jim and his friends have some luck. They get their ship back and leave with the treasure.

10. _____

    No, no pirates go with them. They have to stay on the island.

11. _____

    No, Robert Louis Stevenson didn't know any pirates. He used his imagination to write the story.

> *buried treasure* = gold and other valuable things hidden in a hole in the ground.

12 Questions with *How Much* and *How Many*: Blackbeard, the Pirate (?–1718)

Complete the questions with *how much* or *how many*.

Blackbeard was a pirate who lived 300 years ago. His real name was Edward Teach. He and his men robbed many ships near Charleston, South Carolina.

Questions

Answers

1. __How many__ ships did Blackbeard rob during his career?

   Between 50 and 100.

2. _____ sailors were on his ship, the *Queen Anne's Revenge*?

   About 150.

3. _____ gold was there on his ship?

   Several tons.

4. _____ food did the pirates need on the ship?

   A lot. They stopped often to steal food.

5. _____ money did the British offer as a reward for catching Blackbeard?

   The British offered £100 (100 pounds).

6. Blackbeard often put burning candles in his beard to scare people. _____ candles did he usually put in his beard?

   About 10 candles.

7. Blackbeard asked the city of Charleston for medicine for his sailors. _____ medicine did the city give Blackbeard?

   A lot. It cost about $2,500.

8. _____ time did Blackbeard spend in prison?

   None. He was killed in a fight with the British Royal Navy.

9. _____ wives did Blackbeard have?

   Fourteen. But they didn't get his treasure. He buried it.

Did Blackbeard look like this?

 See the *Grammar Links* Website for more information about Blackbeard.

13 **Questions with *How Much* and *How Many*:** Fill Your Own Treasure Chest

A. Imagine you have a treasure chest. What's in it? Add two other items to the Treasure List. Then complete the list with quantifiers and measure words. Use five or more of the words from the box.

a few	a lot of	box(es)	pound(s)
a little	bag(s)	many	ton(s)

What's inside?

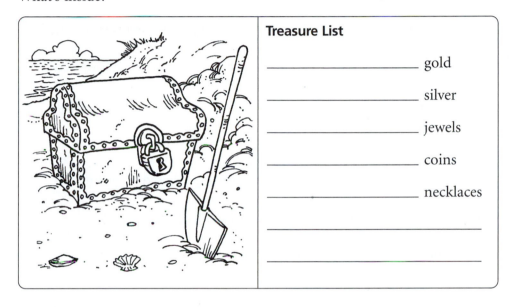

Treasure List

_____ gold

_____ silver

_____ jewels

_____ coins

_____ necklaces

_____

_____

B. Work with a partner. Take turns asking and answering questions with *How much* and *How many* about the things in your treasure chests. To learn about other items added, ask *What else is in your chest?* Ask *How much* and *how many* questions about these items, too.

Example: Student A: How much gold do you have?
               Student B: One ton of gold. How many coins do you have?
               Student A: Six bags of coins.

14 Editing: The Real Treasure Island?

Read about Cocos Island. There are 10 errors in sentences with quantifiers and measure words. Some errors can be corrected in more than one way. The first error is corrected for you.

<u>many</u>

Cocos Island is near Costa Rica. It has ~~much~~ beautiful beaches, any high

mountains, and a lot of flowers and trees. There are also many stories about buried

treasure. Here is one of them.

In 1821, the city of Lima, Peru, had much gold. The people of Lima were worried

about it. They asked a man named Captain Thompson to take it to Spain for safety.

"How many gold do you have?" he asked. "Several tons gold," they said. The captain

promised to take it to Spain. Soon he sailed away with the gold, but he didn't go to

Spain. Instead, he sailed to Cocos Island. Three Spanish ships chased after him, but

they never caught him. On the island, they found only a little coins.

Did Captain Thompson bury the gold on the island? He had only a few time there

to move the gold from the ship. Maybe he did not have time enough. Many explorers

looked on the island, but they didn't find no treasure. Did he drop the gold into the

water near the island? Nobody knows because swimming is dangerous there. There are

alot of sharks in the water. Today, Cocos Island is a national park of Costa Rica. Maybe

the treasure is still there.

Check your progress! Go to the Self-Test for Chapter 16 on the _Grammar Links_ Website.

17

The Good, the Bad, and Their Money

Subjects and Objects; Pronouns

Introductory Task: A Salesman's Story

A. Listen and read this true story about an unusual salesman.

"Jan" (not his real name) was a salesman. He lived in Central Europe, near Karlstein Castle. **Jan** often <u>visited</u> the castle. There, **he** <u>saw</u> many tourists. Some American tourists came one day, and **they** <u>liked</u> the castle very much. They wanted to buy it, and they thought Jan was the owner. The tourists asked, "How much does this castle cost?" Jan gave an answer. The **tourists** <u>had</u> the money, so **they** <u>gave</u> it to Jan for the castle. Then the Americans hired some workers. The **workers** <u>took</u> stones from the castle and put them on trucks. At that point, Jan left for a vacation. Then the real owner of the castle came home and saw the workers and the Americans. He asked, "What are you doing?"

Karlstein Castle

They answered, "**We**'re <u>moving</u> the castle. **We** <u>bought</u> it. It's ours. We're taking it to the United States."

"But this is *MY* castle, not yours! Who are you? Who sold my castle to you?" The **owner** <u>called</u> the police. But **they** <u>didn't find</u> Jan.

Jan traveled and spent lots of money. Soon he had no money, so when he was in Paris, he tried his trick again. He sold the Eiffel Tower to some tourists. But this time, Jan was not lucky. The French **police** <u>caught</u> him and <u>put</u> him in jail.

The Eiffel Tower

> *hire* = give a job to (a person). *a trick* = an action that a person does to fool or cheat someone. *jail* = the place where police put people they arrest.

B. Circle the answer or answers to each question. (Sometimes there are two answers.)

1. Look at the **boldfaced** words in the story. They are the subjects of sentences. The subject tells who or what does the action. What kinds of words are subjects?

    nouns   verbs   pronouns

2. Look at the <u>underlined</u> words. They follow the subjects. What kind of words are they?

    nouns   verbs   pronouns

3. Look at the **boldfaced** words that follow the verbs in the sentences below. They are direct objects.

    The workers took **stones** from the castle.

    The workers put **them** on trucks.

    We bought **it**.

    They didn't find **Jan**.

    The direct object tells who or what receives the action of the verb. What kinds of words are direct objects?

    nouns   verbs   pronouns

GRAMMAR BRIEFING 1

Subjects and Objects—Nouns and Pronouns

FORM and FUNCTION

A. Subject and Object Pronouns

SUBJECT PRONOUNS	OBJECT PRONOUNS
I	me
you	you
he	him
she	her
it	it
we	us
you	you
they	them

(continued on next page)

B. Nouns and Pronouns as Subjects and Objects

1. An English sentence has a subject (S) and a verb (V). In some sentences, the verb has a direct object (DO). Use the word order: S + V (+ DO).

   S   V
   The students left.

   S   V   DO
   They left the room.

2. The subject of a sentence tells who or what the sentence is about. The subject can be:

   • A noun (+ the words that go with it).

   The new doctor was young.

   Mrs. Reed loves the park.

   • A subject pronoun.

   He was young.

   She loves the park.

3. A direct object tells who or what receives the action of the verb. The direct object can be:

   • A noun (+ the words that go with it).

   We looked at **the people**.

   She didn't buy **the funny postcard**.

   • An object pronoun.

   We looked at **them**.

   She didn't buy **it**.

4. Some sentences have prepositional phrases. Prepositional phrases have a preposition + an object of the preposition. The object can be an object pronoun or a noun (+ the words that go with it).

   They talked about the **girl**. They talked about **her**.

   I sat with **Al Jordan**. I sat with **him**.

Subjects and Objects—Nouns and Pronouns

1 **Identifying Subjects, Verbs, and Direct Objects:** The Story of King Midas, Part 1

Look at each **boldfaced** sentence. Circle the subject. Underline the verb. Draw a box around the direct object when there is one.

Long ago, in a country far away, there lived an unhappy king. This king's name was Midas.

(1) King Midas had a fine castle. (2) **He also had a beautiful garden.** It was full of roses. (3) **The king loved his roses.** They smelled beautiful. Midas also had a lot of money and gold, and he loved these things, too. But Midas still wasn't happy.

One day, the king's servants were at work in the garden. (4) **There, they saw a strange man.** (5) **They brought him to the king.** The king recognized this man at once. He was really a god with great powers. King Midas decided to be nice to this powerful god.

"Welcome! Are you hungry? (6) **My servants are bringing food and drink,**" said Midas. The god thanked Midas. (7) **Then they sat down together.** They ate dinner and listened to music.

The god wanted to do something for King Midas in return for his kindness. (8) **So, after dinner, he gave a special gift to the king.** He gave him one wish. (9) **King Midas thought for a long time.** Then he said, "This is my wish: When I touch things, the things will change into gold."

"Are you sure you want that wish?" asked the god.

"Yes," said Midas. (10) **Midas touched a chair.** (11) **It changed.** Now he had a gold chair.

> *a servant* = a person who works in the house of another person.
> *recognize* = know.

2 **Identifying Subject and Object Pronouns; Objects of Prepositions: The Story of King Midas, Part 2**

A. Look at the **boldfaced** pronouns. Write *SP* over subject pronouns and *OP* over object pronouns.

                                         SP

King Midas was excited. **He** touched a cup. **It** changed into gold. Midas
                              1   2

saw some dishes. He touched **them**. More gold. "**I** am so happy!" he cried.
                                  3   4

Then he went out into his garden.

The servants were curious, so **they** followed their king and they watched
                                           5

him. In the garden, Midas touched all the roses. He now had a garden of
  6

gold, but it didn't smell beautiful.

Finally, Midas grew tired. He went inside and sat down. He was hungry.

He said to a servant, "Do **you** have any grapes? Bring some to **me**." The
           7   8

servant brought some fruit and put it down near **him.** Midas touched the
                                9

green grapes, and they changed to gold. They were beautiful, but Midas was

still hungry. He began to worry.

Then his daughter entered the room. **She** was young and beautiful. She ran to
               10

him. "I love **you**," she said. Midas kissed **her**, and she changed to gold. Midas was
 11   12   13

horrified! He found the god and said, "Please help my family! Please help **us**! I don't
                                                   14

want this wish anymore!" The god gave Midas instructions.

Midas went to a river and washed in **it**. Then he touched a
                              15

stone, but **it** didn't change into gold. He went home, and
         16

his daughter ran to meet **him.** Midas was finally happy.
                      17

Today, people still find pieces of Midas's gold in that river.

The story of Midas is a lesson for **us.**
                             18

> *curious* = interested, wanting to know something. *horrified* = feeling a
> terrible shock.

B. Which object pronouns from Part 2 of the story are objects of prepositions?
Write the five prepositional phrases here. The first one is done for you.

1. _to me_____

2. _____

3. _____

4. _____

5. _____

3 Object Pronouns: Getting the Story Straight

Complete the answers to questions about the story of King Midas.
Use object pronouns.

1. Did the servants call the king?   No, the king called _them_.

2. Did the god welcome Midas?   No, Midas welcomed _____.

3. Did the god say, "I invited you to dinner"?   No, he said, "You invited _____."

4. Did Midas pick up the chair?   No, he touched _____.

5. Did Midas eat the grapes?   No, he couldn't eat _____.

6. Did Midas's daughter say, "You love me"? No, she said, "I love _____."

7. Did she change her father into gold?   No, Midas changed _____.

8. Did Midas send the god to a river?   No, the god sent _____.

9. Did Midas and his daughter help the god? No, the god helped _____.

10. Did they say, "We helped the god"?   No, they said, "The god helped _____."

4 Using Object Pronouns: Questions and Answers

Work with a partner. Student A: Ask a question with *Do you know* or *Do you like* + a noun direct object. Student B: Listen and answer with words from the boxes. Take turns.

Example: Student A: Do you know Itza?
           Student B: No, I don't know her. Do you like Jackie Chan movies?
           Student A: Yes, I like them.

Yes, I	like	him.
		her.
	know	it.
No, I don't		them.

Possessive Pronouns; Review of Possessive Adjectives and Possessive Nouns

FORM and FUNCTION

A. Possessive Adjectives and Possessive Pronouns

POSSESSIVE ADJECTIVES	POSSESSIVE PRONOUNS
my	mine
your	yours
his	his
her	hers
its	—
our	ours
your	yours
their	theirs

B. Meanings and Uses of Possessive Adjectives and Possessive Pronouns

1. Possessive adjectives and possessive pronouns show that someone owns or possesses something.

   Possessive adjective: That is **my** car.
   Possessive pronoun: That car is **mine**.

2. Possessive adjectives (PA) are used before nouns (N).

          PA   N
   This is **our classroom**.
             PA   N
   Is this **your book**?

3. A possessive pronoun takes the place of a possessive adjective + a noun.

   Use a possessive pronoun alone. A noun never follows it.

   She has **her paper**. → She has **hers**.
   This is **their room**. → This is **theirs**.

   This is my hat. It is **mine**.
     NOT: It is ~~mine hat~~.

(continued on next page)

C. Possessive Nouns

1. Possessive nouns also show that someone owns or possesses something. To form a possessive noun, always use an apostrophe ('). Add:

   - An *'s* to singular nouns and to plural nouns that do not end in *s*.

     the **man's** book (singular noun)

     Carlos's sister (singular noun)

     the **children's** toys (plural noun that does not end in *s*)

   - An *'* alone to plural nouns that end in *s*.

     the **players'** shirts

     the **Johnsons'** house

2. A possessive noun can be used alone or before another noun.

   That office is **Mr. Smith's**.

   That is **Mr. Smith's office**.

GRAMMAR PRACTICE 2

Possessive Pronouns; Review of Possessive Adjectives and Possessive Nouns

5 **Identifying Possessive Adjectives and Possessive Pronouns: A Millionaire and His Money**

Look at the **boldfaced** words in the conversation. Write *PA* over possessive adjectives and *PP* over possessive pronouns.

A reporter is interviewing Andrew Carnegie some time in the early 1900s. Carnegie was a very rich man. He gave away a lot of money.

Reporter: Mr. Carnegie, you gave away a lot of **your** money.
                                                  PA
                                                  1

Carnegie: Yes, I think it's important for rich people to use **their** money for good
                                                       2

        things. I want to help **my** children and **yours**. **Our** children need public
                                  3   4   5

        libraries, museums, and good schools. The future is **theirs**.
                                                               6

Reporter: Tell me about your life.

Carnegie: My family came here from Scotland. We were poor, and we all worked

   many different jobs. At first, my brother Tom and I worked in a cloth

   factory. **His** job was easy because he was young. I was 12 years old, so **mine**
   7   8

   was a little more work. My salary was low—$1.20 a week. **His** was the same.
                                                                           9

   The factory didn't pay much money to **its** workers.
                                            10

Reporter: Later you worked for the railroad, right?

Carnegie: That's right. Railroads were very important. I enjoyed my work at the

   railroad. I became a supervisor and hired my brother and my cousin Maria.

   His job was in my office, and **hers** was in the telegraph office.
                                 11

Reporter: What other jobs did you have?

Carnegie: Well, after the railroad, I started some businesses—iron, steel. I built

   big factories.

Reporter: The Carnegie Steel Company was **yours**, right?
                                            12

Carnegie: Yes, but I sold that business in 1901. I was 65 years old, and it was time for

   me to use **my** money, not make more money. I want to give something to
            13

   our community and to the world.
    14

Reporter: Thank you, Mr. Carnegie, for **your** time and for being so generous.
                                        15

> *a salary* = money paid for work. *a supervisor* = a person who manages
> workers. *generous* = willing to give money, time, etc., to other people.

6 Possessive Adjectives and Possessive Pronouns: Carnegie Hall

A. Read about Carnegie Hall. Circle the correct possessive adjective or possessive pronoun.

1. Carnegie Hall got (its / his) name from Andrew Carnegie.

2. Carnegie was very rich. (His / Its) money built the hall.

3. The hall is in New York City. (Its / Their) address is 154 West 57th Street.

4. Many famous musicians play at Carnegie Hall. (Their / Theirs) concerts are popular.

5. The Beatles gave a concert there. (Theirs / Their) was sold out—every seat was sold.

B. Two friends are talking about a concert at Carnegie Hall. Write the correct possessive word (adjective or pronoun) that is related to the subject pronoun in parentheses.

Marta: ___My___ brother and I went to a concert last Saturday with some
          1 (I)

friends. It was great, but _____ seats were really far from the stage!
                            2 (we)

Oscar: Were _____ seats in the center or on the side?
             3 (you)

Marta: In the center. _____ was in the next-to-last row. My brother got a
                      4 (I)

seat with his friends. _____ were behind _____.
                       5 (They)   6 (I)

Oscar: Whose concert was it?

Marta: A young Russian girl played the piano. _____ music was beautiful.
                                              7 (she)

Oscar: You know, _____ band is planning a concert.
                 8 (we)

Marta: At Carnegie Hall?

Oscar: I wish!

Marta: Where are you going to have _____ concert?
                                   9 (you)

Oscar: At the student center. Are you coming?

7 Possessive Nouns: Philanthropists

Bill and Melinda Gates

Complete each sentence with the possessive form of the noun in parentheses ( ).

A philanthropist is a person who gives away a lot of money.

A __*philanthropist's*__ goal is to help people.
     1 (philanthropist)

Andrew Carnegie was a famous American philanthropist.

_____ fortune came from steel production.
2 (Carnegie)

This _____ money built many libraries. John D. Rockefeller was an important
    3 (man)

philanthropist, too. He made his money in oil, and he was _____ first billionaire.
                                                   4 (America)

He and his family gave away a lot of money. The _____ gifts to the public add
                                         5 (Rockefellers)

up to millions of dollars. Their _____ name is on many buildings.
                                 6 (family)

_____ money comes from Microsoft. His _____ success made
7 (Bill Gates)   8 (company)

him very rich. These three _____ fortunes came from their businesses, but not
                              9 (men)

all philanthropists are businesspeople. Margaret Rey wrote _____ books, and
                                        10 (children)

Gladys Holm was a secretary, but they became millionaires. These _____ gifts
                                             11 (ladies)

went to hospitals and libraries. Another _____ money came from winning an
                                  12 (woman)

eight-million-dollar lottery. This woman, Eleanor Boyer, gave it all to her church.

8 Using Possessive Nouns, Possessive Pronouns, and Possessive Adjectives: Whose Is It?

Student A: Point to something in the classroom that belongs to someone. Ask a question with *Whose*. Student B: Answer in two ways, with two different possessive words. Take turns. Use possessive nouns, possessive pronouns, and possessive adjectives in your answers.

Example: Student A: *Whose hat is that?*
                 Student B: *That's Ahmed's hat. It's his. Whose knapsack is that?*
                 Student A: *It's mine. It's my knapsack.*

Indefinite Pronouns

FORM and FUNCTION

A. Overview

The indefinite pronouns include:

	SOME-	ANY-	NO-
+ -ONE	someone	anyone	no one
+ -BODY	somebody	anybody	nobody
+ -THING	something	anything	nothing

B. Meanings of Indefinite Pronouns

1. An indefinite pronoun with:

   - The ending *-one* or *-body* refers to people. (These endings have the same meaning.)

   - The ending *-thing* refers to things.

   Someone is here. (A person is here.)

   I didn't see **anybody**. (I didn't see any people.)

   We didn't eat **anything**. (We didn't eat any food.)

   I have **nothing** to read. (I have no book or newspaper, etc.)

2. An indefinite pronoun with:

   - *Some-* refers to a person or thing that is not known or not named.

   - *Any-* often refers to a person or thing that is not specific.

   - *No-* means "not one person" or "not one thing."

   Someone called for you. (I don't know who.)

   Can you help me with **something**? (The thing is not named.)

   Invite **anyone** you want. (not a specific person, all people)

   He'll eat **anything**. (not a specific food, all kinds of food)

   Nobody called. (Not one person called.)

   There's **nothing** to do. (There's not one thing to do.)

(continued on next page)

C. Uses of Indefinite Pronouns in Sentences

1. An indefinite pronoun can be a subject.	**Somebody** is at the door. **Nothing** is wrong.
2. An indefinite pronoun can be the object of a verb or a preposition.	He didn't **say anything**. I want to go **with someone**.
3. In negative statements, use indefinite pronouns with *any-*, not with *no-*.	There **wasn't anyone** home. **NOT:** There ~~wasn't no one~~ home.

Indefinite Pronouns

9 **Indefinite Pronouns: A Thief?**

A. Read this strange but true story. Circle the eight indefinite pronouns. The first one is circled for you.

Mr. X worked at a bank. He did (something) unusual there and got a lot of money, but he didn't take it from anyone. He didn't steal anything. He borrowed people's money for a little time. For years, nobody knew anything about it. Then somebody found out. By then, Mr. X was rich. Very rich! His bank account was full of money. The bank president asked him about it. "I didn't take anything from anyone," Mr. X said. How did Mr. X do it?

B. Continue with the story of Mr. X. Circle the correct pronoun.

At the bank, Mr. X received checks. Customers sent the checks to the bank every month to pay for loans. They often sent their checks early.

Mr. X put the early checks into his own savings account. After several days, he took the money from his account and gave it to the bank. Mr. X kept the interest from the customers' money in his own account. Mr. X didn't cause any problems. (Anyone / (No one)) was hurt. (Anything / Nothing) was lost. The bank received its
          1   2
money on time.

Finally, (somebody / anybody) in the bank noticed Mr. X's savings account. The
                        3
person thought, "(Something / Someone) seems wrong here. Why does Mr. X have
                                  4

all this money?" Then the bank officers learned about it, and they were angry and called the police. The bank officers also told their customers about Mr. X. But the customers were not angry. They didn't lose (nothing / anything). A judge said that
5
(anyone / no one) was hurt, so Mr. X didn't do (anything / nothing) wrong. He
6   7
didn't pay (anyone / anything) to the bank. He got something for nothing.
8

What do you think? Was Mr. X a thief or not?

> *interest* = money paid by the bank to the owner of a savings account.
> *a judge* = a person whose job is to decide what is right or wrong in court. *a savings account* = money that a customer saves in the bank.

C. Work with a group. Discuss your ideas about the story.

1. What do you think about the story?
2. Was anybody hurt? Did anyone lose anything?
3. Was Mr. X a thief? Did he do anything wrong?

GRAMMAR BRIEFING 4

One and *Ones* as Indefinite Pronouns

FORM and FUNCTION

Uses of *One* and *Ones*

1. *One* and *ones* are indefinite pronouns. Use *one* or *ones* instead of repeating a count noun.	The blue **car** is Jack's. That red ~~car~~ is Ann's. *(one)* He has a few new **CDs** and many old ~~CDs~~. *(ones)*
2. The article *the* can come before *one* or *ones*.	This store is closed, but **the one** across the street is open. Do you see those girls? I mean **the ones** near the door.

(continued on next page)

Uses of *One* and *Ones* (continued)

3. Do not use *a/an* + *one*. Use *a/an* only before an adjective + *one*.	I don't have a computer. I need **one**. **NOT:** I need ~~a~~ one. I need **a good one**.
4. *One* is often used after *this* or *that*. Do not use *ones* after *these* or *those*.	That shirt costs $50, but **this one** is only $39. These books are mine. **Those** are, too. **NOT:** Those ~~ones~~ are, too.

GRAMMAR PRACTICE 4

One and *Ones* as Indefinite Pronouns

10 *One* and *Ones*: Yuri's Job at the Bank

Use *one* or *ones* in each sentence. Cross out the word or words it replaces.

1. Yuri works in a bank. It is a small ~~bank~~.
   one

2. Yuri's bank is downtown. It is the bank on the corner of Main Street and Broadway.

3. He likes his job. He thinks it is a good job.

4. Many people have accounts at the bank. Yuri has an account, too.

5. Some people have big accounts. Yuri has a small account.

6. Some customers come in often. Yuri knows the names of the customers he sees

   every day.

7. Do you see the window on the left? Yuri usually works at that window.

8. Yuri handles a lot of money. He handles new bills and old bills.

9. Yuri's bank is not the only bank downtown.

10. I have a bank account. Do you have a bank account?

11 **Using *One* and *Ones*:** Which Do You Like?

Work in a group. Look at the pictures. Take turns asking *Which _____ do you like?*
Give answers with *one* or *ones*.

Example: Student A: *Which glasses do you like?*
Student B: *I like the round ones.*
Student C: *I like the ones on the left.*

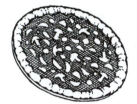

 Check your progress! Go to the Self-Test for
Chapter 17 on the *Grammar Links* Website.

Wrap-up Activities

1   A Trip to Washington, D.C.: READING

Read the paragraph.

    Marek spent several days in Washington, D.C., with his family. They visited the city in the spring, and the weather was nice and warm. They stayed with some friends, so they didn't spend any money on a hotel, but they spent a lot of money on food. They went to several museums and monuments, and they visited the Bureau of Engraving and Printing. That was Marek's idea. He wanted to see lots of money. Marek didn't buy any souvenirs in Washington, but his sister bought some small ones there. They both sent postcards to friends back home.

 See the *Grammar Links* Website for more information about the Bureau of Engraving and Printing.

2   A Trip You Took: WRITING

    Write a paragraph of six or more sentences about a trip you took. Where did you go? How much time did you spend there? Did you buy anything? Did you have fun? Try to use both count and noncount nouns, quantifiers, pronouns (subject, object, and indefinite), and possessives (nouns, adjectives, and pronouns). Use articles carefully.

 See the *Grammar Links* Website for a model paragraph for this assignment.

3   A Trip to the Beach: EDITING

Correct the 10 errors in articles, quantifiers, possessives, and pronouns. Some errors can be corrected in more than one way. The first error is corrected for you.

A Trip to the Beach

    I took *a* trip with four friends to a nice beach. We went in my friend Hiro car.

We had enough money for just a little days. We stayed at small hotel, but we didn't

spend many time in ours rooms. Weather was great, so we were always on the beach.

We didn't eat in no expensive restaurants. We usually bought things like sandwiches

and ate it on the beach. This trip was a lot fun.

---

4 **On My Treasure Hunt:** SPEAKING/LISTENING

Work with a group. Sit in a circle and take turns in order. Each person completes the statement *On my treasure hunt, I found . . .* with a quantifier or measure word + a noun. Student A: Use a noun that starts with *a*. Student B: Repeat Student A's statement and add something that starts with *b*. Continue through the alphabet.

Example: Student A: On my treasure hunt, I found a pound of apples.
Student B: On my treasure hunt, I found a pound of apples and a few bananas.
Student C: On my treasure hunt, I found a pound of apples, a few bananas, and a lot of coins.

5 **How Much Can You Guess?** SPEAKING/LISTENING/WRITING

Step 1 Read the list below. Then find a partner. Write your guesses about your partner. Do not show them to your partner.

Your Partner	Guesses	The Facts
1. The number of movies he or she saw last week	_____	_____
2. The amount of coffee he or she drinks each day	_____ cup(s)	_____ cup(s)
3. The number of brothers and sisters he or she has	_____	_____
4. The amount of fruit he or she eats each day	_____ piece(s)	_____ piece(s)
5. The amount of money in his or her pockets today	$_____	$_____
6. The number of pictures in his or her wallet	_____	_____
7. The amount of time he or she spends on homework each day	_____ hour(s)	_____ hour(s)

Step 2 Take turns with your partner asking questions with *How much* and *How many*.

Example: How much coffee do you drink each day?

Write the facts about your partner. Add up the correct guesses you both have. The winner in the class is the pair with the most correct guesses.

Expressing Future Time

UNIT OBJECTIVES

- **the future with *be going to***
  (We ***are going to*** visit a national park. ***Is*** the weather ***going to*** be good?)

- **the future with *will***
  (The weather ***will be*** cool. It ***won't snow*** in the rain forests.)

- **future time expressions**
  (They're going to leave ***tomorrow morning***. They will be back ***in a few days***.)

Grammar in Action

🎧 Reading and Listening: National Parks

Read and listen to reporter Al Jordan talk about national parks.

1   The Grand Canyon . . . the Florida Everglades . . . Yosemite . . . Yellowstone . . . Do you know any of these names? These are all names of national parks in the United States. These national parks are very beautiful places, and they are for everyone to enjoy. Our national parks are national treasures.

The Grand Canyon

2   Go to any national park, and you will have the chance to see some amazing things. You will find wonders of nature—maybe mountains, volcanoes, great forests, or deserts. There will be some places that are the same as they were thousands of years ago.

3   Our national parks get a lot of use. For example, the Grand Canyon had over 3 million visitors last year. Large numbers of visitors are one reason that the parks are in trouble. Most people agree that our parks have problems. The question is, are we going to solve these problems?

4   Some people say no. They predict that there are going to be more and more visitors, too many visitors for the parks. They say that the parks are going to have more forest fires and more pollution. They are afraid that we are going to lose many of the wild animals in the parks.

5   But other people predict a bright future for our parks. They say that we'll find ways to have more visitors and solve these problems. Fires and pollution won't destroy our parks, and wild animals will be safe there. They predict that in the years ahead, we'll use our parks wisely. Let's hope they are right. Then our parks will continue to be national treasures well into the future.

> *wonders* = great or beautiful things that cause surprise and admiration.
> *predict* = say what you think will happen in the future. *pollution* = dirty and dangerous substances in the air, water, and soil. *wisely* = in a smart and careful way, based on good decisions.

12 OF THE 50 U.S. NATIONAL PARKS

Think About Grammar

A. The words in the boxes are from the reading. Write the missing words.

From the Second Paragraph:	From the Fourth Paragraph:
1. . . . you _____ have the chance to see . . .	4. . . . there _____ _____ _____ be more and more visitors . . .
2. You _____ find wonders of nature . . .	5. . . . the parks _____ _____ _____ have more forest fires . . .
3. There _____ be some places . . .	6. . . . we _____ _____ _____ lose many of the wild animals . . .

Look at the words you wrote. What do they express? Circle your answer.

They are two ways of expressing:　　a. present time.　　b. past time.　　c. future time.

B. Look in the last paragraph for the contracted forms of *will* and *will + not*. Copy them here.

1. They say that we will find ways . . .　　They say that we _____ find ways . . .

2. Fires and pollution will not destroy . . .　　Fires and pollution _____ destroy . . .

18

Yellowstone National Park, from Summer to Fall

Expressing Future Time with *Be Going To*

Introductory Task: Welcome to Yellowstone

A. Listen and read.

David Garcia lives in Montana and often visits Yellowstone National Park. Today, David is driving to the park with his sister Linda, their little brother Ben, and Linda's friend Makiko. It is a sunny day in June.

David: What a beautiful day! This is a great time to come to Yellowstone!

Ben: Are we almost there? I'm hungry.

Linda: Hold on, Ben! In a few minutes, you're going to see the north entrance.

Makiko: David, are we going to see any geysers?

David: You bet! Yellowstone has thousands of geysers. In fact, there are more geysers here than in all the rest of the world.

Ben: But, David, are we going to see one erupt? Maybe they won't do anything today.

Linda: Don't worry! We're going to see Old Faithful—right, David? We know it's going to erupt.

Makiko: How do you know?

David: Old Faithful is predictable. It erupts on a regular schedule—about every 70 minutes, I think.

Ben: Look! There's the entrance to the park!

Old Faithful Erupting

> *a geyser* = hot water and steam shooting up into the air from a natural hole in the ground. *a schedule* = a plan of what is going to happen and when (the times, dates, etc.).

B. Read the statements. Are they true or false? Put a check (✓) in the correct column. Check "It Doesn't Say" when the conversation doesn't give this information.

	True	False	It Doesn't Say
1. David and the others are going to visit Yellowstone.	✓		
2. They're going to eat in a restaurant.			
3. They're going to see Old Faithful.			
4. Old Faithful is going to erupt.			
5. They're going to swim in a geyser.			
6. All geysers erupt at the same times every day.			

Expressing Future Time with *Be Going To*; Affirmative Statements with *Be Going To*

FUNCTION

Expressing Future Time with *Be Going To*

1. Use *be going to* to describe future plans. Use it to describe what someone has decided to do.

    PAST   NOW   FUTURE

    I am going to take

I **am going to take** some pictures.
They **are going to visit** the park in June.
We **are going to go** in a few minutes.

2. Use *be going to* to make predictions or express expectations. Use it to tell what someone believes is going to happen in the future.

I think we **are going to be** late.
It**'s going to rain** today.
You**'re going to love** that movie!

3. Use *probably* to show that plans or predictions are not 100% sure.

I'm **probably** going to stay home tonight.
They're **probably** not going to catch any fish.

4. Sentences with *be going to* often have future time expressions to tell when something is going to happen.

He's going to leave **tomorrow.**
We're going to meet **in an hour.**
The course is going to start **a week from today**.

(continued on next page)

A. Affirmative Statements

Statements with Subject Nouns or Pronouns

FULL FORMS

SUBJECT	BE	GOING TO	BASE VERB
I	am		
He			
She	is		
It			leave.
Jack	going to		stay.
We			come.
You	are		
They			
The girls			

CONTRACTIONS

SUBJECT + BE	GOING TO	BASE VERB
I'm		
He's		
She's		
It's		leave.
Jack's	going to	stay.
We're		come.
You're		
They're		
—		

Statements with There + Be

FULL FORMS

THERE	BE	GOING TO	BE	NOUN
There	is	going to	be	a storm.
	are			strong winds.

CONTRACTIONS

THERE + IS	GOING TO	BE	NOUN
There's	going to	be	a storm.

B. Future Time Expressions

Future time expressions usually come at the beginning or end of a sentence. Future time expressions include:

- *Tomorrow* and *tomorrow + morning/ afternoon/evening/night.*

- *Next* + a specific period of time.

- *In* + an amount of time.

Tomorrow I'm going to buy a map.

He's going to arrive **tomorrow night**.

Next week, they're going to go camping.

I'm going to graduate **next spring**.

In a year, he's going to return.

We're going to leave **in a few minutes**.

Remember! Sentences with *am/is/are going* (to a place) are in the present progressive. Use the present progressive to tell what is happening now. Sentences with *am/is/are going to* + base verb express future time.

Jack is on the bus. He **is going to** school. (now)

Jack **is going to be** at school in 10 minutes. (future)

GRAMMAR PRACTICE 1

Expressing Future Time with *Be Going To*; Affirmative Statements with *Be Going To*

1 Future Time with *Be Going To*: Visiting Yellowstone

A. David, Linda, Makiko, and Ben are on their way to Yellowstone National Park. Read each statement about them. Does the statement express present or future time? Circle your answer.

1. David is driving his car. He's going to Yellowstone.   (present) / future

2. He's going to be in the park in a few minutes.   present / future

3. Ben is in the back seat of the car. He's going with David.   present / future

4. This is going to be Makiko's first visit to Yellowstone.   present / future

5. They are probably going to have a great time.   present / future

6. The car is going slowly because there are many cars on the road.   present / future

7. It's going to be a beautiful, sunny day.   present / future

B. Does *be going to* describe a future plan or express a prediction? Circle your answer.

1. Linda: Smile, Makiko! I'm going to take your picture.   (a plan) / a prediction

2. A park ranger: The geyser is going to erupt in a few minutes.   a plan / a prediction

3. Ben: I'm going to stand here and wait for Old Faithful.   a plan / a prediction

4. Makiko: I'm probably going to need more film for my camera.   a plan / a prediction

5. Ben: I'm going to buy some postcards for my friends.   a plan / a prediction

6. David: Ben and I are going to get something to eat.   a plan / a prediction

7. The ranger: There's probably going to be some rain tomorrow.   a plan / a prediction

> *a ranger* = a person who takes care of a public forest or other natural area.

2 Affirmative Statements: Old Faithful Erupts

Complete the statements using the words in parentheses and *be going to*. Use full forms, not contractions.

A Sign Outside
the Visitor Center

Linda and Makiko are waiting to see Old Faithful erupt. What is going to happen?

1. <u>Linda and Makiko are going to listen</u> for a low sound in the ground.
   (Linda and Makiko / listen)

2. _____ for steam.
   (they / watch)

3. _____ from the geyser's opening.
   (water / shoot)

4. Linda: "_____ the geyser erupt."
   (we / see)

5. _____ high into the air.
   (the water / go)

6. Makiko: "_____ some pictures."
   (I / take)

7. _____ a lot of noise.
   (there / be)

8. _____ lots of tourists there.
   (there / be)

9. _____ lots of pictures.
   (the tourists / take)

10. _____ for 1.5 to 5 minutes.
    (the eruption / last)

11. _____ again in about an hour.
    (it / happen)

12. _____ several eruptions this afternoon.
    (there / be)

3 Future Time Expressions: Faithful to Yellowstone

Complete the sentences with *tomorrow*, *next*, or *in*.

Mark Sloan is camping in Yellowstone National Park. He is a teacher, and he comes here every summer after school gets out. He loves the park.

_____In_____ a few minutes, he is going to go for a

<u> </u>
1

hike through the Hayden Valley area. He hopes to see some

wild animals there. He visited this area last year, and

_____ year, he is probably going to come
2

back again. He expects to return from this hike

_____ three hours. Mark is not like most
3

people who come to Yellowstone: 98% of visitors never go

more than 100 yards from their cars!

Going for a Hike

_____ morning, Mark is going to go fishing, and he is planning another hike for
4

_____ afternoon. _____ evening, there is going to be a ranger telling
5   6

stories at the campground, and Mark is going to be there to hear them.

_____ a few days, Mark is going to go home. _____ week, he is
7   8

going to start his summer job. Then, _____ about eight weeks, the new school
9

year is going to begin.

Mark never gets tired of Yellowstone. There are always new places to discover.

_____ a year, he is going to be back in the park again.
10

🌐 See the *Grammar Links* Website for more information about Yellowstone and other U.S. national parks.

4 Using Future Time Expressions: Your Plans

👥 Work with a partner. Take turns asking *When are you going to . . . + words from the list below. Think of more activities for 7 and 8. Answer your partner's questions with a future time expression. (You can also answer *Never*.)

Example: Student A: **When are you going to take a vacation?**
          Student B: **In about three months.**

1. take a vacation   5. travel by plane
2. go camping   6. do something fun with a friend
3. go for a hike   7. _____
4. visit a new place   8. _____

5 Listening to *Be Going To*: Predicting the Weather

 A. Listen to the weather report for Yellowstone National Park for a Thursday in June. You are going to hear the verbs *be*, *drop*, *have*, and *see*. Listen again, and write the words you hear. Write full forms, not contractions.

Today, temperatures _are going to be_____ in the sixties. There

<u>   </u> a mix of clouds and sunshine. This afternoon, we're
2

probably _____ showers in some areas. Tonight, it
3

_____ cool, with temperatures dropping down into the forties.
4

For tomorrow, the forecast is good. We _____ a sunny
5

day with temperatures in the seventies. Then, tomorrow night, temperatures

_____ into the forties again. And, for the weekend, it
6

_____ partly to mostly cloudy.

B. Work with a partner. Look at the weather information below. Take turns telling the forecast. Use *be going to*.

Example: *On Friday, temperatures are going to be in the seventies.*

FRI	SAT	SUN	MON	TUES
☀	☀	🌤	☁	🌧
70°–78°	75°–85°	72°–79°	65°–75°	64°–69°

C. Continue working with your partner. What is the forecast for your area? What is the temperature going to be? Share your predictions about the weather for today, tonight, tomorrow, and the day after tomorrow. Use *be going to*.

Weather	
Nouns	**Adjectives**
clouds	cloudy
fog	foggy
rain	rainy
snow	snowy
sunshine	sunny
thunder and lightning	stormy

Negative Statements with *Be Going To*

FORM

A. Statements with Subject Nouns or Pronouns

FULL FORMS

SUBJECT	BE	NOT	GOING TO	BASE VERB
I	am			
He				
She	is			
It				leave.
Ann		not	going to	stay.
We				come.
You	are			
They				
The men				

CONTRACTIONS

SUBJECT + BE + NOT	GOING TO	BASE VERB
I'm not		
He's not/He isn't		
She's not/She isn't		
It's not/It isn't		leave.
Ann's not/Ann isn't	going to	stay.
We're not/We aren't		come.
You're not/You aren't		
They're not/They aren't		
The men aren't		

B. Statements with *There + Be*

FULL FORMS

THERE	BE	NOT	GOING TO	BE	NOUN
There	is	not	going to	be	a storm.
	are				strong winds.

CONTRACTIONS

THERE + BE + NOT	GOING TO	BE	NOUN
There's not			a storm.
There isn't	going to	be	
There aren't			strong winds.

Negative Statements with *Be Going To*

6 **Affirmative and Negative Statements with Contractions:** Changing Seasons

A. Complete the sentences in this letter from a ranger at Yellowstone National Park. Use *be going to* + the words in parentheses. Use contractions.

Yellowstone, Aug. 30

Dear Mom and Dad,

Summer is coming to an end, and life __isn't going to be_____ the same
                                        1 (not / be)

around here! Some birds are already traveling south, and the aspen trees are

starting to turn gold. After Labor Day, there _____
                                                        2 (not / be)

so many people in the park. With kids back in school, it _____
                                                                3 (not / be)

so crowded here. We _____ our evening programs
                            4 (not / give)

at the campgrounds anymore, so I _____ so
                                            5 (not / work)

many hours. That means I _____ more time for
                                    6 (have)

my photography. I got some great pictures of a grizzly bear yesterday.

The Canyon Visitor Center _____ open after
                                        7 (not / be)

October 1, so I _____ at the park headquarters
                        8 (work)

instead. It's at the North Entrance to the park, on Route 89. When winter comes,

the other roads into the park _____ open, but the
                                        9 (not / be)

North Entrance is open all year.

Well, I _____ to bed now. Take care!
                10 (go)

Love,

Laura

P.S. Do you want a nice photo of a grizzly?

A Grizzly Bear

Labor Day = a holiday in honor of workers, on the first Monday in
September. *headquarters* = the main office or building of an organization.

B. Work with a partner. Student A: Read a statement with a negative contraction from Part A. Student B: Repeat the statement with a different negative contraction or with the full form. Take turns.

Example: Student A: Summer is coming to an end, and life isn't going to be the same around here.

Student B: . . . life's not going to be the same around here. (or . . . life is not going to be the same around here.)

7 | Affirmative and Negative Statements: Your Plans and Mine

A. List five things you plan to do in the future under WHAT. Write a time expression for each plan under WHEN.

WHAT	WHEN
Examples: have lunch see my parents	at 12:30 in June
1. _____	1. _____
2. _____	2. _____
3. _____	3. _____
4. _____	4. _____
5. _____	5. _____

B. Work with a partner and take turns. Student A: Use information from your list in Part A to say what you are going to do and when. Student B: Listen to the statement. If you have the same plan, say the same statement with *too*. If you don't, then make the statement negative, and tell your own plans for that time.

Example: Student A: I'm going to see a movie this weekend.
Student B: I'm going to see a movie this weekend, too.
OR
I'm not going to see a movie this weekend. I'm going to study.

If you are not 100% sure about your plan, use *I'm + probably* (not).

Example: Student B: I'm going to watch TV tonight.
Student A: I'm probably not going to watch TV tonight. *I'm probably going to write some letters.*

C. Write a paragraph about one of your plans from Part A. Include sentences with *be going to*.

Example: I'm going to have lunch with my friend Oksana today. We are going to meet at 12:30. We are probably going to eat at . . .

See the *Grammar Links* Website for a complete model paragraph for this assignment.

Yes/No Questions and Short Answers with *Be Going To*

FORM

A. Questions with Subject Nouns or Pronouns

QUESTIONS				ANSWERS					
BE	SUBJECT	*GOING TO*	BASE VERB	YES			NO		
Am	I				I **am.**			I'm **not.**	
	he				he **is.**			he's **not**/he **isn't.**	
	she				she **is.**			she's **not**/she **isn't.**	
Is	it				it **is.**			it's **not**/it **isn't.**	
	the bus	**going to**	**leave?**	Yes,			No,		
	we				we **are.**			we're **not**/we **aren't.**	
Are	you				you **are.**			you're **not**/you **aren't.**	
	they				they **are.**			they're **not**/they **aren't.**	
	the girls								

B. Questions with *There + Be*

QUESTIONS					ANSWERS				
BE	THERE	GOING TO	BE	NOUN	YES			NO	
Is	there	going to	be	a storm?	Yes,	there **is.**	No,		there's **not**/there **isn't.**
Are				strong winds?		there **are.**			there **aren't.**

GRAMMAR PRACTICE 3

Yes/No Questions and Answers with *Be Going To*

8 **Yes/No Questions and Short Answers:** Forest Fires

A. Complete the questions using the subjects and verbs in parentheses with *be going to*. Complete the short answers.

David Garcia is with his group. (See the picture on page 284.) They are getting ready to hike to Mud Volcano in Yellowstone National Park.

David: Okay, is everybody ready to go?

Ben: Hey, Dave, _____are we going to see_____ any grizzly bears?
         <u>1 (we / see)</u>

David: No, __we__ probably __aren't__. They don't usually come into
         2   2

this area.

Makiko: _____ any other animals? I'm
                    3 (there / be)

wondering about bringing my camera.

David: We're probably going to see some elk, lots of birds, and

maybe a bison. I heard there was a bison near Mud Volcano

earlier today.

An Elk

Ben: Wow! _____ there when we get there?
                    4 (he / be)

David: I don't know, Ben. I'm not going to make any predictions about bison!

Makiko: _____ some of the area that
                    5 (we / see)

burned in the big fire last year?

David: Yes, _____.
                    6

Makiko: _____ all black and ugly?
                    7 (it / be)

David: No, _____! There are some beautiful
                    8

A Bison

wildflowers growing in that area now. Of course, there are also some black trees.

Linda: We heard that lightning started another fire, near Heart Lake, and it's still burning.

_____ something?
                    9 (the rangers / do)

David: Well, the rangers are going to watch the fire carefully.

Makiko: _____ the fire?
                    10 (they / put out)

David: No, _____ Not right away. You see, fires are part of life in a forest.
                    11

They clear away the old trees so new things can grow.

Ben: Dave? I'm hungry. _____ a snack or something
                    12 (I / get)

pretty soon?

David: Here, have an apple. Now let's get started!

> *put out* = stop from burning. *right away* = very soon, immediately.

9 *Yes/No* Questions: What's Going to Happen?

Write *yes/no* questions with *be going to* and the words in parentheses.

1. It's cloudy now.

   <u>Is it going to rain later?</u>
   _____
   (it / rain later)

2. Makiko has a camera.

   _____
   (she / takes pictures)

3. Ben has an apple.

   _____
   (he / eat it)

4. David has a map.

   _____
   (he / need it)

5. They are going to take a hike.

   _____
   (they / walk far)

6. Ben: I want to see a bison.

   _____
   (I / see one)

7. Linda: Ben, you have one apple.

   _____
   (you / want another)

8. Makiko: We don't have much water.

   _____
   (we / need more)

9. Linda: There isn't much sunscreen in this bottle.

   _____
   (there / be enough for everyone)

10. There are often wild animals near Mud Volcano.

    _____
    (there / be any animals there today)

Wh- Questions and Answers with *Be Going To*

FORM

A. Questions with *Wh-* Question Word as Subject

QUESTIONS					ANSWERS
WH- QUESTION WORD/SUBJECT	*BE*	*GOING TO*	**BASE VERB**		
Who			**take**	pictures?	I am.
What	**is**	**going to**	**happen?**		There's going to be a party.
Which horse			**win**	the race?	I don't know—maybe number 7.

B. Questions with Other Subjects

QUESTIONS						ANSWERS
WH- QUESTION WORD	*BE*	SUBJECT	*GOING TO*	**BASE VERB**		
Who	**are**	you		**call?**		My sister.
Whom*						
What	**is**	Bob	**going to**	**do**	next?	Find a new job.
Where	**are**	they		**go**	on vacation?	To the beach.
When	**am**	I		**see**	you again?	Next week.
How often	**is**	she		**visit**	her family?	Twice a year.

Whom is very formal. It is not common in conversation.

GRAMMAR PRACTICE 4

Wh- Questions and Answers with *Be Going To*

10 **Wh- Questions and Answers:** Linda's Party Plans

A. Write questions with *who*, *what*, and *which* to ask for the missing information.

1. Something is going to happen.

   What is going to happen?
   _____

   There's going to be a party.

2. Someone is going to have a birthday.

   _____

   Makiko.

3. A friend is going to give a party for her.

   _____

   Linda is.

4. Some people are going to be there.

_____

Linda and Makiko's friends.

5. Something is going to happen at the party.

_____

I can't tell you. It's going to be a surprise.

B. Write *wh-* questions to ask for the missing information.

1. The party is going to be on a certain day.

   When is the party going to be?
   _____

2. It is going to start at a certain time.

   _____

3. The party is going to be at a certain place.

   _____

4. Linda is going to invite certain people.

   _____

5. Her friends are going to bring certain things.

   _____

6. They are going to eat and drink certain things.

   _____

7. They are going to surprise a certain person.

   _____

11 Asking and Answering *Yes/No* and *Wh-* Questions: Weekend Plans

A. Work with a partner. Interview your partner about his or her plans for the weekend. Use *yes/no* and *wh-* questions. Take notes on his or her answers.

Example: Student A: What are you going to do this weekend?
         Student B: Friday night, I'm going to go to a club with my friends.
         Student A: Are you going to go dancing?

B. Join another pair to form a group of four. Ask them questions about their plans. Answer all their questions about your partner's plans, and let your partner describe your plans.

Example: Student C: What's Li going to do this weekend?
         Student A: She's going to go to Club Paradise with her friends Friday night. They're going to dance.

Check your progress! Go to the Self-Test for Chapter 18 on the *Grammar Links* Website.

Chapter 19

Olympic National Park, from Winter to Spring

Expressing Future Time with *Will*

Introductory Task: Olympic National Park

A. Listen and read about Olympic National Park.

Look at the map of Washington State. You will find Olympic National Park in the west. This park is unusual. In any season, visitors to the park will see both beautiful green rain forests and snow-covered mountains. This park is also the home of many kinds of wild animals.

Visit the park, and you will probably see herds of elk. Cougars live there, too. In fact, there are more cougars here than in any other national park. Will you see any? No, the cougars will probably avoid you. But in the winter, people sometimes see cougar tracks in the snow.

A Cougar

This spring, many visitors will travel to the beaches of Olympic National Park. They will go there to see Pacific gray whales. The whales pass these beaches each spring on their way north for the summer.

Cougar Tracks

Spring, summer, winter, fall: In any season of the year, Olympic National Park is a wonderful place to visit.

A Pacific Gray Whale

> *herds* = large groups of certain types of animals that live together.
> *avoid* = stay away from.

B. Choose the correct words to make true statements.

1. (You'll find / You won't find) Olympic National Park on a map of Washington State.

2. If you go to the park, (you'll see / you won't see) snow on the mountains.

3. There (will be / won't be) animal tracks in the snow.

4. Visitors to the park (will probably see / probably won't see) cougars.

5. Whales (will pass / won't pass) by the park next spring.

6. The whales (will spend / won't spend) the summer near the park.

C. Complete the statements.

1. The contracted form of *will* is _____.

2. The contracted form of *will* + *not* is _____.

GRAMMAR BRIEFING 1

Expressing Future Time with *Will*

FUNCTION

Using *Will*

1. Use *will* (like *be going to*) to make predictions or express expectations about the future.	I think it**'ll be** sunny tomorrow. All their friends **will come** to the party.

PAST — NOW — FUTURE
it will be

2. Use *will* to describe future plans made at the moment of speaking. (Do not use it to describe plans already made at some time in the past.)	*Sara:* **I'm going to meet** Ann for lunch at Gino's. Do you want to join us? *Al:* Sure. **I'll see** you there at 12:30, okay? (Sara already had a plan; Al is making a plan now, as he speaks.)
3. Use *probably* to show that a prediction is not 100% sure.	You'll **probably** catch some fish. He **probably** won't be there.
4. Sentences with *will* often have future time expressions. (See Chapter 18, Grammar Briefing 1, page 287, for more information on future time expressions.)	I'll be ready **in a minute**. **Next week**, there will be a test. She'll be home **the day after tomorrow**.

Remember! Use *be going to* to describe your plans for the future. Use *will* only when you are deciding on a plan at that moment.

Tom: **I'm going to have** a party this Friday.
            NOT: I ~~will~~ have a party this Friday.

Chris: On Friday? Great, **I'll be** there.

GRAMMAR PRACTICE 1

Expressing Future Time with *Will*

1 ***Will* for Predictions Versus *Will* for Plans:** Everyday Matters

In these sentences, is *will* used to express a prediction or to describe a plan made at the moment of speaking? Circle your answer.

1. We're out of coffee. I'll get some on the way home.   (a plan)/ a prediction

2. I don't think it'll rain today.   a plan / a prediction

3. Someone called you. He'll probably call again.   a plan / a prediction

4. Jack doesn't know about the party yet. I'll call him now. a plan / a prediction

5. Don't worry—they won't forget.   a plan / a prediction

6. We need to hurry, or we'll be late.   a plan / a prediction

7. I'll clean up the kitchen, and you do the living room, okay? a plan / a prediction

8. Would you like a ride? We'll pick you up in 10 minutes.   a plan / a prediction

9. *A*: Don't tell anyone! *B*: Okay, fine. I won't say a word. a plan / a prediction

10. Give her the good news right away. She'll be so happy!   a plan / a prediction

2 ***Will* Versus *Be Going To* for Future Plans:** Getting Ready for a Trip

A. Work with a partner. Read the conversations out loud. Choose the correct form and circle it. Use *will* only for plans made at the moment of speaking. Use *be going to* for plans already made.

Max and Rob are friends. Beth is Max's sister. Max and Rob have plans for a camping trip.

1. Max: Rob and I (are going to go / will go) to Olympic National Park for
                                                     a

    a week.

    Beth: Are you planning to stay at a hotel?

    Max: No, I have a tent, and (we're going to camp / we'll camp).
                                                     b

2. Max: So, do you have everything you need for the trip?

   Rob: I don't have a good sleeping bag.

   Max: Okay, then (I'm going to bring / I'll bring) one for you.

Max with a Sleeping Bag

3. Beth: Max, how are you going to get to the park?

   Max: I didn't tell you? (I'm going to take / I'll take) the 9:00 bus on Saturday.
   a

   Beth: (I'm going to drive / I'll drive) you to the bus station if you want.
   b

   Max: Great! Thanks.

4. Rob: Max, are you going to walk to the bus station?

   Max: No, my sister offered to drive me, so (I'm going to get / I'll get) a ride.

5. Beth: Will you call me from the park?

   Max: Sure. Rob (is going to bring / will bring) his cell phone.

6. Max: Let's talk again before Saturday.

   Rob: Okay, (I'm going to call / I'll call) you Friday night.

B. Listen to the conversations from Part A. Check your answers.

C. Work with a partner. Tell your partner the following two things:
   1. Three things you have decided to do in the future: *I'm going to . . .*
      Example: I'm going to work in international business.
   2. A new idea for a plan for you and your partner: *I'll (meet/call/see/bring) you . . .*
      Example: I'll be your partner tomorrow, too, okay?

Affirmative and Negative Statements with *Will*
■ Affirmative Statements

FORM

A. Statements with Subject Nouns or Pronouns

FULL FORMS				CONTRACTIONS		
SUBJECT	*WILL*	BASE VERB		SUBJECT + *WILL*	BASE VERB	
I				I'll		
You				You'll		
He				He'll		
She				She'll		
It	**will**	**work**	hard.	It'll	**work**	hard.
We				We'll		
You				You'll		
They				They'll		
Ann				—		
The men				—		

B. Statements with *There* + *Be*

THERE	*WILL*	*BE*	NOUN	
There	**will**	**be**	a bus	at 9:00.
			20 people	here.

(continued on next page)

■ Negative Statements

FORM

A. Statements with Subject Nouns or Pronouns

FULL FORMS

SUBJECT	WILL NOT	BASE VERB
I		
You		
He		
She		
It	will not	work.
We		
You		
They		
Jack		
The girls		

CONTRACTIONS

SUBJECT	WILL + NOT	BASE VERB
I		
You		
He		
She		
It	won't	work.
We		
You		
They		
Jack		
The girls		

B. Statements with *There + Be*

FULL FORMS

THERE	WILL	NOT	BE	NOUN	
There	will	not	be	a bus	at 9:00.
				20 people	here.

CONTRACTIONS

THERE	WILL + NOT	BE	NOUN	
There	won't	be	a bus	at 9:00.
			20 people	here.

GRAMMAR **HOT**SPOT!

1. The verb after *will* is in the base form. Do not add -(*e*)*s*.

   He will go home tomorrow.
   NOT: He will ~~goes~~ home tomorrow.

   She will have a good time.
   NOT: She will ~~has~~ a good time.

2. In statements, add *probably* after *will* or before *won't*.

   He**'ll probably** be here soon.
   He **probably won't** stay long.

	WRITE	SAY
1. Contractions of subject pronouns + *will* are common in spoken English and in informal written English.	**He will** call tonight. **He'll** call tonight. (informal)	**He'll** call tonight.
2. Contractions of nouns or *there* + *'ll* are common only in spoken English.	**John will** call tonight. NOT: ~~John'll~~ call tonight.	**John'll** call tonight.
	There will be no class today.	**There'll be** no class today.

GRAMMAR PRACTICE 2

Affirmative and Negative Statements with *Will*

3 **Affirmative and Negative Statements:** A Trip to Olympic National Park

A. Complete the statements. Use the full forms of *will* and *will not* with the verbs in parentheses.

1. (travel)   Max Thomas __will travel__ to Olympic National Park from Seattle, Washington.

2. (meet)   His friend Rob Ryan _____ him there. Rob lives in Portland, Oregon.

3. (spend)   They _____ a week in the park in January.

4. (not/stay)   They _____ in a hotel. They're going to sleep in a tent.

Rob in the Tent

5. (be) The weather _____ different in different areas of the park.

6. (see) *Max*: I hope that we _____ lots of animals.

7. (not/see) *Rob*: I hope that we _____ any bears!

8. (be) There _____ snow for skiing at Hurricane Ridge.

9. (not/be) There _____ any snow in the rain forests.

10. (not/go) Max and Rob _____ to the beach.

B. Replace the full forms of *will* (*not*) in Part A with contractions when possible. In affirmative statements, contract *will* only after a subject pronoun.

Example: 3. ~~They will~~ They'll spend a week in the park in January.

4 Predictions and Expectations: Max and Rob's Trip

A. Work with a partner. Student A: Read aloud a statement about Max and Rob's trip to Olympic National Park. Student B: Repeat the statement but use *will* instead of *be going to*. Use the contractions *'ll* and *won't*.

Example: Student A: They're going to camp in the park.
Student B: They'll camp in the park.

1. They're going to camp in the park.
2. They're going to stay for a week.
3. It's not going to be expensive.
4. It's going to be cool.
5. There isn't going to be much rain.
6. There isn't going to be any snow in the rain forests.
7. They aren't going to go swimming.
8. They're going to go hiking.
9. It's going to be a lot of fun.
10. There aren't going to be any cougars in the campground.

B. Student B: Read aloud a statement from Part A. Student A: Repeat the statement but use *will* and add *probably*. Use the contractions *'ll* and *won't*.

Example: Student B: They're going to camp in the park.
Student A: They'll probably camp in the park.

C. Continue working with your partner. Student A: Name someone or something you want to hear a prediction about. Student B: Make one or more predictions about the person or thing using *will* or *won't*. Take turns. Use *probably* in some of your predictions.

Example: Student A: our next test in this class
Student B: You'll probably get an A. But we won't have a test this week.

Questions with *Will*

■ *Yes/No* Questions and Short Answers

FORM

A. Questions with Subject Nouns or Pronouns

QUESTIONS				ANSWERS					
WILL	SUBJECT	BASE VERB		YES			NO		
	I				I			I	
	you				you			you	
	he				he			he	
	she				she			she	
Will	it	arrive	on time?	Yes,	it	**will.**	No,	it	**won't.**
	the bus								
	we				we			we	
	you				you			you	
	they				they			they	
	the men								

B. Questions with *There + Be*

QUESTIONS					ANSWERS			
WILL	THERE	BE	NOUN		YES		NO	
Will	there	be	a movie	tonight?	Yes, there **will.**		No, there **won't.**	
			many people	there?				

■ *Wh-* Questions and Answers

FORM

A. Questions with *Wh-* Question Word as Subject

QUESTIONS				ANSWERS
WH- QUESTION WORD/SUBJECT	WILL	BASE VERB		
Who		**tell**	him the news?	I will.
What	will	**happen**	next?	There will probably be a meeting.
Which horse		**win**	the race?	Nobody knows.

(continued on next page)

B. Questions with Other Subjects

QUESTIONS				ANSWERS
WH- QUESTION WORD	*WILL*	SUBJECT	BASE VERB	
Who	will	you	**invite?**	All my friends.
Whom*				
What		she	**do?**	She'll probably call us.
Where		they	**live?**	In London.
When		the bus	**arrive?**	In a few minutes.

*Whom is very formal. It is not common in conversation.

TALKING THE TALK

Use *probably* in short answers when you are not 100% sure about something. Use it before *will* or *won't*.

Q: Will it rain tonight?
A: Yes, it **probably will**./No, it **probably won't**.

GRAMMAR PRACTICE 3

Questions with *Will*

5 *Yes/No* **Questions and Short Answers:** January in the Park

Complete the *yes/no* questions using *will* and the words in parentheses. Complete the short answers.

Max and Rob will be in Olympic National Park in January. What will it be like?

1. (there/be) <u>Will there be</u> snow in the park? Yes, <u>there will</u>. There is
   a   b
   almost always snow on the high mountains. Sometimes 100 feet of snow falls on the
   mountains in winter.

2. (there/be) _____ places to ski? Yes, _____.
   a   b
   For example, people ski at Hurricane Ridge from December to March.

3. (it/snow) _____ in the rain forests? No, _____.
   a   b
   It'll be very green there. More than 100 inches of rain falls there each year.

4. Rob: (we/hike) _____ in the rain forests?
   a
   Max: Yes, _____. Wear good boots.
   b

5. Rob: (you/bring) _____ camping supplies?
   a

   Max: Yes, _____. I have a tent and all the equipment we'll need.
   b

6. Rob: (I/need) _____ to bring a map of the park?
   a

   Max: No, _____ We'll get maps at the Visitor Center.
   b

7. Rob: (the nights/be) _____ very cold?

   Max: It depends. The weather is different in different areas of the park.

6 *Wh-* Questions: A Sign of Spring

Read about Pacific gray whales. Then write *wh-* questions about the **boldfaced** words using *who, what, when, where, how much,* and *how many.*

1. In the spring, visitors to Olympic National Park will see **something**.

   Question: *What will they see?* _____
   Answer: Pacific gray whales. They pass the park each year on their way north.

2. The whales will pass the park **at some time**.

   Question: _____
   Answer: In late March and early April.

3. The whales will go **somewhere**.

   Question: _____
   Answer: To the waters near Alaska. This is their summer feeding area.

4. They will travel **a number of** miles to get to Alaska.

   Question: _____
   Answer: 5,000 miles.

5. The whales will eat **something**.

   Question: _____
   Answer: Small shellfish and plants.

6. Maybe it will cost **some money** to watch the whales.

   Question: _____
   Answer: Nothing! The whales will swim close to land, so people will watch them from the beaches.

7. There are no more Atlantic gray whales. They have all died; they are now extinct. But **someone** will protect the Pacific gray whales from extinction.

   Question: _____
   Answer: People who care about wildlife.

 See the *Grammar Links* Website for more information about Pacific gray whales.

Yes/No and *Wh-* **Questions:** The Magic Coin

 A. On three small pieces of paper, write three *yes/no* questions with *will*. Ask about people, places, and things that your classmates know about.

Example: Will Brazil win the next World Cup?
Will we get a big snowstorm?
Will Natasha marry her boyfriend?

 B. Work with a group. Put all your questions into a hat or a bag. Take turns drawing a piece of paper and reading the question out loud. Each member of the group gives a short answer as their prediction. Then toss a coin to get an answer. Take turns asking *wh-* questions about it.

 Heads = *Yes, _____ will.*   **Tails** = *No, _____ won't.*

Example: Student A: "Will Brazil win the next World Cup?"
Student B: Yes, it will.
Student C: No, it probably won't.

Student A tosses the coin.

Student A: Heads. Yes, it will!
Student C: Where will they have the next World Cup?

 Check your progress! Go to the Self-Test for Chapter 19 on the *Grammar Links* Website.

Wrap-up Activities

1 A Trip to Australia: READING

Read this paragraph.

   Makiko and her family are planning a trip to Australia next month. They will be there for about two weeks. First, they are going to spend time in two cities. They have relatives to visit in Melbourne, and they are going to spend three days in Sydney. They will probably take walks, visit museums, and eat in restaurants. Makiko is going to do some shopping, too. However, they won't spend all their time in cities. They are also going to visit a beautiful national park. It is on Fraser Island, the largest sand island in the world. They are going to relax on the beach, swim, and go for hikes in the rain forest. They will probably see wild horses, hundreds of birds, and some kinds of animals that live only in Australia. Makiko is looking forward to the trip.

2 A Future Trip: WRITING

Write a paragraph of seven or more sentences about a trip you will take. It can be any kind of trip: maybe a big trip that will happen some time far into the future, or maybe a short trip to the supermarket next Saturday. Use affirmative and negative statements with *will* and *be going to*. Include at least one time expression.

 See the *Grammar Links* Website for a model paragraph for this assignment.

3 My Trip: EDITING

Correct the eight errors with future time expressions and with *will* and *be going to*. Some errors can be corrected in more than one way. The first error is corrected for you.

My Trip

In a few days, I ~~will~~ *am* going to visit my brother. I am going to leave on next

Saturday. My brother is a student at the University of Florida, but he will has a

vacation next week. I think the weather will to be nice there, so we probably going

to go to the beach. I want to see some movies and sleep a lot, too. I'm going spend

five days with my brother, and I won't probably do any homework during this

time. It going to be a real vacation.

---

4 **Predictions:** WRITING/SPEAKING/LISTENING

Step 1 Use three slips of paper and write three predictions that will make people happy. Use *You* (or *Your* + noun) + *will* or *be going to*.

Examples: You're going to get good news in the mail.
Your grade on the next test will be very good.

Step 2 Work in a group. Put all your predictions into a hat or an envelope. Each person will pull out one slip of paper and read it out loud. After you read your prediction, tell if you are happy about it or not. Give your reasons. Continue, taking turns.

5 **Looking into the Future:** WRITING/SPEAKING/LISTENING

Step 1 Think of words to write on the lines below.

1. Write a job (for example: *doctor*, *taxi driver*). _____

2. Write a noncount noun. _____

3. Write a number. _____

4. Write the name of a place. _____

5. Write a kind of wild animal. _____

6. Write a girl's name. _____

7. Write an adjective. _____

8. Write a plural noun. _____

9. Write the name of a famous (living) man. _____

10. Write the name of a famous (living) woman. _____

Step 2 Form a group of four or six. Give your book to someone in the group, and take that person's book.

Step 3 Go to page A-2. Follow the directions for Unit Eight Wrap-up Activities, Task 5: *Looking into the Future*, Steps 3 and 4.

6 **Vacation Plans:** SPEAKING/LISTENING

Step 1 Congratulations! You are the winner of a wonderful vacation for two! Make some decisions about your trip, such as where you are going, when you are leaving, whom you're going to invite, and what you're going to do.

Step 2 Work with a partner. Take turns interviewing each other about your vacation plans.

Example: Student A: *Where are you going to go on your vacation?*
Student B: *East Africa.*
Student A: *Why are you going to go there?*

Modals; Imperatives

TOPIC FOCUS
Going Into Business

UNIT OBJECTIVES

- **one-word modals and phrasal modals**
  (We *should* talk to a banker. *Could* you go with me? I *have to* go soon.)

- **ability with *can*, *could*, and *be able to***
  (He *can* speak three languages now. He *could* speak English when he was 12 years old. He *'ll be able to* read that.)

- **possibility with *might*, *may*, and *could***
  (I *might* go to the movies tonight. Anna *may* come with me. We *could* go to the 7:00 show.)

- **advice with *should***
  (I think you *should* take a math course. We *shouldn't* talk in class.)

- **necessity with *must* and *have to***
  (All employees *must* fill out tax forms. I *have to* fill out a form. You *don't have to* do anything.)

- **modals for requests, permission, and offers**
  (*Will* you sign this paper for me? *Could* I use this computer? *Can* I help you? *Would* you like some coffee?)

- **imperatives and *let's***
  (Please *come* here. *Don't sit* on that chair! *Let's go* to the store.)

Grammar in Action

🎧 Reading and Listening: Plans and Ideas

Read and listen to this conversation.

Daniel Ruiz and Misha Sova are talking about their jobs and making some plans for the future.

Daniel: You know what? I've been thinking. I'd like to have my own business. I'm tired of working for somebody else.

Misha: Me, too. What do you have in mind?

Daniel: I don't know . . . but I'm a pretty good cook. I **can** bake. I learned from my grandmother. She **could** bake anything.

Misha: So you **might** make bread or cookies or something like that?

Daniel: Yeah. Do you want to help? **Can** you bake anything?

Misha: Sorry, but I'm afraid not.

Daniel: But you made this soup, right? It's great.

Misha: Soup is easy. I make different kinds of soup all the time.

Daniel: Wait a minute. Listen to this: A soup and sandwich shop. My bread, your soup. What do you think?

Misha: Interesting . . .

Daniel: Come on, let's do it.

Misha: But, where? It has to be some place around here, so we don't have to move.

Daniel: What about right here in our neighborhood?

Misha: Well, there aren't that many people here.

Daniel: What about near the college? There are lots of people there.

Misha: Well, we **might** find a place to rent there. But that area **may** be expensive.

Daniel: Hmmm . . . I have a friend with a restaurant near there. Maybe . . .

Misha: You **should** ask her for her opinion.

Daniel: Yeah, I'll do that.

Misha: And we need a name. What **should** we call our place?

Daniel: I think we **should** call it "Daniel & Misha's Soup and Sandwich Shop."

Misha: Or maybe "Soup and Sandwich as You Like It"?

Daniel: Yeah, that **might** work. Well, what are we waiting for? Let's go look for a place!

Misha: Hey, slow down a minute! Did you know that 10% of all new businesses fail in their first year? And in the restaurant business, it's a lot more than 10%. We have to think about this some more.

---

fail = (in business) lose money and close down.

Think About Grammar

A. Look at the **boldfaced** words in the conversation. They are **modals**. Write the five modals on the lines below.

_____   _____   _____

_____   _____

B. Look at the verbs that follow the modals in the conversation. What form of the verb is used after a modal? Circle the answer.

a. verb + *-ing*   b. verb + *-ed*   c. base form of the verb

C. Match these sentences from the conversation with the meanings of the **boldfaced** modals. Write the letters.

_____ 1.	I **can** bake. I learned from my grandmother. She **could** bake anything.	a. Advice (Something is a good idea.)
_____ 2.	Well, we **might** find a place to rent there. But that area **may** be expensive.	b. Ability (Someone knows or knew how to do something.)
_____ 3.	You **should** ask her for her opinion.	c. Possibility (Maybe something is true, or maybe something will happen.)

On the Job

Overview of Modals; Ability—*Can*, *Could*, and *Be Able To*; Possibility—*Might*, *May*, and *Could*

Introductory Task: Skills for the Job

A. Skills are abilities—things that you learn to do. Match the people and the job skills they have. Write the letters.

People		Job Skills
1. An artist	_c_	a. can explain school lessons.
2. A nurse	_____	b. can use a camera.
3. A scientist	_____	c. can draw or paint.
4. A photographer	_____	d. can help sick people.
5. A musician	_____	e. can play music.
6. An interpreter	_____	f. can speak more than one language.
7. A teacher	_____	g. can do experiments in a laboratory.

B. Make a list of your skills (job skills, musical skills, athletic skills, etc.). Write three things that you can do.

I can _____, I can _____, and I can

_____.

C. Work with a partner. Read your skills to each other. Complete the statements below.

Is there a skill you both have?   Yes, we both can _____.

Do you have different skills?

I can _____, but my partner can't. My partner can

_____, but I can't.

Overview of Modals

FORM and FUNCTION

One-Word and Phrasal Modals

1. **Modals** are auxiliary verbs (or helping verbs). They are used with a main verb. The main verb is in the base form:

SUBJECT	MODAL	BASE FORM OF MAIN VERB	
I	**can**	**drive**	a car.
We	**should**	**ask**	someone for directions.

2. Modals add meaning to main verbs. Modals can express:

   - Ability.

     He **can** drive. (He has the ability to drive.)

   - Possibility.

     It **might** rain later. (Maybe it will rain.)

   - Advice.

     You **should** do it. (It's good to do it.)

   - Necessity.

     Everyone **must** pay. (It is necessary.)

   - Requests.

     Will you please help me? (I'm asking you for help.)

   - Permission.

     Can I call you later? (Is it okay for me to call you later?)

   - Offers.

     Could I get you some coffee? (I'm ready to get some coffee for you if you want it.)

3. Most modals are one word. **One-word modals** do not change form. They are the same for all subjects.

I	
We	**may** be away next week.
He	

4. **Phrasal modals** are more than one word. They begin with *be* or *have*. *Be* and *have* change form. Phrasal modals include:

   - *Be able to.*

     We **were able to** drive.

     He **was able to** drive.

   - *Have to.*

     I **have to** pay.

     She **has to** pay.

| Use only one one-word modal with a main verb. | I think you **would** enjoy that movie.
NOT: I think you ~~might~~ would enjoy that movie. |

TALKING THE TALK

| Do not pronounce the *l* in *could*, *should*, or *would*. These words rhyme with *good*. | *Would* and *wood* sound the same. |

GRAMMAR PRACTICE 1

Overview of Modals

1 **Identifying One-Word and Phrasal Modals:** Some Friendly Advice

Read the conversation. Circle the eight one-word modals. The first one is circled for you. <u>Underline</u> the three phrasal modals. The first one is underlined for you.

Daniel Ruiz is talking to his friend Emma. Emma has her own restaurant. Daniel wants to open one. He is asking her for some advice.

Emma: So this is my restaurant! It's not big, but it's mine. (Will) you have some coffee?

Daniel: Yes, please. Thanks. You know, I want to start my own business, too. Can I ask you some questions?

Emma: Sure.

Daniel: Is it really difficult to get started?

Emma: In a word, yes. First, you <u>have to</u> have a good business plan, and then, some money—a lot of money for the first few years.

Daniel: Should I borrow the money from a bank?

Emma: Many people do. But then you have to pay it back. With a bank, the payments must be on a regular schedule. The problem with this is, you might not make much money at first.

Daniel: Well, how else do people get the money to start?

Emma: They borrow from friends and relatives. I wasn't able to get a bank loan, so that's what I did.

Daniel: That's an idea. Ahh, tell me . . . would you invest in my business?

Emma: Well, I don't know. I may be interested. Tell me more about it.

Daniel: Well, I don't have anything definite right now. Can I call you next week?

Emma: Sure.

> *on a regular schedule* = at planned times. *borrow* = take something that belongs to someone else
> to use it and give it back. *invest* = put money into a business in order to make money from it.

2 **Listening for One-Word and Phrasal Modals: News for Misha**

Listen and read. Listen again, and complete the sentences with the modals you hear. Some of the modals are used more than once.

> can   could   have to   may   ✓ might   should

Daniel Ruiz is doing a lot of planning for his new restaurant. He calls Misha (his friend and maybe his future business partner), and he leaves this message on the answering machine:

Hey Misha, it's me. Listen, I have some great news! I learned a lot today from Emma, and she _____might_____ give us some kitchen equipment. But the best part is that I saw a "For Rent" sign on a building today. It's an old restaurant. It's perfect for us! I _____2_____ look at it again tomorrow. _____3_____ you come with me? We _____4_____ act fast, or we _____5_____ lose our chance. The last owners of this restaurant _____6_____ serve about 100 meals a day. But I think we _____7_____ serve even more. We _____8_____ buy a new stove and paint the place, but that won't be too expensive. I'll see you tonight and we _____9_____ talk more then. I _____10_____ go. I _____11_____ talk to my parents about money. See you later.

3 **Editing: Planning a Small Business**

Correct the errors in modals and main verbs. There is one error in each sentence. The first error is corrected for you.

1. Daniel can ~~to~~ bake bread.

2. Daniel's grandmother could baked anything: bread, cookies, cakes, etc.

3. Daniel and Misha may a business together.

4. Misha mights become Daniel's business partner.

5. They should getting some more advice.

6. Daniel have to talk to his parents about borrowing money.

7. Maybe he will be able get some money from his parents.

8. New business owners must often borrows money from a bank.

Expressing Ability with *Can*, *Could*, and *Be Able To*— Affirmative and Negative Statements

FORM

A. Statements with *Can* and *Could*

AFFIRMATIVE

SUBJECT	MODAL	BASE VERB	
I	can	swim	now.
	could		when I was five.

NEGATIVE

SUBJECT	MODAL + *NOT*	BASE VERB	
He	cannot can't	swim	yet.
	could not couldn't		last year.

B. Statements with *Be Able To*

SUBJECT	*BE* (*NOT*)	*ABLE TO*	BASE VERB	
I	am (not)	able to	swim	now.
	was (not)			10 years ago.
	will (not) be			soon.

FUNCTION

Using *Can*, *Could*, and *Be Able To*

Can, *could*, and *be able to* express ability. Use them to describe skills or what someone knows how to do. To express:

- A present ability, use *can* or *am/is/are able to*.

She **can**	type 100 words a minute.
She**'s able to**	

- A past ability, use *could* or *was/were able to*.

They **could**	read and write.
They **were able to**	

- A future ability, use *will be able to*.

He's taking Spanish lessons. Soon he**'ll be able to** speak Spanish.

TALKING THE TALK

The *a* in *can* usually has a very short, soft sound. It is not stressed. The *a* in *can't* is stressed, so it has a longer, louder sound.

I /kn/ SÉE it.

I /KÁNT/ SÉE it.

GRAMMAR PRACTICE 2

Expressing Ability with *Can*, *Could*, and *Be Able To*—Affirmative and Negative Statements

4 *Can* and *Could* for Ability: Ben and Jerry, Ice Cream Makers

Complete the statements. Write *can* or *could*.

Ben Cohen and Jerry Greenfield were good friends in

high school. Later, in 1978, they went into business together.

They began the famous Ben & Jerry's ice cream company.

Ben Cohen has many skills. He __can__
                                      1

do a variety of things. During high school, Ben worked

for an ice cream company. He had a driver's license, so he

_____ drive the ice cream truck. After high school,
        2

he learned to make pottery. He moved to New York City to

learn more about it. In 1974, he got a job as an art teacher in a small school because he

_____ make pottery. He worked in the school kitchen, too, because he
        3

_____ also cook.
        4

Ben and Jerry

Meanwhile, Jerry Greenfield studied science in college because he wanted to become a doctor. For fun, he took a class in Carnival Techniques, so he knows how to do some unusual tricks. For example, he _____ swallow fire! Jerry didn't go to
5
medical school, so he _____ not become a doctor. Instead, he worked as a lab
6
technician. Later, he and Ben took a course in how to make ice cream.

Pottery

Today, Ben and Jerry are successful businessmen. Now they _____ advise others
7
about starting a business. They _____ do a lot to help their communities, too, and
8
they do.

> *a lab technician* = a person who is trained to do scientific work in a laboratory.

 See the *Grammar Links* Website for more information about Ben and Jerry's ice cream company.

5 *Can, Could* and *Be Able To*: Meet the Bookkeeping Staff

A. Cross out *can* and *could*, and write forms of *be able to*. Use contractions with subject pronouns and with *not*.

Paula is the head of the bookkeeping department for a small company.

wasn't able to
She started working there in 1992. At first, she ~~couldn't~~ use a computer, but now
1

she can operate most computers and even fix them.
2

Sharon is the department secretary. She can type 100 words per minute.
3

Sharon could speak three languages when she was eight years old: Chinese,
4

English, and French. She knows where everything is in the office, and she can
5

answer almost any question.

There are two bookkeepers, Tran and Raúl. Tran started as a part-time worker

three years ago. She couldn't work full-time because she was in school. Last year,
          6
Tran graduated and started to work full-time. Raúl began as a bookkeeper

ten years ago. Raúl says, "We can prepare the financial reports in five hours.
                            7
Two years ago, we couldn't do reports that fast. Now we have good equipment,
             8
and we work as a team. There's always a lot of work. In the past, I couldn't take
                                                                            9
work home at night because I didn't have a computer. Now I have a computer,

but I still can't take work home. My family doesn't let me. They say I work all day
          10
and I shouldn't work all night, too."

> *bookkeeping* = keeping records of money received and paid by a
> business. *part-time* = working only part of the usual number of hours.
> *full-time* = working the usual number of hours (about 40 hours a week
> in the United States).

B. Cross out the forms of *be able to* and write *can* or *could* when possible.
Write *No change* when you cannot use *can* or *could*.

1. Paula ~~is able to~~ **can** use a computer.

2. When she started her career, she wasn't able to use computers.

3. Sharon is able to speak three languages.

4. She was able to speak Chinese, English, and French as a child.

5. She is taking Japanese lessons, and soon she'll be able to speak four languages.

6. Sharon is not able to write much Japanese.

7. Two years ago, Tran wasn't able to work many hours.

8. Both Tran and Raúl are able to use bookkeeping programs on the computer.

9. Raúl can't work at home now and probably won't be able to work at home in
   the future, either.

6 *Can* Versus *Can't*: Practicing for a Job Interview

A. Read the list of job skills in the chart below. These are skills a bookkeeper might need.

Skill	Can	Can't
1. Organize files	✓	
2. Prepare financial reports		
3. Type reports		
4. Use a computer		
5. Speak Spanish		
6. Read German		
7. Complete tax forms		
8. Use the bookkeeping program		
9. Order materials		
10. Do an inventory		

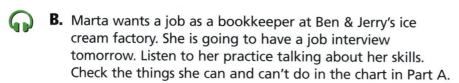

financial = related to money. *tax forms* = papers that show the amount of taxes to be paid. *an inventory* = a list of things (as in a store) that has the number or quantity of each item.

B. Marta wants a job as a bookkeeper at Ben & Jerry's ice cream factory. She is going to have a job interview tomorrow. Listen to her practice talking about her skills. Check the things she can and can't do in the chart in Part A.

C. Work with a partner. Say what Marta can and can't do. Pay attention to the pronunciation of *can* and *can't*.

Example: Student A: *She can organize files.*

Asking About Present Ability with *Can*

FORM

A. *Yes/No* Questions and Short Answers

QUESTIONS				ANSWERS					
MODAL	SUBJECT	BASE VERB		*YES*			*NO*		
Can	you	**cook**?		Yes,	I	**can**.	No,	I	**can't**.
	he	**drive**	a bus?		he			he	

B. *Wh-* Questions and Answers

WH- QUESTIONS WITH *WHO/WHAT* AS SUBJECT				ANSWERS
WHO/WHAT	MODAL	BASE VERB		
Who	**can**	**fix**	the computer?	Irene can. She knows how.
		run	the fastest?	Antonio—no one can catch him.

WH- QUESTIONS WITH OTHER SUBJECTS					ANSWERS
WH- QUESTION WORD	MODAL	SUBJECT	BASE VERB		
What	**can**	he	**play**?		The piano.
Why		Siok	**speak**	French so well?	She learned it as a child.

GRAMMAR PRACTICE 3

Asking about Present Ability with *Can*

7   *Wh-* **Questions with** *Can*: Job Skills

Read the incomplete sentences. Write *wh-* questions with *can* to match the answers.

1. A carpenter can . . .

   Q: *What can a carpenter do?*
   _____

   A: Build things out of wood.

2. A dentist can help . . .

   Q: _____

   A: People with tooth problems.

3. . . . can fix cars.

   Q: _____

   A: A mechanic can.

4. Lifeguards can help people at . . .

   Q: _____

   A: At the beach or a pool.

5. A chef can . . .

   Q: _____

   A: He or she can cook many types of food.

6. . . . can fly a plane.

   Q: _____

   A: A pilot can.

7. A composer can write . . .

   Q: _____

   A: Music.

8. A person can become a doctor after . . .

   Q: _____

   A: After many years of study and training.

8 **Asking and Answering *Yes/No* Questions with *Can*: Can You Do This?**

Walk around your classroom. Ask your classmates *yes/no* questions with *Can you*
based on the statements below. Think of your own question for number 8.
Complete the statements with the names of different classmates.

Example: Student A: *Can you play the guitar?*
           Student B: *Yes, I can.* OR *No, I can't.*

1. _____ can play the guitar.   _____ can't play the guitar.
        a   b

2. _____ can swim.   _____ can't swim.
        a   b

3. _____ can drive.   _____ can't drive.
        a   b

4. _____ can speak three   _____ can't speak three
        a   b
   languages.   languages.

5. _____ can make soup.   _____ can't make soup.
        a   b

6. _____ can sing.   _____ can't sing.
        a   b

7. _____ can use a computer.   _____ can't use a computer.
        a   b

8. _____ can _____   _____ can't _____
        a   b

Expressing Possibility with *Might, May,* and *Could*

FORM

A. Affirmative Statements with *Might, May,* and *Could*

SUBJECT	MODAL	BASE VERB	
It	might		
	may	be	true.
	could		

B. Negative Statements with *Might, May,* and *Could*

FULL FORMS

SUBJECT	MODAL	*NOT*	BASE VERB	
It	might			
	may	not	be	true.
	could			

CONTRACTIONS

SUBJECT	MODAL + *NOT*	BASE VERB	
It	—		
	—	be	true.
	couldn't		

C. Questions with *Could*

Yes/No *Questions and Short Answers*

QUESTIONS				ANSWERS	
COULD	SUBJECT	BASE VERB		*YES*	*NO*
Could	it	be	true?	Yes, it **could**.	No, it **couldn't**.

Wh- *Questions and Answers*

QUESTIONS					ANSWERS
WH- QUESTION WORD	*COULD*	(SUBJECT)	BASE VERB		
Where	could	they	be?		Maybe they're downtown.
Who			be	at the door?	That might be Sam.

FUNCTION

Expressing Possibility

1. Use *might, may,* or *could* to express:

   - Present possibility.

     I don't know where he is. He **may be** at home now.

   - Future possibility.

     I don't know where he'll be tonight. He **may be** at home then.

(continued on next page)

Expressing Possibility (continued)

2. If you are sure about something, use a present or future verb. If you are almost sure, use *probably*.	He **is** (**probably**) at home now. He **will** (**probably**) **be** at home tonight.
3. *Could + not* is different from *might* or *may + not*:	
• *Might not* and *may not* show the speaker is not sure about something.	He **might not** be home. He might be out. She may be married or she **may not** be.
• *Could not* shows the speaker is sure that something is not possible.	He **couldn't** be home—he was here just a minute ago!
4. Use *could* in questions about present possibility. Do not use *might* or *may*.	**Could** they be on vacation? **NOT:** ~~Might/May~~ they be on vacation?

GRAMMAR **HOT**SPOT!

1. *Maybe* is an adverb. It expresses possibility.	I don't know why he's absent. **Maybe** he's sick.
2. *Maybe* can introduce statements with past, present, or future verbs.	**Maybe** they are / were / will be out.
3. Do not confuse *maybe* with the modal *may* + main verb *be*.	adverb **Maybe** he is at home. modal + base verb He **may be** at home.

GRAMMAR PRACTICE 4

Expressing Possibility with *Might*, *May*, and *Could*

9 **Future Possibility:** What Are the Chances?

Match each sentence with its meaning. Write the letters.

_c_	1. He'll get that job.	a.	I'm almost sure he'll get it.
_____	2. He'll probably get that job.	b.	I am sure he won't get it.
_____	3. He might get that job.	c.	I am sure he'll get it.
_____	4. He might not get that job.	d.	Maybe he'll get it—it's possible.
_____	5. He couldn't get that job.	e.	Maybe he won't get it.

10 Present and Future Possibility: Changing Jobs

Complete the statements with *might, may,* or *could* + the information given.

1. Between the ages of 18 and 32, the average American changes jobs nine times.

   Between the ages of 18 and 32, an American worker *may change jobs nine times.*

2. The average retirement age in the United States is 65. But maybe a person will retire at 55 or at 85.

   A person _____

3. Sometimes people change to completely different careers.

   A person _____

4. There are lots of reasons to change jobs. For example, maybe a new job will pay more.

   A new job _____

5. Maybe a new job will be more secure.

   A new job _____

6. Maybe a new job will be more interesting.

   A new job _____

7. Maybe a new job will offer better benefits.

   A new job _____

> *benefits* = special payments for work in addition to money, such as paid vacation time or insurance.

11 *Might Not* and *May Not* Versus *Could Not*: A New Job for Tran?

Complete the statements with *might/may not* or *could not* + the information given.

Tran is considering a new job. She is talking about it with her friend Mary.

1. Tran: Maybe I won't stay at this job.

   Tran says that she *might not stay at her job.* _____

2. Tran: Business is slow. Maybe the company won't keep me.

   Tran says that the company _____

3. Mary: Business won't get that bad. It's not possible.

   Mary believes that business _____

4. Tran: There's a job open at Bankwest. But maybe it isn't full-time.

   Tran thinks that the job at Bankwest _____

5. Tran: It's not possible for me to work just part-time.

   Tran says that she _____

6. Mary: Tran, maybe this city isn't the right place for you.

Mary says that this city _____

7. Tran: It would not be possible for me to move to another city. All my family and friends are here.

Tran says that she _____

8. Tran: Maybe I won't look for another bookkeeping job.

Tran says that she _____

9. Mary: Maybe you won't need a new job.

Mary says that Tran _____

12 *Maybe* Versus *May Be*: What's Going On?

A. Tran is at work, but she isn't working. Make guesses about why not. Write sentences with *maybe* or *may be* + the words in parentheses. Do not add any other words.

1. _Maybe she has no work to do._ _____
   (she / has no work to do)

2. _She may be on her break now._ _____
   (she / on her break now)

3. _____
   (she / doesn't feel well)

4. _____
   (it / is time for lunch)

5. _____
   (it / time to go home)

6. _____
   (she / asleep at her desk)

B. Work alone or with a partner. Make two more guesses about why Tran is not working at the moment. Write one sentence with *maybe* and one sentence with *may be*.

1. _____

2. _____

13 Using *Might, May, Could,* and *Maybe*: No Test Today?

Work with a partner. Imagine that you are going to class. Your teacher planned to give a test today. Talk about reasons why you might not have the test. Use *might, may, could,* and *maybe* in your statements. How many reasons can you think of?

Example: Student A: The teacher might not come to school.
Student B: There may be no electricity or lights.
Student A: Maybe the teacher will forget the test.

14 **Editing:** A Tour of Ben & Jerry's

Correct the 10 errors in modals. Some errors can be corrected in more than one way. The first error is corrected for you.

Daniel and Misha are taking a tour of the Ben & Jerry's ice cream factory in Vermont.

Tour guide: Welcome to Ben & Jerry's! We will ~~taking~~ a trip through the factory
                         take

             building today. Please come this way, everyone.

Daniel: Wow! Look at all the machines!

Misha: And all the ice cream! It might could be fun to work here.

Tour guide: In this room, you can to see the worker prepare some ice cream. She

             musts add the ingredients carefully and then mix them.

Misha: What kind of ice cream is she making? Might it be chocolate? That's my

             favorite kind . . .

Tour guide: Yes, I believe it is chocolate. We'll have some later. Please step this way, everyone.

Misha: Excuse me, when did Ben and Jerry first make their ice cream?

Tour guide: In 1978. They started an ice cream shop in Burlington, Vermont. Back then,

             they can't produce a lot—they had to make it, package it, and deliver it, too.

             But now, in this factory building, the company can makes over 50 different

             flavors of ice cream. These machines are fast, and they could fill 90 cups a minute.

Daniel: Is it okay for the workers to eat some of the ice cream?

Tour guide: Of course!

Misha: Do all the workers here love ice cream?

Tour guide: I don't know. Most people probably love it, but some could not. In the

             next room, we have samples for all of you to taste. They maybe ready now.

             Thank you for coming on the tour, and we hope you have a nice day!

Check your progress! Go to the Self-Test for Chapter 20 on the *Grammar Links* Website.

Chapter 21

Getting Started in Business

Should for Advice; *Must* and *Have To* for Necessity

Introductory Task: Some Advice, Please?

A. Read the list of nine conversation topics in Part B.

 B. Listen to a conversation between a counselor at the Small Business Association and Helen Zajac. Helen wants to start a business, and she needs a loan from a bank. Listen to the counselor: Is he

(a) giving advice (describing something Helen should do) or

(b) explaining what's necessary (telling something she must or has to do)?

Check (✓) the correct column.

	(a) You should . . .	(b) You must/ You have to . . .	
1.	✓		. . . read about loans.
2.			. . . describe your past business experience.
3.			. . . tell the bank how much money you need.
4.			. . . tell the bank what you will buy.
5.			. . . explain why you need these things.
6.			. . . be able to pay back the loan.
7.			. . . give predictions about the future of your business.
8.			. . . call some banks.
9.			. . . meet with several different bank managers.

> *a counselor* = a person who gives advice. *the Small Business Association* = a group that gives advice about starting a business. *a loan* = an amount of money that someone borrows.

C. Work with a group. Think about what is necessary for all students. Then think of some good advice for students learning English. Complete these statements, and share your ideas with the class.

All students must _____.

Learners of English should _____.

Should for Advice

FORM

A. Affirmative Statements

SUBJECT	*SHOULD*	BASE VERB	
She	**should**	**study**	for the test.
The boys			

B. Negative Statements

SUBJECT	*SHOULD* + *NOT*	BASE VERB	
She	**should not**	**talk**	during the test.
The boys	**shouldn't**		

C. *Yes/No* Questions and Short Answers

QUESTIONS				ANSWERS	
SHOULD	SUBJECT	BASE VERB		*YES*	*NO*
Should	I	**buy**	this?	Yes, you **should**.	No, you **shouldn't**.
	we				

D. *Wh-* Questions and Answers

QUESTIONS					ANSWERS
WH- QUESTION WORD	*SHOULD*	(SUBJECT)	BASE VERB		
Who	**should**		**answer**	the phone?	Emily should.
Why		she	**do**	it?	Because she is the secretary.

FUNCTION

Giving Advice

Use *should* to give advice or to state opinions about what is and isn't right.	You **should** study tonight. They **shouldn't** smoke.

To give advice more politely, use *I think* or *I don't think* before *you should*.

I think you should drive more slowly.

I don't think you should do it. It's not safe.

Should for Advice

1 **Affirmative and Negative Statements with *Should*:** Giving Business Advice

Complete the statements with *should* or *shouldn't*.

Advice for the New Store Owner

1. You ___should___ start with good products. Quality is important.

2. You _____ sell bad products. Customers won't be happy, and then they won't come back.

3. You _____ be honest. Customers and employees need to trust you.

4. You _____ start several stores at the same time! Start one store. Your company will grow over the years.

5. You and your staff _____ help your customers. Talk to them and answer their questions.

6. You _____ try to make your customers happy.

7. A person _____ work 365 days a year. Take some time off.

8. Businesspeople _____ always look for new ideas. Keep your eyes and ears open!

products = things that a company makes or produces. *quality* = how good something is. *staff* = the employees who work for a person or an organization.

2 Yes/No and Wh- Questions with *Should*: Asking for Advice

A. Write questions with *should*. Use the words in parentheses.

Helen Zajac is almost ready to open a children's clothing store. She now has a partner, Nino Martin. They need more advice from the counselor at the Small Business Association.

Dick Collins: It's nice to see you again. Do you have some more questions?

Helen: Yes, we do. First, we have a question about taxes. <u>Should we complete</u>
1 (we / complete)

these tax forms for the state?

Dick Collins: Oh, yes. They're very important. You don't want to forget them.

Nino: _____ the tax forms?
2 (when / we / send)

Dick Collins: The best time is in March. That way, you won't miss the deadline.

Helen: What about ads? _____ on the radio?
3 (we / advertise)

Dick Collins: Yes, radio ads can be very helpful for a new business.

Nino: _____?
4 (which radio station / we / use)

Helen: WKLP, I think. It's a popular station.

Dick Collins: Mmmmm, yes. That sounds like a good choice. And think about newspaper

advertising, too.

Helen: Yes, I suppose we should. Also, we'll need sales help in the store. I'd like to hire

someone. But _____?
5 (we / wait)

Dick Collins: No. You can't do everything! You should get some help.

Nino: _____?
6 (how much / we / pay)

Dick Collins: Minimum wage, I think.

Helen: We're not sure about the bookkeeping for the business.

_____ a bookkeeper?
7 (we / hire)

Dick Collins: Well, you should know a little bit about bookkeeping. We have a short course

about the basics. You may want to hire someone to help you while you're learning.

minimum wage = by law, the lowest amount that an employer can pay a worker.

B. Listen to the conversation in Part A, and check your answers.

3 **Using Affirmative and Negative Statements with *Should*:** Some Do's and Don'ts for Shoppers

 Work with a partner. Write a list of 10 statements with advice for shoppers. Use *should* or *shouldn't* and the ideas below or your own ideas. Give the reasons for your advice.

Example: *People should always wait for things to go on sale. They'll save money.*

- look at ads in newspapers, online, etc.
- do business with the same stores or companies
- decide how much to spend before shopping
- buy big-name brands only

- ask questions
- save all receipts
- buy things only with cash
- _____
- _____

Big Deals	
#50241 10:35 a.m. 1/2/04	
Merch	9.99
Merch	1.99
Sub-total	11.98
Sales tax	.60
Total	12.58
Pay type	CASH
Received	20.00
Change	7.42

A Receipt

> *big-name brands* = products made by companies with famous names.

 See the *Grammar Links* Website for advice for online shoppers.

4 **Using *Yes/No* and *Wh-* Questions with *Should*:** Ask a Question, Get Some Advice

A. What advice do you need about school, work, or life in general? Write about a problem or situation on a small piece of paper. Include a question asking for advice with *should*. Sign your name if you want, or sign an invented name (for example, *Tired Student* or *Shy Girl*).

B. Work in a group. Put all the papers into an envelope or a hat. Take turns drawing out and reading a question. Take turns giving advice about each problem or situation.

Example: Student A (reads): *I gave some money to a friend at work two weeks ago. He didn't pay it back. What should I do? This question is from "Working Man."*

Student B: *He should sit with the friend at lunch and talk. Then he should ask the friend for the money.*

Student C: *He should forget about it.*

C. Describe a problem from your group discussion in Part B. Write your advice for the person with the problem. Include statements with *should*.

See the *Grammar Links* Website for a model paragraph for this assignment.

Must and *Have To* for Necessity

FORM

A. Affirmative Statements*

SUBJECT	MUST/HAVE TO	BASE VERB	
I	**must** **have to** **had to**	**show**	my passport.

*For negative statements, see Grammar Briefing 3 in this chapter, page 343.

B. *Yes/No* Questions and Short Answers

QUESTIONS						ANSWERS	
DO/DID	SUBJECT	HAVE TO	BASE VERB			YES	NO
Does	he	**have to**	**take**	a test?		Yes, he **does**.	No, he **doesn't**.
Did	you					Yes, I **did**.	No, I **didn't**.

C. *Wh-* Questions and Answers

QUESTIONS WITH *WHO/WHAT* AS SUBJECT				ANSWERS
WHO/WHAT	HAVE/HAD TO	BASE VERB		
Who	**has to**	**pay**	taxes?	Everyone does.
	had to	**register**	for courses?	All the students did.

QUESTIONS WITH OTHER SUBJECTS					ANSWERS
WH- WORD	DO/DID	SUBJECT	HAVE TO	BASE VERB	
What	**do**	I	**have to**	**do?**	Show your ID card.
Why	**did**	you		**leave?**	Because I had to work.

FUNCTION

Expressing Necessity

1. Use *must* or *have to* to express necessity or state a rule. Affirmative statements with these modals tell what someone needs to do.

   All travelers **must** show their passports.
   All travelers **have to** show their passports.

(continued on next page)

2. Use *must* and *have to* to express:

   • Necessity in the present.

We	**must**	be on time **every day**.
	have to	

   • Necessity in the future.

We	**must**	be on time **tomorrow**.
	have to	

3. To express necessity in the past, use *had to*.

   I **had to** leave early **yesterday** because I felt sick.

4. Use *have to*, not *must*, in questions.

   Do you **have to** work tomorrow?
     NOT: ~~Must~~ you work tomorrow?

   Why **did** they **have to** leave?

TALKING THE TALK

1. *Have to* is more common than *must* in conversation.

   I **have to** go now.
     NOT USUALLY: I must go now.

2. In conversation, *have to* is often pronounced "hafta." *Has to* sounds like "hasta."

WRITE	YOU WILL OFTEN HEAR
They **have to** pay.	They "hafta" pay.
He **has to** wait.	He "hasta" wait.

GRAMMAR PRACTICE 2

Must and *Have To* for Necessity

5   **Expressing Necessity with *Must* and *Have To*: Problems at the Bakery**

A. Listen and read about problems at Kamila and Jon's bakery. Complete the sentences with the words you hear: *must*, *have to*, *has to*, and *had to*.

Kamila: Oh, no! It's raining, and the roof is leaking again. You <u> have to </u> fix it,

                                                                 ₁

Jon. I can't!

Jon: All right, all right. But this bread machine doesn't work, and I can't fix it. Call Bob,

and tell him he _____ come and do it today.

                                                                          ₂

Kamila: Okay. Hey, did you go to the post office?

Jon: No, why?

Kamila: We _____ send the
                      3

         tax forms today, or they'll be late.

Jon: The bookkeeper didn't send them?

Kamila: No, she _____ go home
                        4

         early yesterday. In fact, I _____ drive her. She suddenly felt really sick.
                                              5

Jon: How is she today?

Kamila: I don't know. We _____ call her and find out. Hey, Jon? You know,
                                  6

         I think I _____ sit down. I don't feel well.
                        7

Jon: You can't get sick! Somebody _____ help me here!
                                                8

Kamila: I'm sorry, but I really _____ go home.
                                        9

Jon: So do I _____ do everything myself?
                        10

Kamila: I'm afraid so.

B. Write *yes/no* and *wh-* questions to match the answers. Use *have to* and the words in parentheses.

1. (what/Jon/fix)

   What does Jon have to fix? _____

   The roof.

2. (Kamila/fix/the roof)

   _____

   No, she doesn't.

3. (who/Kamila/call)

   _____

   Bob.

4. (where/someone/go today)

   _____

   To the post office.

5. (who/send the tax forms)

   _____

   Kamila or Jon.

6. (who/leave early yesterday)

_____

The bookkeeper did.

7. (what/Kamila/do/yesterday)

_____

She had to drive the bookkeeper home.

8. (why/the bookkeeper/leave early)

_____

Because she felt sick.

9. (Kamila/go home now)

_____

Yes, she does.

10. (Jon/do everything alone today)

_____

Yes, he does.

6 **Affirmative Statements with _Must_ and _Have To_:** Rules for Employees at the Bakery

A. Jon is talking to Olga, his new employee at the bakery. Complete the statements. Use _must_.

Jon Tells Olga:	The Rules Are:
1. You have to be on time for work.	Employees _must be on time for work._
2. You have to park behind the store.	Employees _____
3. You have to be polite to customers!	Employees _____
4. Remember to wash your hands.	Employees _____
5. Be careful with the bread machine.	Employees _____

an employee = a person who works for a company or for another person.

B. Look at the rules in Part A. Write sentences about Olga using *have to*.

1. *She has to be on time for work.*

2. _____

3. _____

4. _____

5. _____

Must and *Have To* in Negative Statements

FORM

A. Negative Statements with *Must*

FULL FORMS					CONTRACTIONS			
SUBJECT	MUST	NOT	BASE VERB		SUBJECT	MUSTN'T	BASE VERB	
You					You			
The children	must	not	touch	that!	The children	mustn't	touch	that!

B. Negative Statements with *Have To*

SUBJECT	DO/DID	NOT	HAVE TO	BASE VERB	SUBJECT	DO/DID + NOT	HAVE TO	BASE VERB
He	does	not	have to	work.	He	doesn't	have to	work.
	did					didn't		

FUNCTION

Must Not Versus *Not Have To*

1. Use *must not* to say what is not allowed or permitted.	You **must not** leave. (You must stay.)
2. Use *not have to* to say what is not necessary.	You **don't have to** leave. (You can stay if you want, or you can leave.)

Must and *Have To* in Negative Statements

7 *Mustn't* Versus *Don't Have To*: Training a New Employee

Complete the statements with *mustn't* or *don't have to*.

Kamila is speaking to Olga, her new employee at the bakery:

1. It's very important to lock the door at night! You __mustn't_____ forget.

2. Coffee is free to all employees. You _____ pay for it.

3. We all should be polite to customers. We _____ make customers angry.

4. You _____ lose any order forms. We need those!

5. Sometimes the plants in the window need water. But you _____ water them every day.

6. We should be polite all the time, but you _____ smile all the time.

7. You need to park in the parking lot. You _____ park on the street. You'll get a ticket if you do.

8. It's important to wash your hands often. You _____ forget.

9. I usually wear an apron, but Jon doesn't. You _____ wear one. It's up to you.

10. You _____ call me "Mrs. Borawski." It's okay to call me "Kamila."

> *It's up to you.* = You can choose what to do.

8 Affirmative and Negative Statements with *Have To*: Planning a Schedule

Work with a partner. Look at the work schedule for Kamila, Jon, and Olga at the bakery. Make two statements with *have to* about each of the days. Make one statement affirmative and the other negative. Take turns.

Example: Student A: Today is Thursday. Kamila has to work this morning.
She doesn't have to work this afternoon.

Student B: Jon and Olga had to work Tuesday morning.
Kamila didn't have to work Tuesday afternoon.

	Sunday	Monday	Tuesday	Wednesday	Thursday	Friday	Saturday
3 a.m.–9 a.m.	------	Kamila	Kamila	Kamila	Kamila	Kamila	Kamila Jon
9 a.m.–12 p.m.	Olga	Jon	Jon Olga	Jon	Jon	Olga	Kamila
12 p.m.–5 p.m.	Olga	Jon	Jon	Olga	Olga	Olga	

Today ⟶ (Thursday)

 9 **Statements with (*Not*) *Have To* and *Must Not*:** What's Necessary?

 A. Work in a group. Choose an activity from the list below, or think of another activity. Make three or more statements about things that are and are not necessary to do this activity. Use *have to*, *don't have to*, and *must not*. Talk about any disagreements.

Example: Student A: "Play the guitar." You have to use two hands.
Student B: You must not drop the guitar.
Student C: You don't have to know a lot of music.

> bake/cook (something)   plan a trip to (a place)
> become a doctor   play soccer
> borrow a book from the library   play the guitar
> drive a car   rent an apartment
> get a job   send e-mail
> get the bus   speak English

B. Choose two activities from the list in Part A, or think of two other activities. Write about things that are and are not necessary to do each one. Use *have to*, *don't have to*, and *must not*.

Example: To learn a new language, you have to listen to it, and you have to see it in writing. You don't have to take a course, but it helps. You have to find people to talk to, and you have to ask a lot of questions. You have to be patient, and you must not be afraid of making mistakes.

Check your progress! Go to the Self-Test for Chapter 21 on the *Grammar Links* Website.

Chapter 22

Communicating

Requests, Permission, and Offers; Imperatives; *Let's*

Introductory Task: Restaurant Talk

🎧 **A.** Listen to these conversations in Donatello's Restaurant. Circle the words you hear.

1. Marcos is the restaurant manager. He is talking to Anita, a new server at Donatello's. (A server waits on customers.)

    Marcos: Anita! (See / Could you see) what the people at Table 4 need.

    Anita: I'm on my way.

2. Marcos is talking to Mr. Donatello, the owner of the restaurant and Marcos's boss. (Marcos works for Mr. Donatello.) Mr. Donatello is holding a lot of papers.

    Marcos: (May / Can) I help you with those papers?

    Mr. Donatello: Thank you, I appreciate it.

3. Marcos is still talking to Mr. Donatello.

    Marcos: (May / Can) I take my vacation in August?

    Mr. Donatello: I don't see any problem with that.

4. Marcos is on the phone in his office, talking to his wife, Judy.

Marcos: I talked to Mr. D., and it's okay, we can go in August. (Could / Will) you get the plane tickets?

Judy: Sure. I'll do that today.

5. Marcos is still on the phone in his office, talking to his wife.

Marcos: (Let's / Please) rent a movie to watch tonight.

Judy: Okay. What do you feel like watching?

B. What is Marcos doing in each conversation in Part A? Write the number of the conversation. Copy the words from Part A.

4   a. Marcos is making a **request**. He is asking someone to do something. Marcos says,

"Will you get the plane tickets?"

_____ b. Marcos is using an **imperative**. He is telling someone what to do. Marcos says,

_____

_____ c. Marcos is asking **permission**. He is asking if it is okay for him to do something. Marcos says,

_____

_____ d. Marcos is making an **offer**. He is ready and able to do something for someone. Marcos says,

_____

_____ e. Marcos is making a **suggestion**. He wants to do something with the other person. Marcos says,

_____

GRAMMAR BRIEFING 1

Requests

FORM

REQUESTS				RESPONSES		
MODAL	*YOU*	BASE VERB		*YES*		*NO*
Would						
Will	you	help	me?	Yes,	I **will**.	I'm sorry, but I **can't**.
Could					I **can**.	
Can						

(continued on next page)

A. Formal and Informal Requests

1. Use *would*, *will*, *could*, or *can* + *you* to ask someone to do something:

   - Use *can you* or *will you* in informal requests (for example, to a friend).

   - Use *could you* or *would you* in more formal requests (for example, to a person you don't know well).

Sue: Ann, **can you/will you** lend me a dollar? *Ann*: Sure!
Student: **Could you/Would you** repeat the homework? *Professor*: Certainly. Read pages 41 to 76.

2. You can add *please* to make a request more polite. Put *please* after *you* or at the end of a request.

Could you please explain something?
Can you lend me a dollar, **please**?

B. Responses to Requests

1. Do not use *could*, or *would* in answers to requests. Use *can* or *will*.

Professor: **Could/Would** you carry these books to my office for me? *Student*: Yes, I **can/will**.   **NOT**: Yes, I ~~could/would~~.

2. To say "No" politely, you can use *I'm sorry, but* or *I'm afraid* + *I can't*.

Student: Would you please give us the test next week instead? *Professor*: **I'm sorry, but I can't./I'm afraid I can't.**

TALKING THE TALK

Sure is often used to say "Yes" to a request. It is very informal.	*Al*: Will you pass me some pizza? *Sara*: **Sure.**

GRAMMAR PRACTICE 1

Requests

1 **Formal and Informal Requests:** At Donatello's

Work alone or with a partner. Read each conversation at Donatello's Restaurant. Is the situation formal or informal? Circle your answer. Complete the request with an appropriate modal. In each request, more than one modal is possible.

1. A server and a customer are in the dining area. (formal / informal)

   Stan: Could I get you anything else?

   Ms. Greene: Yes, _could_ you bring me some more coffee?

   Stan: Certainly.

2. Two servers are in the kitchen. They are friends. (formal / informal)

   Stan: Hey, Anita! _____ you take this coffee to Table 5?

   Anita: Sure.

3. A server is in the manager's office. (formal / informal)

   Anita: Excuse me, Marcos. _____ you give me any more hours next week?

   Marcos: Maybe. I'll look at the schedule.

4. Two servers are speaking. (formal / informal)

   Stan: Anita, _____ you work next Saturday for me?

   Anita: No problem—I need the hours.

5. A customer and the manager are speaking in the dining area. (formal / informal)

   Marcos: I hope you enjoyed your meal.

   Ms. Greene: Yes, very much. Good food, good service, . . . This was my first time
               here, but I'll be back.

   Marcos: I'm glad to hear it. _____ you please tell all your friends?

2 Making and Responding to Requests: Please?

Work with a partner. Read the situations in the lists below. Student A: Make a request using *can*, *could*, *will*, or *would* + *you*. Include *please*. Student B: Give an answer to the request. Take turns.

Example: Student A: Could you please bring two cups of coffee?
          Student B: Yes, of course.

Formal	Informal
• You're in a restaurant. You want the server to bring you something to drink.	• You're at a pizza restaurant. Your friend works there. You want some free pizza.
• You're a student. You want your advisor to sign a form.	• You're in the library. Your friend is there. You want the answers to the homework.
• You're in a store. You want the person at the cash register to change a bill for you.	• You're a teacher. You want the students to bring their books to class tomorrow.

Permission and Offers

FORM

A. Permission

ASKING PERMISSION

MODAL	SUBJECT	BASE VERB	
Could			
Can	I	leave	early?
May			

RESPONSES

YES		NO	
Yes,	you **can**.	No,	you **can't**.
	you **may**.		you **may not**.

B. Offers

MAKING OFFERS

MODAL	SUBJECT	BASE VERB	
Could			
Can	I	help	you?
May			

RESPONSES

YES	NO
Yes, please.	Thank you, but . . .

FUNCTION

A. Asking, Giving, and Refusing Permission

1. Use *could*, *can*, or *may* to ask permission to do something:

   - *Could* is used in formal or informal situations.

     Could I borrow your pen for a minute?

   - *Can* is informal.

     Can I call you back later?

   - *May* is very formal.

     Dr. Smith, **may** I ask a question?

2. Use *can* or *may* (but not *could*) to:

   - Give permission.

     Informal: You **can** sit with us.
     Formal: You **may** sit down now.

   - Refuse permission.

     Informal: No, you **can't** use my car!
     Formal: You **may not** use notes during the test.

(continued on next page)

B. Making and Responding to Offers

1. Use *could*, *can*, or *may* to offer to do something for someone:

   - *Could* is used in formal or informal situations.

     Could I carry those books for you?

   - *Can* is informal.

     Can we bring something to the party?

   - *May* is very formal.

     May I get you a drink?

2. To accept an offer, you can say *Yes, please.* To say no to an offer, you can use *Thank you, but* + some words of explanation.

   Server: May I take your order?
   Customer: **Thank you, but** we're still looking at the menu. Could you come back in a minute?

TALKING THE TALK

1. There are many ways to respond when someone asks permission.

   Q: May I please use your phone? (formal)
   A: **Certainly./Of course.**

   Q: Can I use your phone? (informal)
   A: **Sure./No problem./Go right ahead.**

2. There are many ways to respond when someone makes an offer.

YES	NO
Thanks!	No, thank you.
I'd appreciate it.	Thanks, but I'm fine.

   Store clerk: Can I help you find something?
   Shopper: **Yes, please.** I'm trying to find . . . /
                  Thank you, but I'm just looking.

Permission and Offers

3 **Functions of Modals:** Welcome to Donatello's

Look at the numbered sentences in the four conversations. Is the speaker asking permission or making an offer? Circle P for permission and O for an offer.

Reporter Al Jordan and his wife, Sara, are customers at Donatello's Restaurant. Stan is their waiter.

P **(O)** 1. Stan: May I help you?

P **O** 2. Al: Could we have a table near the window?

P **O** 3. Stan: Certainly. Here are some menus. Could I get you something to drink?

P **O** 4. Sara: May I have some water, please?

Stan: Certainly.

****

P **O** 5. Sara: Al, can I change seats with you? It's cold by this window.

P **O** 6. Al: Sure. Can I give you my jacket?

Sara: Thanks, but I'll be fine.

****

P **O** 7. Stan: Could I tell you about today's special?

Al: Go right ahead.

Stan: It's fresh trout stuffed with apples and nuts.

Al: Sounds great! Sara?

P **O** 8. Sara: Could I have the trout without the nuts?

Stan: I'm sorry, but I'm afraid that's not possible.

Sara: Then I'll have the chef's salad, please.

****

P **O** 9. Sara: Excuse me, could we close that window? It's cold in here.

P **O** 10. Stan: Can I do that for you?

Sara: Thank you.

---

trout = a fish.

---

4 **Permission:** Formal or Informal Talk?

A. Marcos is at a coffee shop, talking to his friend George. Circle the modal that is correct and appropriate for the informal situation.

Marcos: George, how are you doing?

George: Not good. (Can / May) I talk to you for a minute?
1

Marcos: Sure, you (can / could). You look worried. What's the problem?
2

George: Someone stole my car.

Marcos: Oh, no! When did that happen?

George: Yesterday.

Marcos: (May / Can) I do anything to help?
3

George: Well, I need to go to the city this afternoon for a meeting. (Could / May)
4

I borrow your car?

Marcos: Of course, you (could / can). It's parked right outside the door.
5

B. Marcos is at work now at Donatello's Restaurant. He's talking to a customer about a special party. Circle the modal that is correct and appropriate for the formal situation.

Marcos: Nice to see you again, Ms. Greene. (May / Can) I ask a question about
1

your party on the sixteenth?

Ms. Greene: Certainly.

Marcos: Do you know the number of guests?

Ms. Greene: About 25. I'll know the exact number next week. (Could / Will) I tell
2

you then?

Marcos: Yes, you (can / could). That'll be fine.
3

Ms. Greene: Is smoking allowed in the restaurant?

Marcos: I'm sorry, but no one (could / may) smoke in here. It's the law.
4

5 Permission: Teacher/Student Role-Play

Work with a partner. Look at the situations below. Student A: You are a student asking the teacher for permission. Be formal. Student B: You are the teacher. Respond to your student informally. Take turns.

The student wants to:
- Enter the teacher's office.
- Take the test tomorrow.
- Borrow a dictionary.
- Make a phone call.
- Have more time to do a report.
- Ask a question about the homework.
- Ask for help in the course.
- Other: _____

Example: Student A: Could I leave early today, please?
         Student B: I'm sorry, but you can't. We have a test.

6 **Making and Responding to Offers:** Helping Out

 A. Work with a partner. Student A: Choose a situation. Make offers of help. Student B: Respond to each offer. Take turns.

- Your friend is sick in bed. Offer to: go to the store, make something to eat, get a book, magazine, or movie, etc.

- Your friend is getting ready to have a party. Offer to: buy something, make something, bring something, etc.

- Your friend doesn't know how to choose something that he or she needs to buy (a computer, a phone, a car, clothes for a special event, etc.)

- Your friend has to move to a new place to live.

Example: Student A: *Could I help you with the food for the party?*
Student B: *Thanks! I'd appreciate it. Could you come early?*
Student A: *Sure. I'll come an hour before the party. Can I bring something?*

B. Choose a situation from Part A. Write a conversation between two friends. Include offers of help.

See the *Grammar Links* Website for a complete model conversation for this assignment.

GRAMMAR BRIEFING 3

Would Like for Offers and Requests

FORM and FUNCTION

A. Offers

MAKING AN OFFER

WOULD	SUBJECT	LIKE	NOUN/ INFINITIVE*	
Would	you	like	a drink?	
			to come	with us?

RESPONSES**

YES	NO
Yes, please.	No, thank you.

B. Requests

FULL FORMS

SUBJECT	WOULD	LIKE	NOUN/ INFINITIVE*	
I	would	like	coffee,	please.
			to go,	too.

CONTRACTIONS

SUBJECT + WOULD	LIKE	NOUN/ INFINITIVE	
I'd	like	coffee,	please.
		to go,	too.

*An infinitive = *to* + the base form of a verb.
**See Talking the Talk, page 351, for other ways to respond to an offer.

(continued on next page)

C. Being Polite

1. In offers and requests, *would like* has the same meaning as *want,* but *would like* is more polite.

POLITE	VERY INFORMAL
Would you like a drink?	**Do you want** a drink?
I'd like tea, please.	I **want** tea, please.

2. There are many ways to respond to a request with *would like.*

Teacher: I'd like to talk to you after class.
Student: **OK./Sure.** OR **I'm sorry, but** I have to catch the bus.

GRAMMAR PRACTICE 3

Would Like for Offers and Requests

7 **Requests and Offers with *Would Like*:** A Message for Marcos

Ms. Greene, a customer, faxed this note to Marcos, the manager at Donatello's Restaurant. Cross out the seven forms of *want* and use a form of *would like* instead. Use the contracted form when possible. The first one has been done for you.

MAY 2 10:05 a.m.   877 555 9755 P. 01

FAX TRANSMITTAL

To: Marcos @ Donatello's Restaurant

From: Paula Greene, (877) 555-9755

Date: Monday, 5/2

Page: 1 of 1

    I'd like
~~I want~~ to make some changes in the plans for my party on the 16th. I want to

invite a few more people, so I want to increase the total to 30 or 35. I'll know for

sure by Friday. Do you want me to call you with the exact number?

    Also, I want fresh flowers for all the tables. I want yellow or pink ones, please.

    Perhaps we should talk about some other details. Do you want to call me at my

office? The number is 555-9752.

Thank you.

 See the *Grammar Links* Website for more information about business communication.

8 Using Requests and Offers with *Would Like*: Would You Like Something?

Student A: Choose a role from the list below. Student B: Make an appropriate request using *would like*. Student A: Respond to the request, and make an offer using *would you like*. Take turns.

Example: Student A: I work at a pizza shop.
Student B: I'd like some pizza.
Student A: Sure. Would you like salad, too?
Student B: No, thanks.

worker at a pizza shop	movie ticket seller
librarian	server in a nice restaurant
post office worker	bank teller
salesperson in a sports department	salesperson in a jewelry store

GRAMMAR BRIEFING 4

Imperatives

FORM and FUNCTION

A. Imperatives

AFFIRMATIVE		NEGATIVE		
BASE VERB		*DO + NOT*	BASE VERB	
Stop!		Do not	run.	
Open	your books to page 117.	Don't	talk	during the test.

B. Using Imperatives

1. Use an **imperative** (also called a **command**) to tell someone to do or not to do something. Imperatives are common in:

   - Stating rules.

     Stay on the sidewalk. **Don't walk** on the grass.

   - Giving directions to a place.

     Turn left at the next light, and **go** two blocks.

   - Giving instructions how to do something.

     Heat the milk, but **don't boil** it.

2. Imperative statements do not have a subject. The subject is understood to be *you* (singular or plural).

   (To Laura:) **Call** me tonight.

   (To Lee and Tom:) Please **work** together.

3. You can add *please* to make an imperative more polite. Put *please* at the beginning or end of the statement.

   Please wait here.

   Put the book on the table, **please**.

Imperative statements are strong. People in authority (such as teachers, employers, parents, police officers, etc.) often use imperative statements. It is more polite to use a modal to ask or request (not tell) others to do something.

IMPERATIVE	REQUEST
Call 911! It's an emergency!	**Would you please call** back later?
Read pages 60 to 85.	**Could you read** me the instructions, please?

GRAMMAR PRACTICE 4

Imperatives

9 **Affirmative and Negative Imperatives:** Signs All Around

Look at these signs and symbols. What do they mean? Write an affirmative imperative statement after each plus sign (+). Write a negative imperative statement after each minus sign (–).

1. (+) Fasten your seatbelt.

2. (+) _____

3. (–) _____

EXIT

4. (+) _____

5. (–) _____

6. (+) _____

7. (–) _____

8. (–) _____

10 **Using Affirmative and Negative Imperatives: What Are the Rules?**

A. Work with a partner. Think of rules for three or more of the places and situations below. On a piece of paper, make a list of at least four affirmative and negative imperatives for each place or situation.

Example: Rules for an ESL class:
Bring your book to class. Don't forget your homework.
Don't use a pencil. Use a pen.

an ESL class	a church, temple, or mosque
a college library	a movie theater
a computer lab	a rock concert
your room	a classical music concert
the office of a bank manager	a birthday party
an elegant restaurant	a job interview

 B. With your partner, join others to form a group. Share your list with the group. Explain why you think the rules are necessary.

 C. Choose another place or situation from Part A, or think of another one. Write a list of at least four rules. Use affirmative and negative imperatives.

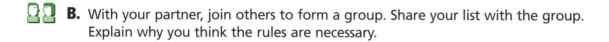
GRAMMAR BRIEFING 5

Suggestions with *Let's*

FORM and FUNCTION

A. Making Suggestions

AFFIRMATIVE			NEGATIVE			
LET'S	**BASE VERB**		**LET'S**	**NOT**	**BASE VERB**	
Let's	**play**	tennis.	Let's	not	**tell**	anyone.
	meet	at the library.			**go**	out tonight.

B. Using *Let's*

1. *Let's* and *let's not* are used to make suggestions. The suggestions include the speaker and his or her listener(s).

   A: I'm hungry. Did you eat?
   B: No, we didn't. **Let's go to** lunch now.
   C: That sounds good!

2. The subject of a statement with *let's* is understood to be *you and I*.

   A: **Let's go** for a run.
   B: You can go—I'm tired.

Suggestions with *Let's*

11 **Making Suggestions with *Let's* (*Not*):** What Do You Suggest?

Make a suggestion with *let's* or *let's not*.

1. Worker: I'd like to talk to you about my schedule. Is this a good time?

   Boss: <u>Let's go into my office. OR Let's not talk now—let's do it tomorrow.</u>

2. Friend 1: I'd like something hot to drink. What about you?

   Friend 2: _____

3. Wife: I don't know what to make for dinner.

   Husband: _____

4. Co-worker 1: The boss is leaving the company. Should we plan a good-bye party?

   Co-worker 2: _____

5. Student 1: Everyone in the class did badly on this test.

   Student 2: _____

12 **Making Suggestions with *Let's* (*Not*):** That's a Good Idea!

Work with a partner. Student A: Read a statement from the list. Make a suggestion using *let's*. Student B: Agree to the suggestion, or disagree and make a different suggestion. Take turns.

Example: Student A: The weather is beautiful today! Let's go to the beach.
         Student B: No, let's not. Let's play tennis.

The weather is beautiful today.	I'm bored.
There's no school today.	I'm hungry.
We have a test tomorrow.	I need some new clothes.
My car isn't running. We can't drive to school.	I'm tired of studying.
Tomorrow is the last day of class!	We need some money.

Check your progress! Go to the Self-Test for Chapter 22 on the *Grammar Links* Website.

Wrap-up Activities

1 **How to Combine Work with Studying:** READING

Read this article from the Dover Community College student newspaper.

Learning on the Job

At Dover Community College, you can take courses and work at the same time, and you can earn college credits on the job. The Cooperative Education Program at the college can help you get a job that is related to your field of study. For example, a student in hospitality management could work at a Dover hotel, or a business student could get a job with a local company. To learn more about the program, go to www.dovercc.edu and click on "Learning at DCC" and then "Cooperative Education." Or you can visit the Cooperative Education Program office in Building A. Go in the main door, turn right, and take the elevator or the stairs to the third floor. You will find the office in Room 315.

2 **Instructions:** WRITING

Write a paragraph giving instructions on how to do something. Give your paragraph a title, such as *How to Make an Ice Cream Cone, How to Buy a Used Car*, or *How to Find a Boyfriend/Girlfriend*. You can begin your paragraph with a sentence like this:

To make a paper airplane, first, take a piece of notebook paper.
OR To get to the airport, you can take the subway.
OR To play Ping-Pong, you need two people, two Ping-Pong paddles, a ball, and a Ping-Pong table with a net.

Use imperatives and modals in your paragraph.

 See the *Grammar Links* Website for a complete model paragraph for this assignment.

3 **How to Make a Good Cup of Tea:** EDITING

Correct the eight errors in imperatives or verbs with modals. Some errors can be corrected in more than one way. The first error has been corrected for you.

To make good tea, you should ~~to~~ have a teapot. No make the tea in a cup. You will need one tea bag for each person. You could to use loose tea instead, but you must not; a tea bag is easier. Put the tea bag in the teapot, and add boiling water. The water must being as hot as possible. Don't using too much water, just one or two cups for each tea bag. Now the tea have to sit for four minutes. Then pour the tea into a cup. I always like my tea with a little milk in it, but you might may like your tea with lemon and sugar.

4 **Pick the Right Location:** SPEAKING/LISTENING

Work with a partner. Think of some cities or places for the following companies. Explain why the places might be right for the company. Use modals in your discussion.

- Ski World
- International Tourist Hotel
- Toy World
- Computers Are Us
- Big Burger & Fries Company
- A to Z Beach Supplies

Example: Student A: Colorado might be a good place for Ski World. Lots of people in Colorado might want ski equipment and clothes.
Student B: People have to use the skis, and Colorado has many ski areas.

Give Some Advice: READING/SPEAKING/LISTENING

Step 1 Read this letter to "Wally Knows What to Do," a business advice column.

Dear Wally Knows What to Do,

I just finished school and have my degree in business. I'd like to work as a bookkeeper. I have two good job possibilities. But I don't know which job to take.

One job is in a large hotel in the city. The pay is OK to start. I need to move to the city for the job. I know that apartments are expensive there, but I really like the city.

The other job is in a small bank in a town nearby. It pays $100 a week less. But I can stay in my apartment, and most of my friends live nearby. On the other hand, I need a car to get to that job. I'm really not sure what to do. What do you suggest?

Vinoth

Step 2 Decide what you think Vinoth should do. Then join one of two groups: Group A, a "go to the city" group, or Group B, a "stay in the small town" group. Share the reasons for your opinion. Make a list of advice for Vinoth. Use modals in your advice.

Step 3 Form a new group with two to four other students. Include students from both Group A and Group B. Try to convince the others in your group to agree with your advice.

 See the *Grammar Links* Website for advice on careers.

Adjectives and Adverbs; Comparisons

TOPIC FOCUS
All About Clothes

UNIT OBJECTIVES

- **adjectives**
  (He often buys *new* clothes. Are clothes *important* to you?)

- **adverbs**
  (That jacket fits you *well*. It's *very* handsome. You're *always* well-dressed.)

- **expressing similarities and differences with** *like*, *the same (as)*, *different (from)*, **and** *as . . . as*
  (He looks *like* his brother. His clothes aren't *the same as* his brother's. Their clothes are quite *different*. Is he *as* tall *as* his brother?)

- **comparative adjectives and adverbs**
  (Swimsuits today are *better* than the swimsuits of 100 years ago. People can swim *more easily* in them.)

- **superlative adjectives and adverbs**
  (This coat is *the warmest* of the three coats. Which coat fits *the best*?)

Grammar in Action

Reading and Listening: At a Halloween Party

Read and listen to the conversation.

Rose O'Malley and Jane Chun are students of fashion design. Right now they're at a college Halloween party. They are wearing costumes that they made. Rose's boyfriend, Doug Noonan, is at the party, too.

Rose: Hi, Jane—what a **great** witch costume!

Jane: This old thing? It's just the same as last year's. Maybe next year I'll make something more interesting. But your costume is **wonderful**—you're Cinderella, right?

Rose: Uh-huh.

Jane: Nice shoes. They **really** look like glass! And that dress fits **perfectly**. So where's your **handsome** prince?

Rose: Doug? He's here, somewhere. Look for a cowboy. He **always** wears cowboy clothes for Halloween.

Jane: I see two cowboys over there.

Rose: Where? There are so many people … oh, there's Doug. He's the taller one.

Jane: Yeah, I see him now. This party is really crowded. It's more crowded than last year's party.

Rose: True, but this party's better—people are wearing more interesting costumes this year.

Jane: The band's not bad, either. Hey, look at the guy in the old bathing suit!

Rose: Now that is the funniest costume here tonight.

Jane: And there are two more witches, too.

Rose: Hmm, yeah. Well, their costumes are pretty good, but you're the best witch here tonight. Hey, look over there—it's Frankenstein!

Jane: Boy, he looks scary. Rose, do you think a costume tells something about the person wearing it? Wait—forget that question—I mean, look at *me*! Come on, let's go get something to eat.

Rose: Okay, but I have to go slowly. These are the most uncomfortable shoes in the world. How could Cinderella dance in glass slippers!

---

fashion design = the business of planning and making clothes.
Halloween = a holiday celebrated on October 31, when people often dress in costumes. *a prince* = a son of a king or queen.

Think About Grammar

A. Complete the following sentences from Rose and Jane's conversation. Look for **boldfaced** words.

1. Rose: Hi, Jane—what a _____ witch costume!

2. Jane: But your costume is _____—you're Cinderella, right?

3. Jane: So where's your _____ prince?

The words you wrote in sentences 1–3 are **adjectives**.

4. Jane: Nice shoes. They _____ look like glass!

5. Jane: And that dress fits _____.

6. Rose: He _____ wears cowboy clothes for Halloween.

The words you wrote in sentences 4–6 are **adverbs**.

B. Look at the sentences in Part A. Then circle your answers below.

1. (Adjectives / Adverbs) modify nouns. (They describe people, places, and things.)

2. (Adjectives / Adverbs) can modify verbs. (They can give more information about an action.)

C. Use words from the chart to complete statements based on the conversation.

Comparative Adjectives	Superlative Adjectives
better	the best
taller	the funniest
more interesting	the most uncomfortable

1. Doug Noonan is _taller_____ than the other cowboy.

2. Rose thinks this year's party is _____ than last year's party.

3. The costumes this year are _____ than last year's costumes.

4. Rose thinks the old bathing suit is _____ costume at the party.

5. There are three witches, but Jane is _____ witch of all.

6. Rose thinks her Cinderella shoes are _____ shoes in the world.

Statements 1–3 compare **two people or things** (two cowboys, two parties, two costumes).

What kind of adjectives are used in these statements? Circle your answer:

comparatives / superlatives

Statements 4–6 compare **three or more people or things** (all the costumes at the party, the three witches, all the shoes in the world).

What kind of adjectives are used in these statements? Circle your answer:

comparatives / superlatives

23

People in the Clothing Industry
Adjectives and Adverbs

Introductory Task: Getting Clothes by Magic?

A. Listen and read about clothing production in the story of Cinderella and in real life.

Most people know the story of Cinderella. She's the poor girl who went to a dance, fell in love with a **handsome** prince, and lived **happily** ever after.

Cinderella went to that dance wearing a **very** beautiful dress and a pair of **unusual** shoes—glass slippers. Where did she get these **terrific** clothes? Her fairy godmother produced them, just by saying some magic words. Cinderella didn't have to sew anything, she didn't have to go shopping, and all her clothes fit **perfectly**. And she didn't have to try on ten pairs of glass slippers in some shoe store. ("No, those slippers aren't pretty **enough**. No, no, these are **too** big!")

In real life, people **never** get their clothes from fairy godmothers, and there's no magic in clothing production. We **usually** buy our clothes, and it almost **always** takes a lot of work to produce them. Think of a simple cotton shirt, for example. Who made it? Well, first there was the farmer. He grew the cotton. Then there were the factory workers. They made the cloth. A designer drew the shirt, and more factory workers cut and sewed it. Then a buyer ordered it for the store. A lot of people worked **hard** to bring that shirt to you, the customer!

He's using a sewing machine.

> *a fairy godmother* = in stories, a woman who can make wishes come true. *produce* = make or create.

B. Complete the answers to the questions. Use **boldfaced** words from the story.

1. What kind of prince did Cinderella marry?   A <u>handsome</u> prince.

2. What kind of shoes did she wear to the ball?   _____ shoes.

3. What kind of clothes did she have?   _____ clothes.

The words you used in answers 1–3 are **adjectives**.

4. How beautiful was Cinderella's dress?   _____ beautiful.

5. How pretty was the first pair of slippers in the store?   Not pretty _____.

6. How big was the next pair of slippers?   _____ big.

The words you used in answers 4–6 are **intensifiers (adverbs of degree)**.

7. How often do people get their clothes from fairy godmothers?   _____.

8. How often do people buy their clothes?   _____.

9. How often does it take a lot of work to make clothes?   Almost _____.

The words you used in answers 7–9 are **adverbs of frequency**.

10. How did Cinderella end up?   She lived _____ ever after.

11. How did Cinderella's clothes fit?   _____.

12. How did people work to produce that cotton shirt?   _____.

The words you used in answers 10–12 are **adverbs of manner**.

C. Circle your answers to these questions.

1. What kind of clothes do you like?

   a. unusual   b. traditional   c. new   d. other: _____

2. How happy are you with the clothes you have?

   a. very happy   b. kind of happy   c. not happy   d. other: _____

3. How often do you make your clothes?

   a. often   b. sometimes   c. never   d. other: _____

4. How did you get dressed today?

   a. quickly   b. carefully   c. sleepily   d. other: _____

D. Work in a group. Are these statements true or false?

1. Most people in my group like unusual clothes.	True	False
2. Most people in my group are very happy with their clothes.	True	False
3. Most people in my group often make their clothes.	True	False
4. Most people in my group got dressed quickly today.	True	False

Adjectives and Adverbs

FORM and FUNCTION

A. Adjectives

1. Adjectives modify or give information about nouns. They tell us more about people, places, and things.

   That is a **beautiful** beach.

   They live in a **little red** house.

   He looks **sad**.

2. An adjective usually comes before the noun it modifies.

   They are **good** workers.

   It is a **Japanese** car.

3. Adjectives can also come after *be* and other linking verbs, such as *feel*, *look*, *seem*, *smell*, *sound*, and *taste*.
   (See Chapter 26, Grammar Briefing 4, page 418, for more information on linking verbs.)

   That jacket is **beautiful** and **warm**.

   I feel **great**.

   It looks **funny**.

B. Adverbs

1. Adverbs often modify or give information about:

   - Verbs.

     He works **fast**.

   - Adjectives.

     The model is **very** thin.

   - Quantifiers.

     There is **too** much noise.

2. There are several kinds of adverbs. For example:

   - **Adverbs of frequency** tell how often something happens.
     (See Chapter 7, Grammar Briefing 5, page 125, for more information on adverbs of frequency.)

     He is **always** late.

     They **rarely** go shopping.

     I **never** met him.

   - **Adverbs of manner** tell how something happens.
     (See Grammar Briefing 2, page 372, for more information on adverbs of manner.)

     They spoke of their son **proudly**.

     She smiled **cheerfully**.

     The clothes fit **well**.

   - **Intensifiers**, or adverbs of degree, make the words they modify stronger or weaker in meaning.
     (See Grammar Briefing 3, page 376, for more information on intensifiers.)

     It's **very** expensive.

     These shoes aren't big **enough**.

     Slow down—you're talking **too** fast!

Adjectives and Adverbs

1 **Identifying Adjectives:** The Emperor's New Clothes, Part 1

🎧 **A.** Listen and read Part 1 of this famous story by Hans Christian Andersen. Then work with a partner to find and circle the 19 adjectives in the numbered sentences. <u>Underline</u> the words they modify. The first two are done for you.

(1) Once upon a time, there was a (foolish) <u>emperor</u>. (2) <u>He</u> was (crazy) about clothes. One day, two men arrived at his castle. They told the emperor that they were weavers, but that was a lie. (3) "We can weave magical cloth," they said. (4) "It is very beautiful and very unusual. (5) The cloth is sometimes invisible— you must be smart and good at your job to see it." (6) The emperor thought, "This is excellent news! (7) They can make me some magical clothes, and I'll learn which people are stupid or useless." He gave the men money and a room in the castle, and they pretended to weave the cloth. Meanwhile, the news about the cloth traveled all through the city.

(8) After a week, the emperor sent an honest old advisor to check on the work. (9) There was no cloth, so he saw nothing, but the weavers cried, "Isn't it beautiful?" (10) The old man was upset. (11) "The cloth is invisible! What does this mean?" he asked himself. (12) "Am I bad at my job? Maybe I shouldn't be an advisor to the emperor! Oh no! I must not tell anyone the truth."

A Weaver Working at a Loom

> *an emperor* = the ruler of a group of countries. *a lie* = a false and dishonest statement. *invisible* = impossible to see.

👥 **B.** Talk with your partner. What do you think is going to happen in Part 2 of the story? What is the old man going to say to the emperor? Use adjectives to describe the people in the story.

2 Adjectives: Ready, Set, WRITE!

Form teams of three or four people. Each team must find a space to write on the blackboard (or use a large piece of paper). The teacher will say a letter of the alphabet. Write all the adjectives you can think of that start with that letter. Stop writing when the teacher says "Stop." Compare all the lists of adjectives. Then start again with a new letter.

Example: Teacher: *Write adjectives beginning with "g."*
Team A writes: *good, great, green, gentle, graceful, . . .*

3 Identifying Adverbs: The Emperor's New Clothes, Part 2

Listen and read Part 2 of Hans Christian Andersen's story. Then work with a partner to find and circle the 14 adverbs (two adverbs of frequency, six adverbs of manner, and six intensifiers). The first adverb is circled for you.

The emperor's advisor went back to the castle and said that the cloth was (very) beautiful. He was too afraid to tell the truth. After a few days, the weavers came to the emperor and proudly said, "See our wonderful cloth!" All the emperor's advisors were there, as they always were, and the old man waited nervously. But the emperor was very foolish. He looked, saw nothing, and thought, "It's invisible! Oh no—maybe I'm not smart enough to be the emperor! I must keep this a secret." So he smiled cheerfully, and he ordered some clothes for a parade that Sunday.

When there was a parade, it was the emperor's custom to walk through the streets. So that Sunday, people came out and waited eagerly to see the emperor's new clothes. All the people expected to see the clothes. Only people who were too stupid or useless couldn't see them, right? So when the emperor walked proudly past them, all the people said, "What wonderful clothes! They fit the emperor so well!" But a small boy was there, and this boy never told lies, so he said loudly, "But he isn't wearing any clothes!" Then all the people laughed at their foolish emperor.

eagerly = in a way that shows great interest and desire.

Adverbs of Manner

FUNCTION

Meaning and Use of Adverbs of Manner

Adverbs of manner modify action verbs. They tell how something happens or the way someone does something.	He <u>sews</u> **quickly**. The man <u>called</u> my name **loudly**. We <u>waited</u> **eagerly** for the news.
Adverbs of manner can answer questions with *how* + an action verb.	Q: How does she draw? A: **Beautifully**.

FORM

Placement and Spelling of Adverbs of Manner

1. Adverbs of manner usually follow the verb. In sentences with verb + object, they follow the object. (See Chapters 17 and 26 for more information on objects of verbs.)	I drove **carefully**. I <u>drove</u> his car **carefully**. **NOT:** I drove ~~carefully~~ his car.
2. Form -*ly* adverbs of manner from adjectives:	
• For most adjectives, add -*ly*.	graceful → graceful**ly** quiet → quiet**ly**
• For adjectives that end in *y*, change the *y* to *i* and add -*ly*.	easy → eas**ily** happy → happ**ily**
• For adjectives that end in a consonant + *le*, drop the *e* and add -*y*.	gen**tle** → gently comforta**ble** → comfortably
3. The adverb form of *good* is *well*.	They're **good** singers. They sing **well**.

GRAMMAR **HOT**SPOT!

1. Some words that end in *-ly* are adjectives, not adverbs of manner. These adjectives include *friendly, lonely, lovely, silly,* and *ugly*.

    She was a **friendly** person.

    She spoke in a **friendly** way.
       NOT: She spoke ~~friendly~~.

2. Some words can be either adjectives or adverbs of manner. These words include *hard* and *fast*.

ADJECTIVE	ADVERB OF MANNER
They're **hard** workers.	They work **hard**.
It's a **fast** train.	It travels **fast**.

3. Remember, use adjectives (not adverbs of manner) with linking verbs.

    (See Grammar Briefing 1 on page 369 for examples of linking verbs.)

    Q: How is he today? How does he feel?
    A: He feels **bad**. He's still pretty sick.
       NOT: He feels ~~badly~~.

Adverbs of Manner

4 **Adjective Versus Adverb of Manner:** People in the Fashion Industry

Work with a partner. Make statements about these people in the fashion industry. Use the words next to the pictures. Make statements with (a) adjective + noun and with (b) verb (+ object) + adverb of manner. Take turns.

Example: Student A: 1. He's a careful tailor. He measures things carefully.
         Student B: 2. He's a quick . . .

Adjective	Noun	Verb (+ Object)
1. careful	a. a tailor	b. measure things
2. quick	a. a worker	b. sew
3. quiet	a. man	b. speak

Adjective	Noun	Verb (+ Object)
4. good	a. a photographer	b. do her job
5. graceful	a. a model	b. model clothes
6. cheerful	a. people	b. talk

Adjective	Noun	Verb (+ Object)
7. fast	a. typists	b. type
8. hard	a. workers	b. work
9. good	a. employees	b. do their jobs

10. professional	a. a designer	b. design clothes
11. good	a. an artist	b. draw
12. creative	a. a thinker	b. think

 See the *Grammar Links* Website for more information about the fashion industry.

5 **Answers to Questions with *How*; Adjectives Versus Adverbs of Manner: A New Model**

Read the conversation between a fashion designer and her assistant. Circle the correct word.

Designer: What did you think of the new model? How does she seem to you?

Assistant: She seems (terrific / terrifically). She's lovely. She smiles (easy / easily).
1   2

Designer: How did she move in front of the camera?

Assistant: Very (good / well)—she moved very (graceful / gracefully), I thought.
3   4

Designer: And how did she get along with the photographer?

Assistant: They worked (good / well) together. He thought she did a (good / well) job.
5   6

Designer: You saw the photos, right? How were they?

Assistant: (Beautiful / Beautifully). Really.
7

Designer: How did the clothes look?

Assistant: (Perfect / Perfectly)!
8

Designer: Well, you sound (happy / happily)
9

with this girl's work.

Assistant: Yes, I am, and I think you'll be

(happy / happily) with it, too.
10

6 Adjectives with -ly Versus Adverbs of Manner: Annika, High-Fashion Model

Work with a partner. Read about Annika, a high-fashion model. Which two words can you use in each sentence? Circle them. Say the statements.

Example: Student A: Annika has beautiful clothes.
Student B: Annika has lovely clothes.

1. Annika has _____ clothes.   beautiful, comfortably, lovely, well

2. She always dresses _____.   good, beautiful, fashionably, nicely

3. She never wears _____ clothes.   cheaply, ugly, old, messily

4. Her clothes always fit her _____.   well, perfect, beautifully, comfortable

5. She and her friends talk about fashion _____.   seriously, silly, friendly, constantly

6. Do you think she's a _____ person?   beautifully, friendly, lonely, happily

7 Adverbs of Manner: The Way to Do It

Work with a partner. Take turns reading aloud directions 1–8 and making statements with adverbs of manner.

Example: Student A: Tell something you do carefully.
Student B: Shave! I always shave carefully.

1. Tell something you do carefully.

2. Tell something you handle gently.

3. Name someone who writes neatly.

4. Name someone who smiles easily.

5. Tell something you can do well.

6. Tell something you don't do cheerfully.

7. Tell something people talk about constantly.

8. Tell something people shouldn't do fast.

Intensifiers

FUNCTION

Meaning and Uses of Intensifiers

1. Intensifiers, or adverbs of degree, include *almost, enough, extremely, fairly, hardly, really, too,* and *very.* An intensifier may modify:

   - A verb.

     I **really** <u>don't like</u> this music.

   - An adjective.

     These shoes aren't <u>wide</u> **enough**.

   - A quantifier.

     We spent **too** <u>much</u> money.

   - Another adverb.

     I don't go shopping **very** <u>often</u>.

2. *Very* and *extremely* make the words they modify stronger in meaning.

   It was cold. → It was **very** cold. → It was **extremely** cold!

3. Some intensifiers make the words they modify weaker in meaning:

   - *Almost* = nearly but not completely.

     I'm **almost** ready—one more minute . . .

   - *Fairly* = more than a little, but not very.

     It's **fairly** heavy, but I can pick it up.

   - *Hardly* = almost not at all.

     I **hardly** studied. I didn't have time.

FORM

Placement of Intensifiers

1. Use most intensifiers before the verb, adjective, quantifier, or other adverb that they modify.

   I **almost** <u>fell</u> asleep.

   It was **extremely** <u>difficult</u>.

   We have **hardly** <u>any</u> money.

   She sings **fairly** <u>well</u>.

2. The intensifier *enough* goes after an adjective or adverb.

   Is the water <u>hot</u> **enough**?

   We don't see you <u>often</u> **enough**.

   Enough is also a quantifier.
   (See Chapter 16, Grammar Briefing 1, page 246, for information on the quantifier *enough* + noun.)

   There aren't **enough** chairs.

1. Do not confuse *hard* and *hardly*.

   - *Hard* is both an adjective and an adverb of manner. It means "with force or effort."

   > He's a **hard** worker. He works **hard**.

   - *Hardly* is an intensifier. It means "almost not at all." Use it in affirmative statements.

   > He **hardly** works. = He doesn't work much./He almost doesn't work at all.
   > **NOT:** He ~~doesn't hardly work~~.

2. The intensifiers *too* and *very* are not the same.

   - Use *very* + an adjective or an adverb. It makes the adjective or adverb stronger in meaning.

   > *Q:* Is she a good runner?
   > *A:* Oh yes, she's **very** good. She can run **very** fast.

   - Use *too* + an adjective, adverb, or quantifier. *Too* means "more than is good or wanted."

   > This coffee is **too** <u>hot</u>. I burned my tongue.
   > You're driving **too** <u>fast</u>. It's dangerous.
   > We have **too** <u>much</u> work. We can't do it all.

GRAMMAR PRACTICE 3

Intensifiers

8 **Identifying Intensifiers:** Bill Bowerman, Shoe Designer

Read Al Jordan's report on Bill Bowerman. Circle the seven intensifiers. <u>Underline</u> the words they modify. The first one is done for you.

Bill Bowerman wasn't a shoe designer, but he invented the modern running shoe. His ideas (really) <u>changed</u> athletic shoes and had a very big impact on the shoes we wear today. Bowerman was a track coach at the University of Oregon from 1948 to 1973. The runners on his teams were extremely successful. But he thought their running shoes weren't good enough. Then, one day at breakfast, he looked at the waffle iron in his kitchen, and he got an idea. So he took the waffle iron to his workshop, and he used it to make a new kind of rubber sole. His invention hardly seemed important at that time, but it was the start of really big changes in athletic shoes. Bowerman and a young graduate student named Phil Knight decided to start their own business. They had just a few hundred dollars—were they too optimistic? Not at all. You probably know their company: It's called Nike. Today, you can see the name "Nike" on running shoes and athletic clothes almost everywhere.

> *have an impact on* = influence or make a change in. *optimistic* = sure that the future will bring good things.

9 *Too* Versus *Very*; *Hard* Versus *Hardly*: Shoe Shopping

A. Rose and Jane are shopping for running shoes for Jane. Complete the three conversations. Use both *too* and *very* in each conversation.

1. Rose: Jane, these shoes are _____ expensive. Can you afford them?

a

   Jane: No, I can't. They're _____ expensive for me.

b

2. Rose: Excuse me, could you get the next smaller size in this style?

   Salesman: I'm sorry, but we don't have that size. That pair's not right?

   Jane: I'm afraid not. They're _____ good-looking, but they're _____

a   b

   big for me.

3. Rose: How are those shoes?

   Jane: They don't really fit. They're _____ wide for me.

a

   Rose: You have _____ narrow feet!

b

B. Complete each conversation with *hard* and *hardly*.

1. Rose: I think this is our fifth shoe store.

   Jane: I'm so tired I can _____ walk.

a

   Rose: Do you always have to look so _____ to find the right shoes?

b

2. Jane: There are too many customers in this store. It's going to be _____ to

a

   get the salesman's attention.

   Rose: And there's _____ any place to sit down. Let's come back later.

b

3. Jane: Let's go home! I'm tired. I got up early and worked really _____ today.

a

   Rose: I'm sorry you had no luck finding shoes.

   Jane: That's okay. I _____ ever find shoes the first time I go shopping.

b

	MORE FORMAL	LESS FORMAL
In conversation, people often use informal intensifiers. These include *really, pretty, kind of* (pronounced "kinda"), and *sort of* (pronounced "sorta").	These shoes fit **very** well.	These shoes fit **really** well.
	My brother is **fairly** tall.	My brother is **pretty/kind of/sort of** tall.

10 Informal Intensifiers: Athletic Clothes

 Listen to four conversations between people in stores. They are using informal intensifiers. You will hear each conversation twice. Which statement gives the main idea of the conversation? Circle *a* or *b*.

Conversation 1: (a) The shoes fit fairly well.   (b) The shoes don't fit.

Conversation 2: (a) The shirt is too big.   (b) The shirt is very big.

Conversation 3: (a) It's a fairly good jacket.   (b) It's an extremely good jacket.

Conversation 4: (a) The shoes are extremely expensive.   (b) The shoes are fairly expensive.

11 Intensifiers: Shopping Together

A. Work with a partner. Imagine that you are two family members or two friends with very different ideas about clothes. You are shopping for clothes together. Act out a conversation about clothes or shoes that you see in the store. Use intensifiers from this list:

almost, enough, extremely, fairly, hardly, kind of, pretty, really, sort of, too, very

Example: Student A: Mom, I really like this skirt. And it's not very expensive.
Student B: What! That skirt is too short!

B. Write a conversation between two family members or two friends who are clothes shopping together, as in Part A.

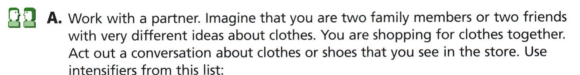 See the *Grammar Links* Website for a complete model conversation for this assignment.

 **Check your progress! Go to the Self-Test for Chapter 23 on the *Grammar Links* Website.**

Chapter 24

Clothes and Shopping
Expressing Similarities and Differences

Introductory Task: Different Tastes

 A. Listen and read about two brothers. Circle the **boldfaced** words about things that are the same or equal. <u>Underline</u> the **boldfaced** words that show things are different.

Doug and Ralph Noonan are twins. Doug is exactly **as tall as** Ralph, and people all say they **look like** each other, but in many ways, they **are different from** each other. For example, their tastes in clothes are completely different.

Doug wants to **look the same as** his friends. Their clothes come from big and famous companies, and they are all fairly traditional. In fact, Doug's clothes aren't very different from his father's. Doug often buys his clothes online. The prices he pays **aren't as low as** the prices in stores, but Doug hates to shop in stores.

Ralph loves to look for clothes in secondhand clothing shops. He likes colorful shirts with unusual hats and jackets. He doesn't want to **look like** other people. Ralph likes to **be different**. But he doesn't want to pay a lot for clothes. He **doesn't spend money as freely as** Doug does.

Doug and Ralph often tell each other, "Hey, you can borrow my clothes anytime you want." But the response **is always the same**: "No, thanks!"

> *a taste* = a liking or preference. *secondhand* = used, not new. *borrow* = take something that belongs to someone else to use it and give it back.

B. Circle the words that make a true statement about the twins and their clothes.

1. People say Doug and Ralph (look like / don't look like) each other.

2. Doug (is as tall as / isn't as tall as) Ralph is.

3. Doug's taste in clothes (is the same as / isn't the same as) Ralph's.

4. Doug's clothes (look like / look different from) his friends' clothes.

5. Ralph wants to (look the same as / look different from) other people.

6. Their shopping habits (are the same / aren't the same).

C. Talk with a partner or a small group. Share your answers to these questions: Do you ever borrow clothes from anyone? Whose taste in clothes is like yours? Are your clothes the same as all your friends' clothes?

GRAMMAR BRIEFING 1

Expressing Similarities and Differences

FORM and FUNCTION

A. The Same (As)

Use *the same* (*as*) to say that things are equal or completely alike.

SUBJECT	LINKING VERB*	*THE SAME*	(*AS* + NOUN PHRASE**)
The two shirts	**look**	**the same.**	
One shirt	**is**	**the same**	**as** the other shirt.

B. Like

Use *like* to say two things are similar but not exactly the same.

SUBJECT	LINKING VERB*	*LIKE*	NOUN PHRASE**
These shoes	**are**	**like**	those shoes.
I	**look**		my father.

*Linking verbs include *be, feel, look, seem, smell, sound,* and *taste*. (See Chapter 26, Grammar Briefing 4, page 418, for more information about linking verbs.)

**Noun phrase = a noun (or pronoun) and its modifiers. (*A shirt, someone new,* and *my blue jacket* are all noun phrases.)

(continued on next page)

C. *Different (From)*

Use *different* (*from*) to say that two things are not the same.

SUBJECT	LINKING VERB*	*DIFFERENT*	(*FROM* + NOUN PHRASE**)
The two ties	**are**	**different**.	
The tie on the left	**is**	**different**	**from** the tie on the right.

*Linking verbs include *be, feel, look, seem, smell, sound,* and *taste.* (See Chapter 26, Grammar Briefing 4, page 418, for more information about linking verbs.)

**Noun phrase = a noun (or pronoun) and its modifiers. (*A shirt, someone new,* and *my blue jacket* are all noun phrases.)

D. Using *The Same (As)*, *Like*, and *Different (From)*

1. After *the same as*, *like*, and *different from*, we often use:

   • Possessive nouns.

   • Possessive pronouns.

   • Demonstrative pronouns.

      The demonstratives *this* and *that* are often followed by the indefinite pronoun *one*.

   | Your car looks like **Jack's**. |
   | His work schedule is the same as **mine**. |
   | These flowers don't smell like **those**. |
   | That book is the same as **this one**. |

2. *The same (as)*, *like*, and *different (from)* can also be used in negative statements and questions.

   | *We're* and *were* **don't** sound **the same**. |
   | Our new boss **isn't like** our last one. |
   | How is softball **different from** baseball? |

GRAMMAR **HOT**SPOT!

Compare and contrast things of the same kind.

| **His clothes** are like his **father's**. (This sentence compares clothes.) |
| **NOT**: His clothes are like his ~~father~~. (This sentence compares clothes and a person.) |

Expressing Similarities and Differences

1 *The Same (As), Like, and Different (From):* Men's Shirts

A. Complete the statements about the shirts in the picture. Write *the same*, *the same as*, *like*, *different*, or *different from*.

Bob   Doug   Mr. Noonan   Ralph

1. Doug's shirt and Ralph's shirt are _different_____.

2. Ralph's shirt is also _____ Bob's.

3. Doug's shirt looks exactly _____ his friend Bob's shirt.

4. Doug's shirt and Bob's shirt look _____.

5. Both Doug's shirt and Bob's shirt look _____ Mr. Noonan's shirt, but Mr. Noonan's has short sleeves.

6. Ralph's shirt and his father's are not _____. They are _____.
   a   b

B. Correct the errors in these sentences.

1. Ralph looks like his ~~brother's.~~ brother

2. Ralph's clothes don't look like his brother.

3. Doug's shirt is the same Bob's shirt.

4. Mr. Noonan's shirt is different Ralph's.

5. Their shirts don't look same.

6. Do the twins look like their father's?

7. Ralph's shirt isn't like to Doug's.

2 Possessive Pronouns and Demonstratives in Comparisons: At the Mall

A. Jane is shopping with her friend Rose. Use pronouns and demonstratives in place of the underlined words.

1. Jane: That sweater is a beautiful color on you.

   Rose: Thanks. What about ~~this sweater~~ *this one*?

   Jane: That sweater is nice, too, but I really like the blue sweater.

2. Rose: Do you like any of these earrings?

   Jane: Those gold earrings are nice. They're the same as these gold earrings.

   Rose: Yes, they are, and they're a lot like your gold earrings, too!

3. Rose: The heels on these shoes are very high. They're not comfortable.

   Jane: Try this pair. These heels are a little different from those heels.

4. Rose: Look at that black dress in the window. It's the same as my black dress.

   Jane: Really? Is it exactly the same as your black dress?

   Rose: Well, almost—that black dress has a different belt.

5. Jane: Let's look at sunglasses for a minute. Oh, I like these sunglasses!

   Rose: Those sunglasses look good on you.

B. Work with a partner. Read the conversations in Part A out loud. Did you and your partner make the same changes? (Remember, you can use *this* and *that* alone or with *one*.)

3 Using *The Same (As)*, *Like*, and *Different (From)*: In Your Classroom

Work with a partner. Find things in the classroom to compare, such as people's books, school supplies, and clothes. Take turns making affirmative and negative statements about them. Use *the same*, *the same as*, *like*, *different*, and *different from*.

Example: Student A: Your book is the same as mine.
          Student B: All the people in the room are different.

As . . . As with Adjectives and Adverbs

FORM and FUNCTION

A. Overview

	AS + ADJECTIVE/ADVERB + *AS*		(VERB)
This jacket is	**as expensive as**	that one	(is).
He doesn't work	**as hard as**	you	(do).

B. Comparisons with *As . . . As*

1. Use *as* + adjective or adverb + *as* to:

   - Say that two people or things are the same or equal in some way.

     She swims **as well as** her brother does. (They swim equally well.)

   - Ask if they are the same.

     Can she swim **as far as** her brother?

2. Use *not as* + adjective or adverb + *as* to say that someone or something is not equal to another.

   I'm **not as tall as** he is. (I'm shorter.)

   I can't **run as fast as** you can. (I'm slower.)

3. After *as . . . as*, you can use:

   - A possessive noun or possessive pronoun.

     Your books are as heavy as **Jack's.**

     My books aren't as heavy as **yours.**

   - A demonstrative pronoun.

     These sunglasses aren't as expensive as **those.**

     The demonstratives *this* and *that* are often followed by the indefinite pronoun *one*.

     My computer isn't as fast as **that one.**

4. You can often use a verb in the second part of a sentence with *as . . . as*. This verb is a form of *be*, the auxiliary *do*, or a modal.

   You **are** as fast as Brad (**is**).

   You **ran** as fast as Brad (**did**).

   You **can** run as fast as Brad (**can**).

TALKING THE TALK

1. In formal English, a pronoun used after *as . . . as* is a subject pronoun. A verb often follows the pronoun.

   Are you as tall as **he** (**is**)?

2. In informal conversation, the pronoun is often an object pronoun. There is no verb after an object pronoun.

   Are you as tall as **him**?

As . . . As with Adjectives and Adverbs

4 *As . . . As* with Adjectives: A Tale of Two Malls

Reporter Al Jordan is describing two shopping malls. Complete the sentences with (*not*) *as . . . as* and the adjectives in parentheses.

No other mall is ___as big as___ the West Edmonton Mall in Alberta,
       1 (big)

Canada. It has more than 800 shops. The Mall of America in Bloomington, Minnesota, is

_____ the West Edmonton Mall, but it's big, too—big enough to hold
       2 (not / large)

32 Boeing 747s, or over 24,000 school buses!

The first of these two malls, the West Edmonton Mall, opened in 1981. The Mall of America is

_____ the Canadian one. Construction on the mall in Minnesota began
       3 (not / old)

in 1989, and it opened in 1992.

Tourists are almost _____ shoppers at these malls. That's because at
                          4 (common)

both malls, entertainment is _____ shopping. Both malls have popular
                                 5 (important)

amusement parks, and the restaurants are just _____ the stores.
                                                    6 (interesting)

People even come to these malls to get married.

Each of the two malls gets millions of visitors a year. The average visitor to the Mall of

America stays for three hours, which is three times _____ a typical
                                                          7 (long)

shopping mall visit. Maybe these malls are _____ Disney World,
                                                8 (not / popular)

but they're not just ordinary malls. Do you want to get more information about them?

It's _____ pie—just telephone, or look up the malls on the Internet.
         9 (easy)

---

typical = having the usual qualities of a group, person, or thing.
as easy as pie = very easy.

 See the *Grammar Links* Website for more information on malls.

5 **Pronouns after *As . . . As*:** All in the Family

A. Listen to these four conversations. They take place between two brothers, their parents, and a boyfriend and girlfriend. Circle the words you hear.

1. Doug: Mom and Dad are the same age, right?

   Ralph: No, he's not as old as (she is / her).

2. Doug: I'm going to ask Mom for the car.

   Ralph: Try Dad. Mom's really busy. He isn't as busy as (she is / her) right now.

a

   Doug: Yeah, but he doesn't say "Yes" as often as (she does / her).

b

3. Mr. Noonan: The boys are so tall now! I'm not as tall as (they are / them) anymore.

a

   Mrs. Noonan: Well, that's normal. What about our parents? They aren't as tall as

   (we are / us).

b

4. Rose: Your brother seems really nice.

   Doug: Oh, yeah? As nice as (I am / me)?

a

   Rose: Don't be silly. Ralph plays tennis, too, right? Is he as good as (you are / you)?

b

   Doug: I can usually beat him, but I'm not as fast as (he is / him).

c

   Rose: My sister plays, too, but not as often as (I do / me).

d

B. Work with a partner. Read aloud the conversations in Part A, but use the words you did not circle.

6 Using *As . . . As*: Two Brothers and Their Clothes

A. Work alone or with a partner. Look at the information in the chart about the twins Doug and Ralph. The checkmarks tell who does what. Complete the statements with *as* + adverb + *as*. Add *not* where needed.

	Doug	Ralph
1. Often goes to stores		✓
2. Often shops online	✓	
3. Dresses comfortably	✓	✓
4. Dresses traditionally	✓	
5. Spends his money carefully		✓
6. His clothes fit well	✓	✓
7. Takes care of his clothes well	✓	✓

shop online = use the Internet to buy things.

1. Doug _doesn't go to stores as often as_ _____ Ralph does.

2. Ralph _____ Doug does.

3. One brother _____ the other one does.

4. Ralph _____ Doug does.

5. Doug _____ Ralph does.

6. Doug's clothes _____ Ralph's do.

7. One brother _____ the other one does.

B. Work with a partner. Take turns asking the questions below. Use *as* + adjective/adverb + *as* in your answers.

Example: Student A: How is Doug different from Ralph?
Student B: Doug doesn't go shopping as often as Ralph.

1. How is Doug different from Ralph?

2. How is Ralph different from Doug?

3. How are the brothers the same?

4. How are their clothes the same?

5. How are you different from Doug or Ralph?

7 Using *As . . . As* with Adjectives and Adverbs: Similarities and Differences

A. Work with a partner. Student A: Tell your partner about a person you know well. It can be a friend or family member. Describe two ways in which you and this person are the same, and describe two ways in which you are different. Use *as* + adjective/adverb + *as*. Student B: Ask one or more questions with *as . . . as*. Take turns.

Example: Student A: My brother is as tall as I am. He works as hard as I do. He isn't as old as I am, and he doesn't go out as often as I do.

Student B: Does your brother speak English as well as you do?

B. Write a paragraph about the person you described to your partner. Describe at least two ways that you and this person are the same, and describe two ways you are different. Use *as* + adjective/adverb + *as*.

Check your progress! Go to the Self-Test for Chapter 24 on the *Grammar Links* Website.

Chapter 25

Clothes of Yesterday and Today
Comparatives and Superlatives

Introductory Task: Cowboy Clothes

A. Listen and read about cowboy clothes in the United States.

The first cowboy clothes appeared in the 1800s. They were clothes that were practical for the work of cowboys in the West. Cowboy clothes today are in many ways the same as these clothes from over 100 years ago. But lots of people wear cowboy clothes today, not just cowboys in the West.

The most familiar item of cowboy clothing may be the cowboy hat. The cowboy hat has a wider brim than other men's hats and a taller crown, or top part. Some cowboy hats are called "Stetsons." J. B. Stetson was the most famous designer and maker of cowboy hats in the 1800s. Other cowboy hats have specific names, too. The largest ones, for example, are called "ten-gallon hats."

Cowboy boots are also very familiar. They have narrower toes than most men's boots, and their heels are higher. These heels are useful to a cowboy on a horse. They help his feet stay in the stirrups (the two metal loops that hang from his saddle). A Texas bootmaker produced the first real cowboy boots in the 1870s.

Chaps are less familiar to most people today than cowboy hats and boots. A pair of chaps covers a cowboy's legs and protects them better than his blue jeans do. Chaps are tough and practical, for a good reason. A cowboy's clothes all have to be tougher and last longer than most people's clothes.

---

practical = designed to be useful. *familiar* = well-known, not new or strange. *tough* = strong, not easy to tear or break.

B. Work alone or with a partner. Complete the sentences about comparisons in the reading.

1. The most familiar item of cowboy clothing may be the cowboy hat.

   This statement compares the cowboy hat to <u>other kinds of cowboy clothes.</u>

2. The cowboy hat has a wider brim than other men's hats.

   This statement compares _____ to other men's hats.

3. J. B. Stetson was the most famous designer and maker of cowboy hats in the 1800s.

   This statement compares J. B. Stetson to _____

4. Chaps are less familiar to most people today than cowboy hats and boots.

   This statement compares chaps to _____

5. A pair of chaps covers a cowboy's legs and protects them better than his blue jeans do.

   This statement compares _____ to _____

C. Work in a group. Talk about these questions: What kinds of cowboy clothes do you see people wearing? Who wears them? Where do you see cowboy clothes? Do you own any cowboy clothes?

See the *Grammar Links* Website for more information about cowboy clothes.

Comparatives

FORM and FUNCTION

A. Meaning of Comparative Adjectives and Adverbs

Comparative adjectives and adverbs help describe differences between two people or things.

Ann is tall, but her brother is **taller** than she is.

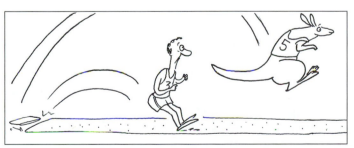

Kangaroos can jump **farther** than people.

(continued on next page)

B. Forming Comparative Adjectives

1. To form the comparative of most one-syllable adjectives: Add -(e)r.	old → old**er** nice → nic**er**
2. For one-syllable adjectives ending in 1 vowel + 1 consonant: Double the final consonant and add -er.	b**ig** → big**ger** h**ot** → hot**ter**
3. For two-syllable adjectives ending in y: Change the y to i and add -er.	happy → happ**ier** pretty → prett**ier**
4. For most adjectives of two syllables or more: Use more + the adjective.	famous → **more** famous beautiful → **more** beautiful

C. Forming Comparative Adverbs

1. To form the comparative of most one-syllable adverbs: Add -(e)r.	fast → fast**er** late → lat**er**
2. For most adjectives of two syllables or more: Use more + the adverb.	often → **more** often happily → **more** happily

D. Irregular Forms—Adjectives and Adverbs

Some adjectives and adverbs have irregular comparative forms.

ADJECTIVE	ADVERB	COMPARATIVE
good	well	**better**
bad	badly	**worse**
far	far	**farther/further**

GRAMMAR **HOT**SPOT!

Some two-syllable adjectives can form the comparative with -er or more.	narrow → narrow**er** OR **more** narrow handsome → handsom**er** OR **more** handsome friendly → friendl**ier** OR **more** friendly

Comparatives

1 Comparative Adjectives and Adverbs: Form Practice

A. Write the comparative form of each adjective in the correct column.

1. friendly	5. narrow	9. big	13. fashionable
2. practical	6. early	10. good	14. bad
3. late	7. lucky	11. strong	15. intelligent
4. far	8. handsome	12. careful	16. sweet

-er	more . . .	-er OR more . . .	irregular
later	more practical	friendlier, more friendly	farther/further

B. Write the comparative form of each adverb in the correct column.

1. quietly	5. early	9. cheaply	13. fast
2. far	6. often	10. frequently	14. slowly
3. late	7. smoothly	11. carefully	15. easily
4. badly	8. well	12. hard	16. quickly

-er	more . . .	irregular
later	more quietly	farther/further

Sentences with Comparatives

FORM and FUNCTION

A. Sentences with Comparative Adjectives and Adverbs

	COMPARATIVE ADJECTIVE/ADVERB	*THAN*		(VERB)
Is your brother	**taller**	**than**	you	(are)?
Kangaroos can jump	**farther**		people	(can).

1. Use sentences with comparative adjectives and adverbs + *than* to describe differences between two people or things.

    He's 25, and I'm 20. He's **older than** I am.

    She finished the test **sooner than** we did.

2. You can often use a verb in the second part of a sentence with a comparative. It is a form of *be*, the auxiliary *do*, or a modal.

    You **are** faster than Brad (**is**).

    You **ran** faster than Brad (**did**).

    You **can** run faster than Brad (**can**).

B. Comparative Sentences with *Less . . . Than*

1. You can also make comparisons with *less* + adjective/adverb + *than*. *Less* is the opposite of *more*. *Less . . . than* has the same meaning as *not as . . . as*.

    A bike is **less expensive than** a car. (A bike is not as expensive as a car.)

    I call home **less often than** my brother. (I don't call home as often as he does.)

2. Do not use *less . . . than* with one-syllable adjectives or adverbs. Use *not as . . . as* instead.

    This coat is **not as** warm **as** that one.
    NOT USUALLY: This coat is less warm than that one.

C. Comparative Sentences Without *Than*

You can omit *than* and the second part of the comparative sentence when the meaning is clear.

He's thin, but his sister is **thinner**. (= *thinner than he is.*)

The express bus is faster than the local bus, but the express bus comes **less often**. (= *less often than the local bus comes.*)

Sentences with Comparatives

2 **Comparative Adjectives and Adverbs; Comparisons with *Less*:**
100 Years of Bathing Suits

A. Write the comparative forms of the adjectives and adverbs in parentheses.
Use *-er* or *more* when there is a plus sign (+). Use *less* when there is a minus
sign (–). Add *than* where needed.

The bathing suits that are

common today are very different

from the bathing suits of

100 years ago. People—especially

women—can swim <u>more easily</u>
                    1 (+ easily)

in modern bathing suits. The swimsuits of the past were _____ in the water.
                                                            2 (– comfortable)

That's because the old suits were heavy, and they got _____ when they were wet.
                                                        3 (+ heavy)

Those suits covered most of people's bodies, and women sometimes wore black wool stockings

with them. Can you imagine anything _____ or _____
                                        4 (+ hot)   5 (+ uncomfortable)

that? Swimsuit fabrics today are _____, and this helps people swim
                                    6 (+ light)

_____ swimmers of the past. Bathing suits are _____ now,
    7 (+ fast)   8 (+ small)

too. One hundred years ago, people showed their bodies _____ in public.
                                                          9 (– freely)

Which style of bathing suit do you think is _____? The suits of the past
                                              10 (+ good)

were _____ for swimming. But they protected people from sunburn
      11 (– practical)

_____ bathing suits do today.
    12 (+ well)

B. Use the words given to write comparative statements based on the information in
Part A. Use the comparative form of the adjective or adverb or use *less . . . (than)*.

1. the swimsuits of the past/be/comfortable/swimsuits today
   The swimsuits of the past were less comfortable than swimsuits today.

2. the swimsuits of the past/be/heavy/swimsuits today

   _____

3. wool/be/hot/modern swimsuit fabrics

   _____

4. people today/can swim/fast/people 100 years ago

    _____

5. the swimsuits of the past/be/practical for swimmers

    _____

6. swimmers in the past/could move/easily/swimmers wearing today's swimsuits

    _____

7. today's swimsuits/be/good for swimmers

    _____

8. today's swimsuits/be/attractive/the swimsuits of the past

    _____

 See the *Grammar Links* Website for more information about bathing suits of the twentieth century.

3 | *Not As . . . As* Versus *Less . . . Than*: Two Lifeguards

Work alone or with a partner. Look at the information in the chart comparing two lifeguards. Write four statements about each one. Use *not as . . . as* in statements with one-syllable adjectives and adverbs. Use *less . . . than* in the other statements.

Chris and Dana both work as lifeguards at Bella Vista Beach.

Chris	looks stronger, can swim farther, is more experienced, is more confident
Dana	can swim faster, works harder, can communicate better, is more punctual

Chris   Dana

1. *Dana doesn't look as strong as Chris.* _____

2. _____

3. _____

4. _____

5. _____

6. _____

7. _____

8. _____

> *a lifeguard* = a person whose job is to help swimmers in danger at a beach or pool. *confident* = sure that you can do something well.
> *punctual* = arriving on time, not late.

4 Comparative Statements with Adjectives: Changes in Tennis Clothes

 Work alone or with a partner. On a piece of paper, write at least six statements comparing the clothes of the two tennis players. Player A is wearing tennis clothes from the year 1880. Player B is wearing a modern tennis dress. Use *be* or *look* + comparative forms of these adjectives: *modern, cool, good, heavy, light, practical,* and *short.*

Example: *Player B's dress looks more practical than Player A's dress.*

Player A   Player B

5 Making Comparative Statements: Comparing People and Things You Know

Divide the class into two teams. Team A: Choose a category and an adjective or adverb from the chart. Make a comparative statement.

Examples: Cities, *big*: *Rome is bigger than Hong Kong.*
Clothes, *comfortable*: *High heels are less comfortable than running shoes.*

For a statement with the correct comparative form, score one point for your team. Both teams cross out that box; that adjective or adverb will not be used again. Team B: Now it's your turn. Continue until all the boxes are crossed out.

Cities	Food	People	Clothes	Animals
big	sweet	famous	expensive	common
far	good	tall	comfortable	useful
crowded	popular	handsome	warm	slowly
easily	healthy	well	fashionable	fast

Superlatives

FORM and FUNCTION

A. Forming Superlative Adjectives and Adverbs

1. To form superlatives, use *the* and change the adjective or adverb as follows:

   - For most one-syllable adjectives and adverbs: Add -(e)*st*.

     old → **the** old**est**

     late → **the** lat**est**

   - For one-syllable adjectives that end in 1 vowel + 1 consonant: Double the final consonant and add -*est*.

     big → **the** big**gest**

     hot → **the** hot**test**

   - For two-syllable adjectives that end in *y*: Change the *y* to *i* and add -*est*.

     happy → **the** happ**iest**

     pretty → **the** prett**iest**

   - For most adjectives and adverbs of two syllables or more: Use *most* + adjective/adverb.

     famous → **the most** famous

     slowly → **the most** slowly

2. Some adjectives and adverbs have irregular superlative forms.

ADJECTIVE	ADVERB	SUPERLATIVE
good	well	**the best**
bad	badly	**the worst**
far	far	**the farthest/furthest**

3. Some two-syllable adjectives can form the superlative with either -*est* or *most*.

   narrow → **the** narrow**est** OR **the most** narrow

   handsome → **the** handsom**est** OR **the most** handsome

   friendly → **the** friend**liest** OR **the most** friendly

B. Meaning and Use of Superlatives

Use superlative adjectives and adverbs to describe differences in a group of three or more people or things.

England has several important cities, but London is **the most important** one.

Dan can beat all his teammates in a race. He runs **the fastest** of them all.

C. *The Least* + Adjective or Adverb

The least is the opposite of *the most*.

Q: Of those three cars, which one is **the least expensive**?

A: The Honda. The other two cost more.

(continued on next page)

D. Sentences with Superlatives

	SUPERLATIVE ADJECTIVE/ADVERB	(NOUN)	(PREPOSITIONAL PHRASE)
Louis is	**the best**	student	in the class.
You work	**the hardest**		of all the people in our office.
Which is	**the least crowded**	part	of the beach?

1. Sentences with superlatives often have prepositional pharases with *in* or *of* to identify the group.

   It was the most beautiful dress **in the store**.
   That shop stays open the latest **of all**.

2. A noun often follows a superlative adjective. You can omit the noun or use the pronoun *one*, if the meaning is clear.

   Bruno's pizzas are | the best pizzas / the best / the best ones | in town.

GRAMMAR PRACTICE 3

Superlatives

6 **Superlative Adjectives and Adverbs:** Form Practice

A. Write the superlative form of each adjective in the correct column.

1. friendly
2. practical
3. late
4. early
5. narrow
6. good
7. lucky
8. handsome
9. cheap
10. big
11. pretty
12. careful
13. informal
14. bad
15. far
16. interesting

the -est	*the most*	*the -est* OR *the most*	irregular
the latest	the most practical	the friendliest, the most friendly	

B. Write the superlative form of each adverb in the correct column.

1. well
2. quietly
3. late
4. early
5. noisily
6. often
7. happily
8. politely
9. fast
10. frequently
11. far
12. carefully
13. badly
14. slowly
15. hard
16. successfully

the -est	*the most*	irregular
the latest	the most quietly	the best

---

7 **Superlative Adjectives and Adverbs:** Remembering the Clothes of the Sixties

Write the superlative form of the adjective or adverb in parentheses. Circle the nine prepositional phrases with *in* or *of* that identify the groups. The first one is circled for you.

Mrs. Noonan, Doug and Ralph's mother, is describing clothes back in the 1960s.

Doug and Ralph always laugh at pictures of me from the 1960s.

They think my clothes were ___the funniest___ thing (in the world.)
                            1 (funny)

Now I look at those old photos, and I smile, too. My skirts were very

short—I wore _____ skirts of all my friends. I wore
              2 (short)

them with very tall boots, but they weren't _____
                                             3 (tall)

boots you could buy. Back then, I had _____ hair
                                        4 (long)

of all my friends, and I pressed it with a hot iron to make it straight.

Isn't that _____ thing? I wore some pretty awful colors, too, but they weren't
           5 (crazy)

_____ colors of the sixties. In fact, my high school classmates voted me
6 (bad)

"Best-Dressed Girl in the Class of 1968."

My sons laugh _____ 7 (hard) at pictures of me with my

brother, their uncle Jim. In the 1960s, Jimmy dressed like a hippie.

He wore blue jeans with _____ 8 (wide) legs he could find.

Our parents hated them, but they were more patient than a lot of other

parents were. I remember my best friend's father—he hated all the

changes. He got upset _____ 9 (easily) of all the parents

in the neighborhood. Oh, how he yelled at poor DeeDee about her

clothes! For my parents, _____ 10 (difficult) thing of all was Jimmy's hair. He had

_____ 11 (curly) hair in the family, and it was pretty long. Girls thought he was

_____ 12 (handsome) boy in his class. Jim certainly looks different now. These days,

he dresses _____ 13 (formally) of all the men in the family.

8 Editing: Back at the Halloween Party

Correct the eight errors in sentences with comparative and superlative adjectives and adverbs. The first error is corrected for you.

Do you remember the Halloween party from page 364? Jane is now dancing with the man in the Frankenstein costume, and Rose is talking to Doug.

Rose: What a great party! It's ~~best of~~ better than last year's party, isn't it? The costumes

are wonderful.

Doug: Did you see the other two guys in cowboy outfits? Theirs are the better

than mine.

Rose: No, yours is the better one of all!

Doug: Well, it's good enough. You look terrific in that Cinderella outfit.

Rose: Thanks, but it's not the more interesting one here tonight.

Doug: What are you talking about? Whose costume is better than you? Nobody's.

Rose: Well, what about the sixties outfit on that blonde girl over there? She's wearing

shortest skirt in the room, isn't she? It's about three feet more short than mine is.

Doug: Oh, that's Dominique.

Rose: You talked to her for a very long time.

Doug: Yeah, well, uh, she seemed lonely. Listen, do you want to dance?

Rose: Dance? Doug, I can hardly stand up. These are the uncomfortablest shoes in

the world. Let's just leave. But please don't walk too fast.

9 Using Superlative Adjectives and Adverbs: An Opinion Survey

  A. Form a group. Each person in the group chooses a question to research in the class. Find out what your classmates think. Report their answers to your group.

1. What is the best restaurant in this area?

2. What is the most exciting sport to watch?

3. What is the most important quality in a friend?

4. Who works the hardest in this class?

5. Who comes to school the earliest?

6. Who understands grammar the best?

7. Who lives the farthest from school?

8. Write your own question: _____

Example: Student A: I asked, "What is the best restaurant in this area?" A lot of people said Nini's has the best pizza. The best Japanese food is at Ichiban. There isn't one best restaurant. It depends on the food you like.

B. Choose question 1, 2, 3, or 4 from Part A. Write a paragraph giving your answer to the question and the reasons for your opinion.

See the *Grammar Links* Website for a model paragraph for this assignment.

Check your progress! Go to the Self-Test for Chapter 25 on the *Grammar Links* Website.

Wrap-up Activities

1 **Playing Cowboys:** READING

Read this paragraph.

   On the wall in my parents' room, there is an old photograph of my brother and me. My mother took this picture when I was about three years old. In the photo, my brother and I are standing in the kitchen. My brother is only two years older than I am, but in the photo, he is much taller. We are wearing the same white cowboy hats, brown cowboy jackets, blue jeans, and cowboy boots, and we are smiling happily. In those days, the TV shows we liked the best were shows about cowboys. We really liked to put on these clothes and play cowboys.

2 **What I Remember:** WRITING

Think of a photograph of two or more people, perhaps friends or family members, perhaps a photo of you and someone else. It can be a photo you have or one that you remember well enough to describe. Who is in the photo? What are they doing? What are they wearing? Write a paragraph about the photo, and try to use adjectives (including comparatives and superlatives) and adverbs, such as adverbs of manner and intensifiers.

 See the *Grammar Links* Website for a model paragraph for this assignment.

3 **A Wedding Day Photo:** EDITING

Correct the eight errors in statements with adjectives and adverbs. Some of them can be corrected in more than one way. The first error is corrected for you.

Wedding Photograph

                       an old photograph
   There is ~~a photograph old~~ of my parents on the wall in our living room at

home. It is nicest photo from their wedding day. They are standing together and

smiling happy. My mother is wearing a long white dress and holding some prettiest

flowers. My father is wearing a dark suit. They look too young. My mother doesn't

look very different now, but she is more heavy than she was, and her hair is shorter.

My father is more heavier, too, and he doesn't have hardly any hair.

---

4 **Pet Peeves:** SPEAKING/LISTENING

Step 1 A pet peeve is something that always annoys you. Do you have any pet peeves? Think of something that people do that bothers you.

Step 2 Form a group. Tell your group about a pet peeve you have. Describe when, where, and how people do this thing. Use adverbs of manner, intensifiers, and adverbs of frequency.

Example: Some drivers really annoy me. They never think about other people on the road. They drive thoughtlessly. For example, they don't use their turn signals, and then they turn suddenly.

Step 3 Vote on the most and least annoying pet peeves in your group.

5 **All in the Family:** SPEAKING/LISTENING

Work with a partner. Student A: Interview your partner about his or her family. Find out the answers to the questions below. Student B: Answer the questions. Compare the people you talk about to yourself. Take turns.

Example: Student A: Who is the youngest person in your family?
Student B: My brother Emil. He is eight years younger than I am.

1. Who is the youngest person in your family? Who is the oldest?

2. Who is the most serious person in your family? Who is the funniest?

3. Who speaks English the best?

4. Who works the hardest?

5. Who do you talk to the most often?

6. What can you do better than anyone in your family?

Verbs and Objects; Past Progressive Tense; Time Clauses

TOPIC FOCUS
Adventure and Excitement

UNIT OBJECTIVES

- **verbs that take direct objects**
  (She **bought a car**. She **liked it**.)

- **verbs that take direct objects and indirect objects**
  (She **gave me the directions**. I **read them** to **the driver**.)

- **verbs that do not take direct objects**
  (They **traveled** across the desert. They finally **arrived**.)

- **linking verbs**
  (It **looked** dangerous, but the stuntman **seemed** confident.)

- **verbs that can take infinitives as direct objects**
  (He **wanted to fly** airplanes. He **decided to become** a pilot.)

- **the past progressive tense**
  (In June, he **was making** a film. The filmmakers **were working** underwater.)

- **sentences with past time clauses**
  (I was standing on the beach **when I took this picture. While we were fishing**, we saw a shark.)

Grammar in Action

Reading and Listening: A Sense of Adventure

Read and listen.

An Astronaut

1   On July 20, 1969, millions of people around the world were sitting in front of television sets. They were waiting to see a very exciting moment in human history. All these people were watching when astronaut Neil Armstrong stepped onto the surface of the moon. They saw Armstrong become the first person to walk on the moon.

2   When Armstrong was on the moon, he could look back at our beautiful blue planet. The earth looks blue because of its oceans. Oceans cover 71 percent of the earth's surface. While Armstrong was learning about the moon, ocean explorers were making discoveries, too. One of the most famous of these explorers was Jacques Cousteau.

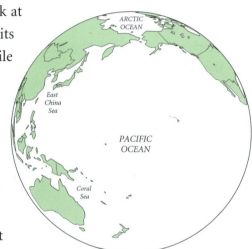

3   Cousteau was an ocean scientist and a filmmaker. He sailed around the world to explore the oceans. Cousteau made many exciting discoveries. He learned secrets of the seas, and he taught them to other people. With his films, he showed audiences some of the amazing things that exist underwater. He gave us new ways of thinking about our oceans.

4   Like Neil Armstrong, Jacques Cousteau had a sense of adventure. Both men explored new places and took great risks. Their work put them in a lot of danger, but they loved the excitement of exploration.

5   Most of us want to work in nice, safe jobs, but some people like to do jobs that involve excitement and risk. Some of them try to find jobs where they can help people in danger. Firefighters are an example. Others risk their lives in front of an audience. Circus performers and race car drivers are good examples. Explorers, firefighters, circus performers, and race car drivers—their work may be very different, but they are all people with a strong sense of adventure.

Jacques Cousteau

---

discoveries = things people find or learn that were not known before.
an audience = the people watching a movie, concert, show, etc. *a sense of adventure* = a liking for experiences that are exciting, dangerous, or unusual.
performers = people who do something for others to watch and enjoy.

Think About Grammar

A. Complete these statements from paragraphs 1 and 2 of the reading.

1. On July 20, 1969, millions of people around the world _____ in front of television sets.

2. All these people _____ when astronaut Neil Armstrong stepped onto the surface of the moon.

3. While Armstrong _____ about the moon, ocean explorers were making discoveries, too.

The verbs you wrote are in the **past progressive tense**. These verbs have two parts. What are they?

_____ or _____ and the base form of the verb + -_____

B. Complete these statements from paragraphs 3 and 4 of the reading.

1. Cousteau made _____.

2. . . . and he taught _____ to other people.

3. Both men explored _____ and took _____.

The words you wrote are **direct objects**. They tell who or what received the action of the verb. What types of words are they? Circle one or more answers.

nouns/noun phrases   verbs   pronouns   adverbs

> *a noun phrase* = a noun and the words that modify it.

C. Complete these statements from paragraph 3 of the reading.

1. He learned the secrets of the seas, and he taught them to _____.

2. With his films, he showed _____ some amazing things underwater.

3. He gave _____ new ways of thinking about our oceans.

The words you wrote are **indirect objects**. They tell the people to whom or for whom the subject did the action. What types of words are they? Circle one or more answers.

nouns/noun phrases   verbs   pronouns   adverbs

D. Complete these statements from paragraph 5 of the reading.

1. Most of us want _____ in nice, safe jobs . . .

2. . . . but some people like _____ jobs that involve excitement and risk.

3. Some of them try _____ jobs where they can help people in danger.

The words you wrote are **infinitives**. What is an infinitive? Circle your answer.

An infinitive = *to* + _____

the base form of a verb   the -*ing* form of a verb   a past tense verb

26

Looking for Excitement
Verbs and Objects

Introductory Task: Circus Thrills

 A. Listen and read about Gregor, the lion tamer. Some of the verbs are **boldfaced**. The <u>underlined</u> words are direct objects.

Gregor has a dangerous job. He is a lion tamer in a circus. When Gregor performs, he enters a big cage full of lions. He **shouts** at the lions and **watches** <u>them</u> closely. Then he calls one lion to the center of the cage. He **waves** <u>his whip</u> at the other lions. The lion in the center **stands** quietly. Gregor **shouts** <u>commands</u> at the lion. Then he opens the lion's mouth. The lion's teeth are big and sharp! Carefully, Gregor **puts** <u>his head</u> into the lion's mouth. The people in the audience hold their breath. Some **put** <u>their hands</u> over their eyes—they can't watch. Finally, Gregor steps away from the lion, and the crowd cheers. The lion tamer **stands** in the spotlight and **waves** to the people.

B. Work alone or with a partner. Look at each use of the **boldfaced** verbs in Part A. Check (✓) one or both columns for each verb.

	Is Used with a Direct Object	Is Used without a Direct Object
1. shout	✓	✓
2. watch		
3. wave		
4. stand		
5. put		

C. Work with a partner. Think of sentences using each of the following verbs. Does the verb take a direct object? Circle your guesses. Then compare answers with the class.

1. want   (always / sometimes / never)

2. have   (always / sometimes / never)

3. sleep   (always / sometimes / never)

4. arrive   (always / sometimes / never)

5. study   (always / sometimes / never)

GRAMMAR BRIEFING 1

Verbs with Objects

FORM and FUNCTION

A. Direct Objects and Indirect Objects

1. A **direct object** (DO) is the person or thing that receives the action of a verb.	DO I called **my friend**. DO I bought **a CD**.
2. An **indirect object** (IO) tells to or for whom an action happens.	IO I gave a present to **my friend**. IO I bought **him** a CD.
3. Direct and indirect objects can be:	
• Nouns (or noun phrases).	We didn't see **Julia**. We saw **some other friends**. We told **our friends** about you.
• Object pronouns: *me, you, him, her, it, us, them*.	I didn't reach **her**. I gave the message to **him**.

B. Transitive Verbs

1. A **transitive verb** is a verb that must take a direct object. Examples include *hit, cut, want,* and *have*.	The player **hit** the ball. I'll **cut** the cake. They **want** more time. Do you **have** a car?
2. Some transitive verbs can take an indirect object, too. Examples include *describe, do, send,* and *teach*.	He **described** the game to his listeners. Could you **do** something for me? I'll **send** you a postcard. She **taught** me a new word.

Verbs with Objects

1 **Identifying Direct and Indirect Objects:** Katya, Circus Star!

Read about a real circus performer. Look at the **boldfaced** objects. Write *DO* over direct objects and *IO* over indirect objects.

A Circus Acrobat
on a Trapeze

Do you like **the circus**? Katya does. She does **amazing tricks**
　　　　　　　　1　　　　　　　　　　　　　　　　2

for **audiences** all over North America. She's a circus acrobat. High
　　　3

up in the air, Katya swings **her body** around and around the
　　　　　　　　　　　　　4

trapeze. Sometimes she uses only **one arm**! An announcer describes
　　　　　　　　　　　　　　5

her act to **the audience**. People look up at her and wonder, "How can she do **that**!"
6　　　　7　　　　　　　　　　　　　　　　　　　　　　　　　　　8

Katya's real name is Ekaterina Odintsova. She was born in Russia and studied at a

special sports school there. Her teachers taught **her many tricks**. Later, a European
　　　　　　　　　　　　　　　　　　9　　　10

circus wanted **Katya** in their show, so she did **her act** for **people** in Europe. Then in
　　　　　11　　　　　　　　　　　　　12　　　　13

1996, she joined "The Greatest Show On Earth"—the Ringling Bros. and Barnum &

Bailey Circus.

People in the audience often say things like "Her act scared **us**. It looked so
　　　　　　　　　　　　　　　　　　　　　　　14

dangerous!" Many children send **her letters**. Katya sends **them photos**. Someday
　　　　　　　　　　　　15　　16　　　　　　　　17　　18

Katya would like to teach. Right now, she's the Queen of the Clouds.

Bros. = (abbreviation for) Brothers.

 See the *Grammar Links* Website for more information about circus acrobats.

2 Object Pronouns: A Dangerous Trick

Complete the sentences using object pronouns for the direct and indirect objects in parentheses.

Reporter Al Jordan is in Las Vegas, Nevada. He sent his wife this e-mail message about an amazing show.

Bullets

From: ajordan@WRJY.com (Al Jordan)

To: jordan54478@westnet.com (Sara Jordan)

Subject: You won't believe it

Sara, Last night I saw this great show. It was truly amazing. I have to tell _you_____
1 (Sara)

about _____.
2 (the show)

There were two men on the stage. First, one man showed a gun and a bullet to three police

officers. He asked the police to check _____. They did, and then they gave
3 (the gun and bullet)

_____ back to _____. The man's partner carried a glass
4 (the gun and bullet)   5 (the man)

window to the stage. He put _____ in front of the man with the gun. Then he
6 (the glass window)

walked back, opened his mouth, and waited. The man with the gun aimed _____
7 (the gun)

at his partner and fired. His partner caught the bullet with his teeth!

A camera operator recorded the act for the audience. Then she showed

_____ the film. It was in slow-motion, so we could see the bullet break
8 (the others in the audience and me)

the glass and then see the second man catch the bullet with his teeth. Really, you have to believe

_____! These guys have a great act. I wouldn't try _____ for a
9 (Al Jordan)   10 (their act)

million dollars. Love, Al

a stage = a raised floor in a theater where actors or musicians perform.

Sentence Patterns for Verbs with Direct and Indirect Objects

FORM

A. Verbs with Two Possible Patterns

1. With some transitive verbs that take both a direct object (DO) and an indirect object (IO), two sentence patterns are possible. The indirect object can come:

   - After the direct object (with *to* or with *for*).

	DO	IO
I gave	**the papers**	to **her**.

   - Before the direct object (without *to* or *for*).

	IO	DO
I gave	**her**	**the papers**.

2. These two sentences pattern are possible with verbs including:

   - Verbs that take *to* + indirect object: *bring, send, teach, give, show, tell, sell, take,* and *write.*

     I **sent** a letter **to** Jack. I **sent** Jack a letter.

     She **gave** flowers **to** her friend. She **gave** her friend flowers.

   - Verbs that take *for* + indirect object: *buy, find, get,* and *make.*

     I **bought** some coffee **for** you. I **bought** you some coffee.

     We **got** tickets **for** our friends. We **got** our friends tickets.

B. Verbs with One Pattern Only

With some transitive verbs that take both a direct and an indirect object, only the pattern with *to* or *for* is possible. These verbs include:

- Verbs that take *to* + indirect object: *announce, explain,* and *introduce.*

  He **explained** the lesson **to** us.
  NOT: He explained ~~us~~ the lesson.

- Verbs that take *for* + indirect object: *answer, open, close,* and *perform.*

  Would you **open** the door **for** me?
  NOT: Would you open ~~me~~ the door?

Sentence Patterns for Verbs with Direct and Indirect Objects

3 **Patterns for Sentences with Direct and Indirect Objects:**
Making an Action Movie

Karate

A. Use the words in parentheses. Write commands with direct object + *to/for* + indirect object.

Jack O'Brien is directing a Hollywood action movie. It will have karate fighting and dangerous situations. O'Brien is giving commands to people around him.

1. To his secretary:

   Get my assistant for me!
   _____
   (get / my assistant / me)

2. To his assistant:

   _____
   (find / a new stuntman / me)

3. To his secretary:

   _____
   (send / a "Get Well Soon" card / the last stuntman)

4. To his assistant:

   _____
   (bring / the writer / me)

5. To the writer:

   _____
   (write / some new lines / the actors)

6. To his assistant:

   _____
   (tell / my new ideas / the writer)

7. To his secretary:

   _____
   (get / a new computer / the writer)

8. To his assistant:

   _____
   (give / these clothes / the new stuntman)

9. To the new stuntman:

   _____
   (teach / some karate moves / the actors)

10. To the secretary:

   _____
   (make / some more coffee / us)

> *a stuntman* (*or stuntwoman*) = a person who takes the place of an actor
> to do something dangerous for a film.

B. Work with a partner. Student A: Read aloud a command from Part A. Student B: Restate the command putting the indirect object before the direct object. Take turns.

Example: Student A: Get my assistant for me!
Student B: Get me my assistant!

4 **Patterns for Sentences with Direct and Indirect Objects:** Hollywood Stunt Actors

The following statements have a direct object + *to/for* + an indirect object.
Circle *to* or *for*. Rewrite each statement with the indirect object first if possible.
Write "No change" after statements with only one possible pattern.

David is a student at the USA International Stunt School. He's learning to do stunts for movies. Read what David says about the school.

1. My best friend got an application for the Stunt School (to / (for)) me.
   My best friend got me an application for the Stunt School.

2. The director introduced the teachers (to / for) the new students.
   No change.

3. The director announced some changes (to / for) the group.

4. The instructors teach karate (to / for) the students.

5. For the fire safety class, the instructor got safety goggles (to / for) me.

6. The instructor answered my questions (to / for) me.

7. For the climbing class, the instructors gave ropes (to / for) us.

8. The instructors explained each stunt (to / for) the students.

9. One instructor showed a bomb stunt from his last movie (to / for) the class.

10. The director bought new safety equipment (to / for) everybody.

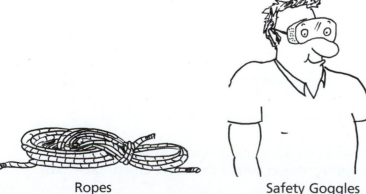

Ropes   Safety Goggles   A Bomb

5 Using the Indirect Object + Direct Object Pattern: Sorry to Hear About Your Accident

A. Work in a group of three or four. Your friend David had an accident doing a stunt for a movie. He broke both his legs. Now he is at home in bed. Talk about things you can do for David. Use sentences with verb + indirect object + direct object. Include the verbs *take*, *give*, *send*, *buy*, *get*, *write*, and *make*.

Example: Student A: I can take him something to read.

B. Work with a partner. Student A: You are David. Your friend is visiting you. Ask for help using verb + indirect object + direct object. Include the verbs *bring*, *buy*, *find*, *get*, *make*, and *tell*. Student B: Listen and answer.

Example: Student A: Would you bring me a video?
Student B: Sure. What video would you like?
Student A: Could you make me something to eat?
Student B: Sure. I'll make you some chicken soup, okay?

C. Write five or more sentences about things you plan to do for David. Use verb + indirect object + direct object.

Example: I'm going to make him something to eat.

Verbs with and without Direct Objects

FORM and FUNCTION

A. Intransitive Verbs

1. An **intransitive verb** does not take a direct object. There is no person or thing receiving the action of the verb. Intransitive verbs include *arrive, be, come, fall, go, sit, sleep, stand, wait,* and *walk*.	The baby **is sleeping**. When will the plane **arrive**? Let's **walk**. Where should we **go**?
2. Verbs without a direct object are often followed by an adverb or prepositional phrase.	The baby **is sleeping** now. The plane **arrived** at 10:15. Let's **walk** faster. Where should we **go** for lunch?

(continued on next page)

B. Verbs That Can Be Transitive or Intransitive

Some verbs can be transitive or intransitive. They can be used with or without direct objects.

These verbs include *begin, cook, hear, play, start, study,* and *watch*.

TRANSITIVE	INTRANSITIVE
She **cooked** dinner last night.	She **cooks** every night.
We **played** soccer.	We **played** together.
Did you **hear** the news?	Speak up! We can't **hear**!

Verbs with and without Direct Objects

6 **Verbs with and without Direct Objects:** Take a Walk with Monsieur Blondin

A. Work alone or with a partner. Look at each **boldfaced** verb. Does it have a direct object? Write *T* over transitive verbs and *I* over intransitive verbs. Circle the direct object after each transitive verb.

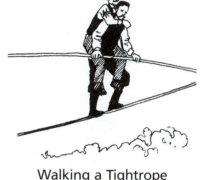

Jean François Gravelet **had** a dangerous job. He was "The

Great Blondin," a circus performer and a tightrope walker. In

1859, a railroad company **offered** a reward for crossing Niagara

Falls on a tightrope. Blondin **wanted** the money, so he agreed

Walking a Tightrope

to do it. On June 30, special trains **traveled** to the falls. They **carried** hundreds of

people from New York and Canada. All these people **were going** to the falls to see

the famous tightrope walker. Would he **make** the trip safely, or would he **fall**?

Blondin **set** his rope across the river. It was 1,100 feet long. Then he **climbed** up.

He **stood** on the rope, holding a long pole in his hands, and the crowd **watched**

and **waited**. Then Blondin **began** his walk. The crowd saw the rope moving in

the wind, and they **heard** the falls, sounding like thunder below. Blondin **walked**

across the rope, over Niagara Falls, and **arrived** safely on the other side. There, a
17

man from the railroad company **was waiting**. He **gave** Monsieur Blondin his
18   19

reward. But Blondin was not finished. On August 19, he **went** back across the
20

falls, and this time, he **had** another man on his shoulders!
21

B. Work with a partner. Imagine you are at Niagara Falls on the day of Monsieur
Blondin's stunt. Will you watch, or will you close your eyes? Tell your partner
what you will do and explain why. Do you usually like to watch people do
dangerous things? Give an example.

7   Using Verbs with and without Direct Objects: To Jump or Not to Jump

A. Bungee jumpers use a special cord or rope, a bungee.
It stretches and then springs back again. Look at the
pictures of these bungee jumpers. Write at least six
statements about the people in the pictures. Use at
least three transitive verbs and at least three
intransitive verbs. Mark these verbs *T* and *I*.

A Bungee Jumper Wearing a Harness

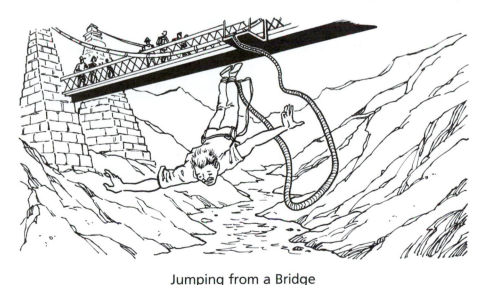

Jumping from a Bridge

Example: One person is in the air. Some people are watching. They are watching the jumper.

B. Share your sentences with the class.

Linking Verbs

FORM and FUNCTION

1. A **linking verb** is a special kind of intransitive verb. It links a subject to a word that describes the subject.

   Linking verbs include *be, become, feel, look, seem, smell, sound,* and *taste*.

   He **is** a pilot.

   I **feel** fine.

   The car **sounds** strange.

   The tea **tasted** funny.

2. Linking verbs do not take objects. They are often followed by:

   • Adjectives.

   She seemed **happy**.

   The flowers smell **nice**.

   • Noun/noun phrases.

   He became **an actor**.

   You are **the winner**.

GRAMMAR **HOT**SPOT!

1. The verbs *smell* and *taste* can be:

   • Linking verbs.

   This coffee **tastes great**. (*Great* describes *this coffee*.)

   Dinner **smells good**.

   • Transitive verbs (with direct objects).

   You should **taste this soup**. (*Taste* is an action verb.)

   I **smell smoke**.

2. The verb *look* can be:

   • A linking verb.

   He **looks sad**.

   You **look great** in that suit.

   • An intransitive verb for an action.

   I didn't see it—I **wasn't looking**.

   Look at that!

Linking Verbs

8 Linking Verbs: Pick a Verb

Use linking verbs to complete the statements. More than one verb may be possible.

1. TV weatherman to audience: The air will _become/be_ drier and cooler.

2. Director to young actor: Don't _____ nervous.

3. Bungee jumper to instructor: This doesn't _____ hard.

4. Doctor to stuntman: You'll _____ better tomorrow.

5. Customer to waiter: This coffee doesn't _____ good.

6. Car owner to auto mechanic: My car _____ funny.

7. Neighbor to neighbor: Your flowers _____ great.

8. Teacher to two children: I hope you'll _____ friends.

9 Look, Smell, and Taste: Is It a Linking Verb?

Underline the verbs in these sentences. Are they linking verbs? Check (✓) your answers.

	A Linking Verb	Not a Linking Verb
1. I'm looking for my keys.		✓
2. He looks sick.		
3. Look at me!		
4. The math problems don't look easy.		
5. The pizza smells great.		
6. I can't smell anything because of my cold.		
7. I tasted all four kinds of ice cream.		
8. Which one tastes the best?		

10 **Using Linking Verbs:** What's Your Opinion?

Work in a group. Take turns giving opinions using the different linking verbs. Talk about the things in the lists below. You can also add other people or things to the lists.

Example: Student A: Tonya and Mike look busy.
Student B: My voice sounds strange because I have a cold.

People and things in the classroom:	I my voice (a classmate)
People and things outside the school:	my best friend people on the street the weather (a famous person)
Smells and tastes:	chocolate onions the food in the cafeteria pizza

be
become
feel
look
seem
smell
sound
taste

GRAMMAR BRIEFING 5

Verbs with Infinitives as Direct Objects

FORM and FUNCTION

Using Verb + Infinitive

1. An **infinitive** is *to* + the base form of a verb. Some verbs can have an infinitive as a direct object. These infinitives function as nouns.

NOUN DIRECT OBJECT	INFINITIVE DIRECT OBJECT
I like **music**.	I like **to dance**.
He's learning **English**.	He's learning **to swim**.

2. Verbs that can take infinitives include *decide, learn, prefer, expect, like, prepare, forget, love, start, hate, need, try, hope, plan,* and *want*.

We **decided** to go.

They **expected** to win the race.

I **forgot** to call you.

Ann **hates** to swim.

I **hope** to go there some day.

I **tried** to find them.

In informal spoken English, the *to* in an infinitive often sounds like "ta".

WRITE	YOU WILL OFTEN HEAR
I plan to become an artist.	I plan "ta" become an artist.
Paula hopes to buy a car.	Paula hopes "ta" buy a car.

GRAMMAR PRACTICE 5

Verbs with Infinitives as Direct Objects

11 **Infinitives as Direct Objects:**
The Paris–Dakar Rally

🎧 Read and listen. Complete the statements with the missing infinitive or noun direct objects that you hear.

Reporter Al Jordan is talking with Felipe Torino, a driver in this year's car race from Paris to Dakar.

Al: I'm here in Paris, France, for the start of the

Paris–Dakar car rally, and I'm talking to Felipe

Torino. He's preparing ___to start___ the race in
                              1

a few hours. Felipe, how do you feel right now?

Felipe: Great! I really want _____ this!
                                  2

Al: This is a hard race. Why did you decide _____ it?
                                                3

Felipe: I love _____, and I love _____. Racing is my life,
                   4   5

you know?

Al: Well, Felipe, let's talk about your chances in this race. There are 160 cars entered this year.

Usually, fewer than half arrive in Dakar. Do you expect

_____?
        6

Felipe: It's going to be hard, I know, but I hope

_____ there!
         7

Al: Tell me, how did you prepare for this race?

Felipe: Well, I entered some short races, just for practice. And I started _____
                                                                                    8

French and Arabic. They're pretty useful languages for this trip.

Al: Did you take courses?

Felipe: Nah, I prefer _____ by talking to people.
                              9

Al: I see. Now, you plan _____ your own repairs during the race, right?
                                     10

Felipe: Oh, yeah. You really need _____ how to do all that.
                                          11

Al: Can you get supplies during the race? And water?

Felipe: Yeah, sure, we stop in a lot of cities along the way. But I want _____ a lot
                                                                              12

of water with me, for the desert sections.

Al: You'll also need _____!
                               13

Felipe: That's for sure. Well, I want _____ to a few friends before the race.
                                              14

Al: Okay, then. Good luck to you, Felipe. We'll look for you at the finish line!

🌐 See the *Grammar Links* Website for more information on the Paris–Dakar Rally.

12 Using Infinitives as Direct Objects: What Do You Want to Do?

A. Take a piece of paper and write at least three things you would like to do or hope to do in the future.

Example: ski in the Olympics, go to business school, get married

B. Work with a partner. Exchange papers, and ask each other about the activities. Use questions from the charts below or think of your own questions. Use infinitives as direct objects.

Example: Student A: Why do you want to ski in the Olympics?
          Student B: Because I hope to win a medal.
          Student A: When did you learn to ski?
          Student B: In 1998.

Why		want to . . .
Where	do you	expect to . . .
		hope to . . .
When		plan to . . .

Do you	want to . . .
	love to . . .
	hate to . . .

When	did you	learn to . . .
		start to . . .

Do you ever	forget to . . .
	try to . . .

C. Tell the class something about your partner.

D. Write a paragraph about one of the things you would like or hope to do. Include sentences with verb + infinitive.

Example: In 1998, I learned to ski. Now I really love to ski. I would like to be in the Olympics . . .

See the *Grammar Links* Website for a complete model paragraph for this assignment.

13 Editing: Charles Lindbergh

Read about Charles Lindbergh, the first person to fly across the Atlantic Ocean alone. Correct the nine errors with direct and indirect objects, linking verbs, and infinitives. Some errors can be corrected in more than one way. The first error is corrected for you.

     Charles Lindbergh was born in the United States in 1902. He went to college and

started to ~~studied~~ ^{study} mechanical engineering, but he left school. He was looking for

adventure. Lindbergh wanted for become a pilot, so he bought an old war plane, and

he taught himself to fly. He performed in air shows in the 1920s and gave airplane

rides people. He also gave to people flying lessons. Lindbergh decided on fly solo

(alone) across the Atlantic Ocean. On May 20, 1927, he took off from Long Island,

New York, on his historic flight. It was a long flight. After nine hours, he felt to

be very tired. After 23 hours, he saw Ireland, but he didn't land there. He wanted

to reach France. He continued on, and he arrived his plane in Paris 33 hours and

9 minutes after starting. His trip made him famous.

     Airplanes became more popular because of Charles Lindbergh. He explained

people the importance of flying. He showed to people some things that airplanes

could do.

Check your progress! Go to the Self-Test for Chapter 26 on the *Grammar Links* Website.

Chapter 27

Ocean Adventures

Past Progressive Tense; Past Time Clauses

Introductory Task: The Deepest Dive

A. Listen and read the following true story.

The captain of the ship was worried. The wind was strong, and the ocean was rough, maybe too rough. Was a dive possible? "I was wondering the same thing myself," Jacques Piccard later wrote. Piccard and Don Walsh were working for the U.S. Navy, and they were preparing to make the deepest dive in history.

It was January 23, 1960. Piccard and Walsh were on a ship near Guam in the Pacific Ocean, above the deepest part of the sea. They were getting ready to enter the *Trieste*, a small submarine designed for deep ocean dives. How deep was the ocean there? No one knew. Did anything live at the bottom, under the great pressure of the ocean? Scientists around the world were waiting to find out.

At 8:23 a.m., the dive began. The *Trieste* went down slowly for more than four hours before it reached the ocean floor. It stopped almost 35,800 feet down.*
Piccard and Walsh looked out. To their surprise, a flat fish about one foot long was lying on the bottom. It wasn't doing anything special, but when they saw it, the two men shook hands in excitement. No one expected fish like that to live so deep in the ocean.

The *Trieste*

After 20 minutes on the bottom, they started back up. They reached the surface at 4:56 p.m. Planes were circling in the sky, and photographers were waiting to take pictures. When Piccard and Walsh came out of the *Trieste*, they received a hero's welcome.

*Compare this depth (35,800 feet) to the height of Mt. Everest, the tallest mountain in the world at only 29,028 feet!

---

rough = in violent motion, not calm or smooth. *a hero* = a person who is brave and does something good.

B. Work alone or with a partner. <u>Underline</u> the verb in each of the following statements about the story. Does it describe a completed action or an action that was in progress at a certain time? Check (✓) your answer.

	Completed Past Action	Past Action in Progress
1. Piccard and Walsh <u>made</u> their dive on January 23, 1960.	✓	
2. They <u>were working</u> for the U.S. Navy at that time.		✓
3. After four hours, the *Trieste* was still going down.		
4. At the bottom, a fish was lying on the ocean floor.		
5. Scientists were waiting for information from the *Trieste*.		
6. The *Trieste* returned to the surface at 4:56 p.m.		
7. Later, Piccard wrote about the dive.		

GRAMMAR BRIEFING 1

Past Progressive Tense—Affirmative and Negative Statements

FUNCTION

Using the Past Progressive

Using the **past progressive tense** (or **past continuous**) for actions in progress at a certain time in the past. The action began before that time. It possibly continued after that time.

PAST — 10:00 — NOW — FUTURE
I was studying.

Q: What **were** you **doing** at 10:00 last night?
A: I **was studying**.

PAST — last year — NOW — FUTURE
We were working.

Q: Where were you and your wife last year?
A: We **were working** in New York.

FORM

A. Affirmative Statements

SUBJECT	WAS	BASE VERB + -ING	SUBJECT	WERE	BASE VERB + -ING
I			We		
He			You		
She	was	working.	They	were	working.
It			The men		
The man					

(continued on next page)

B. Negative Statements

FULL FORMS			
SUBJECT	*WAS/WERE*	*NOT*	BASE VERB + *-ING*
I			
He			
She	was		
It			
The cat		not	sleeping.
We			
You	were		
They			
The girls			

CONTRACTIONS		
SUBJECT	*WASN'T/WEREN'T*	BASE VERB + *-ING*
I		
He		
She	wasn't	
It		
The cat		sleeping.
We		
You	weren't	
They		
The girls		

GRAMMAR **HOT**SPOT!

Non-action verbs are not usually used in the past progressive. Use the simple past instead.

She **seemed** nervous.
  NOT: She ~~was seeming~~ nervous.

I **didn't want** it.
  NOT: I ~~wasn't wanting~~ it.

(See Chapter 9, Grammar Briefing 2, page 150, for more information on non-action verbs.)

GRAMMAR PRACTICE 1

Past Progressive Tense—Affirmative and Negative Statements

1 **Affirmative and Negative Statements:** A Grouper Goes to Hollywood?

A. Write the verbs in parentheses in the past progressive tense. Use contractions in negative statements.

This is a true story about the ocean scientist and filmmaker Jacques Cousteau.

Cousteau and his team _____were making_____ a movie. They _____
                              1 (make)   2 (work)

in the Indian Ocean, east of Africa, and they _____ the film underwater.
                                                  3 (shoot)

A photographer later said, "An underwater film is never easy, but we _____
                                                                        4 (have)

an unusual problem with this one." He _____ about a problem with a
                                          5 (talk)

grouper, a three-foot-long fish. The fish _____ trouble for the divers.
                                              6 (cause)

It _____ them. This fish was like a friendly pet. It ate food from the
      7 (not / attack)

divers' hands, and they named it "Ulysses." But, as one diver said, "Ulysses liked to get in

front of the cameras. Maybe he _____ to become a movie star. But we
                                        8 (try)

_____ a film about groupers!" The filmmakers _____
   9 (not / make)   10 (not / get)

any work done, so finally, they called up to their ship, "Send down the shark cage!" They

_____ trouble with sharks. They needed the cage for Ulysses. They put
   11 (not / have)

the grouper "in jail" and finished their work in peace. Then Ulysses went free.

> *a shark cage* = a box made of steel bars that divers can enter for
> protection from sharks.

B. Answer the questions with complete sentences. Use past progressive verbs.

1. Where was Cousteau working?

   _____

2. What was he doing there?

   _____

3. Who was working with him?

   _____

4. What problem were the filmmakers having?

   _____

5. What was the fish doing?

   _____

2 **Action and Non-Action Verbs:** A Caribbean Vacation

A. Complete the sentences with the verbs in parentheses. Use the
past progressive tense when possible. Use the simple past for
non-action verbs.

   Reporter Al Jordan and his wife, Sara, are showing their friend Gail
some photographs from their vacation on Grand Cayman Island in the
Caribbean.

1. Al: Sara took this picture of me. We __were snorkeling_____ .
                                              a (snorkel)

   Gail: You _____ an underwater camera, I guess.   Al Snorkeling
                  b (use)

Sara: Yeah, we _____ one of those single use ones.
        c (have)

I _____ it!
  d (love)

2. Al: Here's a good picture of Sara. We _____ on a
                                          a (be)

boat on a trip to Stingray City. You can find lots of stingrays there

and feed them.

Sara: This was when our guide _____ about safety, and
                                  b (talk)

you _____, Al. You _____ pictures.
    c (not / listen)   d (take)

Al: Hey, I _____ everything!
           e (hear)

A Stingray

3. Sara: Gail, look at this one. Al _____ a stingray.
                                    a (feed)

Al: I _____ a squid for it.
     b (hold)

Sara: But he didn't let go of the squid soon enough.

Al: Because I _____ to pat the sting ray. They like that, if you touch them
                c (plan)

gently on the underside.

Sara: But the stingray _____ in the squid, like a vacuum cleaner, and it got
                        d (suck)

Al's hand, too.

A Squid

Gail: Ouch!

Sara: After that, I _____ to try to feed them!
                    e (not / want)

4. Al: Here's a picture of Sara on Seven Mile Beach. We _____ on the beach
                                                         a (walk)

at sunset.

Gail: What a beautiful place!

Sara: Oh, it _____ wonderful. The sun, the water—and the air
              b (be)

_____ so good! It _____ like a different world.
    c (smell)   d (seem)

B. Listen to the conversations in Part A. Check your answers.

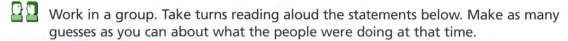

3 **Using the Past Progressive:** Guess What They Were Doing

Work in a group. Take turns reading aloud the statements below. Make as many guesses as you can about what the people were doing at that time.

Example: Student A: **The man was all wet.**
Student B: **He was swimming.**
Student C: **He was taking a shower.**
Student A: **He was walking in the rain.**

1. The man was all wet.
2. The children were hot and sweaty.
3. The man's heart was beating very fast.
4. The woman was very cold.

5. The children's feet were all muddy.
6. The people's eyes were full of tears.
7. The man's hands were black with oil.
8. The children had big smiles.

4 **Storytelling with the Past Progressive and the Simple Past:** A Fish Story

Work in a group. Look at the picture, and read this story:

One morning last summer, Bobby, his father, and his uncle Ted were on a fishing trip. It was about 9:00. Bobby . . .

Then something happened . . .

Use the past progressive tense to describe what was happening at 9:00: What was Bobby doing? What were his father and his uncle doing? Then use the simple past to complete the story. What do you think happened next?

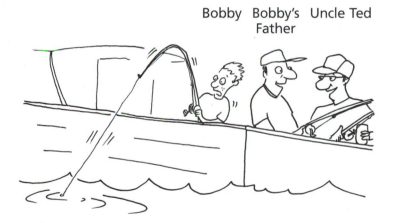

Bobby   Bobby's   Uncle Ted
Father

5 **Using the Past Progressive:** On Vacation

Find a photo of yourself on vacation or having fun with friends or family, or find a picture in a magazine of someone on vacation. Write a paragraph describing what was happening at the time the picture was taken. Use the past progressive tense for actions in progress at that time.

Example: **At the time of this picture, I was taking a vacation with my family. We were staying in . . .**

See the *Grammar Links* Website for a complete model paragraph for this assignment.

Past Progressive Tense—*Yes/No* and *Wh*- Questions

FORM

A. *Yes/No* Questions and Short Answers

QUESTIONS

WAS/WERE	SUBJECT	BASE VERB + -ING	
Was	I		
	he		
	she	**doing**	a good job?
	it		
Were	we		
	you		
	they		

ANSWERS

YES			NO		
Yes,	I		No,	I	
	he	**was.**		he	**wasn't.**
	she			she	
	it			it	
	we			we	
	you	**were.**		you	**weren't.**
	they			they	

B. *Wh*- Questions and Answers

QUESTIONS WITH *WH*- QUESTION WORD AS SUBJECT

WH- QUESTION WORD	WAS	BASE VERB + -ING	
Who	**was**	**calling**	me?
What		**making**	that noise?

ANSWERS

I was.
My watch.

OTHER *WH*- QUESTIONS

WH- QUESTION WORD	WAS/WERE	SUBJECT	BASE VERB + -ING
Who/Whom*	**were**	you	**calling**?
What	**was**	he	**doing**?
Whose book	**was**	she	**reading**?
Which channel	**were**	you	**watching**?
Where	**were**	they	**going**?

ANSWERS

My sister, but she didn't answer.
He was building something.
Mine.
Channel 2.
To a movie.

Whom is very formal. It is not common in spoken English.

Past Progressive Tense—*Yes/No* and *Wh-* Questions

6 **Identifying Questions in the Past Progressive Tense:** Asking About Field Study in Belize

Check (✓) the questions in the past progressive tense.

Shana Washington is studying marine biology in college. She wants to go on a field study trip to Belize. Another student, Laurie Powers, just returned from field study in Belize, so Shana is asking Laurie some questions.

1. _____ Did you go to Belize with other students?

2. ✓_____ What were you doing there?

3. _____ Were you working with biologists?

4. _____ Were all the students doing research?

5. _____ Where were you staying?

6. _____ Were you also traveling around Belize?

7. _____ Was it a good place for snorkeling?

8. _____ Did you do any scuba diving there?

9. _____ How was the food?

10. _____ How did you apply for this trip?

> *marine biology* = the study of ocean plants and animals. *field study* = learning outside the classroom by working with professionals.

7 ***Yes/No* Questions and Short Answers:** A Conversation About Field Study

Complete the questions using the subject and verb in parentheses. Use the past progressive tense. Complete the short answers.

College students Shana Washington and Laurie Powers are talking about Laurie's field study experience in Belize.

Shana: <u>Were you studying</u> marine biology in Belize?
              1 (you / study)

Laurie: No, _____. Some other students were, but my interest is
                  2

in environmental planning. So I was learning about the Holchan Marine Sanctuary.

Shana: _____ with scientists at the sanctuary?
             3 (you / talk)

Laurie: Yes, and with fishermen and other people in the area, too. I wanted to know how it's

working. And it's doing well! There are more fish there now than there were 10 years ago.

Shana: What about the other students? _____ research, too?
4 (they / do)

Laurie: Yes, _____. For example,
5

my friend Liz was studying coral.

Shana: _____ it underwater?
6 (she / study)

Coral

Laurie: Yes, _____. She was scuba diving with a group.
7

Shana: _____ pieces of coral to take home?
8 (they / collect)

Laurie: Oh no! The coral is protected. They were taking inventory.

Shana: Taking inventory? I'm not sure I understand. _____
9 (they / check)

how much coral there was?

Laurie: Yes, that's right.

> *environmental planning* = planning to protect the air, water, and land.
> *a sanctuary* = an area where wildlife is protected by law.

8 *Wh*- Questions: A Week on Wee Wee Caye

A. Write *wh*- questions to match the answers below. Use the past progressive tense.

Laurie Powers spent a week with some other college students doing field study on a little island in Belize.

1. Where was Laurie staying? _____

   Laurie was staying **on the island of Wee Wee Caye.**

2. _____

   She was doing **underwater research** there.

3. _____

   She was working with **other college students and their professor.**

4. _____

   They were living **in small cabins with no electricity.**

5. _____

   They were studying **coral reefs.**

6. _____

   They were doing this **because coral reefs are in danger from pollution.**

B. Work with a partner. Take turns asking and answering the questions in Part A. Do not use the complete statements as answers. Use only the **boldfaced** words.

9 Using *Wh-* Questions and Answers: Murder at Sea

Work with a partner. You are going to read about the murder of a millionaire. The murder takes place on a ship. Two detectives are on the ship. There are three suspects. Take turns asking questions to get the whole story.

Student A: Look at page A-3.

Student B: Look at page A-4.

> *a millionaire* = a person who has a million dollars or more. *a detective* = a police officer who gets information about crimes and tries to catch criminals. *a suspect* = a person who might be guilty of a crime.

GRAMMAR BRIEFING 3

Main Clauses and Time Clauses

FORM and FUNCTION

Clauses, Main Clauses, and Time Clauses

1. A **clause** is a group of words that has a subject (S) and a verb (V).	S V S V He likes her, and she likes him. S V S V When I saw them, I smiled.
2. A **main clause** (or independent clause) is a clause that can stand alone as a complete sentence.	main clause When he saw the fish, **he tried to catch it**. complete sentence **He tried to catch it.**
3. A **time clause** begins with a time expression (such as *before, after, when,* or *while*). It gives information about the time of the action or situation in the main clause. A time clause is never a complete sentence. It cannot stand alone.	S V I go fishing **when** I have time. S V He changed his clothes **before** he went out. **After the storm passed**, the sun came out. NOT: ~~After the storm passed~~.
4. A **time clause** can come before or after the main clause in a sentence. Use a comma after a time clause that comes before the main clause.	I saw a shark **while I was on the boat**. **While I was on the boat**, I saw a shark.

1. *Before* and *after* can also be used in prepositional phrases. (These are not time clauses. They have no verb.)

   Let's meet **before the game**.

   After the movie, we went for pizza.

2. *After* must be in a time clause or a prepositional phrase. Do not use *after* alone. Use *afterward* to mean "after that."

   After we had dinner, we went to a movie.

   We met for dinner. **Afterward**, we went to a movie.
   NOT: ~~After~~, we went to a movie.

(See Chapter 10, Grammar Briefing 4, page 173, for more information on prepositions of time.)

GRAMMAR PRACTICE 3

Main Clauses and Time Clauses

10 Identifying Clauses: Shark Attack!

Look at the **boldfaced** words in the following sentences. Do they form a clause? Write *yes* or *no*. When your answer is *yes*, <u>underline</u> the subject and verb.

1. <u>George Ellis</u> <u>is</u> a diver and a photographer.   yes

2. **A little while ago**, he was working in the ocean near Australia.

3. He saw a shark **while he was taking pictures underwater**.

4. **At that moment**, the shark was swimming about 30 feet away.

5. **After Ellis saw the shark**, he started back to his boat.

6. The shark attacked him **before he could reach the boat**.

7. **It didn't bite him**, but it took away his camera.

8. **Then a friend pulled him out of the water.**

9. **After that experience**, Ellis began to study sharks.

10. He plans to continue his work. **Before then**, he'll need a new camera.

11 Identifying Main Clauses and Time Clauses: Cousteau's Story

Look at the nine **boldfaced** sentences in this true story about Jacques Cousteau. <u>Underline</u> the seven main clauses. Circle the four time clauses in complete sentences. Cross out the two incomplete sentences (like ~~this~~).

(1) **Jacques Cousteau and Frédéric Dumas were making an underwater film.**

(2) **They were diving near the islands of Cape Verde.** These islands are in the Atlantic

Ocean near Africa. (3) **While the two men were filming, they suddenly saw a large** shark. (4) **When they first saw it, it was swimming about 40 feet away.** Cousteau later wrote, "I shouted, and Dumas closed in beside me." Both of them were thinking about shark attacks. This shark was a great white, a man-eater. (5) **When they realized this, their hearts began to pound.** They felt terribly afraid. (6) **After the shark saw the two divers.** (7) **It turned instantly.** Then it raced away from them. The shark seemed to be afraid of the two men! (8) **After Cousteau and Dumas could laugh about it.** (9) **But before they could laugh, they had to get out of the water.**

 See the *Grammar Links* Website for more information about sharks.

Past Time Clauses

FORM and FUNCTION

A. Overview

A **past time clause** tells when in the past the action (or situation) in the main clause happened.	He called me **after he got home**. *Q:* When did he call you? *A:* After he got home.

B. Sentences with *Before/After/When* and the Simple Past

1. Sometimes the action in one clause was complete and then the action in the other clause followed.

   PAST   NOW   FUTURE
   It ended. We left.

                  1   2
   When the class **ended**, we all **left**.

2. In these sentences, use the simple past tense in both clauses.

   PAST   NOW   FUTURE
   simple   simple
   past   past

   I **stopped** at the store before I **went** home.
   After I **got** home, I **found** your message.

3. To introduce the time clause, use:

   • *Before* when the action in the time clause happened later.

                1   2
   We **had** dinner **before** we **went** out.

   • *After* or *when* when the action in the time clause happened earlier. (*When* = immediately after.)

                2   1
   We **had** dinner **after/when** they **arrived**.

(continued on next page)

C. Sentences with *When/While*, the Past Progressive, and the Simple Past

1. Sometimes the action was already in progress at the time the second action happened.

> action in progress   second action
> **It was raining** when **I woke up** this morning.

2. In these sentences, use the past progressive for the action already in progress. Use the simple past for the second (or interrupting) action.

PAST   **simple past**   NOW   FUTURE

past progressive

> second action   action in progress
> The phone **rang** while I **was sleeping**.
> action in progress   second action
> While I **was sleeping**, the phone **rang**.

3. In the time clause, use:

- *While* or *when* + past progressive (for the action in progress).

> **While/When** we **were standing** at the bus stop, it started to rain.

- *When* + simple past (for the second action).

> **When** it started to rain, we were standing at the bus stop.

Past Time Clauses

12 **Statements with Past Time Clauses:** The First Man to Sail Around the World Alone

A. Read about a great adventure. Underline the nine past time clauses. In each sentence with a past time clause, write *1* above the action that happened or started first and *2* above the action that followed or started later.

                1   2

1. After Francis Chichester turned 65, he decided to sail around the world alone.

2. When he announced his plan, many people laughed.

3. Chichester got a small sailboat and named it the *Gipsy Moth IV*.

4. When he started out from England, he sailed south toward Africa.

5. He began a journal while he was making the trip.

6. He reached Australia after 15 weeks at sea.

7. When he got there, big crowds of people were waiting for him.

8. He rested there before he began the next part of his trip.

9. Chichester then had to cross the Pacific Ocean.

10. After he experienced a terrible storm, he wrote about feeling helpless and afraid.

11. Chichester grew thin, tired, and weak after so much time at sea.

12. While he was crossing the Atlantic, people around the world started to talk about him.

13. When he reached England on May 28, 1967, his family and thousands of others

    welcomed him home.

B. On a piece of paper, rewrite the nine sentences with time clauses from Part A. Change the position of the time clause. Remember to use a comma after a time clause that comes before a main clause.

Example: **Francis Chichester decided to sail around the world alone after he turned 65.**

13 Statements with *When* or *While* Past Time Clauses: Accidents

A. Circle the correct verb tense.

Four patients are waiting to see the doctor on their cruise ship. The first

patient tripped and fell while she (danced /(was dancing)). She thinks her arm
                                                       1

is broken. The second patient (cut / was cutting) his steak when his knife
                                          2

(slipped / was slipping), and he cut his hand. The third patient was in bed.
       3

He (fell / was falling) out of bed while he was turning over, and he
       4

(hurt / was hurting) his back. And the fourth one (fished / was fishing)
       5   6

when she (got / was getting) a fishhook caught in her ear!
            7

   When each accident happened, the person (went / was going) directly
                                                       8

to the doctor's office. When they (got / were getting) there, a nurse
                                       9

(gave / was giving) them medical forms to fill out.
   10

A Fishhook

B. Complete each sentence with the verb in parentheses. Use the simple past tense or the past progressive.

1. When the four people hurt themselves, they _____ on a cruise ship.

(travel)

2. The four patients _____ when the doctor arrived.

(wait)

3. When the first patient saw the doctor, she _____ her accident.

(describe)

4. Patient #1: When I hurt myself, I _____.

(dance)

5. Patient #1: I think I _____ my arm when I _____ the floor.

a (break)   b (hit)

6. Patient #2: I cut my hand while I _____ my steak.

(cut)

7. Patient #3: I was just turning over when I _____ out of bed.

(fall)

8. Patient #4: I _____ when this happened.

(fish)

14   **Using Statements with Past Time Clauses:** The Story of Your Life

On a piece of paper, complete the following sentences with information about your life. Each sentence must have a main clause and a past time clause.

Example: *I started school after we moved to Sarajevo.*

1. When I was born, my parents were living in . . .
2. Before I started school, . . .
3. I started school . . .
4. I learned to read . . .
5. While I was growing up, . . .
6. When I reached the age of _____, . . .
7. After . . .
8. Before . . .

15   **Editing:** Sylvia Earle, Marine Biologist and Ocean Explorer

Correct the 10 errors in verb tenses, time clauses, and punctuation of time clauses. Some errors can be corrected in more than one way. The first error is corrected for you.

             fell
Sylvia Earle was ~~fall~~ in love with the ocean. When she was a little girl. While she

growing up in New Jersey, she paid close attention to the natural world. When she

was 16, she was making her first deep sea dive. Then she decided to become an ocean

scientist. It was seeming the perfect career for her.

In 1970, she and her team of scientists lived underwater for two weeks. While they were living underwater they was doing research. After, they returned to the surface, and they discovered that they were being famous!

In 1979, Earle walked alone on the ocean floor 1,250 feet below the surface. She wore a special suit, when she did this.

Later, Earle got a very important job. She became chief scientist of the U.S. National Oceanographic and Atmospheric Administration. While she got this job, she became the first woman to hold the position.

Earle is working to save our oceans from pollution and too much fishing. In 1998, *Time* magazine named her a "Hero for the Planet."

 See the *Grammar Links* Website for more information about our oceans.

16 Storytelling with Past Time Clauses: A Tall Tale

Work in a group of three or four. Choose a friend in the class who is not in your group, and invent a tall tale about that person. Describe something that happened while your friend was making a trip by boat. Maybe he or she saw something strange, did something brave, or met someone famous. Decide where he or she was traveling, what happened, and what he or she was doing at that time. Decide what happened afterward. When your story is ready, tell it to the class. Include sentences with past time clauses with *after*, *before*, *when*, and *while*.

> *a tall tale* = an exciting story that is impossible to believe.

Example: Student A: This tall tale is about Karine.
Student B: Last summer, Karine was sailing a little boat across the Atlantic.
Student C: One night, while she was sleeping, a big whale swallowed her boat.
Student A: When she woke up, she was inside the whale.

 Check your progress! Go to the Self-Test for Chapter 27 on the *Grammar Links* Website.

Eleven

Wrap-up Activities

1 The Apollo 13: READING

Read this paragraph about an adventure in space.

On Saturday, April 11, 1970, the spaceship *Apollo 13* began a trip to the moon. When the *Apollo 13* took off, many Americans were watching it on TV. Three astronauts were making the trip: James Lovell, Fred Haise, and Jack Swigert. For the first two days, things went well. But at about 9:00 p.m. on April 13, when they were 200,000 miles from the earth, there was an explosion. An oxygen tank blew up. When this happened, the astronauts lost most of their air, water, and power. For the next four days, there were many scary moments. The astronauts grew cold, tired, hungry, and thirsty. People at NASA were racing the clock to find a way to bring the men home, and people around the world were following the story in the news. Finally, on April 17, the astronauts landed safely in the Pacific Ocean.

> *NASA* = the U.S. government organization for space research and travel.
> *race the clock* = try to complete something quickly before time runs out.

2 What Happened? WRITING

Write about an experience from your life. It could be a good, bad, funny, or scary experience. Tell when it happened. Where were you, and what were you doing at that time? Explain what happened and how you felt. Include some sentences with past time clauses. Try to use verbs that do and do not take objects, including infinitive direct objects.

 See the *Grammar Links* Website for a model paragraph for this assignment.

3 My Car Accident: EDITING

Correct the 10 errors in the paragraph. There are errors in verb tenses and forms, time clauses (and their punctuation), and objects of verbs. Some errors can be corrected in more than one way. The first error is corrected for you.

An Accident

One day last year, ~~I'm~~ *I was* driving in my car, and it rained very hard. Suddenly, I saw that the car ahead of me was stopping. I wanted slow down, so I stepped on the brake. Unfortunately, when I did that, nothing was happening. After I hit the brake again my car slowed down, but it was too late. I was hitting the car in front of me. After I hit that car, the one behind hit me. All three drivers got out at the side of the road. I showed to them my driver's license, and they showed their licenses for me. There was no damage to their cars, but mine needed get some repairs. So after, I drove to a garage.

---

4 Interview a Daredevil: SPEAKING/LISTENING

Work with a partner. Student A: You are a daredevil (a person who takes great risks). You are planning to do a dangerous stunt. Decide what the stunt is, where and when you will do it, and why you want to do this stunt. Some ideas might be:

- bungee jump off the Statue of Liberty.
- cross the Atlantic Ocean in a small boat.
- jump over a car on a motorcycle.

Student B: You are a reporter. Find out about this daredevil's stunt. Ask questions about:

- what he/she plans (hopes, expects) to do.
- why he/she decided to do this.
- when he/she plans to do this.
- where he/she will try to do this.

Then report to the class about your partner's plans.

5   A Surprise: SPEAKING/LISTENING

Think of a time when somebody or something surprised you. Was it an unexpected visit? Was it a sudden event, such as an earthquake or an accident? Was it some news you received?

Form a group of three or four. Take turns telling what surprised you. Ask each other questions: *Where were you? What were you doing at that time?* Describe what you were doing and what happened afterward. Use statements with past time clauses.

Example: I got a phone call from my friend, and she had two tickets for a concert. When she called, I was trying to study. But I was thinking about the weekend. I was happy when she told me about the tickets. After we finished talking, I tried to study again, but it was too hard.

6   Alibi for a Robbery: SPEAKING/LISTENING

Work with the whole class. Imagine you are on a cruise ship in the Mediterranean Sea. There was a robbery on the ship at 10:00 last night. Someone stole a lot of money from the captain's desk. Two students play the parts of suspects—maybe they are the robbers! The others in the class are detectives.

Step 1 Suspects: Go outside the room, and plan your alibi (the story about what you were doing at the time of the robbery). You say you were together last night from 9:00 to 11:00, somewhere on the ship. Your stories must be the same.

Step 2 All other students: While the suspects are outside the room, write on the board some questions to ask them about last night. Include *wh-* and *yes/no* questions in the past progressive tense. Then erase the questions.

Step 3 The first suspect comes into the room alone. The detectives take turns asking questions.

Example: Detective 1: What were you doing at 10:00 last night?
            Suspect: I was reading in the library.
            Detective 2: Was anybody reading there with you?

Step 4 The first suspect goes out of the room, and the second suspect comes in for questioning.

Step 5 Bring in the two suspects. They can listen while the detectives talk about the case. If the two suspects' stories match, they will go free. If their stories don't match, ARREST THEM!

Exercise Pages

Task 4: A Race, Page 41

To the teacher: Tell the students to write a list with the names of everyone in the class. Spelling counts. If you have an international class, you can also ask them to write where each person is from.

Task 6: Who's Missing from the Family Tree?, Page 78

Student B: This is Kim Hewitt's family tree. Answer your partner's questions. What are the missing names on the family tree? Ask your partner. Write the names.

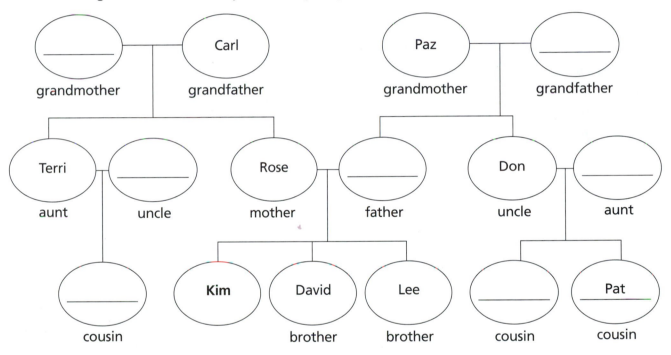

grandmother   Carl grandfather   Paz grandmother   grandfather

Terri aunt   uncle   Rose mother   father   Don uncle   aunt

cousin   Kim brother   David   Lee brother   cousin   Pat cousin

10 Listening to Prepositions: The Runaway Puppy, Page 171

Description 1

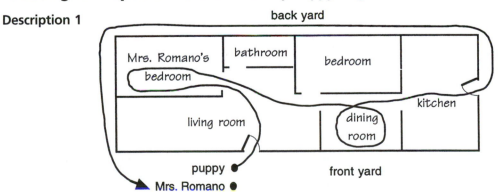

back yard

Mrs. Romano's bedroom   bathroom   bedroom   kitchen

living room   dining room

puppy ●

▲ Mrs. Romano ●   front yard

8 Using *Yes/No* Questions and Short Answers: French and American Inventors, Page 203

B. The people in the chart were all French or American inventors. Each person was also a scientist, a teacher, or a businessperson. Find the missing information about them by asking your partner questions with *Was*. Take turns.

Example: Student A: Was Louis Pasteur a man?
Student B: Yes, he was. Was Louis Braille a scientist?
Student A: No, he wasn't.

Inventor's Name	Man/Woman	Profession	Nationality
Edouard Benedictus		a scientist	
Louis Braille	a man		French
Elizabeth Lee Hazen		a scientist	
James Naismith		a teacher	American
Louis Pasteur	a man		
Ruth Wakefield	a woman		American
Madame C. J. Walker		a businessperson	

Task 4: Mystery Inventions, Page 229

Picture A shows a foot-warming device. A man wore it under his clothes in cold weather and breathed warm air into the funnel at the top. The air traveled down the tubes and into his boots.

Picture B shows an early pair of roller skates.

Picture C shows a swimming device. A man rested on top of it and used his hands and feet to turn the pedals and work the propeller at the back.

Task 5: Looking into the Future, Page 313

Step 3 Use the words your classmate wrote in Step 1 on page 313 to complete the paragraph below:

_____'s Future
(your classmate's name)

In 10 years, you will be a famous _____. You will be rich because people will pay
1

for your advice on _____. You will live in a _____-room house in
2   3

_____ with your pet _____, whose name will be _____.
4   5   6

In your house, you will have a wonderful collection of _____ _____.
7   8

_____ and _____ will be your neighbors. Life will be good.
9   10

Step 4 Read the paragraph to your classmate and the rest of the group. Talk about the predictions. Do you believe them?

9 *Wh-* **Questions and Answers:** Murder at Sea, Page 433

Student A: Take turns with your partner asking and answering *wh-* questions in the past progressive tense. Ask the questions you need to ask in order to fill in the missing information. Fill in the information (in items 1, 3, 5, 7, 9, and 11), and then discuss the final question about the story.

Example: *What were the detectives doing?*

1. Detectives Sam and Nora Sherlock were _____ing _____.

2. It was going to Belize.

3. One night, the ship was rocking and rolling because _____.

4. Passengers were feeling sick because of the movement of the ship.

5. The Sherlocks were trying to read in _____. Suddenly, they heard a gunshot.

6. They hurried to the door. Millionaire Bill Bucks was lying on the floor outside. He was dead. Who shot him?

7. The captain asked the Sherlocks for help. They were already _____ing

   _____.

8. They started with Bucks' wife, Tiffany. She said, "Yes, I heard the shot. I was in our cabin. I was writing a postcard to my mother."

9. The Sherlocks asked for the postcard, and Mrs. Bucks gave it to them. They looked at it closely. They were _____ing the postcard. There was a picture of the ship on one side. On the other side, the handwriting was small and neat. The message began, "Dear Mother."

10. Then the Sherlocks questioned Bill Bucks' secretary, Ms. Wideout. She said, "No, I didn't hear the shot. I was praying in my cabin." She was crying and holding a small prayer book.

11. Next, the Sherlocks questioned Bill Bucks' sister Betty. "I didn't hear anything—I was wearing headphones because _____."

12. The Sherlocks turned to the captain and said, "_____ is lying. She is our number one suspect." Whose name did they say? Why?

9 *Wh-* Questions and Answers: Murder at Sea, Page 433

Student B: Take turns with your partner asking and answering *wh-* questions in the past progressive tense. Ask the questions you need to ask in order to fill in the missing information. Fill in that information (in items 2, 4, 6, 8, and 10), and then discuss the final question about the story.

Example: **Where was the ship going?**

1. Detectives Sam and Nora Sherlock were taking a vacation on a cruise ship.

2. It was going to _____.

3. One night, the ship was rocking and rolling because it was traveling through a storm.

4. Passengers were _____ing _____ because of the movement of the ship.

5. The Sherlocks were trying to read in their cabin. Suddenly, they heard a gunshot.

6. They hurried to the door. _____ was lying on the floor outside. He was dead. Who shot him?

7. The captain asked the Sherlocks for help. They were already thinking of questions to ask people.

8. They started with Bucks' wife, Tiffany. She said, "Yes, I heard the shot. I was in our cabin. I was writing a postcard to _____."

9. The Sherlocks asked for the postcard, and Mrs. Bucks gave it to them. They looked at it closely. They were studying the postcard. There was a picture of the ship on one side. On the other side, the handwriting was small and neat. The message began, "Dear Mother."

10. Then the Sherlocks questioned Bill Bucks' secretary, Ms. Wideout. She said, "No, I didn't hear the shot. I was praying in _____." She was crying and holding a small prayer book.

11. Next, the Sherlocks questioned Bill Bucks' sister Betty. "I didn't hear anything—I was wearing headphones because I was listening to music."

12. The Sherlocks turned to the captain and said, "_____ is lying. She is our number one suspect." Whose name did they say? Why?

Appendixes

Cardinal and Ordinal Numbers

CARDINAL NUMBERS	ORDINAL NUMBERS	CARDINAL NUMBERS	ORDINAL NUMBERS
1 = one	1st = first	11 = eleven	11th = eleventh
2 = two	2nd = second	12 = twelve	12th = twelfth
3 = three	3rd = third	13 = thirteen	13th = thirteenth
4 = four	4th = fourth	14 = fourteen	14th = fourteenth
5 = five	5th = fifth	15 = fifteen	15th = fifteenth
6 = six	6th = sixth	16 = sixteen	16th = sixteenth
7 = seven	7th = seventh	17 = seventeen	17th = seventeenth
8 = eight	8th = eighth	18 = eighteen	18th = eighteenth
9 = nine	9th = ninth	19 = nineteen	19th = nineteenth
10 = ten	10th = tenth	20 = twenty	20th = twentieth

CARDINAL NUMBERS	ORDINAL NUMBERS
21 = twenty-one	21st = twenty-first
30 = thirty	30th = thirtieth
40 = forty	40th = fortieth
50 = fifty	50th = fiftieth
60 = sixty	60th = sixtieth
70 = seventy	70th = seventieth
80 = eighty	80th = eightieth
90 = ninety	90th = ninetieth
100 = one hundred	100th = one hundredth
200 = two hundred	200th = two hundredth
1,000 = one thousand	1,000th = one thousandth
1,000,000 = one million	1,000,000th = one millionth

Telling Time

It's 9:00.
It's nine o'clock.

It's 2:05.
It's two-oh-five.

It's 3:10.
It's three-ten.

It's 10:15.
It's ten-fifteen.
It's a quarter past ten.

It's 7:30.
It's seven-thirty.
It's half past seven.

It's 11:45.
It's eleven forty-five.
It's a quarter to twelve.

The Days of the Week

WEEKDAYS	
Monday	Mon./M.
Tuesday	Tues./Tu.
Wednesday	Wed./W.
Thursday	Thurs./Th.
Friday	Fri./F.

THE WEEKEND	
Saturday	Sat./S.
Sunday	Sun./S.

The Months of the Year

1	January	Jan.	7	July	Jul.
2	February	Feb.	8	August	Aug.
3	March	Mar.	9	September	Sept.
4	April	Apr.	10	October	Oct.
5	May		11	November	Nov.
6	June	Jun.	12	December	Dec.

(continued on next page)

Dates

In the United States, people write dates as "(month)/(day)" or "(month)/(day)/(year)."

10/1 = October 1

1/10/05 = January 10, 2005

To say dates, people usually use the ordinal number for the day of the month; for example, say "October 31st" or "the 31st of October."

APPENDIX 4

Irregular Count Nouns

Nouns with Irregular Plurals:

person/people	man/men	woman/women	child/children
tooth/teeth	foot/feet	mouse/mice	

Nouns with the Same Form for Singular and Plural:

deer (one deer, two deer)	sheep	fish

Nouns with Only a Plural Form:

clothes	pants	jeans	shorts	(eye)glasses	sunglasses	scissors

APPENDIX 5

Possessive Nouns

To form the possessive of:

1. Any noun that does not end in *s*: Add *'s*.

   My friend has a name. → my friend's name

   The baby has a toy. → the baby's toy

   Her children have teachers. → her children's teachers

2. A noun that ends in *s*:

   • Add only *'* to any plural noun that ends in *s*.

   My friends have names. → my friends' names

   The babies have toys. → the babies' toys

   • Add *'s* to any singular noun that ends in *s*.*

   The waitress has a job. → the waitress's job

   Charles has a book. → Charles's book

*You will also see the possessive form of names that end in *s* spelled with *'* only: *Charles' sister*.

Common Noncount Nouns

LIQUIDS	SOLIDS	THINGS WITH PARTICLES	GROUPS OF SIMILAR THINGS	WEATHER	SCHOOL SUBJECTS	ABSTRACT IDEAS	OTHER
coffee	bread	cereal	cash	fog	biology	advice	air
juice	butter	corn	clothing	lightning	business	education	mail
milk	cheese	dirt	equipmen	train	economics	entertainment	music
oil	cotton	dust	food	snow	English	fun	pollution
soda	gold	pepper	fruit	weather	history	homework	smoke
soup	ice	rice	furniture		math(ematics)	information	traffic
tea	meat	salt	jewelry		science	love	
water	plastic	sand	money			luck	
	silver	sugar	trash			peace	
	wood					work	

Irregular Verbs

BASE FORM	SIMPLE PAST FORM	BASE FORM	SIMPLE PAST FORM	BASE FORM	SIMPLE PAST FORM
be	was, were	drink	drank	hide	hid
become	became	drive	drove	hit	hit
begin	began	eat	ate	hold	held
bend	bent	fall	fell	hurt	hurt
bite	bit	feed	fed	keep	kept
blow	blew	feel	felt	know	knew
break	broke	fight	fought	lead	led
bring	brought	find	found	leave	left
build	built	fly	flew	lend	lent
buy	bought	forget	forgot	lose	lost
catch	caught	get	got	make	made
choose	chose	give	gave	mean	meant
come	came	go	went	meet	met
cost	cost	grow	grew	pay	paid
cut	cut	hang	hung	put	put
do	did	have	had	quit	quit
draw	drew	hear	heard	read	read

(continued on next page)

Irregular Verbs (continued)

BASE FORM	SIMPLE PAST FORM	BASE FORM	SIMPLE PAST FORM	BASE FORM	SIMPLE PAST FORM
ride	rode	sit	sat	tell	told
ring	rang	sleep	slept	think	thought
run	ran	speak	spoke	throw	threw
say	said	spend	spent	understand	understood
see	saw	stand	stood	wake up	woke up
sell	sold	steal	stole	wear	wore
send	sent	swim	swam	win	won
shake	shook	take	took	write	wrote
shut	shut	teach	taught		
sing	sang	tear	tore		

APPENDIX 8

Summary Chart of Modals

MODAL	FUNCTION	EXAMPLE
can	to express present ability	He can play the piano.
	to ask, give, or refuse permission	Can I park here?
		Yes, you can.
		No, you can't park here.
	to make requests	Can you do something for me?
	to make offers	Can I help you?
could	to express ability in the past	He could speak two languages when he was a child.
	to express present or future possibility	He's not in school. He could be sick.
		We could leave tomorrow or the next day.
	to ask permission	Could I please leave now?
	to make requests	Could you spell your name for me?
	to make offers	Could I do that for you?
have to	to express necessity in the past, present, and future	I had to miss class yesterday.
		He has to work on weekends.
		We have to leave in a few minutes.

(continued on next page)

Summary Chart of Modals (continued)

MODAL	FUNCTION	EXAMPLE
may	to express present or future possibility	He's not in school. He may be sick. It may rain later.
	to ask, give, or refuse permission	May we use our notes during the test? You may begin now. You may not leave early.
	to make offers	May I help you?
might	to express present or future possibility	He's not in school. He might be sick. It might rain later.
must	to express present or future necessity	You must always wear gloves at work. I must remember to call them tonight.
	to say what is not allowed	People must not smoke inside the building.
should	to give advice	I think you should buy the blue shirt.
	to state opinions about what is right or wrong	They should build more schools.
will	to express future plans and predictions	I'll see you later! It will probably rain tomorrow.
	to make requests	Will you please call me tonight?
would	to make requests	Would you please repeat that?
would like	to make requests	I'd like some coffee.
	to make offers	Would you like some help?

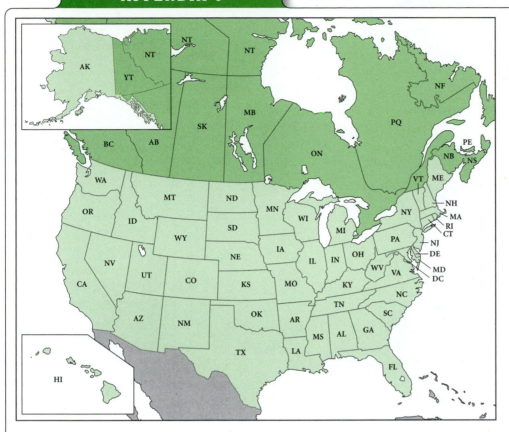

Names and Abbreviations of the 50 States

AL	Alabama	IN	Indiana	NE	Nebraska	SC	South Carolina
AK	Alaska	IA	Iowa	NV	Nevada	SD	South Dakota
AZ	Arizona	KS	Kansas	NH	New Hampshire	TN	Tennessee
AR	Arkansas	KY	Kentucky	NJ	New Jersey	TX	Texas
CA	California	LA	Louisiana	NM	New Mexico	UT	Utah
CO	Colorado	ME	Maine	NY	New York	VT	Vermont
CT	Connecticut	MD	Maryland	NC	North Carolina	VA	Virginia
DE	Delaware	MA	Massachusetts	ND	North Dakota	WA	Washington
FL	Florida	MI	Michigan	OH	Ohio	WV	West Virginia
GA	Georgia	MN	Minnesota	OK	Oklahoma	WI	Wisconsin
HI	Hawaii	MS	Mississippi	OR	Oregon	WY	Wyoming
ID	Idaho	MO	Missouri	PA	Pennsylvania	DC*	District of Columbia
IL	Illinois	MT	Montana	RI	Rhode Island		(*not a state)

Names and Abbreviations of the 10 Canadian Provinces and Three Territories

AB	Alberta	NF	Newfoundland	PE	Prince Edward
BC	British Columbia	NT	Northwest Territories	PQ	Quebec
MB	Manitoba	NS	Nova Scotia	SK	Saskatchewan
NB	New Brunswick	NT	Nunavut	YT	Yukon Territory
		ON	Ontario		

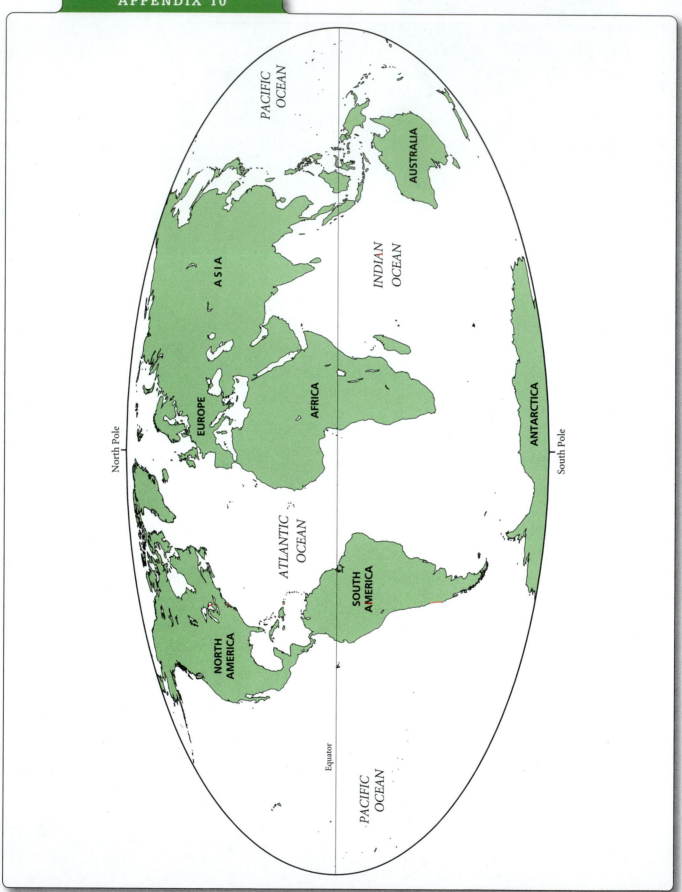

Grammar Glossary

action verb   A verb that expresses an action. Action verbs can be transitive (take direct objects) or intransitive (do not take direct objects).

> She **bought** a new CD.
> They **exercise** every morning.

adjective   A word that modifies (or describes) a noun. Adjectives often come before the nouns they modify. They also come after linking verbs.

> You have a **beautiful** sweater.
> The coffee smells **good**.

adverb   A word that modifies (or describes) a verb, an adjective, another adverb, or a complete sentence.

> He talks **quickly**.   She is **very** tall.
> We ran **really** fast.   I saw it **yesterday**.

affirmative statement   A positive sentence. Affirmative statements do not have *not* with the verb.

> I like chocolate.   We need more chairs.

article   The words *a/an* and *the*. Articles introduce and identify nouns.

> **a** dog   **an** apple   **the** cat
> **the** apples

auxiliary verb (also called *helping verb*) A verb that is used with a main verb to help form tenses and to form questions and negative statements. Forms of *do* and *be* are often used as auxiliary verbs. The modals (e.g., *can, should, will*) are also auxiliary verbs.

> Rachel **doesn't** have time for lunch.
> I**'ll** wait for you.   **Is** she sleeping?
> They **can** swim.

base form of a verb (also called *base verb*) A verb without *to* in front of it or any endings after it.

> make   do   eat   be

clause   A group of related words that has a subject and a verb.

> Because I was absent, . . .
> Today is Sunday.   . . . when he arrived.

common noun   A noun that is not the name of a particular person, place, thing, or idea.

> cat   sugar   people   education

comparative   A form of an adjective or adverb used to describe two things that are different.

> The earth is **bigger** than the moon.
> Jack works **more quickly** than Joe does.

conjunction   A word that connects words, groups of words, or two complete sentences.

> April **and** May are months.
> Is he married **or** single?
> I'll be there Monday, **but** I can't come Tuesday.

consonant   A letter of the alphabet that represents a sound made by blocking or partially blocking the flow of air from the mouth. Consonants include *b, c, d, f,* and *g.*

contraction   The combination of two words into one. In contractions, letters are replaced with an apostrophe (').

> they will → **they'll**
> we are → **we're**
> is not → **isn't**

count noun   A noun that names a person, place, thing, or idea that can be counted. There can be one, two, three, or more.

> boy (one boy, two boys, three boys)
> foot (one foot, two feet, 100 feet)

definite article   The word *the. The* is used with singular, plural, and noncount nouns when both the speaker and the listener know which specific person, place, or thing the noun is naming.

> **The** sun rises in the east.
> Here is **the** book you wanted.

demonstrative   *This, that, these,* or *those* used as an adjective or a pronoun. *This* and *these* describe things that are near. *That* and *those* describe things that are not so near.

> **This** book is mine.
> **That** is your book over there on the desk.

■ **direct object**   A noun, pronoun, or noun phrase that directly receives the action of the verb in a sentence.

> Jack ate **the cake**.   Ramon likes **me**.

■ **first person**   Referring to the speaker or writer of a sentence. *I*, *me*, *we*, and *us* are first person pronouns. *Am* is the first person singular form of the present tense of *be*.

■ **formal**   Used in many official, professional, or public situations. For example, people often use formal language for academic or business purposes or when speaking to strangers.

> Formal: How do you do?
> Informal: Nice to meet you!

■ **helping verb**   See *auxiliary verb*.

■ **imperative**   A type of sentence used for giving orders. Imperatives can also be used for making offers and requests. The main verb in an imperative sentence is in the base form.

> Help her!   Please don't touch that.
> Have a cookie.

■ **indefinite article**   The word *a* or *an*. *A/an* is used to introduce a singular count noun.

> Their new baby is **a** boy.
> **An** apple is a kind of fruit.

■ **indefinite pronoun**   A pronoun that refers to a person or thing and is not specific about who or what.

> **Somebody** took my book.
> Did you take **anything** from my bag?

■ **independent clause**   See *main clause*.

■ **indirect object**   A noun, pronoun, or noun phrase that indirectly receives the action of the verb in a sentence. It tells to whom or for whom the action of the verb occurred.

> Jack gave **Mary** a book.
> Mary bought a new hat for **him**.

■ **infinitive**   *To* + the base form of a verb. Infinitives can be used as nouns.

> Peter loves **to swim**.
> They wanted **to come**.

■ **informal**   Used in casual, relaxed situations. For example, people often use informal language with friends.

> Informal: *Q:* How's it going? *A:* OK, thanks.
> Formal: *Q:* How are you? *A:* Fine, thank you.

■ **information question**   See *wh-* question.

■ **intransitive verb**   A verb that does not take a direct object.

> John **runs** every day.
> I **worked** while the children **slept**.

■ **irregular**   Not following an expected pattern; different from the usual. For example, *do* is an irregular verb because its past tense form is *did*. It does not add *-ed*, the usual pattern for forming the simple past tense.

> Irregular verbs: go/went, sing/sang
> Nouns with irregular plurals: man/men, person/people

■ **linking verb**   A verb that is followed by an adjective or a noun referring back to the subject. Linking verbs include *be*, *feel*, *seem*, *smell*, and *become*.

> She **is** a teacher.   Ralph **feels** sick.
> The coffee **smells** great.

■ **main clause**   (also called *independent clause*) A clause that is or could be a complete sentence.

> **Today is Sunday.**
> When he called, **I wasn't home**.

■ **main verb**   The verb that can be used alone in a sentence (in simple present and simple past tense statements) and that carries the most important verbal meaning in the sentence. Main verbs often occur with auxiliaries.

> Carol **ate** breakfast today.
> Mark is **working** now.   I won't **forget**.

■ **measure word**   A word used to express a specific or exact amount of something.

> a **cup** of sugar   a **bag** of food
> two **pounds** of apples

- **modal** An auxiliary verb used to express ability or possibility, to ask for or give permission or advice, to make offers and requests, or to express necessity. Modals include *can, could, may, might, should, must, will,* and *would*.

    Harriet **can** play the guitar.
    We **should** learn Spanish.

- **modify** Tell more about or change the meaning of a word or phrase. For example, adjectives can modify nouns, and adverbs can modify verbs.

    She's a **beautiful** woman.
    They sang **well**.

- **negative statement** A sentence that is not positive. Negative statements usually contain *not*.

    I do not like chocolate.
    He never forgets to call.

- **non-action verb** (also called *verb with stative meaning*) A verb that tells states of mind or senses, not actions. A non-action verb is not usually used in the progressive tenses.

    I know the answer.
    NOT: I ~~am knowing~~ the answer.

- **noncount noun** A noun that names something that cannot be counted.

    water   freedom
    information   sugar

- **noun** A word that names a person, place, thing, or idea.

    king   New York City   house   peace

- **noun phrase** A noun and its modifiers.

    my house
    the beautiful blue bowl on the table

- **object** See *direct object, indirect object,* and *object of a preposition*.

- **object of a preposition** A noun, pronoun, or noun phrase that comes after a preposition.

    from **Ben**   to **them**   at **the party**

- **object pronoun** A pronoun that can be the object of a verb or preposition: *me, us, you, them, him, her,* or *it*.

    I called **her** last night.
    They sent a package to **us**.

- **past tense** See *simple past tense*.

- **past progressive tense** (also called *past continuous tense*) A verb tense that describes actions in progress in the past.

    At six o'clock last night, the sun **was shining**.

- **phrase** A group of related words that does not contain both a subject and a verb.

    on the table   the big black dog

- **plural** More than one. Pronouns and nouns can be plural (for example, *they, dogs*). Plural verb forms are used with plural subjects.

    The **books are** on the table.
    The **children go** to school.

- **possessive** A noun, pronoun, or adjective that shows ownership or possession.

    John's car is new.   This book is **mine**.
    This is **my** book.

- **preposition** A word that takes a noun or pronoun as an object. Prepositions often express meanings like time, location, or direction.

    at 10 o'clock   **in** the building
    into the house

- **prepositional phrase** A preposition and its object.

    We met **at ten-thirty**.
    Let's go **into the house**.

- **present progressive tense** (also called *present continuous tense*) A verb tense that describes actions happening at the moment of speaking or over a longer, indefinite period of time in the present.

    I **am writing** postcards right now.
    We **are studying** English this semester.

- **present tense** See *simple present tense*.

- **pronoun** A word that replaces a noun or noun phrase. See *object pronoun, indefinite pronoun, possessive,* and *subject pronoun*.

    John is my friend. **He** is my friend.
    I have the tickets. I have **them**.

- **proper noun** A noun that names a particular person, place, thing, or idea. Proper nouns begin with capital letters.

    Mary Larson   Paris
    Christmas   Buddhism

- **quantifier**   A word or phrase that comes before a noun and tells how many or how much.

  Many people like to travel.
  They don't need **much** money for the trip.

- **question**   A sentence used to ask for information. It has a question mark (?) at the end. See *yes/no question* and *wh- question*.

- **regular**   Following a set pattern. For example, verbs that add -*ed* to the base form for the simple past tense are regular verbs.

  Regular verbs: stop/stopped, pick/picked
  Nouns with regular plurals: cat/cats, boy/boys

- **second person**   Referring to the listener or reader of a sentence. The second person pronouns are *you* and *yours*.

- **short answer**   An answer to a *yes/no* question that includes: *Yes/No,* + subject pronoun + auxiliary verb or *be* (+ *not*).

  Do you like fish? **No, I don't.**
  Are you tired? **Yes, I am.**

- **simple past tense**   A verb tense that describes actions and states that began and ended in the past.

  We **visited** some friends last weekend.
  John **was** here yesterday.

- **simple present tense**   A verb tense that describes habits, routines, and things that are generally or always true.

  We often **meet** for breakfast.
  Fish **swim** in the sea.

- **singular**   One. Pronouns and nouns can be singular (for example, *I, she, book*). Singular verb forms are used with singular and noncount subjects.

  The book is on the table.
  The sugar is in the bowl.

- **statement**   See *affirmative statement* and *negative statement*.

- **subject**   The noun, pronoun, or noun phrase that the action or experiences the state in a sentence. The subject usually comes before the verb.

  John is a teacher.   **We** like chocolate.
  Do **you** need help?

- **subject pronoun**   A pronoun that can be the subject of a sentence. *I, we, you, they, he, she,* and *it* are the subject pronouns.

  I like pizza.   Do **you** know the answer?
  Who was **she**?

- **superlative**   A form of an adjective or adverb used to compare three or more things or actions.

  The Nile is the **longest** river in the world.
  She dances the **most gracefully** of all.

- **syllable**   A word or part of a word that has a single vowel sound.

  One-syllable words: house, cat, they
  Two-syllable words: houses, study, father

- **third person**   Referring to people other than the speaker/writer or listener/reader of a sentence. For example, *he, she, it, they, him, her,* and *them* are third person pronouns; *goes* is a third person singular verb.

- **time clause**   A clause that begins with a time expression (for example, *when, while, before,* or *after*).

  After I slept, I felt better.
  John exercises **before he has breakfast**.

- **transitive verb**   A verb that takes a direct object.

  My brother **wrote a letter** to me.

- **verb**   A word for an action or a state, such as a state of mind. All sentences have verbs.

  They **didn't like** the food.
  She **was swimming** when I arrived.

- **verb with stative meaning**   See *non-action verb*.

- **vowel**   A letter of the alphabet that represents a sound made by the unblocked flow of air through the mouth; *a, e, i, o,* and *u* are vowels.

- ***wh-* question** (also called *information question*) A question that begins with a *wh-* word (*who, whose, what, where, when, why, which, how*) and asks for information. *Wh-* questions cannot usually be answered with *yes* or *no*.

  Q: **What do you want to eat?**
  A: Some pizza.

- ***yes/no* question**   A question that can be answered with *yes* or *no*.

  Q: **Are you hungry?**
  A: Yes, I am./No, I'm not.

Index